AF805742

Management for Professionals

More information about this series at http://www.springer.com/series/10101

Jacques Chlopczyk • Christine Erlach
Editors

Transforming Organizations

Narrative and Story-Based Approaches

Springer

Editors
Jacques Chlopczyk
Zentrum für systemische Forschung und Beratung GmbH
Beyond Storytelling Partners
Mannheim, Germany

Christine Erlach
NARRATA Consult
Burscheid, Germany

ISSN 2192-8096 ISSN 2192-810X (electronic)
Management for Professionals
ISBN 978-3-030-17850-5 ISBN 978-3-030-17851-2 (eBook)
https://doi.org/10.1007/978-3-030-17851-2

© Springer Nature Switzerland AG 2019
This work is subject to copyright. All rights are reserved by the Publisher, whether the whole or part of the material is concerned, specifically the rights of translation, reprinting, reuse of illustrations, recitation, broadcasting, reproduction on microfilms or in any other physical way, and transmission or information storage and retrieval, electronic adaptation, computer software, or by similar or dissimilar methodology now known or hereafter developed.
The use of general descriptive names, registered names, trademarks, service marks, etc. in this publication does not imply, even in the absence of a specific statement, that such names are exempt from the relevant protective laws and regulations and therefore free for general use.
The publisher, the authors and the editors are safe to assume that the advice and information in this book are believed to be true and accurate at the date of publication. Neither the publisher nor the authors or the editors give a warranty, express or implied, with respect to the material contained herein or for any errors or omissions that may have been made. The publisher remains neutral with regard to jurisdictional claims in published maps and institutional affiliations.

This Springer imprint is published by the registered company Springer Nature Switzerland AG.
The registered company address is: Gewerbestrasse 11, 6330 Cham, Switzerland

Acknowledgements

The work as editors on this book put us in many varying roles throughout the last year: we were treasure seekers and visionaries, we were coaches and sparring partners, we were guides and learners. It was a great pleasure to encounter and discuss with all the professionals within the newly emerging field of narrative and story-based work in organizations along the way.

We thank the authors for their precious contributions in this book, helping to strengthen the awareness for storytelling organizations and the work with stories in transformational processes.

A special gratitude is extended to the BEYOND STORYTELLING network and community. Throughout the past years, this growing community of practitioners committed itself to the advancement of the theory and practice of narrative work in organizations and communities. For us, this community exemplifies innovation, support and learning.

Mannheim, Germany
Burscheid, Germany
January 2019

Jacques Chlopczyk
Christine Erlach

Contents

The Narrative Approach to Transforming Organizations

Jacques Chlopczyk and Christine Erlach

Abstract

The chapter introduces the book *Transforming Organizations—Narrative and Story-Based Approaches*.

Acknowledging the current sense of urgency to transform and adapt to the changing business environment and the social and technological developments, the chapter outlines the contribution of the emerging field of narrative work in organizations to rethink the approaches and tools organizations can use to enable change and transformation.

This emerging field of practice explores the potential of working with narratives and stories in the organizational field. Besides a general introduction, the chapter outlines the shared assumptions of the authors and provides a thematic overview to the contributions in the book.

1 Introduction

Throughout the recent decades, a plot has emerged that situates the world on the edge of a fundamental transformation that will alter how our societies, our economies, and the organizations that we work with operate.

There are many books written about this transition and what it means for societies, economies, organizations and individuals. And this transition has been given many names. But no matter how we call it, the pressure to change, adapt, and

J. Chlopczyk (✉)
Zentrum für systemische Forschung und Beratung GmbH, Beyond Storytelling Partners, Mannheim, Baden-Württemberg, Germany
e-mail: jacques.chlopczyk@beyondstorytelling.com

C. Erlach
NARRATA Consult, Cologne, Germany
e-mail: christine.erlach@narrata.de

© Springer Nature Switzerland AG 2019

J. Chlopczyk, C. Erlach (eds.), *Transforming Organizations*,
Management for Professionals, https://doi.org/10.1007/978-3-030-17851-2_1

transform can be felt everywhere. There is a substantial agreement that something is changing in a very fundamental way.

If we zoom out and take a macro-perspective, we are now entering a configuration that can best be described as a new industrial revolution with the widespread proliferation of new technologies throughout the world, enabling new ways of working, of value creation, and of connection between different actors in different market places.

It is of course not the case that transformation or change is something new. Organizations have always transformed to adapt to changing markets, new technological developments, altered behavior of customers, and changed expectations of their workforce. Yet, it seems that the pace is perceived as getting higher and the story why change is needed is changing.

While these stories are different around the globe, a common denominator is a sense of urgency, based on the assumption that if organizations do not act now, they will be out of the picture in the near future. New business models and automatization will disrupt existing value chains, rendering existing modes of value creation no longer economically viable. For organizations that means that they have to reinvent their business models, the way they situate themselves in their markets (or strive for new monopolies), and redefine their very purpose of existence.

Going through transformation is a challenging thing, as organizations need to find a balance between stability and change, between learning and unlearning, between envisioning a new future while at the same time being grounded in their daily operations.

To support organizations in these transitions, a diverse and multifaceted field of practice evolved in the course of the last century, establishing different methods, approaches, and practices to facilitate transformation. The intention behind this book is to give an emerging approach to organizational transformation a platform.

2 Working with Stories in Organizational Transformation: An Emerging Field of Practice

At the core of this narrative approach is the assumption that human beings think, act, and feel in stories and that organizational change can be understood as a change and a transformation of the stories told in and about the organization—about its purpose, development, history, and way of operating (cf. Chlopczyk 2017).

Humans think and act in stories. Ask anyone about their work biography or the strategy of their company, and they will respond with something that approximates a story with a beginning, a middle, and an end. Humans are storytelling animals (Gottschall 2012).

In the last years, we see a heightened interest in storytelling. From digital marketing to leadership development, this interest in storytelling aims at engaging audiences, inspiring employees and customers, and influencing opinion leaders and important stakeholders.

From our point of view, this new focus on storytelling seems to be a reaction to ever more mediated forms of communication. Good storytelling promises to cut through the noise of our digitally informed lives and engage hands, hearts, and minds of employees and stakeholders.

But this focus on story*telling* alone neglected other ways in which we can work with stories in organizational transformation. Humans not only tell stories; they think, feel, remember, and enact stories. And working with stories in organizations caters to this "narrative condition" of humans.

The approaches described in this book go beyond a single focus on the telling of stories and show the various ways in which the human capability for storied perception of the world, of storied thinking and doing, can be a powerful partner in organizational transformation. In this sense, working with stories in organizations is not only about telling them in order to engage and convince others but about collaborative sensemaking and organizational healing (cf. Chapter "Six Perspectives on the Role of Story in Creating Flourishing Organisational Futures" by Arthur, this volume).

Enriching the mainstream path of the predominant focus on storytelling with a much wider range of ways of working with narrations, the book outlines approaches and methods that put their focus on story listening and the collaborative transformation of the stories that guide and inform organizational life—thus enlarging the notion of what it means to work with stories in organizational transformation.

In doing so, the book also showcases the many roots of narrative work. As with many approaches to organizational transformation, working with stories is an eclectic field—adopting and tailoring methods from marketing, facilitation, and therapy to the specific context of organizational transformation.

Before we outline the different contributions of the book, we want to share some basic assumptions that are inherent in these practices and in many contributions to this book. These assumptions form a conceptual or theoretical background to the chapters in this volume.

3 Stories Make Worlds: Basic Assumptions of a Narrative and Story-Based Approach to Organizational Transformation

This book looks at change or transformations in organizations from a specific point of view. This is the case with every written text and every field of practice—there are assumptions that we take for granted to develop our arguments and make sense of the topics and issues we deal with and that inform our actions and decisions while working in a specific field.

Narrative work has many roots. The key assumptions that follow guided us as editors and most of the authors in this book in developing their ideas regarding the role of narratives and stories in organizational transformation:

- *The social construction of reality*: This way of thinking about organizations and social interactions in general presumes that meaning is generated in the interaction between humans. In a wider sense, this also means that the representation of reality is something that is not giving but developed through interactions with others. Human knowledge, values, and behaviors are thus always situated in and contributing to a certain construction of reality. For organizational transformation, this puts the patterns of meaning-making and the discourses and taken-for-granted beliefs that make up a specific organizational reality in focus (cf. Gergen 2002).

- *Narrative versus paradigmatic thinking*: Humans think, act, and feel in stories. While this seems something very natural to assume, this mode of thinking has not been in focus in modern organizations or theorizing about organizational behavior. There is a preference for numbers, facts, and "scientific thinking." Yet, in the recent decades, we witnessed a turn toward narration in many different fields (cf. Sarbin 1986; Rhodes and Brown 2005)—but essentially also in the way the workings of the human mind are theorized. Jerome Bruner characterized this as "narrative thinking," a way of thinking that is fundamentally oriented toward making sense of human action in the social context it is situated in. While the ultimate goal of paradigmatic or scientific thinking is the establishment of truth, narrative thinking aims to establish plausibility of the behaviors of humans in action based on their motives, thus making meaning through the emplotment of chains of events into coherent narrations (Bruner 1986; Chlopczyk 2017).
- *Organizations as storytelling systems*: Taking this as a starting point, we also assume that larger social structures, including organizations, are constituted through story and narration. Yuval Harari (2014) sees the ability of the human kind to use "fictional language" for things that do not exist in the material world—such as capitalism, religions, and also organizations—as the main reason to be able to collaborate in larger groups. As long as there is a critical mass of people believing in a fictional idea and as long as they share their beliefs with stories of their experiences, it will persist. Organizations in this sense are fictional ideas (i.e., not fixed objects or entities independent of the person describing it) that constitute themselves through all the internal, external, and contextual narrations (Müller 2017) that are told about it. Imagine, nobody told any stories about an organization any longer, it would simply stop to exist. David Boje (2008) developed the concept of organizations as "Storytelling System" in order to understand the role and dynamics of stories in organizations to provide a sense of stability and orientation while at the same time adapting to shifting environmental and internal challenges (cf. Chapter "Change and Transformation in the Storytelling Organization" by Chlopczyk, this volume).
- *Organizational transformation as a change in the stories told in organizations*: Taking the idea of the storytelling organization serious also means that organizational transformation needs to be reconceptualized. Instead of thinking in structures and processes, the focus lies on the ongoing conversations in which the past, present, and future of an organization are told in stories. Stories then become the very stuff that organizational transformation is about. Strategies to enable organizational transformation then focus on what kind of conversations are happening in the organization and what kind of stories are told.

- *Change as a dialogical practice*: Within the practice of organizational transformation, we have many ideas how change works. The approaches presented in this book share the basic idea that change is a profoundly dialogical practice. There is a bulk of existing practice that operates based on that assumption (Bushe and Marshak 2015), but it is not yet common sense. A collaborative way of working through transformation is important not only because it embodies a different kind of attitude toward collaboration but because it is more efficient in a world in which true value lies in finding appropriate responses in a complex environment through the involvement of others in finding solutions. The role of change agents is not meaning-making and then transferring the meaning to others but the enablement of everyone involved in a certain field or system to make meaning together. A changed understanding of the organization or one's role within it emerges from a dialogical, co-creative effort involving all relevant stakeholders.

These basic assumptions are more or less explicitly visible in the way our authors present their ideas and recall their experiences in facing transformational processes through a narrative and story-based approach toward organizations.

4 Chapter Overview

This book is about narrative work and story-based approaches in transforming organizations. It contributes to the development of this perspective through expanding the notion of the "storytelling organization" and outlining major conceptual approaches to narrative work in organizations. Additionally, the authors describe specific approaches, tools, and case studies in supporting organizations and individuals in times of transition based on narrative work:

Wolfgang Tonninger opens with an essayistic approach to narratives told and lived. His chapter builds bridges between art, politics, and organizational work, focusing the process of identity construction. The chapter traces the dynamics of identity formation within an art project based around a fictional character and the voices of the author-artists. This serves as a backdrop to highlight the dialogical and constructivist nature of personal, social, and organizational identities underlining the role of performance of identity within transformation processes in organizations.

The contribution by *Jacques Chlopczyk* provides a theoretical framework for mapping the narrative field in the context of transformational processes. He describes the conceptual roots of the notion of the "storytelling organization" and the function of stories in organizations and develops an overview of the role of stories in organizational transformation.

This conceptual introduction is followed by the chapter from *Mary Alice Arthur* in which six perspectives on how story can support more flourishing organizational futures are described. Deeply rooted in participative processes, the chapter highlights how working with story can ignite and sustain change, support collaborative sensemaking, and enable organizational healing.

Chené Swart focuses on re-authoring practices as a way to enable change in organizations. Her chapter outlines basic assumptions of this approach and exemplifies how collective meaning-making, deconstruction of societal discourses, and the imagining of futures support the development of new and different stories as a basis for organizational transformation.

The creation of future stories is a core dynamic in organizational transformation. Starting from the distinction between open and closed story worlds, *Michael Müller* describes ways to create master plots for new organizational futures. The chapter also provides an insight into the mapping of the stories present in an organization through narrative interviews.

Stephanie Bachmair focuses on the interaction between story and process in organizational transformation in her chapter. In her account of Storywork, sensitive listening, impactful authentic telling, and co-creating are integrated. She illustrates the practice of Storywork with cases from leadership, brand, organizational, and strategy development along the Storywork cycle.

Working with an organizations' mythos lies at the core of the approach to organizational transformation presented by *Silvia Zulauf*. She describes the power of organizational myths pulsating throughout its history, its doctrines and beliefs, and its vision of the future. She outlines examples and a process through which leaders, organizations, and change agent can meaningfully engage with myth in organizational transformation.

Rick Peters and *Karin Thier* describe *Learning Histories*—an approach developed to unearth the implicit knowledge and hidden values in organizations. This analytical framework enables to make the narrations and assumptions that guide organizational behavior visible and create a solid foundation for change processes.

Focusing explicitly on the role of leaders in organizational transformation in the context of agile work settings, *Jaana Rasmussen* describes new narrative competencies that leaders should embrace for being able to give meaning and to support sensemaking in their organizations. A case study introduces the power of story listening and of authentic stories for being a role model toward the team members. A framework for the creation of powerful stories is described.

Taking a wider conceptual stance, the chapter by *Jeffer London*, *John B. McGuire*, and *Filipa Santos* focuses on the role of conversations in organizational transformation. They illustrate how "dialogue experiments" and other co-creative methods can be used and integrated in organizational transformation through a change in the content and the way people are talking with each other in the organization. The chapter highlights the capacity of storytelling for making beliefs visible and changing organizational behaviors to bring about positive change.

Yannis Angelis discusses the concept of disruptive Storywork merging serious game concepts and first-person story development. In this approach, disruptive interventions are used as catalysts for the individual and collective future stories to emerge. A case study shows that the newly crafted narratives have a transformational effect for the individual and the organization.

Metaphorical storytelling is the topic of *Brooke Hessler* and *Elizabeth D. Woodworth*. Using organizational metaphor analysis as a conceptual framework and taking the mythological creature of the chimera as a starting point, the chapter focuses on how professionals can envision themselves and their organizations as multifaceted or hybrid organisms—reflecting on their past, present, and future to envision new stories to live into.

In dealing with falls and failures in private and business lives, understanding the story we live through is crucial. In her chapter *Katarina Veselko* uses smaller- and larger-scale business examples of the processes at work in getting through adversity. Juxtaposing the *Rising Strong*™ process with the hero's journey, the chapter explores the role of storytelling in building resilience in times of transition.

Griet Bouwen, *Marianne Schapmans*, and *Chené Swart* explore the transformation of an organization committed to the future of travel and hospitality describing the history of its evolution. Leveraging the synergies between appreciative inquiry, generative journalism, and re-authoring work, a new practice has been built that enables stakeholder engagement, organizational transformation, and a visible impact on the societal discourse around travel and hospitality.

Enabling individuals to make new career choices is the topic explored by *Marieke Genard*. In her chapter she describes how stories can be used in the context of career coaching. A seven-step process is introduced and illustrated by two cases. The cases show how stories of people's past and the development of future stories support the coachees to envision their personal and professional development.

Human resources and personnel development departments are strong players in every organizational transformation. *Melanie Gabert* describes her work with stories at a personnel development department on its way to a new role model and a changed professional identity. She shows how stories are an effective tool for dealing with constant change and how various narrative approaches are beneficial for developing and supporting the workforce of tomorrow.

Taking a broader perspective, *Joanna Sell* reviews the ways in which time can be perceived in the organizational context in different cultures. Highlighting the impact of how people see past, present, and future on the dynamics of transformation in organizations, she proposes a new approach toward challenges caused by differing time perceptions across cultures.

What becomes visible throughout the different chapters is the potential, versatility, and diversity within this emerging field of narrative and story-based approaches to organizational transformation. While the topics and entry points might be different for the authors, they share the conviction that in rethinking change and transformation through the lens of narrative, organizations have powerful means to reinvent themselves in the twenty-first century.

References

Boje, D. M. (2008). *Storytelling organizations*. London: Sage.

Bruner, J. (1986). *Actual minds, possible worlds*. Cambridge: Harvard University Press.

Bushe, G. R., & Marshak, R. J. (2015). *Dialogic organization development: The theory and practice of transformational change*. San Francisco, CA: Berrett-Koehler Publishers.

Chlopczyk, J. (2017). *Beyond Storytelling*. Heidelberg: Springer.
Gergen, K. J. (2002). *Konstruierte Wirklichkeiten - eine Hinführung zum sozialen Konstruktionismus*. Stuttgart: Kohlhammer.
Gottschall, J. (2012). *The storytelling animal. How stories make us human*. New York: Houghton Mifflin Harcourt Publishing.
Harari, Y. N. (2014). *Sapiens: A brief history of humankind*. London: Harvill Secker.
Müller, M. (2017). *Einführung in narrative Methoden der Organisationsberatung*. Heidelberg: Carl Auer.
Rhodes, C., & Brown, A. D. (2005). Narrative, organizations and research. *International Journal of Management Reviews, 7*, 167–188.
Sarbin, T. (Ed.). (1986). *Narrative psychology: The storied nature of human conduct*. London: Praeger Press.

Jacques Chlopczyk is a social psychologist, systemic consultant, and facilitator working with organizations and communities. He is lecturing on organizational transformation, systemic consulting, and facilitation at the center for systemic research and consulting and other institutions. He is co-initiator of the Beyond Storytelling network and conference.

Christine Erlach is one of the founders of NARRATA Consult (www.narrata.de), a consulting network focusing on the development and application of narrative methods in the fields of knowledge management and cultural change management. Since 1998 she has been specializing in finding and transferring tacit knowledge and cultural values and beliefs in organizations. She uses narrative methods for nudging reflection and learning processes, concerning formerly hidden values and beliefs in change processes. The consultant and facilitator is lecturing at the HdM Stuttgart and has published diverse book contributions concerning the narrative and story-based approach to knowledge management and to cultural change.

The Sun Is Still in My Eyes. Reflecting on the Constructiveness of Life

Wolfgang Tonninger

> *A story isn't about a moment in time, a story is the moment in time.*
>
> W. D. Wetherell

Abstract

This article has the intention to build bridges between art, politics, and organizational work, by scrutinizing the process of identity construction (with its stages of selecting, compiling, and re-presenting) between the author and the artist in a recent movie project. Exploring a co-constructed biography as a film collage, we introduce a practice of coexistence that goes beyond the discourse of essence and establishes a surface zone where the self is transcending its narrowing borders of self-assessment and gets in touch with the other.

This brings us to a second layer, where the article is about the aesthetics of mediation and how this detour of mediation helps us to talk and reflect about ourselves in new ways—also and especially in organizational contexts—protecting participants from becoming vulnerable targets in the dominant discourse when the workshop is over and the drive of the intervention fades out. The common ground of this practice is called externalization, focusing on inspiring relations instead of the core content, subject, and problem and embracing the irritation when witnessing ourselves performed by others.

Taking serious the constructiveness of life, we learn to decipher even the treasures we find in the opaque rooms of our biographies as invitations to open new windows into the commonly owned possibility land and raising the question

W. Tonninger (✉)
ALMBLITZ – stories that change, Abtenau, Austria
e-mail: wolfgang.tonninger@almblitz.com

© Springer Nature Switzerland AG 2019

J. Chlopczyk, C. Erlach (eds.), *Transforming Organizations*,
Management for Professionals, https://doi.org/10.1007/978-3-030-17851-2_2

how this playful and dynamic approach to personal identification can also transform the way we deal with corporate identity in a world of permanent change.

1 How It All Began

It happened in the early 1990s when two young men ran into each other during an exhibition in an annex of a castle south of Vienna. One of them is the artist, the other is the other—that should be sufficient for the moment. What followed was a curious dialogue bridging two summers and two worlds before they were drifting apart again.

Almost 25 years later, they meet again. All of a sudden the telephone rings. A call crossing worlds and decades. The artist is planning to make a film collage[1] about a time in his life and asks the other, the author of this text, me, to "play" a part in it which is not yet defined initially. So, to keep the process open, they start to mix up and shake various pieces of their biographies instead of dousing them in the fixing path of a total recall. In a process of de- and reconstructing, new biographic possibilities are developed out of a fantasized re-membering—allowing new alter egos to show up and transform the concept of a cut in stone identity into a loosely joined net of sparkling personages.

The people appearing in the film collage speak for various personages or drafts of the artist, the director. The artist is observer, as such playing a role without owned voice. For him the film collage serves as a mirror with some cracks. And like a puzzle, he is cut into pieces and rebuilt in the collage. Through these cracks he is reflected and transformed into someone else, the other. And this other is more than one.

One voice of the other is me, digging in my childhood and providing snippets of texts, weaving a skin which spans over multiple biographies, embodying a character which is rooted in another childhood. The artist and I are brotherly sharing this character, Alma, a 15-year-old girl, who offers me a form I can mold myself into. During the process of writing, Alma became a mask through which one layer of my true face was uncovered. Looking back it seems crucial that the process of distancing and the process of adoption were happening almost simultaneously. Alma was invented by the text as it appeared. She represented me in the film collage. And she transcended me at the same time inviting parts of my self to be reseen and rewritten through the lens of the artist. At the end, Alma served as a medium through which our biographies overlapped. We looked at her from different angles, so that our eyelines could meet mysteriously in her glance.

[1]The movie "The order of the past/The sun is still in my eyes/A collage by Wilhelm Singer," can be watched under the following link: https://vimeo.com/225214681.

2 The Process of Identity Construction

The starting point of this process of identity construction and reciprocal acquisition of biographies[2] is the tension field between the revolutionary and the bourgeois in a certain timeframe in the 1970s. Between the one (the artist), who was brought up in a squat, politicized from the beginning, breastfed by a revolutionary dialogue between artists in a world of permanent transgression, and the other (the author), framed in a catholic-minded petite bourgeoisie. The one wishing nothing more than order, the other nothing more than turmoil, unhinging everything this world is nicely made of.

This tension field has provided the framing and became the driving source of my writing. Through this tension field, we became con-texts of each other. And we were able to mix up like communicating vessels. Reflecting this membrane, it was easy for me to sort out the private from the personal, the historical from the metaphorical dimension.

It was Kirsten Hastrup[3], a Danish anthropologist, who experienced this in an exemplary way and accompanied our reflections. In her book (*A Passage to Anthropology*), she remembers her encounter with Eugenio Barba and his idea of a theater play about her life as an anthropologist. And how in this process of inventing herself as a character in this play she step by step developed and transformed her sense of being a person and the concept of her self: "*When my history became mythical, it became real.*" (Hastrup 1995, p. 139)

> Myth and history are equally true renderings of the past; they differ mainly in their being two distinct modes of representation. Myth is an allegorical representation of the past, whereas history is perceived as literal. In our culture we have given priority to literal-mindedness and have largely relegated metaphor to a parasitic position upon literal language. We have repressed the knowledge that metaphors induce action, and thus are history. (Hastrup 1995, p. 139)

We live, we experience, and we reflect—as human beings first and biographical subjects second. Or seconds later, when the experience is seen with the eyes of the teller.[4] We go through the world with a quill in the hand. So, the world comes through language in our brain. And, surprise! At the end of the day, our world looks

---

[2]In rethinking and enriching this text, I accidentally stumbled upon a quote by Kathy Weingarten (1991, p. 29) who also uses the term "reciprocal" when describing the social constructionist view as follows: "the experience of self exists in the ongoing interchange with others . . . the self continually creates itself through narratives that include other people who are reciprocally woven into these narratives."

[3]Thanks to David Epston who set the track to Kirsten Hastrup in Bordeaux 2015, introducing a narrative format called "Insider Witnessing." He compared the "aha moment" when you see yourself through the eyes of a well-informed other—and this other is not talking to you directly but to someone else—with witnessing a performance of yourself in the leading role.

[4]The distinction between life as lived (reality), life as experienced (experience), and life as told (expression) is fundamental (Bruner 1984)—not just for ethnographers or anthropologists but also for systemic versed facilitators who work in the organizational field. Because any change is fueled by reflection, and it is kind of common sense that there are inevitable gaps between reality, experience, and expression where reflection can enter the room and we turn back upon ourselves to start telling stories about our stories.

Table 1 Juxtaposition of Myth and History by ©ALMBLITZ—stories that change

	Myth	History
The rendering of the past	Allegorical	Literal
Diversity versus linearity	Metaphor	Truth
The function of the language	Performant	Representational
Movement versus fixation	Allusion context	Kernel essence
The focus of the storyteller	Possibilities	Reality
Enrichment versus reduction	Plural	Singular

like we are. We are forming and being formed at the same time. And this holds not only true for individuals but also for business artifacts like corporations, as socio-cultural entities being performed every moment by multiple interactions between individuals. But while it seems quite reasonable that social identities are constructed, there is a resistance in holding the same true for individuals, even if we bring to our mind that the role we embody marks the field where the world (or the organization) meets the person (Table 1).[5]

Experiencing the metaphorical dimension in our biographies[6] means also to experience the constructive nature of our identity. That identity is not something pre-given, untouched like the essence or the kernel inside a person, but socially constructed. It correlates with the insight that any storified immediacy is by nature mediated. Especially, when we enter the field of storywork, we leave the place of pure authenticity and handkerchiefs, because it needs a teller to start our work, a person who opens the door of privacy and enters the room of dialogue. Respecting this essential movement, storywork is not circulating around this kernel trying to squeeze the essence out and fix it but the process of enriching a set of multiple possibilities on very different layers, as Joe Lambert (2018, p. 11), the alchemist of digital storytelling, underlines: "*The process of identity construction in the twenty-first century will be as accelerated, fluid, and dislocating as has virtually all aspects of our current economic and social experience within our societies.*"

In other words, in the process of identity construction between Wilhelm Singer and me, we have been exploring the ambiguities of our cultural and social positions—with a timeline fraying out in different directions and dimensions. Kirsten Hastrup (1995, p. 132) describes the process of writing her role in Eugenio Barba's play as "*an essentially creative process in which discovery merges with*

[5]Worth additional reading are the thoughts from William James (1925, pp. 128–129) about the character: "We may practically say that he has as many different social selves as there are distinct groups of persons about whose opinion he cares. He generally shows a different side of himself to each of these different groups. Many a youth who is demure enough before his parents and teachers, swears and swaggers like a pirate among his 'tough' young friends. We do not show ourselves to our children as to our club companions, to our customers as to the laborers we employ, to our own masters and employers as to our intimate friends."

[6]It is important to point out with Freedman and Combs (1996, p. 1) that this metaphorical dimension is less about poetics than politics: "The metaphors through which we organize our work have a powerful influence on both what we perceive and what we do."

definition. My recollections made me discover a person who was defined as such at the same stroke. The stories often seemed to write themselves through me and they were certainly personal."

Deep reading this quote one has to replace the word "definition" with the word "invention" to get the full scale of meaning. It is like opening a modern climbing route in a wall, you will not just orient yourself by the obvious cracks, dihedrals, ledges, and chimneys, but try to invent a line which only becomes real through your climbing moves. The route is the result of a creative discovery. Similarly, the searching for identity and the forming of identity go hand in hand, in the moment you leave the realm of epistemology and focus on the discursive nature of identity. No wonder, that Kirsten Hastrup (1995, p. 132) talks about her "position to speak" when she is reflecting her fieldwork experiences as an anthropologist:

> It is part of the fieldwork condition to be unknown, and sometimes invisible; but it is also part of the game gradually to establish a position to speak from—that is, an identity. I realized that this, perhaps, was not exclusively related to fieldwork but was a general human condition: identities are invented, not given.

We are forming and being transformed at the same time. You need a rock to climb and a language to story. "Story is a verb," as Chené Swart (2013) once formulated in a workshop in Vienna—underlining the dynamics of this process of narrating and re-narrating of what and who we are.

3 The Representation as a Performance

Starting to write for the movie collage of Wilhelm Singer, I was forced to transcend my literal biography and think about the representation of myself. Being the informant of somebody else's story was revealing new aspects of my biography and affecting the "*implicit choices between stories to be told and points to remain unspoken.*" (Hastrup 1995, p. 132f)[7]

Talking about your self is different than staging yourself. No matter if your categories are cinematic or theatrical, in the moment you are thinking about yourself as a performed role, you don't ask anymore "Who am I?", but "What does the audience need to know to understand the construction of myself, to understand my performed self?".[8] The result of this process is a socially constructed identity or a histrionic biography, where meaning becomes an effect of "experiential densities" as

[7]After all, these choices about one's personal contribution every employee in the organizational context also has to make. For bringing in the whole person is less an option than a management myth.

[8]Slightly exaggerating what Michael White (1988, p. 10) said about the construction of the self, this theatrical approach makes it may be a bit more perceptible what "putting into circulation" means: "As 'self' is a performed self, the survival of alternative knowledges is enhanced if the new ideas and new meanings that they bring forth are put into circulation."

Kirsten Hastrup (1995, p. 139) points out. The fact, that our self is a construct that is nurtured from social contexts is, from a narrative standpoint, not disappointing but a massive opportunity to realize that representation is a creative process not a substantive category.

> Writing oneself is … an essentially creative process in which discovery merges with definition. My recollections made me discover a person who was defined as such at the same stroke. The stories often seemed to write themselves through me and they were certainly personal. (Hastrup 1995, p. 132)

Internalizing this playing mode becomes possible on the basis of a principal externalization. We are not lost anymore in the validation of subjective sensitivities but deal with the significance of personages we impersonate on stage. While reflecting on our doubles "*we are forced to admit that sameness and otherness are not objective qualities but categories of thought*" (Hastrup 1995, p. 143) and that identity is always relational and inventive.

> I could neither identify with nor distance myself from Kirsten on stage. She was neither my double nor an other. She restored my biography in an original way, being not-me and not-not-me at the same time. I was not represented, I was performed. (Hastrup 1995, p. 141)

Instead of digging into the depths of the problematic subject, we focus on the process of subjectivation. By disclosing the process of positioning, reflecting, and shaping, we resist the temptation of all psycho-disciplines to internalize the pillars of story and fix them within the rigid terms of essence and truth.[9]

An interesting detail was the artist's reaction during the first screening of the movie in Potsdam, Germany. While he was watching the movie, some nervous giggling flashed through his face, accompanied by a kind of dry cough. It had something dollish, like the personages on the screen were wandering through him who became an interface between reality and fiction, a vessel through which our biographies were marinated.

Something similar happened to me. Being transformed into pieces of texts spoken as a voice-over by a young girl, I was not longer me. I witnessed a representation which sublated my presence in a dialectic sense. At the end, I found myself in a new, meandering state between me, my text, the girl, and Wilhelm Singer and couldn't tell anymore where the revolution came into my bourgeois life. Maybe the performance itself was the revolution relieving me from the burden of identity "*as a skin-bound container with fixed contents (resources).*" (Freedman and Combs 1996, p. 17)

[9]A paragraph that could be written equally for the organizational context: Companies often get stuck in their belief systems and miss alternatives when the one and true and only story is challenged. Paralyzed that a story doesn't work anymore, they initiate the blaming process instead of moving the pillars of the story in a playful way.

4 Breathing Artifacts

On the background of these reflections, we have also to question the opposition between authenticity and artificiality. When we are forming a narration about ourselves, we are circling around ourselves with words; we are molding and being molded at the same time as Walter Benjamin (1969, p. 93f) in his reflections on Nikolai Leskov once noted:

> The storytelling that thrives . . . is itself an artisan form of communication, as it were. It does not aim to convey the pure essence of the thing, like information or a report. It sinks the thing into the life of the storyteller, in order to bring it out of him again. Thus traces of the storyteller cling to the story the way the handprints of the potter cling to the clay vessel.

Following this metaphor and adding a clay that never hardens than you grasp what storywork differs from storytelling. Storywork is about the dynamics of identity construction, while storytelling tries to fix the meanings damming up the stream of free floating significance. We are formed while we are forming. We are made as artifacts when we enter the site of construction.

This is what happens to me: Being displayed I become an object for myself, and a subject for the others, the audience, who is witnessing this performance. And this transformation into an object is another overseen aspect of externalization where we can choose out of two possibilities: (1) to place the problem outside of us and (2) to gain a position to speak which puts a distance between us and the problematic self. When I was writing the texts for the movie collage of Wilhelm Singer, I felt like a Campbell's Soup Can—that something mystical happens to me in the moment I start to select and re-author certain moments in my life; that this very ordinary life is suddenly transposed to canvas and becomes art, like an objet trouvé.[10]

When we enter the stage, we become breathing artifacts, and in this process, we don't have to suffer the loss of authenticity. It is more like entering a different layer, occupying a certain place from where to reflect about ourselves and to talk about ourselves. The Norwegian writer Karl Ove Knausgård (2016) remembers a moment in his adolescence, when he took a plane from Kristiansund to Bergen. When the plane took off, he looked out of the window and saw the familiar landscape slowly disappearing up to the moment that he could see the moving clouds and the landscape beneath and suddenly felt overwhelmed by a very intense sense of the world. It was a moment he could not forget anymore and called it by himself a moment of world vibe which was set up by two different units—(1) a presence in the moment, in the "here and now," and (2) the opposite, the feeling of being apart, cut off, outside of something. And for him this particular simultaneity of presence and distance from the world serves as the place of art par excellence.

---

[10]I replace the "discarded object" and talk about a "discarded moment" which suddenly starts to sparkle on the background of a tension proposed by the artist and gains an aesthetic value.

5 Bridges into the Organization

Much has been said about T-group settings and experiential learning in organizational work,[11] and about the difficulties to create kind of cultural islands or safe containers where cultural rules of what one can and cannot say are not dominating behaviors and dialogic patterns. But even if we can grasp the talking stick and feel free to speak to the campfire in an open and vulnerable manner, what happens when the heroes come home, back to organizational reality, hierarchy, and power games? I would like to call this question the blind spot of dialogic organizational work, when facilitators are not available anymore and a third layer of learning starts, the layer of disenchantment and reinforcing the old cultural patterns.[12]

In this context stories are seen as means to open the hearts of the participants by sharing special moments of truth, to build some common empathy, and to create an experience of "unity in diversity."[13] But this is not the point where the heroes' journey ends. It's the beginning, the very important and crucial part of open sharing before the narrative work of de- and reconstruction starts, followed by the mediated narrative process of mirroring and externalization—circumnavigating and playing with the tides of power. Jumping on the narrative train means to focus on the cracks in the mirror of self-assessment and the process of construction.[14] To leave the realm of mere vulnerability and enter a playing and telling mode where identity conclusions are being tested and re-authored.

Like in the movie collage "The sun is still in my eyes," the starting point is preferably a blank stage and what we call a "tension field."[15] This tension field facilitates the search for the fork as the basis of the story[16] and offers a reflecting surface where people and stories can meet up. Shared moments of decision assure that we don't remain abstract and intellectual but encourage conversations on sensual events we really experienced. Later in the process, this tension field serves as driving

[11]For a quick overview, I recommend Edgar Schein's (2015) foreword to the book *Dialogic Organization Development: The Theory and Practice of Transformational Change*.

[12]Like a dieter experiences a long-term backlash called yo-yo effect.

[13]A concept first shared independently by Paolo Freire and Victor Turner.

[14]It is not a mere coincidence that Barbara Myerhoff and Jay Ruby (1982, p. 2) use the same metaphor of the crack in the mirror when writing about the essential role of reflexivity—pointing out that holding up a mirror is not enough: "Reflexive, as we use it, describes the capacity of any system of signification to turn back upon itself, to make itself its own object by referring to itself: subject and object fuse . . . Within the self, detachment occurs between self and experience, self and other, witness and actor, hero and hero's story. We become at once both subject and object. Reflexive knowledge, then, contains not only messages, but also information as to how it came into being, the process by which it was obtained."

[15]In the movie collage project, the tension field was between a revolutionary and a bourgeoisie approach to the world with a book as a missing link, *The Aesthetics of Resistance* in which the author Peter Weiss invented himself as part of a revolutionary becoming. In business context this tension field can be everything, which helps to define certain crossings from which we can reflect our positioning and decide where to go.

[16]In reference to Jorgé Luis Borges' (1998) image of a "forking in time, rather than in space".

source and lighthouse of approval ensuring that we are heading in the right direction. In overcoming their private story roots, people can write themselves into this tension field in a new and still personal way. But it's not only people who enter the stage; the stage becomes an open platform which is step by step enriched by sounds, colors, objects, entities, and archetypes. Not a cultural island—in a T-group sense of an island where culture is suspended—but an experimental laboratory where the clash of cultural building blocks is freely performed along an open timeline.

The process from the shared moments to the performed roles[17] is crucial in this game of social construction because we are permanently shifting between being informants and audience, objects of subjectivation, and subjects of meaning making, voices which are influential in a company's quest[18] as well as in a so-called association of life.

> Re-membering conversations are shaped by the conception that identity is founded upon an 'association of life' rather than on a core self. This association of life has a member-ship composed of the significant figures and identities of a person's past, present, and projected future, whose voices are influential with regard to the construction of a person's identity. (White 2007, p. 129)

Can you see the experimental stage already? This rich and inspiring mixture of entities and voices from various characters (stakeholders) which are inscribing themselves in the companies' social body? We take place in the audience and listen to the stories unfolding. And at the end we "*come to be performer and observer of the same show.*" (Goffman 1956, p. 49) And if this show is good, the story will instigate new perception, new action, and new movement.

These are the criterions we as facilitators bring in this playful approach in dealing with company culture and the pillars of a company identity. Listening to all the different voices a company's culture is made of, we become anthropologists or even ethnographers of organizations offering them a mirror to see the richness of their being. A mirror with a crack, of course, so we don't waste time with self-adulation but enter a moving process of action and reflection.

With the effect that people—and companies as social entities—are no longer isolated "*from the very contexts of their own lives*"; and no longer blind "*to life as it is produced, and as we produce it.*" (White 1995, p. 42) As people proceed from the moments portal (sharing personal moments of transformation) to the actual storywork section (remembering contexts and de-constructing discursive fixations) and finally enter the rehearsal and enactment stage (reconstructing the story in front of an audience), they start tasting the process of construction and gradually develop

[17]That is also a process from mere telling to writing things down and polishing meanings—from feeling it, to rethinking it, to showing it, to seeing it, to hearing it, to mixing it. Similar to the seven steps process from Joe Lambert (2018, p. 89).

[18]Instead of producing these kinds of well-known and lifeless vision statements, we let "preferred stories" enter the stage. And instead of talking about resources, which are fixed inside of someone, we talk about knowledges, as something that "develops and circulates among people" Freedman and Combs (1996, p. 17).

an awareness of how they are part of this process and how they can exert their influence on what they are and what they want to be. Leaving behind the tyranny of "realness" and "authenticity," we enter a stage where meaning making in a new and playful way becomes possible.

6 Epilogue

In the workshop we[19] did in Hamburg, we experienced the processes of remembering and re-authoring as communicating vessels. Up to the moment when the roles we invented behaved like positions in a systemic structural constellation work. When out of the blue, one participant stood up, entered the stage, and embodied another persons' life with gestures, perceptions, and words.

It was a new and secret moment of authenticity where the borders of sameness and otherness have been transcended. A moment when our questions were no longer gathering information, but generating a new experience. When the metaphors we created induced action, the performance became performant. A moment when story was not fixed any longer in its "about-mode" of representation, but became itself a moment in time.[20]

References

Benjamin, W. (1969). The storyteller: Reflections on the works of Nikolai Leskov. In *Illuminations: Essays and reflections*. New York: Schocken Books.

Borges, J. L. (1998). The garden of the forking paths. In *Collected fictions* (pp. 119–128). New York: Viking.

Bruner, E. M. (1984). The opening up of anthropology. In E. M. Bruner (Ed.), *Text, play and story. The construction and re-construction of self and society. Proceeding of the 1983 annual meeting* (pp. 1–16). Washington, DC: American Ethnological Society.

Freedman, J., & Combs, G. (1996). *Narrative therapy: The social construction of preferred realities*. New York: W. W. Norton.

Goffman, E. (1956). *The presentation of self in everyday life*. University of Edinburgh, Social Sciences Research Centre, Monograph No. 2. https://monoskop.org/images/1/19/Goffman_Erving_The_Presentation_of_Self_in_Everyday_Life.pdf.

Hastrup, K. (1995). *A passage to Anthropolgy: Between experience and theory*. London: Routledge.

James, W. (1925). *The philosophy of William James* (Modern Library ed., pp. 128–129). New York: Random House.

Knausgård, K. O. (2016). Alles, was am Himmel ist. In *Das Amerika der Seele: Essays 1996–2013*. München: Luchterhand Literaturverlag.

[19]The artist Wilhelm Singer and the author of this text.

[20]Now, line-editing this text, I was reading the input-quotation by W. D. Wetherell again and was shocked that I deleted one essential word: "A story isn't about a moment in time. A story is about the moment in time." Suddenly this chosen intro quote I have stolen from Joe Lambert (2018) has a different meaning, but I decided to leave both versions. Also, because it seems significant that I was reading what I wanted to see.

Lambert, J., & Hessler, H. B. (2018). *Digital storytelling: Capturing lives, creating community* (5th ed.). New York: Routledge.

Myerhoff, B., & Ruby, J. (1982). *A crack in the mirror: Reflexive perspectives in anthropology*. Philadelphia: Pennsylvania Press.

Schein, E. (2015). Dialogic organization development: Past, present, and future. In G. R. Bushe & R. J. Marshak (Eds.), *Dialogic organization development: The theory and practice of transformational change* (pp. vii–xiv). San Francisco: Berrett-Koehler Publishers.

Singer, W. *The order of the past/the sun is still in my eyes*. A collage by Wilhelm Singer. https://vimeo.com/225214681

Swart, C. (2013). *Re-authoring the world: The narrative lens and practices for organisations, communities and individuals*. Randburg: Knowledge Ressources Publishing.

Weingarten, K. (1991). The discourse of intimacy: Adding a social constructionist and feminist view. *Family Process, 30*, 25–305.

White, M. (1988). Saying hullo again: The incorporation of the lost relationship in the resolution of the grief. *Dulwich Centre Newsletter, 3*, 7–11.

White, M. (1995). The politics of therapy. In *Re-authoring lives: Interviews and essays*. Adelaide: Dulwich Centre Publications.

White, M. (2007). *Maps of narrative practice*. New York: W. W. Norton.

Wolfgang Tonninger studied philosophy and literature. Writing along the interfaces between culture, nature, and technology. Video producer, systemic coach, and storyworker. Living the balancing act between creation and organization development—concentrating on the soft facts of corporate culture.

Founder of ALMBLITZ—a platform focused on narrative organization development, corporate culture, and creative working with stories. Co-founder and chief editor of "gangart"—a project for regional development. Co-founder and coach of "fairMATCHING"—an exploration and implementation platform to accompany people with escape background in their search for work.

Member of the ACC (Austrian Coaching Council), the umbrella association for coaching in Austria. Considers curiosity in storied lives as part of his DNA: "The shortest distance to the other is once around the world."

Change and Transformation in the Storytelling Organization

Jacques Chlopczyk

Abstract

Working with stories in organizations is based on a set of ideas and assumptions. This chapter aims to provide an overview of the conceptual roots of the notion of the "storytelling organization" and the function of stories in organizations and develops an overview of the role of stories in organizational transformation.

The article also highlights the role of stories in the stabilization and change of organizations and shows starting points for working with narrative methods and stories within a broad distinction between episodic and continuous change. It is intended to give a framework for understanding the use and impact of narrative and story-based approaches in supporting organizations in transition.

1 The Storytelling Organization

1.1 Images of Organizations and the Storytelling Organization

The phrase "the storytelling organization" is one possible answer to the question of what an organization is. Over time, very different answers were given to this question with different concepts, ideas, and theories. From Frederick Taylors' account of the scientific organization to more recent concepts like networked organizations, a diverse set of ideas have been put forward to think about, design, and create organizations.

A fruitful categorization of these different concepts was made by Gareth Morgan as early as 1986. In his book *Images of the Organization* (Morgan 1986), he

J. Chlopczyk (✉)
Zentrum für systemische Forschung und Beratung GmbH, Beyond Storytelling Partners, Mannheim, Baden-Württemberg, Germany
e-mail: jacques.chlopczyk@beyondstorytelling.com

© Springer Nature Switzerland AG 2019

J. Chlopczyk, C. Erlach (eds.), *Transforming Organizations*,
Management for Professionals, https://doi.org/10.1007/978-3-030-17851-2_3

describes different approaches to organizations, ranging from the image of the organization as a machine through the understanding of organization as a political system to the idea of the organization as a "brain" and learning system. These are metaphorical descriptions aiming to capture the very essence of different ways of looking at organizations.

With the choice of a metaphor for the description of an organization, different aspects come to the foreground, and other aspects move into the background. For example, the metaphor of the organization-as-machine focuses on processes, the optimization of energy flows (efficiency and effectiveness), and the interchangeability of individual components.

On the other hand, aspects such as the negotiation of different interests (the realm of the political metaphor); the creation, storage, and transfer of knowledge and information (the realm of the metaphor of the brain); or the complex relationships between organization and environment (the realm of the metaphor of the organism) move in the background (see Morgan 1986) with the choice of the organization-as-machine metaphor.

This effect of a guiding metaphor for describing an organization is not limited to theorizing about an organization but is understood as something that shapes the everyday life in an organization: depending on the metaphor or image of the organization that its members (and its customers and stakeholders) have, they will act, decide, and collaborate differently.

Thus, Gareth Morgan's concept of images of the organization can be extended to the cognitive representation of the organization by the people who work in and with it. The organization is above all an "organization in the head" (see Müller 2017) of all observers of the organization: the market, the employees, the executives, the competitors, and the shareholders. And this "organization in the head" determines to a large extent the organizational behavior—the action people take, the way interactions structure itself, and the choices that are made.

The image and the concept of the storytelling organization, first developed by David Boje (cf. Boje 2008), add another image that focuses on the practice and effects of storytelling in organizations. As a central idea, this approach assumes that organizations can be seen as storytelling systems that use narratives and stories to make sense and give orientation in the stream of activities and events that make up "the organization."

1.2 Homo Narrans and Sensemaking in Organizations

The concept of the storytelling organization is fundamentally linked to the assumption that narration and the telling of stories is a central paradigm of human communication (Fisher 1984). From this point of view, *Homo sapiens* is fundamentally a "homo narrans": a storytelling creature.

That humans are in fact telling stories is not by any stretch a new paradigm. But the significance of understanding humans as storytelling animals reaches far beyond the transmission of events in the form of plotted accounts of what happened in the past.

Jerome Bruner (1990) and others (see Sarbin 1986) assign narrative structures a central role in the cognitive organization of humans. People remember, think, and act in narrative structures (see Laszlo 2008). Stories and story-like forms play a central role for humans to orient and organize themselves in their environment: Story "[represents] structurally [. . .] a cognitive organization concept for the making of meaning" (Simoudis 2004, p. 11).

This fundamental role of stories and narrative structures for humans is reflected in the concept of the storytelling organization. It accounts for the efforts of human beings in organizations to remain able to act meaningfully in the complex organizational environments they find themselves in. Stories, from this perspective, "delineate emplotment and causality out of [. . .] potentially chaotic and disorganized [. . .] life at work" (Rhodes and Brown 2005, p. 173f.).

In this way, storytelling and narrative understanding are closely connected to what Karl Weick called "sensemaking" (Weick 1995; Sonenshein 2010). This "sensemaking" with regard to events and actions in organizations (Weick 1995) is one of the central functions of narrative structures and stories in organizations.

This process does not only give rise to ordered behavior and action but also has a correspondence in the representation of "the organization" by its members and its constituents. This "organization in the head" emerges as an action-guiding map (Müller 2017)—a representation of what the organization is and how it works.

This meaning making does not take place in isolation on an individual level but through conversations and the sharing of stories (cf. London et al. Chapter "We Become What We Talk About—How Experimenting with Dialogue Can Change an Organization's Culture" in this volume; Ford 1999). The exchange with others, the sharing and co-creation of meaning, plays a central role in this process. In this sense, an organization is constituted through a network of conversations in which what is seen as real and meaningful is developed and constituted (Gergen et al. 2004).

Thus, the idea of the storytelling organization is an expression of a social constructionist understanding of organizations and represents organizations as a set of relatively stable interactions and representations created by and through human interaction that enables coordinated, goal-oriented behavior and linked activities within the organization.

Stories are one central medium, and telling stories is a key activity through which these frameworks are created, maintained, enacted, and changed. The concept of the storytelling organization therefore focuses primarily on the construction of meaning, the dynamic process through which experiences come to be understood, and the guiding force of stories in the way people act within organizations.

1.3 Meaning Making Through Stories

Structurally, stories involve the description of a development over time. The basic structure of a story unfolds along a timeline—events and actions in stories are subjected to a regime of a temporal order of "before" and "after" and are linked via the construction of a plot, which relates the actions of the actors and the events to each other and integrates them into a meaningful whole. In doing so, stories are characterized by the fact that they consider both the action (the chain of action) as well as the underlying motives of the actors involved.

Thus, stories relate two different worlds (see Bruner 1990): The "landscape of action" and the "landscape of consciousness." On the level of action—of what actually happened—there are the elements of a grammar of stories. This grammar delineates building blocks that are necessary for something to be understood as a story: context (time and place), actors, and action.

"The level of consciousness," on the other hand, is concerned with the subjective experience of the actors: what the actors know, feel, think. Or do not know, do not feel, and do not think. The level of consciousness relates to the unseen drivers, emotions, and motivations that guide the actor's behavior, decision-making, and so on (Bruner 1990).

Stories and narratives build a relation between these two levels and enable a reconstruction of events as well as the associated goals and motives of the actors involved. This construction of the motives, interests, and emotions is necessarily a "creative re-description of the world such that hidden patterns and hitherto unexplored meanings can unfold" (Kearney 2002, p. 12). Intentions and motives of the actors are not accessible by observation but must be developed (constructed) via the "landscape of consciousness."

In this sense, the logic of stories is not a rational-scientific logic in the search for truth but a logic that focuses on the plausibility of the evolving story and the constructed landscape of consciousness. This plausibility is established through the reference to a socially shared framework of what constitutes plausibility. In Bartlett's terms, this is a "social framework of rationality" (see Bruner 1990; Bartlett 1932).

It is a rationality that relates to human emotions, motives and intentions, and their embeddedness in a certain social context with its own norms, values, and regular forms of behaving. When a narrative account of events and the related motives is constructed or told, the person perceiving the story determines if the story is plausible or not, i.e., can the events and actions be understood and are they making sense?

Thus, the content and structure of the narrated stories, the role of the characters, and their motives are often based on existing genres and archetypical plots. In their description of events, people in organizations draw on a culturally mediated repertoire of narrative structures and motifs.

In the sciences of literature, different authors have sought to classify archetypical plots. For instance, genres like comedy, romance, or tragedy have been elaborated by Frye (see Bruner 1986; Laszlo 2008). Also, Elsbree defined archetypical plots (1982).

While these researchers focused on literary genres, such archetypical plots can also be organization-specific containing prototypical roles and actions and expressing certain values, norms, and ideas. The stories and narratives make up what I would like to call the organization's *story-field*.

This *story-field* is in a constant state of change and encompasses all potential stories to be told in and about organization. New stories are carried into the organization, and existing narratives are reinterpreted and renegotiated. The story-field is part of the collective memory of the organization and its environment and represents the repertoire for the narrative framing of events and developments within an organization.

2 Key Perspectives on the Storytelling Organization

The description of organizations as storytelling systems enables new perspectives on leadership, design, and consulting for and within organizations. As described earlier, certain images or concepts allow us to describe phenomena that we would not be able to see or describe with another image. What comes into focus if we follow the image of the storytelling organization?

Social Construction of Reality The image of the storytelling organization is closely linked to a constructionist point of view. What people think is real and the rules, norms, and values that people follow in the organization are a collaborative co-production.

In doing so, people fall back on interpretations and stories stored in the collective memory of society and organization. This "repertoire" for the construction of reality is interwoven with the continuous creation of meaning and serves to make the unknown comprehensible and ultimately to guide and facilitate actions, in which the collaborative construction of reality is referenced, constituted, and realized (Gergen 2002).

Stories and Narratives as Organizing Factors of the Organizational Process The interaction in the organization is characterized by narrative structures. While scripts define prototypical chains of action (see Schank and Abelson 1977), stories make it possible to understand new developments and unforeseen events, using elements of collective memory and shared story frames.

These narrative structures are an organizing force within the organization, connecting its past with potential futures. Stories and narratives are central to action-guiding cultural interpretive patterns, values, and norms as well as organizational identity. The concept of storytelling organization therefore focuses the dynamics that cause fragmented stories and small narratives to become part of the collective memory of the organization—the shared repertoire of meaning and symbols that constitutes the realities of and within the organization.

Authorship The authorship of the stories and narratives that shape an organization takes place everywhere in and around an organization. While not all stakeholders have the same visibility or power to have their story heard, they nevertheless contribute to the definitions of an organizations' culture and identity.

The authorship of the identity-defining stories is distributed. There is no monopoly on telling the story of an organization. Yet, an organization is not an apolitical space, and the question of whose voices are considered legitimate participants to an organizations discourse is an important and decisive factor in the storytelling organization.

The image of the storytelling organization thus also puts the focus on the mechanisms of mainstreaming and marginalization and the mechanics of power in a given environment. Which voices are included and excluded within a given moment? Who is allowed to partake in the organizational discourse?

Plurality and Diversity There are always different versions of the same event. The conception of the storytelling organization is based on the understanding that organizations are inherently diverse, with different accounts of what the organization is and can be. This focus on diversity and plurality embraces differences between voices and actors as something very inherent to organizational life. This diversity is not seen as a challenge to the integrity or coherence of the organization.

Instead, all these different voices and actors are seen as resources for the development of accurate representations of the challenges within and outside of the organization and the actions that are appropriate to respond. Only through an appropriate integration of plurality and diversity can organization succeed in responding to the ongoing demands for adaptation to an ever-shifting environment.

Before we turn to the discussion of change and transformation and the role of story and narrations within such processes, we will further examine the different functions of stories in organizations, expanding and deepening the dynamics through which stories provide orientation, constitute, and contribute to organizational memory, identity, and culture.

3 The Function of Stories in Organizations

3.1 Providing Orientation

The stories told in the organization serve to coordinate, evaluate, and interpret actions. This orienting function of stories allows for an understanding of what is happening in the organization, the events that have led to the current state, or where the organization is heading to.

This also enables an understanding of the intentions and interests of the actors—the protagonists, antagonists, and secondary characters. The explanations associated with a story thus also serve the purpose creating a "secure ground" or shared frame of understanding on the basis of which future actions and events can be interpreted.

But interpretations of past events may change over time. This can be observed in organizations in the event of leadership changes or in times of crisis, when past events are reassessed. In addition, the interpretation of situations always takes place on the basis of currently available information. These are often incomplete or fragmented and not accessible to all actors equally.

Organizations are often confronted with different, sometimes contradictory stories. Especially against this background, organizations spend a lot of time "retrospectively reconstructing plausible stories in order to explain where they stand, even if no such story has brought them exactly to this point" (Weick 1998, p. 14).

Yet, the function of stories is not limited to the past. The future of the organization is also constantly being redesigned, and every organization needs stories that are geared toward a possible future. Thus, there will be a series of stories in a company outlining possible developments, future goals, and ways in which the organization or individual actors achieve these goals.

Especially in times of change, these forward-looking stories have a particularly important role to play in anticipating developments and forming a common image of the future. Strategic processes in particular can be understood from this perspective as the development of credible future stories (Barry and Elmes 1997). Developments in the market, in society, and in technology are analyzed and extrapolated into the future.

Without storied accounts of where the organization has come from and where it is going to, orientation within the organization is missing.

3.2 Knowledge and Organizational Memory

The importance of narrative structures for human thinking, remembering, and acting has already been mentioned. Especially Schank and Abelson (1995) have emphasized this function of stories: "virtually all human knowledge is based on stories constructed around past experiences (p. 1)."

Storytelling serves to convey knowledge. Stories make it possible to partake in the experiences of others and to participate in the narrator's experience as a kind of representative: "This reliving of others' experience is the historical role of storytelling in society in the context of human action (Snowden 2004, p. 204)." The stories that are told in an organization and the stories that are remembered in the organization are a crucial part of the collective memory of the organization.

The collective memory of an organization includes all memories, individual or shared, of the organization members. The collective memory is encoded in various media: it includes discussions (verbal medium), files and documents (text- and image-based media), or visual elements such as architecture, decor, or even gestures (see Boje 2008).

These elements of collective memory, the organization's implicit and explicit knowledge, are embedded in and related to different stories and narratives. Therefore, stories also provide good access to the knowledge available in the organization (cf. Erlach 2017; Angelis 2017) and can be used to convey knowledge in organizations.

Especially stories which are developed around important, emotional events have a special significance and are particularly well available when a situation has to be reinterpreted or described. In the collective memory founding, myths and stories about dramatic events (i.e., takeovers, bankruptcies, serious strategic reorientations) often play an important role (see Clement and Clement 2017; Zulauf, "Keeping Your Mythos Alive: How to Nourish and Nurture a Business's Mythos Through Corporate Transformations" in this volume) for the organizational identity and culture.

3.3 Culture and Identity

Organizational culture can be understood as a system of shared patterns of thinking, feeling, and acting as well as the norms, values, and symbols within an organization. Organizational culture enables the coordination of actions and mutual understanding and has a normative and limiting effect on behavioral choices. The stories told in and about the organization point to these cultural norms, values, and beliefs.

Stories also convey the elements that make up the organizational identity. Identity refers in particular to the answer to the question "Who are we?" and "What does that mean?" The narratives related to the organization make it possible to perceive consistency and stability over a period of time. A shared narrative is a necessary prerequisite for understanding oneself as a group or community: "A community cannot be a community without a shared narrative (Rappaport 2000, p. 6)."

Chené Swart (2013, p. 31) speaks of "taken-for-granted beliefs" in this context. Assumptions and beliefs are no longer questioned, and, often, these "taken-for-granted-beliefs" are no longer consciously accessible. Awareness and dialogical reformulation of these cultural and identity-creating narratives are at the heart of many successful transformation processes.

The three described functions of stories in organizations—giving orientation, collective memory, and culture and identity—are central to establishing a sense of stability in the organization. The interpretation of events in familiar terms enables the joint coordination of actions. Collective memory is made up of shared interpretive patterns and norms of action. Narratives about the organization support and enable the perception of organizational continuity, identity, and transport cultural values.

On the other hand, all three functions are involved in organizational transformation: new stories and the change of core narratives play a key role in successful change. Stories are the medium by which a transformation is described, articulated, and translated into action and behavior.

4 The Storytelling Organization in Transition

4.1 Stability and Change in the Storytelling Organization

Organizations are in a constant field of tension between stability and change. Changing market conditions, new shareholders, and technological developments are forcing organizations to adapt. On the other hand, organizations need to create a degree of stability and security to achieve certain results and outcomes.

Just as scripts, stories, and narratives are constantly confirmed by their enactment and performance (cf. Tonninger, Chapter "The Sun Is Still in My Eyes. Reflecting on the Constructiveness of Life" in this volume) and stabilize the organization, it can be assumed that there is a tendency in organizations (and social systems in general) to maintain stability once it is achieved.

Deviations from the usual are often answered in existing scripts and concepts. Successful change is therefore understood as a process that makes it possible to translate the relevant and decisive developments in the organization's environment into internal structures and processes in such a way that the organization is capable of responses that cater to these developments.

In the process of organizing, stability arises when organizations extrapolate their past experiences to the here and now and the future. Changes can be made when the organization puts its experience and assumptions to the test and reviews its fit with current developments. This dual challenge of the dynamics between stability and change needs "Organizations that both believe and doubt their previous experiences [to] retain greater flexibility and adaptability" (Weick 1998, p. 17).

From the perspective of the storytelling organization, change is about rewriting and renegotiating scripts, stories, and narratives (and the archetypical plots of the organization) in order to accommodate changes in the organization's environment:

> In a healthy storytelling organization, the story lines told in the halls, board rooms and restaurants, accurately map the environment and direct stakeholders to change in anticipatory and responsive ways. In an unhealthy storytelling organization, the processing of data into story and the recall of relevant precedent stories is not working to give accurate readings of the environment. (Boje 1991, p. 16)

4.2 Working with Stories in Organizational Transformation: An Overview

4.2.1 Framing Transformations: Storytelling for Change

In the storytelling organization, narration and change are inextricably linked. The stories told in factory halls, conference rooms, foyers, and offices shape the understanding of the transformation at hand. At the same time, change finds its expression in new and newly told stories:

> In the storytelling organisation, stakeholders and consultants perform stories that make sense of and influence change. Story performance and change are intertwined. Stories are created, old stories are remembered, some are revised, and stories about the future are performed in the collective dialogue among organisational stakeholders as they make sense of and even affect organisational change. (Boje 1991, S. 9)

Organizational transformation in organizations is often conceived and understood in the framework of episodic change—a change that is confined to a set period of time (see Weick and Quinn 1999). For example, the introduction of interdisciplinary teams or a new strategy is understood as a time-limited phase, at the end of which the new work structures and routines should be firmly anchored.

Such episodic changes are accompanied by a narrative framing of change that describes what the change is needed for and what role the different actors play in this transformation. Here, stories and narratives have an orientation function to mark that there is a time that is dedicated to the establishment of a new way of working.

In these cases, the development of a *change story* has an important function. It sets the frame of interpretation for the upcoming changes. In the process of formulating a change story, stories and existing narratives are used to make unfolding changes understandable and comprehensible.

For this purpose, people and organizations often rely on familiar "story frames" and metaphors. Thus, in organizations the image of the "journey" is often used, when changes are framed. But also, slogans and mottos serve as a means to make certain interpretations of changes and certain archetypical plots more accessible.

On the other hand, stories can also serve to shake up the organization and make people aware of the need for change. The goal here is to break through established beliefs by a new story and to convince relevant stakeholders. Stephen Denning developed the concept of "springboard stories" defining it as "a story that enables a leap in understanding by the audience as well as to grasp how an organization or complex system may change" (Denning 2001, p. xviii).

In springboard stories and the narrative framing of change processes, the focus is often clearly on storytelling with the goal of making a persuasive case for the reasons, the goals, and the steps planned for a certain transformation. While these stories are often developed by actors with high power (e.g., management or corporate influencers), the careful crafting of these change stories is important as they might reflect only a dominant position or assert who has the right to interpret the upcoming changes. Without careful consideration of the stories that already exist in the organization, a straight top-down approach might alienate or marginalize important actors and voices in the organization.

In the narrative framing, not only the change is described, but also the role of the different actors in the process of transformation is implied. Like every story, a change story also includes certain roles for the actors involved, deliberately designed or implied. If the occupation of the roles in the change story is not designed to address the interests, wishes, and needs of the involved stakeholders, the envisioned protagonists of change can become antagonists. Because for every story, there are (potential) counterstories that tell events in a different, perhaps contradictory, way. And these stories can pave the way to new information or unlock access to the commitment of marginalized actors in the field.

4.2.2 Storylistening: Inviting Diversity and Broad Participation

Different stories and narratives in the organization reflect emerging changes. Often, it is the case that emerging developments are reflected in emerging stories. These stories are not complete and fully elaborated stories yet, but, first, rough descriptions of developments and events.

David Boje (2008) calls these stories *ante narratives*. The prefix "ante" contains two different meanings. On the one hand, it means "before" and thus marks the fact that these rudimentary stories are not yet full-fledged narratives. The second meaning refers to the fact that an "ante narrative" could become a full-fledged narrative. The narration of a rudimentary story resembles a bet "... that a pre-story wants to become a full-fledged narrative" (Boje 2008).

This allows these ante narratives to be used to diagnose the fit between the organization's current focus and the actual changes in its environment. The conscious use of the "story-field" of the organization succeeds through the creation of contexts in which these emerging stories can be shared and evaluated together and a development of an elaborated story can be achieved.

Against this background, the potential of large-group formats in the tradition of whole system approaches can be appreciated (see Holman et al. 2007 for an overview). Before an accurate understanding of the current situation arises and a corresponding recalibration of the organizational patterns can take place, the relevant perspectives and stories must be given space (see Boje 2008, p. 214f.).

The basic idea is that new solutions and ideas emerge when existing boundaries between different patches of the story-field of the organization are (temporarily) dissolved with the aim to facilitate the free exchange of different interpretations, stories, and narratives. Through the awareness of different points of view and later convergence, a new narrative develops.

The role of the people supporting the transformation in such processes is to account for the diversity of the voices and stories shared through inviting groups and individuals whose voices are not heard in the organizational dialogue (Boje 1991, p. 9ff.). "Counter-stories" to a dominant story and ante-stories are therefore not seen as an obstacle to the implementation of a particular change but as necessary counterweights that point to missing information or interests not considered yet.

4.2.3 From Implicit to New Stories: Re-authoring Practices

Stories and narratives also provide access to the norms and values, the unconscious "taken-for-granted beliefs" of an organization. As Christine Erlach (2017) demonstrates with the example of a project management review, cultural values and norms can be tapped through stories.

In these cases, methods of qualitative social research were used to make the "company in the head" accessible. Thus, the self-descriptions of the organization can be collected through interviews and analyzed with qualitative and interpretative research methods.

Within this general approach, we can also consider the movement of making implicit stories explicit in order to transform them (see Swart 2013; Chapter "Transforming Organisations Through the Re-authoring Lens and Practices" in this volume). Because, often, it is precisely the particularly powerful "story frames" and discourses that are inaccessible, as they are so engrained in a certain way of seeing the world that they become invisible (see Rappaport 2000).

One way to better understand these narrative structures is to trace their genesis and to reconstruct the "historical context" from which they came (see Tonninger and Bräu 2016). The core element of this process is to raise awareness for the historical origins of the stories and the factors that lead to their continuation. The goal is to distinguish anew between facts and the representation of them in order to create a freedom of choice which stories an organization wants to live into.

5 The Potential of Narrative Work in Organizations

In the constant field of tension between change and stability, the stories told in and about the organization also change. Existing stories are overwritten, remembered, or forgotten. New stories are developed or adopted.

Working with stories does justice to the "homo narrans" in organizations. Just as people tell and retell their individual stories, the narrative approaches invite organizations to consciously design and use their story-field. From the harvesting of critical knowledge to the sustainable monitoring of change processes, the toolbox of narrative approaches provides access to the "storytelling animal" in the organization.

Storytelling methods can be used to formulate and design effective "change stories" to convince stakeholders of upcoming changes and "shake up" the organization.

However, the narrative work is not limited to the "anecdote enhancement" (see Snowden 2004) in the sense of a marketing-oriented storytelling approach. Narrative work in organizations emphasizes the process of the co-construction of stories and the power that resides in shared authorship of the stories an organization wants to live into.

It also means that the voices "on the margins" of the organization are important and necessary: not solely because they often reflect important developments first, allowing for early adaptation to changing environmental conditions. Rather, because these "silent" voices tell alternative stories that can shape the future of the organization decisively and profitably.

They tell about desires and needs, unused resources, and alternative identities. If these voices are successfully being integrated into a common narrative, then the competition for "correct" interpretations of reality makes space for a collectively designed search for meaning, which the organization further develops dialogically with all stakeholders. But working with stories is not limited to the accompaniment of change processes. It is a transdisciplinary approach that builds bridges between professions and the past and the future.

References

Angelis, Y. (2017). E-learning with impact: The role of narrative structures and methods in designing and delivering E-learning in a corporate environment. In J. Chlopczyk (Ed.), *Beyond Storytelling – Narrative Ansätze und die Arbeit mit Geschichten in Organisationen*. Heidelberg: Springer.

Bartlett, F. C. (1932). *Remembering: A study in experimental and social psychology*. Cambridge: Cambridge University Press.

Barry, D., & Elmes, M. (1997). Strategy retold: Towards a narrative view of strategic discourse. *Academy of Management Review, 22*, 429–452.

Boje, D. M. (1991). Organizations as storytelling networks: A study of story performance in an office-supply firm. *Administrative Science Quarterly, 36*, 106–126.

Boje, D. M. (2008). *Storytelling organizations*. London: Sage.

Bruner, J. (1986). *Actual minds, possible worlds*. Cambridge: Harvard University Press.

Bruner, J. (1990). *Acts of meaning*. Cambridge: Harvard University Press.

Clement, U., & Clement, H. (2017). Alles begann in einer Garage. Gründungsmythen in der Unternehmenskultur. In J. Chlopczyk (Ed.), *Beyond Storytelling – Narrative Ansätze und die Arbeit mit Geschichten in Organisationen*. Heidelberg: Springer.

Denning, S. (2001). *The springboard*. New York: Routledge.

Elsbree, L. (1982). *The rituals of life: Patterns in narratives*. New York: National University Publications.

Erlach, C. (2017). Wissenstransfer mit Geschichten. In J. Chlopczyk (Ed.), *Beyond Storytelling – Narrative Ansätze und die Arbeit mit Geschichten in Organisationen*. Heidelberg: Springer.

Fisher, W. R. (1984). Narration as a human communication paradigm: The case of public moral argument. *Communication Monographs, 51*, 1–22.

Ford, J. (1999). Organizational change as shifting conversations. *Journal of Organizational Change Management, 12*, 480–500.

Gergen, K. J. (2002). *Konstruierte Wirklichkeiten: Eine Hinführung zum sozialen Konstruktionismus*. Stuttgart: Kohlhammer.

Gergen, K. J., Gergen, M. M., & Barrett, F. J. (2004). Dialogue: Life and death of the organization. In D. Grant, C. Hardy, C. Oswick, & L. Putnam (Eds.), *The Sage handbook of organizational discourse* (pp. 39–59). London: Sage.

Holman, P., Devane, T., & Cady, S. (2007). *The change handbook*. San Francisco: Berrett-Koehler.

Kearney, R. (2002). *On stories*. London: Routledge.

Laszlo, J. (2008). *The science of stories: An introduction to narrative*. London: Routledge.

Morgan, G. (1986). *Images of organization*. Newbury Park: Sage Publications.

Müller, M. (2017). *Einführung in narrative Methoden der Organisationsberatung*. Heidelberg: Carl Auer.

Rappaport, J. (2000). Community narratives: Tales of terror and joy. *American Journal of Community Psychology, 28*(1), 1–24.

Rhodes, C., & Brown, A. D. (2005). Narrative, organizations and research. *International Journal of Management Reviews, 7*, 167–188.

Sarbin, T. (Ed.). (1986). *Narrative psychology: The storied nature of human conduct*. London: Praeger Press.

Schank, R. C., & Abelson, R. (1977). *Scripts, plans, goals, and understanding*. Hillsdale, NJ: Earlbaum Associates.

Schank, R. C., & Abelson, R. (1995). Knowledge and memory: The real story. In R. Wyer (Ed.), *Knowledge and memory: The real story*. New York: Taylor and Francis.

Simoudis, G. (2004). *Storytising. Geschichten als Instrument erfolgreicher Markenführung*. Groß-Umstadt: Sehnert.

Snowden, D. (2004). Narrative patterns: The perils and possibilities of using story in organizations. In E. Lesser & L. Prusak (Eds.), *Creating value with knowledge*. Oxford: Oxford University Press.

Sonenshein, S. (2010). We're changing—or are we? Untangling the role of progressive, regressive, and stability narratives during strategic change implementation. *Academy of Management Journal, 53*, 477–512.

Swart, C. (2013). *Re-authoring the world*. Randburg: Knowres Publishers.

Tonninger, W., & Bräu, U. (2016). *Wegmarken im Möglichkeitenland*. Heidelberg: Carl Auer.

Weick, K. (1995). *Sensemaking in organizations*. Thousand Oaks: Sage.

Weick, K. (1998 [1979]). *Der Prozeß des Organisierens*. Frankfurt: Suhrkamp.

Weick, K. E., & Quinn, R. E. (1999). Organizational change and development. *Annual Review of Psychology, 50*, 361–386.

Jacques Chlopczyk is a social psychologist, systemic consultant, and facilitator working with organizations and communities. He is lecturing on organizational transformation, systemic consulting, and facilitation at the center for systemic research and consulting and other institutions. He is co-initiator of the Beyond Storytelling network and conference.

Six Perspectives on the Role of Story in Creating Flourishing Organisational Futures

Mary Alice Arthur

Abstract

Recently storytelling has gained ground not only as a communications tool but also as a leadership imperative. It is important for leaders to understand and employ story applications across their work. In this chapter, I outline six perspectives on how story can support more flourishing organisational futures and pair them with three major waves of how we can focus our work with stories within rising complexity. These six perspectives indicate practical business applications.

The benefits to the wise use of story are more effective, connected and cohesive individuals, groups and full systems. Story is one of the major "attractor factors" in the working world, whether it is packaged as vision, mission, values, ways of working or culture. It is alive and well, and every organisational system is a mirror of its impact.

1 Story Is the New Black

These days we call everyone a storyteller—our authors, songwriters, business leaders, activists, celebrities, social media stars—even our politicians. Over the past decade especially, storytelling has gained ground not only as a marketing and communications tool but also as a leadership imperative. Leaders are flocking to

This chapter has been previously published on www.getsoaring.com. The concept of the three waves arose out of a conversation with David Hutchens (www.davidhutchens.com) and David Drake (www.momentinstitute.com).

M. A. Arthur (✉)
SOAR (Significant Orientations, Amazing Results), Columbus, OH, USA
e-mail: mary-alice@getsoaring.com

© Springer Nature Switzerland AG 2019

J. Chlopczyk, C. Erlach (eds.), *Transforming Organizations*,
Management for Professionals, https://doi.org/10.1007/978-3-030-17851-2_4

learn how to tell a better story because they believe it will underpin their success and power up their influence.

In these times of complexity, many story advocates are focusing on the old adage that "who tells a better story wins",[1] without realising the many other powers inherent in story. I want to offer *six perspectives* on how story can support more flourishing organisational futures and pair them with the *three major waves* of how we can focus our work with stories in this time of ever-increasing complexity. This is a look at practical application partnered with the future story of Story.

It's helpful to take a more detailed look at how story can work inside of organisational, community and human structures. After all, stories are how we make sense and meaning of the world. They are the lens through which we form our sense of identity, meaning and agency. We are motivated and stimulated by stories. They are the way our neural network files and orders data and experiences into a structure we can retrieve.

This little word "agency" is an important one. What I believe I am capable of, where I decide to take action and what action I decide to take are wrapped up on my story. It seems we humans are compelled to make meaning, so the stories we tell ourselves, in fact, are more powerful than all the data to the contrary. Our stories create our map of reality, and if a new piece of information does not fit this map, it is easy for us to be blind to it or to disregard it. Placing information inside a story helps it to land in us, just like a beautiful box makes us want to open it or a good taste helps the medicine go down.

Stories are human currency and, therefore, they are also the currency of organisation. We trade stories every time we meet, in large and small ways. They focus our attention and tell us what is valued and acceptable in the culture we are part of and what not to do. They enliven and underpin vision and mission—in fact when they are no stories attached to these, they become ossified, merely words on paper that have no meaning.

Stories are like a chemical reaction in the background that is always bubbling away. Or maybe even better as an analogy—organisational culture is like a bowl of yogurt. Yogurt is a living culture (in fact, if something is called "yogurt" that has been so processed that nothing is living any more, don't eat it!). And to stay a living culture, it needs feeding. The higher the quality of nourishment the yogurt receives, the more life, the more generativity will be in it. Organisational cultures are the same. And the nourishment? *Stories*. The more generative the stories that are shared, the more generative the culture. It is no use ignoring this process—stories happen regardless. Humans are made that way!

[1] With great respect to Annette Simmons wonderful book "Whoever Tells the Best Story Wins: How to Use Your Own Stories to Communicate with Power and Impact", Amacom 2015.

2 The Six Perspectives

The six perspectives (Fig. 1) map three different levels of how to apply stories organisationally. They are:

1. Story as a leadership practice
2. Seeing self and story as positive change agents
3. Story as a learning practice
4. Story as a process partner
5. Story as a resonance tuner
6. Story as part of the art of practicing humanity

Let's take a closer look at the first two—*story as a leadership practice* and *seeing self and story as positive change agents*.

2.1 First Story Wave: Influence

2.1.1 Story as a Leadership Practice

Story has gained visibility rapidly within the corporate world as a tool for influence and for good reason. From a leadership point of view, Story can do all of these things:

Fig. 1 The six perspectives and three waves of story (illustrations author's own)

- Awaken the latent leadership potential in everyone.
- Create the frame for collective action.
- Share the goals and challenges for the future/path/journey.
- Illuminate and reinforce mission, vision, values, ethics, stance, etc.
- Strengthen or work with the collective field within a business, industry or community.
- Make "safe enough" spaces for people to show up more fully/allowing the dissenting voice to be heard/enabling the hard conversations to be had without breaking the system.
- Create collective muscle for "leaning in".

The first four points in this list fall under what I'd call *Leadership Storytelling*. It makes good sense for leaders of all ages and stages to learn how to tell strong and well-crafted stories in order to pave the way for people to both work well together and to know how their part fits into the whole. Humans need meaning and humans at work also need purpose. We need to know the *Why* as well as the *What* in order to engage fully.

From a human relations perspective, this is called "line of sight". If I can see how what I'm doing matters and how it fits into the overall goals of the organisation, then I'm more motivated, more committed. The more committed I am, the more likely I am to bring energy, enthusiasm and creativity to my working life. Organisational structures with low employee engagement and low motivation often suffer from a negative or non-existent story base.

I remember working on a major merger process for a telecommunications business. Throughout the process, there were many times when the senior leadership circle didn't have any news to share or they were at one of those places where fog was more prevalent than clear vistas. Their natural inclination was to say nothing. "We don't have anything to say", they told me. However, this is the time to keep communicating; otherwise people will make up their own stories about what's going on. They always do! If you know this is the human default, it is much easier to plan accordingly.

Perhaps you recognise these typical personnel survey results:

- I love my team, but what do the rest of you do?
- I wonder what the leadership team is for? Who really makes the decisions around here?
- Fortunately head office is far away from us!
- Our communication is "______!" (fill in your favourite negative word).

It's a good thing to inquire into the story base people are part of that lead to these results. Often the final comment comes when people don't know how to name that the story they are living and working within is either not sustainable or downright debilitating.

The last three points

- Strengthen or work with the collective field within a business, industry or community.
- Make "safe enough" spaces for people to show up more fully/allowing the dissenting voice to be heard/enabling the hard conversations to be had without breaking the system.
- Create collective muscle for "leaning in".

fall under what I'd call *StoryWork.*

Being able to work with the stories already alive in workplace or community is paramount to people feeling like they are heard, invited to contribute and able to listen to others. We can never make totally safe spaces for people to share their stories, but we can make *safe enough* spaces. From a community or societal point of view, this is absolutely pivotal now, as fear of "the other" and fragmentation grows.

Once we share stories, we can never see each other in the same way again. We forge some understanding and find a little common ground, a place to meet. We begin to see behind the curtain.

In the merger process I described above, two senior leadership teams were combined into one. It was a challenging and emotional process for everyone involved. For some time it didn't feel like the teams would be able to understand each other, let alone do the hard work it would take to merge the two structures. We began with an appreciative interview between the teams, sharing stories about our experiences of high-performing teams and our dreams for the success of the merger. This work provided a ground where the teams could meet.

From that ground, we began to discover the very different ways of working that existed in the two teams. They were using the same words but meaning different things. This cleared up much of the confusion between them and paved the way for the ongoing work of moving along together.

We build connection, as well as the collective muscle for leaning in—staying together, rather than falling apart—when hard stories or big emotions arise or when difficult discussions need to be had. We also build a space for the dissenting voice to show up. In many organisations, it can be unsafe to bring emotions to the table, to question or to disagree. Is questioning, for example, a way to deeper understanding or a demonstration of unpreparedness? That depends on the culture.

A West German friend recently told me she discovered that very difference when she first met her East German husband's family. In her family, questions indicated curiosity to know more about the other. In his family, they represented something entirely different! She found herself wondering why they were so silent and had to learn that the lack of questions didn't indicate a lack of willingness to engage with her. It simply meant they had grown up in a different culture.

2.1.2 Seeing Self and Story as Positive Change Agents

It is important to realise that stories are a potent support in positive change making. At this point in history, we seem to be mesmerised by stories of violence, fear, anger and war. Stories can also be used to help us grow courage, collaboration and connection. It all depends on what you are using your stories *for.*

For me, *seeing self and story as positive change agents* has these components:

- Working with my own StoryField[2]/creating emotional resilience so I can also listen to others, even if their stories are very different to mine
- Discovering/exploring the stories in the field around me
- Using StoryWork to help develop the potential for positive change
- Reinforcing the Heliotropic Principle
- Embodying the Principle of Enactment

None of us is a single narrative; each of us is the intersection of the stories we hold about ourselves and all the stories others hold about us. And to add to that mix, the stories we receive from:

- Our family constellation and our peers
- Our ethnic groupings, religious or belief practices
- Our regional or national identity
- Our surrounding gender and societal roles
- Society at large

We are each easily the most amazingly unique story cocktails! We are literally "StoryFields".

Some stories are ingrained in us while growing up, others slip in unannounced and yet others—like national identity—co-opt us, either willingly or not. Because of the way stories work in the brain, we are less stereotypers than "story-o-typers[3]", applying our stories of people, places and things like an overlay to help us make sense of the world.

Since story is our lens on the world and therefore the filter for how we take action, becoming more aware of your own storylines is important. The more you have worked with your own stories and the dissonance within yourself, the more you can be resilient around stories you don't agree with or find confronting. Other people's stories are literally just someone else's perspective on the world, but it might not feel that simple!

This awareness is vitally important for leaders: firstly, because leaders receive projections from those around them, perhaps someone's expectations or fears of someone in an authority position or perhaps their wounding from a previous hierarchical system or their more basic need for a mother or father figure, and secondly because your own unresolved material means you can be more easily triggered and therefore less in balance when making decisions.

[2]I first heard the term "story field" used around a conference called by US peace activist Tom Atlee in 2007. I have continued to play with this concept writing about it in an unpublished paper in 2009. He now calls this work "storycology".

[3]I've loved this term since I first heard it but admit to not remembering the source. Apologies to whoever you are!

Every system is already full of stories—learning how to identify, work with and shape these is also a key leadership role. Within the merger process, we used Appreciative Inquiry as our foundation for working with the stories inherent in the two systems coming together. The Advisory Team identified three key elements they believed would immediately catapult the new organisation into a leadership role in the ICT industry. They named these elements *passionate people*, *raving fans* and *irresistible leadership*. They held as a target, engaging one third of the full system of 1700 personally in the inquiry. The team designed and hosted 17 four-hour "Fusion Forums" where equal numbers of employees from both organisations were invited to share stories.

Through listening to, collecting and distilling core factors from these stories, the team, those engaged in the exercise and through them the wider organisation, began to build a comprehensive picture of the core factors required to bring the three key elements to life. Discovering and sharing the stories unleashed great energy and put the focus on the positive potential of the merger process, rather than on what each side would need to give up in order to come together.

Both the Heliotropic Principle[4] and the Principle of Enactment come from Appreciative Inquiry practice field. The Heliotropic Principle takes its meaning from the way sunflowers (and all growing things) turn to follow the path of the sun. Our stories can shine a light on positive change that can be made, and they encourage people to turn in that direction too.

The Principle of Enactment might be subtitled "The Gandhi Principle" or *be the change you want to see in the world.* In New Zealand, people used to call this "start in the way you mean to go on". Tell the stories that encourage you to act in new, open and more courageous ways. Act in ways that help you embody your vision and keep telling stories that will help others to act like that too.

2.1.3 Additional Remarks on the First Wave of Story: Influence

So back to that word *Influence*. For me, this is *the first wave of how we work with stories*. Leaders—and others—want stories to help them create influence: *See it my way*, *follow me*, or *our product is better*. There is a power in stories. The question is what we are using that power to do. And here we touch the interlaced practices of ethics, morality and power.

There is no innocent story—although there might be innocent intentions. Every story creates a perspective and asks you to step in and try it on for a while. "Hear me", "listen and help me figure out what I think", "this moment meant this", "I'm

[4]Both of these principles are tenets of the practice field of Appreciative Inquiry. To quote the Center for Appreciative Inquiry (www.centerforappreciativeinquiry.net): The Heliotropic or the Anticipatory Principle: I*mage Inspires Action.*

Human systems move in the direction of their images of the future. The more positive and hopeful the image of the future, the more positive the present-day action. The Enactment Principle: Acting "As If" is Self-Fulfilling: To really make a change, we must "be the change we want to see". Positive change occurs when the process used to create the change is a living model of the ideal future.

asking for your support", "I'm like/not like you", and "here's something I want to share/help you understand". And just like any other tool out there—a bulldozer or a hammer or a weapon—it is the intention you use it with that makes all the difference.

We are in the age of influence, and that makes it important to remember that storytelling is also what makes us human. This gift can be used in any way we decide. Our stories can hold us down or they can lift us up. We can choose.

The first wave of how we work with stories focuses on *influence*. This is the most obvious power of story and storytelling, the ability to transmit potent and important ideas and concepts in such a way that people will take action. The two perspectives that fall under this first wave are *story as a leadership practice* and *seeing self and story as positive change agents*. It makes good sense for leaders to get proficient at telling stories, but they must also increase their skills at working with the stories already inherent in the systems they lead. In this way they can be a generative impact on the future story they want to lead into.

2.2 Second Story Wave: Collective Sense and Meaning Making

2.2.1 Story as a Learning Practice and Process Partner

The human mind is organised around stories. We capture our experiences and make sense of the world through the stories that form our lens on reality. Since our knowledge is captured in story form, it makes sense to use stories as one of the fastest mediums for organisational and group learning. With these applications, story can move from an influencer to a game changer.

The next two perspectives are:

- Story as *a learning practice*
- Story as *a process partner*

Story can form the basis of a *systemic learning practice* in these ways:

- As an organisational currency
- As a medium for learning in various configurations
- As a knowledge management tool
- For making collective sense and meaning
- Creating connections and learning pathways

Whether you know it or not, story already *is* your organisational currency. The stories people share about the organisation, their experience of it, the products or services you deal in and the people they work with and serve are creating the culture you work in. These stories not only pattern the space, they create the map of the territory.

Let's unpack that a bit. The stories being told pattern the space for similar stories to be shared. That means the more negative stories are told, the more negative stories are welcomed in. A complaint culture tends to become a downward spiral, sucking the life force out of an organisational structure. Or think of an organisation where the prevailing storytelling sets up a "them and us" pattern.

One of my clients was an interisland ferry line connected to the national train service. Historically staff there had come from seafaring families with generations of stories about "management" and the enduring legacy of a dockside strike in the 1950s which had ended badly for everyone. The main Story currency was a negative one. Young people arrived every summer as bright and shiny new workers with plenty of good ideas. How long did they stay that way? My non-scientific staff survey indicated about 3 months. That's how long energy and motivation can last in a prevailingly negative system.

Story will trump fact (and I don't use this phrase lightly!). As Peter Drucker[5] supposedly said: "Culture eats strategy for breakfast". So what kind of currency are people around you at work dealing in? Are the stories they are sharing bringing others down or are they intended to lift up the culture?

As both a medium for learning in various configurations and a knowledge management tool, storytelling and story sharing help make the most of organisational wisdom and keep people connected. Early in the 2000s, for example, NASA used stories to spotlight the work of innovative scientists in their geographically widespread organisation. Not content with merely publishing these stories in the usual in-house magazine, they took the bold step of putting stories on a face-to-face basis by taking their featured storytellers on the road and offering interactive sessions.

The more people who interacted with the storytellers of innovation, the more innovation there would be was their thinking. It worked. Storytelling helped to make tacit knowledge visible and shareable. This makes stories one of your key knowledge management tools.

When you focus on what you are learning and how to deepen and integrate it with others, new individual and collective pathways open up. It's more energising, focusing and enlivening to be on the learning edge together. This in itself creates new pathways of connection. As individuals and small groups make sense together, the collective wisdom of the field rises.

Story is also a powerful process partner. It can:

- Strengthen, clarify and deepen individual and collective processes
- Support change and transformation processes
- Strengthen respect, trust, empowerment and engagement
- Create shared understanding/expand perspectives
- Build capacity for deep listening, witnessing and harvesting
- Create capacity for being in the "not knowing" or Groan Zone[6] together

[5]But did he really? This is a very popular quote, but there is no citation for it in the literature. However, the "trueness" of it means it has had a long life.

[6]So named by facilitator Sam Kaner and his colleagues. See more about it in his book "Facilitator's Guide to Participatory Decision-Making", Jossey-Bass Business & Management Series, 3rd edition, 2014.

Story is a potent partner to other individual and group processes. Since it naturally deepens the connection between participants and allows knowledge sharing, it also strengthens the impact of the process it is used in tandem with.

Process facilitators often talk about the need to create safety so people can engage. (It is important to recognise that it might not be possible to create "safe" space for everyone. However, it IS possible to create "safe enough" space.) Sharing stories can help. Stories of experience in the workplace help us build a picture of what it's like in different parts of the business. Stories about culture help us to understand why people come at the same thing in different ways. Stories of challenges help us to learn how to meet them; stories of success fill us with energy. These connections build the relationship necessary to approach the turbulent waters of complexity and change with enough "stick-to-it-ness" to stay together even when the going gets tough. This is especially needed when change and transformation are on the menu.

Most of us don't willingly go into change. Remember those old maps from the Middle Ages with the words: "Here be dragons!" at the edge? When we believed the world to be flat, we also believed we could fall off the edge. There's some of that belief still in the deepest parts of the human psyche. We know that the journey over the borders to the unknown will affect us in fundamental ways. It could be that we never return. But if we do, we could be forever changed. And none of us is sure exactly what that will mean.

It can be helpful to have a map. In my own work, we often start with a powerful question, which can point the way to the stories needed to add a powerful spark to group process work. In this case, the question provides the *context*, which can lead to different *contents*. Questions act as the doorway to stories, and stories act as the doorway to new and different conversations. This in turn can lead to new collective sense and meaning making as a way of deepening vision and values and exploring the learning edge for individuals, groups and the wider system (Fig. 2).

Sharing stories does what I call "*depthing the field*". When we listen carefully to each other, witness each other and harvest the gold from our stories together, it is like growing a collective root system. In a healthy forest system, trees share information and nutrients through their root systems. These in turn are connected by the mycelium sheath, which acts as a conduit for the flow and makes trees a community. The same is true for people—when we share a root system, we more easily share information, knowledge and wisdom. We become a learning field. We find some common ground and, from there, the possibility for higher ground. Stories are the mycelium sheath of the human community.

In this world of increasingly one-way talk and ever-shorter soundbites, so many are hungry to be seen and valued. With so much information passing by so rapidly, the capacity for deep listening and witnessing seems to be missing. When we are listened to, we can in turn listen to others. In these times of conflict, building emotional resilience and offering your presence are some of the most important work you can do to strengthen respect, trust, empowerment and engagement.

And finally, working with storytelling can create capacity to be in the "not knowing" together. In participatory practice, the space between divergence and convergence—literally the space between ideas and action—is called *emergence*.

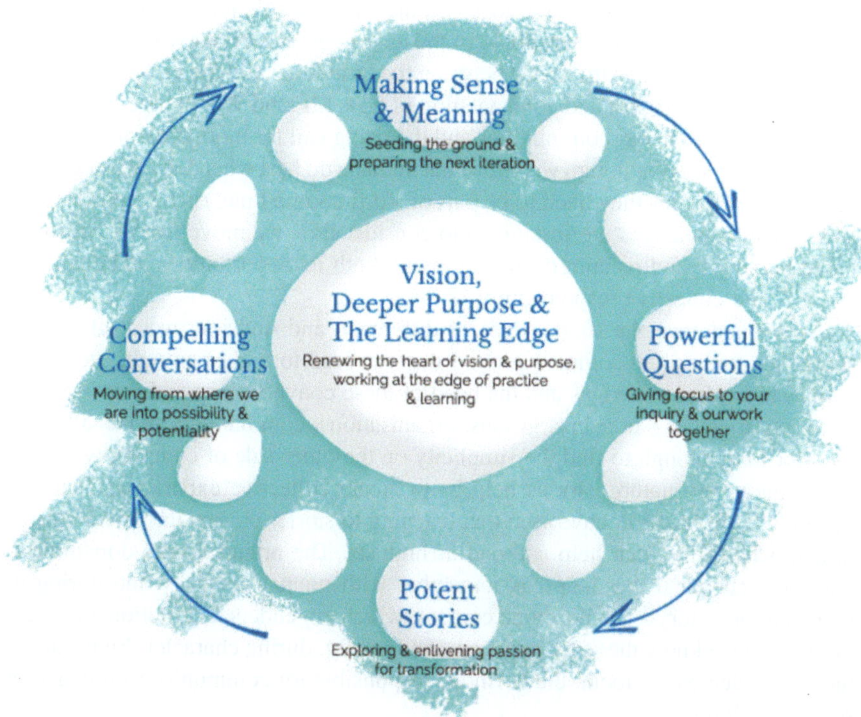

Fig. 2 Story as a process partner—a map (illustrations author's own)

This space of emergence was named "the Groan Zone" by San Francisco-based facilitator Sam Kaner and his colleagues, because this foggy place of "not knowing" can appear terrifying, even painful. It *can* make you groan out loud!

But just in case you think you'd never want to go there, it could as easily be called the "Grown Zone" because it is a place of fertile possibility *IF* you can stay in it well together. Stories help us to find the connection and trust enough to keep going together instead of falling apart. They offer us a red thread to keep finding each other in the complexity of daily life and amidst the differences that would otherwise pull us apart.

2.2.2 Collective Sense and Meaning Making: Exploring the Second Wave of Story Further

So many of us are focusing on story and storytelling as a tool for getting the word out there, but I think what comes next in the future story of Story is working with the bounty our stories carry. The next wave is the realisation that *stories are key in creating collective sense and meaning making*. Creating a medium for collective sense and meaning making is a game changer, especially in conflicted systems. Stories are the ideal change partner.

It is time to move beyond the focus on the single hero's journey and look at the journey we can make together. Some of the major tensions in our world can be seen, from my perspective, as the dance between the individual and the collective. On one side we have the inquiry and confrontation of how ME and WE fit together. We can see the fault lines in our communities and the rising call for more control, more rules and regulations, even though we know that humans do best when they are engaged in creating the changes they need to be part of. At the same time, rising environmental and societal challenges are forcing us to consider how we move from a consumer-based paradigm and reclaim citizenship, with both its opportunities and challenges for self- and collective responsibility.

As we negotiate the sharp edges of difference and division, we need to make spaces for finding the common ground that can lead to higher ground. Stories can help us to explore the edges and the heart of these conversations and can encourage us to stay together—in teams, groups, organisations, communities and as a humanity—for long enough to find the simplicity on the other side of complexity.

By their very nature, stories help us to create collective experience. Scientists mapping brain function have seen that listening to stories creates important changes in neurochemistry[7] that help us bond as humans. The brain releases dopamine—a feel-good chemical that helps us remember with greater accuracy and during the rising arc of a story—the hormone cortisol, which engenders an emotional reaction, even when we know the story is fiction. And finally, during character driven stories, the brain releases oxytocin, the hormone responsible for community feeling and the sense of belonging.

For this reason, stories are especially powerful at helping groups of people make collective sense and meaning together. For the past 7 years, I've been working with a simple but powerful process called *Collective Story Harvest.*[8] This method revolves around strategic selection of listening themes, aimed at specific sense making.

Using the stories of projects, initiatives, teams, organisations, communities, personal and leadership learning journeys, groups work together to comb through the narrative to find the gold that will take both the storyteller(s) and the group further. In doing so, they build teamwork, the ability to listen between the lines, strategic thinking, energy and commitment. By working together in this way, the learning is more deeply nuanced and considered, both for the group and the storyteller(s).

By combining storytelling and a focused harvesting strategy, this simple method uses targeted listening to dig into the often hidden learning in experience. Choosing a number of "listening arcs" focuses attention on key elements and offers new doorways into the story. The selection of listeners is also a strategic choice, enabling

[7]There are many references to the chemistry of the brain during storytelling. This article by Paul Zak reflects the impact of oxytocin on the brain during narrative: https://www.ncbi.nlm.nih.gov/pmc/articles/PMC4445577/

[8]Collective Story Harvest is a methodology developed by Mary Alice Arthur, Monica Nissen and Toke Paludan Møller as part of the Art of Hosting practice field (www.artofhosting.org).

a diverse group of individuals to add their unique skills or expertise to the group learning.

The second wave of how we work with stories focuses on *collective sense and meaning making*. This is the unsung power of story—its ability to create common ground and, from there, open a doorway to common action. The two perspectives that fall under this second wave are *story as a learning practice* and *story as a process partner*. In group contexts especially, storytelling and storywork can serve as a bridge building between disparate groups and groups connected by mission, but not by function, focus or geography. As the intangible currency of organisation, story is a strategic choice for knowledge transfer, connection and enhanced collective wise action.

2.3 Third Story Wave: Healing and Wholing

2.3.1 Introducing the Third Story Wave

In these days of social media likes, fake news and alternative facts, it's easy to see that influence, and how to wield it is in top of mind for most leaders. For this reason, I see storytelling as one of the key leadership capacities—being able to tell a compelling story about an organisation's mission, about your community's potential or about your own vocation is key to creating a more potent future or even having one! There are two ways story can power your leadership edge.

Next on the list for leaders, however, needs to be StoryWork. Using stories to make collective sense and meaning builds a foundation for common ground. To get to higher ground, however, a leader must be able to shape the stories in the field to be more generative or make a new story to take people in a new direction. The ability to recognise and also work with the stories already alive in your organisation, group or team speaks to the leader's role as *StoryShaper* or *StoryMaker*.[9]

Let's take a look at the final two perspectives:

- Story as a resonance tuner
- Story as part of the art of practicing humanity

2.3.2 Stories as a Resonance Tuner

Everyone knows how music can set the tone. Pop music can make you want to sing along. African drum music can make you want to dance. The municipality of Copenhagen even used classical music playing outside the back entrance of the

[9]These are terms I created as part of my work on StoryFields in 2009. For me they have subtly different meanings. A StoryShaper is someone who works with the material inherent in the system to direct it towards a certain vision or goal. A StoryMaker creates a story or narrative arc to move the field in a certain direction. Both of these are leadership skills.

Fig. 3 A workshop wish that indicates a deeper story (photo taken by author)

main train station as a way of keeping young people from loitering. How tastes change over the centuries! The important thing to remember about music is that the more you hear it, the more you resonate with it. You literally *attune* to the tune you are hearing.

Stories also carry a resonance. Stories of challenges overcome can make us feel uplifted. Stories of violence and abuse can make us go into fear. Stories of injustice can ignite a fire in us for change. That's not surprising, considering that neuroscientists[10] have tracked the brain patterning of story listeners and storytellers. When we are listening to a story that compels us, our brains light up in the same way the storyteller's brain lights up. We are literally—both from a mental and physical perspective—experiencing the story at the same time as the teller and the other listeners. This is called *mirroring*.

Neural coupling[11] is the name for the way the brain can be stimulated to take on the ideas and experience within the story as its own. Scientists have also told us that one of the reasons stories are more impactful than facts is that they activate many more parts of the brain, including the motor, sensory and frontal cortexes.

The bad news about this, from a leadership perspective, is that when negative stories continue to circulate, they begin to create a negative resonance that spirals out. The good news is positive stories, as we learned previously, release the very hormones that create a sense of community and intimacy. Good stories we share together make us want to be part of community. They make us want to share more.

Stories speak to our experiences but also to our longings, like this sticky note (Fig. 3) from a woman in the circle at the start of a challenging merger process in the charity Habitat for Humanity: *I hope for us to come home together*, they are

[10]There is plenty written on this, but a good place to start is Jonathon Gottshall's 2012 book "The Storytelling Animal: How Stories Make Us Human", First Mariner Books.

[11]Greg J Stephens, rije Universiteit Amsterdam, "Speaker-Listener Neural Coupling Underlies Successful Communication" in Proceedings of the National Academy of Sciences 107 (32):14425-30 August 2010.

placeholders for our fears, wishes and dreams. For this reason, they act like a tuning fork, vibrating us into the resonance of the story we are in. Story acts as a resonance tuner by:

- Setting the tone
- Building resonance
- Shifting the tone/recalibrating systems
- Using harmonics

You might say a story is the quickest link between two people. We have only to look around us in a political sense to see that the stories that continue to be shared set the tone, whether they are true or not.

2.3.3 Leadership Stories Build a Resonance Throughout the Wider System

People continue to look to leaders (and by this I mean leaders at every level and capacity) to see how to navigate the system they are in. What you *say* is equally as important as what you *do*. When these two align, it is called integrity. Some also call it authenticity.

In the same way, stories can also be used to shift the resonance or recalibrate the system. To their chagrin, many leaders have found out that facts cannot trump a compelling story—only a story can trump another story. If you want to change the course of the system you are leading or living in, you need to find the compelling story that will help you gain traction to shift the system.

The Corrymeela Peace Centre[12] in Northern Ireland delivers some fantastic training on how to work with long-term conflict situations. Their iceberg model shows how conflict escalates and also what the stages of de-escalation are. And like any iceberg, nine tenths of the challenge is under the waterline. What's under the waterline in conflicts is *narrative*. Long after the direct actors in a conflict have come to resolution, the conflict can still continue because the vicarious actors—all those people attached to those directly involved—keep telling the same old story.

And just like a good piece of music is rich and engaging, stories can be used to create harmonics in the system—to spotlight or pinpoint something you want to value or enhance in the moment it is happening or needed. When I'm working with groups, I call that "speaking to the thought bubble", and I imagine myself telling the story I'm sharing directly to the invisible thought or question hovering over people's heads in that moment. Leaders have the platform to tend to system harmonics.

2.3.4 Stories as Part of the Art of Practicing Humanity

Storytelling is what makes us uniquely human, and it seems we can't function without them. Throughout our human history, we've used them to share knowledge, to capture our learning and experience, to make sense and meaning of the world and

[12]Corrymeela Peace Centre www.corrymeela.org

to test our ideas about what it means to be a good human and a valuable member of society. I call stories "the library of humanity".

Everything we have ever known still lives on in our stories—and much that we've forgotten. I remember reading in an old copy of National Geographic about a scientist studying volcanos in Hawaii, who'd hit a dead end. He finally asked elders there about their old stories and found precisely the missing piece in a legend about the fire goddess Pele.

Seeing story in this perspective begs the question about what part of the library we're focusing on at the moment. Perhaps we've been playing on the fear shelf or in the competition section for too long. Perhaps we've gotten lost in the consumer periodicals or we've been rereading the scarcity manual too many times. Maybe it's time to focus on other stories.

2.3.5 How Can We Awaken More Humanity in Our Structures and Organisations?

As our societies face increasing complexity, they are also facing a growing wave of social isolation. The workplace is still a major meeting point for humanity, and most people spend more time at work than they do with their own families. That makes a sense of connection, belonging and purpose at work increasingly important. Employee engagement depends on it.

What does it mean to be human these days? Story is—at its very nature—about the art and practice of being human. It supports our awakening humanity by:

- Creating shared understanding/expanding perspectives
- Welcoming and engaging diversity
- Building bridges of empathy and commitment
- Creating a more resilient foundation through strengthened relationships
- Encouraging self-responsibility
- Creating a bigger now
- Reclaiming the fuller truth of our own stories
- Meeting in our humanity and sharing what it is to be human

Stories and storytelling are a fundamental building block for creating shared understanding. We use them all the time with colleagues, especially in the process of acculturation of a new staff person. The anecdotes we share help us to navigate the workplace and make sense of the codes of behaviour that lurk beneath the surface. Just as a traveller needs translation help in a new country with a new language, employees support each other to learn about local working customs by sharing stories.

Stories can be the bridge builder across the divides and a way for welcoming and engaging diversity. Especially in global organisations with diverse ethnicities, races and languages, storytelling can help to create better teamwork by creating more tolerance and acceptance around different ways of engaging with the same issues. It can also highlight and make useful unique ways of dealing with challenges or creating innovation.

Remember that there are multiple definitions of "culture" operating in the workplace. Each person arrives with their own unique story lens on the world, which is impacted by the culture they were raised in and operate in now. Each organisation also has its own unique cultural mix, the "how we do it around here" that makes it recognisable. On the way to embedding storytelling in the workplace as part of the culture, it needs to be used intentionally and with supportive, well-hosted process so that there is "safe enough" space for sharing and so that good listening and sense making is encouraged.

In these times of complexity and ongoing change, creating resilient community in the workplace is a top priority. As those of us who have lived in the earthquake zone can attest (and this is my experience after 30 years in New Zealand!), a resilient community is not the community with more resources but the more connected community. Creating spaces for people to meet and share their stories—of work, of learning, of life—is an important ingredient in strengthened relationships and community that lasts. It is creating and tending the connected community.

In my early 20s, I had a 3-month internship at IBM's International Education Centre in La Hulpe, Belgium. I was curious to find out what it was like inside of this renowned organisation. I remember many of the people there told me they valued their collegial community and the stories they shared above all else, even more than the many resources and opportunities of such a global enterprise. Some had even left only to return again, saying: "I just couldn't find the kind of conversations I have here anywhere else!"

Stories also create what Open Space founder Harrison Owen[13] calls "a bigger now". They create an extended present moment, where time stops: an opportunity to take a look at a snapshot of life in the midst of the ever-flowing river and make sense of it and a little momentary pause in proceedings in which to rest and reflect. Organisationally, this is a great gift. To be able to consult our collegial and human experience in story form makes it possible to alter the focus; gain new, fresh perspectives; and be in *this* moment, rather than in the past or future.

As human beings, we tell ourselves stories continually. Some of stories remain consistent—even stuck—while others get reedited. If we let them, and sometimes in the light of someone else's listening, stories can help us to claim—maybe even reclaim—our understanding of an experience. Perhaps the truth of our experience might be quite different from someone else's experience of the same moment or a deeper truth that only reveals itself over time. The longer we live with and work with a particular story, the more nuanced it can become and the more it sheds light into the past and offers a new perspective on the future.

[13]Harrison Owen, "Expanding Our Now: The Story of Open Space Technology", Berrett-Koehler Publishers, Inc., 1997.

As Christina Baldwin[14] says: "As you change the story you're living in the now, you change your expectations of your own capacity in the future. Ask yourself: *Are we telling the version of this that is foundational for where we want to go?* The next level is the social field of story—first we take our experience and make meaning out of it, then we take our social experience to make connection".

And finally, sharing stories help us to meet in our humanity and inquire into what it is to be human. All of us have challenges. All of us have coping strategies. All of us have hopes and dreams, fears and frailties. Listening to others helps us to make sense of the wonderful or frightening mess we find ourselves in. Hearing how others cope encourages self-responsibility and action. And this, in turn, helps us to work well together.

2.3.6 The Third Story Wave: Closing Remarks

Both of these last two perspectives of story—*Story as a resonance tuner* and *Story as part of the art of practicing humanity* are part of the last wave. After influence and collective sense and meaning making, what is the next level of the future story of Story? The third wave of story lies in healing and wholing.

Winston Churchill famously said: "We shape our buildings and thereafter they shape us". After more than 20 years of working with groups and after supporting hundreds of institutions, large and small, I've become aware of the fragmentation, stress and even trauma that institutional and societal structures can impose on those who live and work in them.

When I moved to New Zealand in my mid-twenties, I worked in the same team as Andrew Stevens, one of the last people who had spent their entire career at the New Zealand Wool Board. During that time he'd had many different roles, and many different managers, but always a Wool Board family to come back to. Those were still the days where you could smoke in the office and have a cheap, hot meal in the staff cafeteria at lunchtime. I was there when Andrew retired, but I'd moved on before the Wool Board itself became a thing of the past.

I found that same sense of "family" network at the New Zealand Tourism Department when I arrived there. The New Zealand Tourism Department was one of the oldest national tourism functions in the world. Many colleagues who had joined the Department as cadets at aged 17 were now in their fifties and still at work there. But even then, things were becoming much more unpredictable. There were no longer secure career paths into foreign service and life-long rising through the ranks. When sudden and continual restructuring became the norm, trauma was the result. Change fatigue became a constant organisational companion.

In the case of regional, multinational or global organisations—like aid agencies or the European institutions—trauma is multiplied by the fractal nature of the

[14]As quoted in her interview during the Story the Future Online Summit, September 2018 (www.storythefuture.com). See her excellent book: "Storycatcher: Making Sense of Our Lives Through the Power and Practice of Story", New World Library, 2005/More about Christina's work: www.peerspirit.org

StoryField. People carry their own individual and family traumas, of course, but if in their role they also represent their country (and thereby their national traumas), or the trauma of a specific group, then this also needs to be managed while dealing with a variety of cultural divides and at the same time working inside a structure that can create traumatising impacts to individuals through their very size and bureaucracy.

The trauma inflicted by our structures is exacerbated by the idea that people at work should focus on the work and leave their emotions and private lives—essentially the identity that makes them human—at home. This is a concept that, in itself, leads to fragmentation. What suffers is the potential to be a whole person operating within a context that encourages wholeness and holistic or systemic thinking.

At the micro level, I've noticed that when any group meets, first healing is needed. This need may be expressed overtly—as in "Now I need you to listen to me!"—or covertly: the group is uncomfortable, there is something unspoken in the room, and people feel stuck or trapped. Either way, the need is like a threshold the group must step over in order to do good work together and to stay together long enough to do it. Storytelling can take a group over the threshold, enabling them create enough understanding to form the basis of a new conversation and, from there, wiser action. The understanding and community feeling that arises from storytelling can build the foundation for a future.

With so much fragmentation in our societies and organisations, coming back together again—*wholing*—is what we now need to explore. If we truly want to galvanise the potential in our organisations, if we want more energy and commitment in our teams and if we want to share resources and have more vibrancy in our communities, then we need ways to bring the pieces together again or introduce them in the first place!

This third wave of the future story of Story—working with storytelling as a medium for healing and wholing—is not an end in itself, but it is necessary. It takes us back around the cycle again, this time to influencing with integrity and on again to making new sense and meaning together that will take us to the next level of wholeness. It is time for the new paradigm leader—the Story Activist, the one who uses storytelling and storywork to help create a more flourishing future—to get to work.

The third wave of how we work with stories focuses on *healing and wholing*. This is the most hidden power of story and storytelling, the ability to transmute the conflict, pain or trauma of the past into strength for the future. The two perspectives that fall under this third wave are *story as a resonance tuner* and *story as part of the art of practicing humanity*. With the ever-increasing complexity and conflict in human society, it makes sense to pay attention to how we can clear the way for more generative co-working on our most challenging issues.

3 A Closing Thought

Story is a key component in organisational life—and in human life within organisations!—so it makes sense to become proficient at working with it, good at spotting it in action and wise in its application. The benefits to the wise use of story are more effective, connected and cohesive individuals, groups and full systems. Story is one of the major "attractor factors" in the working world, whether it is packaged as vision, mission, values, ways of working or culture. It is alive and well, and every organisational system is a mirror of its impact.

It might be said that every story takes you on a journey, whether that is a complete hero's journey into life's biggest challenges and beyond or a small step towards another individual or into personal understanding. To go beyond merely surviving, to thriving and even further to flourishing means taking hold of your story, challenging your perspectives and riding the waves.

References

Arthur, M. A. (2009). *Mapping the StoryField*. Unpublished work.

Baldwin, C. (2005). *StoryCatcher: Making sense of our lives through the power and practice of story*. Novato, CA: New World Library.

Gottshall, J. (2012). *The Storytelling Animal: How stories make us human*. Boston, MA: First Mariner Books.

Kaner, S. (2014). *Facilitator's Guide to Participatory Decision-Making* (3rd ed.). San Francisco, CA: Jossey-Bass Business & Management Series.

Owen, H. (1997). *Expanding Our Now: The story of open space technology*. San Francisco, CA: Berrett-Koehler.

Simmons, A. (2015). *Whoever Tells the Best Story Wins: How to use your own stories to communicate with power and impact*. New York: Amacom.

Stephens, G. J. (2010). Speaker-listener neural coupling underlies successful communication. *Proceedings of the National Academy of Sciences, 107*(32), 14425–14430.

Mary Alice Arthur is a Story Activist, using Story to help make positive systemic shift and for applying collective intelligence to the critical issues of our times. Her art is in creating spaces where people can find the stories that take them to their most flourishing future. Building the capacity for participatory practice supports people to take back the power of their stories, so they can make wiser choices. She is a sought-after process consultant and event host and an engaging speaker. As an international steward of the Art of Hosting (www.artofhosting.org), she teaches participatory practice and story work around the world. Through *Story the Future* (www.storythefuture.com), she is spreading the meme of Story Activism, supporting people to develop their skills and practice and engaging in leading edge conversations about the power and potential in our world. Contact her through www.getsoaring.com and @StoryActivist.

Transforming Organisations Through the Re-authoring Lens and Practices

Chené Swart

Abstract

In this article you will be invited into the transformational nature of the re-authoring lens and practices for organisational work. Re-authoring work facilitates ways of seeing and doing that invites individuals, communities and organisations to take back the pen in the authoring of their lives and their worlds. It builds on the human capacity to weave meaning into narratives in our given world. As we do this work, the beauty, dignity and knowledges of individuals and communities are deeply honoured. You will be taken on a journey through the theory and practices in three examples that show how collective meaning-making, deconstruction of societal discourses, and the imagining of futures and human dignity open magical doors into unknown worlds. Re-authoring work opens up new possibilities and imagined futures wherein human beings co-author their relationships with all things of the world.

This chapter has been translated and or adapted from the following published documents: Connect your story manual; Rooting Narrative Work: A letter to Re-authoring in Re-authoring Futures Con-Texts; Moments to Stories—Chené Swart's Moments Portal, Re-Authoring Futures—What's in a title?; and A conversation about re-authoring futures with Chené Swart in blog posts on the www.beyondstorytelling.com website. A prior version of this chapter has been published by Chené Swart on www.transformations.co.za under the title, Re-authoring the World: Unfolding Ideas and Practices. Reused here with permission from the author Chené Swart.

C. Swart (✉)
TRANSFORMATIONS, Pretoria, Gauteng, South Africa
e-mail: chene@transformations.co.za

© Springer Nature Switzerland AG 2019

J. Chlopczyk, C. Erlach (eds.), *Transforming Organizations*,
Management for Professionals, https://doi.org/10.1007/978-3-030-17851-2_5

1 The Roots of Re-authoring Ideas and Practices

The re-authoring ideas and practices are rooted in a deep friendship that started at the end of the 1970s between two social workers, Michael White from Australia and David Epston from New Zealand, whose practices were initially called re-authoring therapy, now better known as narrative therapy (Epston and White 1990). Their use of the word 're-authoring' was inspired by the work of Barbara Myerhoff (1986: 145) who wrote about people as 'authors of themselves'.

In the last 20 years, narrative therapy ideas have been translated into various fields and are used across the world as a powerful lens and practice for organisational transformation.

As I began my studies in narrative therapy in 2002, 're-authoring' was one of the many big words in the lexicon of new words that washed over me like a tsunami, words that I had to both make sense of and translate into my mother tongue, Afrikaans (a form of Dutch), and into my South African context. In 2010, when the fresh eyes and continuous curiosity of Peter Block looked upon my explanations of what narrative therapy means for somebody interested in community and organisational work, I saw the word 're-authoring' again. It was as if this word could really hold the complexity and beauty of the ideas and practices in a way that helped people to enter.

When I stepped into the corporate world in 2005 with these narrative therapy ideas and practices, a journey of translation unfolded, in a no-nonsense and no-big-words context. Five years into translating these ideas, I wrote a book, *Re-authoring the World* (Swart 2013), with what some people considered a presumptuous title. I realised that the re-authoring work, amongst many things, also re-authors the world in big and small ways. The transformational nature of the re-authoring work is what most caught my attention and imagination.

Although the majority of the translated ideas and practices that I use in my work firmly stands on the shoulders of narrative therapy, my re-authoring practice has also been infused by Peter Block's community work (2008); Gervase Bushe and Bob Marshak's *Dialogic Organizational Development* (2015a); Jeff Zimmerman's (2018) interpersonal neurobiology; Hans Ulrich Gumbrecht's (2004, 2014) writings on meaning and presence; many conversations with my colleagues Tom Carlson (2015–2017), Griet Bouwen, and Marianne Schapmans (2015–2018); and my beloved country, South Africa.

These ideas and practices are part of my life, my work and my body, and by now, I don't know where it begins and where it ends, where it came from and how and when it entered.

In this article you will be introduced to the explorations of the following questions: What is the re-authoring lens and practices? What does the re-authoring work offer the field of organisational transformation? How can organisational transformation be invited through collective meaning-making, deconstruction of societal discourses, counter-narratives (Lindemann Nelson 2001) for the future and human dignity?

2 What Does the Word 'Re-authoring' Mean?

2.1 Is Re-authoring Work Storytelling?

In organisational work today, we cannot even imagine that there was once a time when the words story, storytelling and narrative were 'soft' words that only the bravest would dare to try out or use in this field.[1]

But what do story or storytelling practices have in mind? Do we merely document and relay the stories of what is? Maybe in a humane way and touching way? Do we draw on the human capacity to be moved and touched so that we can influence and sell our products, our leadership vision, new organisational strategy or the brand of our company? Do we merely use story as an 'authentic' method to influence others? Have we extracted the heart of stories and casted it as an empty tool for marketing purposes?

The dilemma in working with stories today is that it has been captured. Because of countless storytelling training programmes in organisations, 'good' leaders are now expected to tell 'good' stories in a compelling way as stories are used as a marketing tool to influence and convince.

In addition to this pursuit of the 'good' story that will sell and influence, most people believe they don't have a story, or their story is not worth telling or seems too insignificant to share. Therefore, working with narratives in organisations has become increasingly difficult as you have to wade through all of the meanings and the effects created by these dominant understandings of the storytelling industry.

In this maze of meaning in storytelling work, re-authoring work opens magical doors into untold stories through human dignity and connectedness. This re-authoring lens and practices open up moments as a portal into the multiplicity of stories of people's and community's lives, beyond the good and right single story. It does not wish to influence, convince or to merely retell familiar stories. Re-authoring work dares to invite communities into collective meaning-making as they reimagine a future as part of a context, as part of this world, whilst transforming familiar and dominant stories on their way.

2.2 What Is Re-authoring Work?

Re-authoring work facilitates ways of *seeing* and *doing* that invites individuals, communities and organisations to take back the pen in the authoring of their lives and their worlds.

This section is a short introduction into the way we see human beings and the world as well as the practices we employ in working with individuals and organisations in transformational ways.

[1]Read more about the topic of storytelling in Jacques Chlopczyk's chapter, Why Storytelling, Why Now?: Circling around a buzzword (pp. 20–26), in Re-authoring Futures: Con-texts.

The rest of the article will show how this lens and practices play out in three organisational examples focusing on collective meaning-making through significant moments, co-creating counter-narratives for the future, the deconstructing of societal discourses and transformation through human dignity.

2.3 Our Lens: What Do We See?

In this understanding, a lens is a way to see humanity and the world that opens up possibilities and exposes that which presents itself as fact and given. In re-authoring work, we see human beings and the world in ways that open up moments as doorways into transformation.

Human Beings Taking back the pen in the authoring of our lives and our worlds builds on the human capacities to make meaning and to make story (White 2007) through language and through our bodies. In the re-authoring work, human beings are seen as knowledgeable about life and are connected to various communities and social histories from which they draw conclusions about their identities, their relationships and the world. In addition, human beings are seen as the keepers of a multiplicity of stories of their lives with values, dreams, commitments and hopes that move them forward.

Moments The smallest unit of a story is a moment (Zimmerman 2018). Through our meaning-making capacity, we can weave various moments into narratives. These narratives are quite powerful as they shape and maintain people's and communities' identities and relationships and how they see the world.

The Way Things Are The re-authoring lens also provides a way of seeing the world or 'the way things are' built upon societal discourses that have been crafted in history across time in a certain context and influence how we see ourselves, one another and the future. 'The way things are' is not seen as facts and can therefore move or shift in an instant.

Transformation In re-authoring work, transformation can happen in a moment, as if by magic (Gumbrecht 2004). Transformation is invited when our meaning-making and story-making capacity is ignited in connectedness to other human beings in spaces of dignity. In these spaces of dignity, a different kind of knowing and being is invited where meaning can shift and new possibilities become available that have not previously been seen or noticed. In these transformative moments, the future and its possibilities open up from a deep knowing of experience with the past and the present.

2.4 Our Practices: What Do We Do?

The lens described in the previous section brings a particular kind of seeing and therefore invites alternative ways of doing called practices. In re-authoring work, our practices invite moments and counter-narratives, deconstruct the context and facilitate the movement between meaning and presence built on re-dignifying practices as we do so.

Invite Moments Re-authoring work creates conversations or processes that invite participants to make meaning of significant moments in their lives that have often been shifted to the background or have been treated as mere exceptions. These significant moments are then further explored and enriched through the social and cultural histories that they grow from as they offer new possibilities for conclusions about identity, relationships and the future.

Deconstructing the Context Moments and meanings that get individuals and communities stuck are cast in a larger context with taken-for-granted ideas and beliefs about what is good and right in a particular time and age, sometimes also called the status quo or the norm. Re-authoring ideas and practices therefore unpack and challenge these favoured ideas and practices and its influence on people and communities and question 'the way things are' (White 2004). Through this set of practices, what is taken for granted can be unveiled, and emerging counter or alternative moments can be enriched into narratives that can re-author the future.

Invite Counter-narratives Re-authoring work is an invitation into the joy of being authors and co-authors of our world. A joy that speaks of our 'acts of refusal' and 'protest' (White 2004) about the 'way things are', the folding of the richness of our lives into our identities and relationships and the invitation to 'remember' (Myerhoff 1982) our communities and the kindling of hope through alternative or counter-narratives that dream of a different future.

Both the listener and the teller are transported to other worlds in these processes and conversations that invite narratives that move us forward to transform the way things are and therefore also the future. Re-authoring work opens up new possibilities and imagined futures wherein human beings can co-author their relationships with all things of the world.

Host Conversations Based on Re-dignifying[2] Practices The re-dignifying practices are invitations to:

[2]In many conversations Tom Carlson and I shared between 2015 and 2017, Tom spoke about the 're-dignification of the other'. Over the years I have referred to practices of respect in various ways, but since my conversations with Tom, I have come to call these practices, re-dignifying practices.

- Situate the storyteller outside of or separate from the story (Carlson and Epston 2017) in ways that set them up as the 'primary authors' (White 2005: 9) of the narrative
- Create spaces for human connectedness
- Honour, understand and work with the importance of language in the construction of identity, meaning, community and the naming of the future
- Ask transformative questions and listen in ways that individuals and communities can again become surprised and fascinated with their own lives
- Be aware of the privilege and power that our position in organisational work holds by deconstructing power and using privilege towards the common good

The re-dignifying practices will be discussed in more depth towards the end of this article.

Facilitate the Movement Between Presence and Meaning We facilitate the movement between 'presence' and 'meaning' (Gumbrecht 2004) as the ground from where transformation can unfold.

Gumbrecht (2004) talks in this regard about the oscillation between meaning and presence, or in this article, we will talk about the facilitation of movement between moments as a portal into presence and the embodied meaning that grows from these moments.

In Western society, we live in meaning-making cultures, and we cannot but ask 'what does this mean'? Therefore, we are invited to pause in these significant moments before we too quickly move to the meaning of these moments. Once we pause in these moments with all our senses, with the presence of nature, the arts and our relationships, we can move to meaning, which is then embodied meaning.

When we facilitate the opening up of moments through the above-mentioned portals, we put into motion a continuous movement that might sound like:

- Take me to a moment using all your senses.
- Where did the remembering of the moment take you?
- Is there a moment that will help me understand why you were taken to this place?

Once we have explored significant moments, we then ask, 'so what does this moment mean?' These answers give us an embodied meaning that grows out of the different senses of our experience. And as we do, the magic of transformation is on its way!

The unpacking of moments, the deconstructing of the context, the invitation for counter-narratives, the re-dignifying practices and the facilitation of the movement between meaning and presence are re-authoring practices that facilitate the transformation of identity, relationships, organisational culture and ultimately the future. These practices will be further explored through examples in the following sections.

What are the gifts of re-authoring work in the transformation of organisations?

3 Transforming Organisations Through Re-authoring Work

What are the contexts in which organisations would want to transform? Is it about making our organisations better? Do we want 'more value for the shareholder' so that the 'bottom line' can improve? Do we want our organisations to transform to have less absenteeism and more 'engaged' employees? Do we feel the consequences of our inability to be an inclusive work environment where diversity is celebrated? Are we scared of the pace of change and innovation and all the prophets calling out our certain death if we don't adapt or are not agile enough? Are we afraid that we are not at the cutting edge of change?

3.1 Re-authoring Work and Organisational Transformation

In this multiplicity of calls for organisational transformation, the re-authoring work offers a lens and a set of practices that invite organisations to make meaning collectively through significant moments as they co-author the organisations' culture and future, to deconstruct the societal discourses that impact them and to build on human connection and dignity whilst doing so.

Re-authoring work strongly builds on the hope that through our authorship and co-authorship, we are able to shift something in our organisations and consequently also in our world.

Through the re-authoring lens, transformation can happen in a moment but is also supported as part of a continuous process of becoming and never an end state or the crossing of a finish line.

What do we see and do differently in adopting the re-authoring lens and practices? How can we imagine and build futures that are worth living into—for our organisations and communities?

3.2 Transformation Through Collective Meaning-Making

The first lens and practice for transformation that we will explore is the invitation for organisations to make meaning collectively through significant moments.

3.2.1 The Importance of Moments as Transportation and as Experience

Moments That Transport Us For many years I asked participants to tell a story relating to a theme. Time after time their perplexed faces and questions showed their strong belief that they don't have a story to tell or that their story is not significant or important enough to tell or be heard. But if you ask people to take you to a moment, soon a story will unfold.

In re-authoring work, moments are the smallest unit of experience (Zimmerman 2018). But do not be fooled by size! Moments are small enough for anyone to enter.

Moments hold the potential to unlock a whole new world that might transform all we take for granted in an instant.

Maybe this seeming simplicity invites people to dare to speak about a moment without knowing exactly what they will say. And therefore, the effect and impact always surprise participants as they are transported to long forgotten places and sometimes even unknown spaces as they 'remember' (Myerhoff 1982). The key to this approach is asking people not to tell *about* a moment but to *take us to a moment* in which a topic or theme was/is/became relevant and important to them.

Creating Moments Through Experience When we talk about significant moments, we have the moment in which we ask a group or a person about the moments and take us to:

- A moment that you would like more of
- A moment that took you forward

We also have an intersection of the present moment in which we ask the question, as well as the space for human dignity and connectedness that has been created for the question to be asked in, which is also a moment.

As we focus on significant moments, the work we do with organisations happens on two levels: it is both the invitation to remember moments that might be long forgotten and through this remembering to also collectively create moments in the present with the organisation.

At the same time, these moments transform when you invite the past moments to join. And sometimes the past speaks louder now than it did in the moment we experienced it, because it happens in a certain context. This makes for a possible moment of transformation.

3.2.2 The Gift of Moments in Organisational Work

Putting moments at the heart of the work invites organisations to move away from the battle ground of opinions, views, analyses and the correctness and rightness thereof. When moments are centred, we move towards collectively making meaning of these moments anew that creates the possibility for new ways of looking, new ways of relating and new interpretations of reality.

Moments activate the imagination, body and the senses and invite a different kind of conversation with different ways of knowing. As human beings we are bodily beings in which each significant moment calls forth the possibility to engage all our senses. When we are taken to these embodied moments, we experience what Gumbrecht calls 'presence', a moment when we feel 'the soft touch of the world on our skin' (2004: 106).

The magic of asking to be taken to significant moments is that people are remembering specific situations or moments in which a theme had relevance to them. With this seemingly simple invitation, we invite people to take us there, to re-experience the moment, which according to Zimmerman (2018) opens the possibility of re-authoring.

Moments that matter or moments that we want more of in organisational life open up the possibility for collective meaning- and sense-making and provide the ground from where we can imagine a different future as the moments become evidence of the possibility. These significant moments provide organisations with a rich treasure chest of real-life experiences of the possibilities of an alternative future for an organisation to live into.

As we unshackle moments out of the shadows of time (Carlson and Swart 2015–2017), we bring them forward into the future because they are no longer bound to time. When these moments are here, now, we can imagine what it means for the future. We can see the future in a certain sense. Leonhard Cohen has a line in a song in which he sings that there is a crack in everything where the light can shine through. For me, these moments of collective meaning-making are the moments in which the pen is all of a sudden back in our hands.

3.2.3 An Example

In 2017 I was asked by the administrator general of Tourism Flanders,[3] Peter de Wilde, to facilitate an open gathering of employees in which we collectively explored and made meaning of the transformational nature of tourism. The same invitation was then extended to partners in the tourism industry to also join the effort of collective meaning-making later the same year.

How could we invite collective meaning-making through moments to open up the possibilities of our co-search in a way that is useful and relevant for the employees and partners of Tourism Flanders?

These moments that were shared by nearly 50 employees and 150 partners from the tourism sector become evidence that stood as an alternative in the context of taken-for-granted beliefs and ideas of tourism as a purely economic endeavour.

Employees and partners of Tourism Flanders rediscovered why they are involved in this industry, saw themselves connected to one another anew and started imagining together what Flanders as a flourishing destination could be and look like.

It brought energy and excitement to collectively become co-authors of what this new initiative might mean for the industry and for the department. As these different groups explored significant moments, the gathering also became a significant moment in itself, one that marked the small beginnings of a journey collectively making meaning, collectively dreaming and collectively taking action.

The moment questions we explored in the gatherings were:

- Take us to a moment when you travelled where something shifted for you? Where were you? What happened? Who was with you? When did this moment happen?

[3]In the chapter Re-authoring the Future of Travel and Hospitality: An Inquiring and Generative Re-authoring Practice in Tourism Flanders that I co-authored with Griet Bouwen and Marianne Schapmans, you will find a description of the transforming organisational practice and ideas of re-authoring work.

What did you smell, see, hear and feel? Was there art, beauty or nature in this moment?
- Who would not be surprised that this is the moment you have chosen to take us to today? To which moment will they take us to, to help us understand why they would not be surprised?
- What would you call this moment if you had to give it a name like the title of a book?

The meaning questions we explored were:

- What transformed in this moment you spoke about?
- What is the influence of this moment on your life?
- What in the travel experience invited the transformation?
- Which insights from the moment can be carried into our work and lives?

As we collectively make meaning, we become witnesses to one another's experiences in a way that builds relationships, connectedness and community. We dare to see life and possibilities through the eyes of the other which also creates a sense of belonging and intimacy. We are not only witnessing others, but we are also listening to ourselves, re-experiencing the moments anew through our retelling.

One of the participants in the workshop stood up and said that when he thought of the moment, the memory of the moment was even stronger than the moment itself. Re-authoring work taps into the richness of the moment and beyond. As if the moment transcends time.

If we invite real-life moments to inform our futures and explorations, we do not fall into the trap of seeing, in this case transformative tourism, through our well-established and well-known opinions and frames of reference. By using significant moments in our meaning-making, we invite the possibility that the exploration becomes transformative in nature.

Working with moments within the re-authoring practices invites people with all their capacities and gifts to bring their insights, commitments, passions and wisdom as they reconnect with the theme at hand, reconnect with one another and are seen and heard in a dignified way.

Since these two gatherings, Tourism Flanders have embarked on think tanks of exploration around important themes in transformative tourism, have completed a large-scale listening exercise where they harvested the stories of 1600 participants around this topic and have sponsored small projects of exploration and are now in the final phase of documenting and communicating the way forward.[4]

[4]If you are interested in reading more about this transformative exploration, follow the link https://www.toerismevlaanderen.be/toerismevandetoekomst

3.3 Transformation Through Deconstructing Societal Discourses

Secondly, the re-authoring lens and practices provide ways of seeing and doing wherein the taken-for-granted ideas and beliefs or societal discourses of the contexts in which organisations function are 'disrupted' (Bushe and Marshak 2015b: 29) so that possibilities for transformation can open up.

This work acknowledges that everyone, every organisation and every community are part of a context with taken-for-granted beliefs and ideas that supports and invests in the stories that are told by and about them and others.

3.3.1 What Is Water? What Is Air?

To bring back the authorship and co-authorship in organisations requires that we again see the water that we swim in or the air that we fly in. Like the fish in water and the bees in the air, we take for granted that there is such a thing as water or air. The fish might ask, what is water? The bees might ask what is air?

As human beings we take for granted our way of life, our thinking, what is normal and acceptable, what is a good organisation and what is success. Until we understand that we were given the water and air through long histories, traditional power, our communities, markets and the stories we are told, we might remain mere characters in the larger story of our organisations and the world.

Societal discourses or taken-for-granted beliefs and ideas present the world we are living in as fixed, as a world that cannot change, as fact and one that we have been handed, facts that are also without choice or any other alternatives or possibilities in the present.

These beliefs and ideas are hidden through language, power, knowledge and years of tradition which makes it invisible. When one dares to ask questions about them, or to them, we often hear the answer: 'This is just the way it is in our organisation'. Within the hidden nature of these beliefs and ideas, we give meaning and experience their impact on our lives and our organisations as we unknowingly contribute to the organisational future. Societal discourses or taken-for-granted beliefs and ideas have something in mind for us, because they shape how we are in the world.

These taken-for-granted beliefs and ideas make people, teams or organisations the problem as it situates problems inside people (White 2004) or organisations. These kinds of problem stories that the societal context supports are insufficient and incomplete descriptions because it does not speak of the potential and the possibilities that organisations or communities can live into and choose from.

Once we accept that 'this is just the way things are', we become mere characters in this story of the organisation because the stories we then tell and re-tell are shaped and maintained within this organisational context. As mere characters we never bring our gifts and passions fully to the organisation, and we hold no hope and wait for the paycheck at the end of the month.

The re-authoring lens and practices therefore open the possibility to dare to say and see that something is amiss. It makes clear that the world is not what it can be in terms of the future. Re-authoring practices give the platform for the context to be named and to understand the influence of the context on the team or organisation. The joy of this re-authoring work is that once we understand the givenness of this world, we can see the stories that are valued and supported and choose again where, how and what we want to re-author in this world.

3.3.2 How Do We Deconstruct Societal Discourses?

Re-authoring work is about making these hidden taken-for-granted beliefs/societal discourses visible through powerful questions about the influence the context has on various aspects of our lives.

In addition, we also deconstruct societal discourses by making visible counter or alternative moments in which communities and organisations show up and transform this so-called fixed world. What a joy it is to unveil these precious moments and through living and telling counter stories change and rewrite the context along the way. We fold these counter-moments back into time (Carlson 2017) as the first taste and act of protest in re-authoring the future!

The re-authoring practices bring into focus the unique context that these moments take place in and help organisations and individuals to see and know how they shape the context and are shaped by the context. In a sense these practices provide authorship in relationship with the context. A relationship where organisations write themselves into existence and as they do, they are shifting the context by becoming authors and co-authors of their place in the world and therefore their future.

3.3.3 An Example

Everyone Deserves a Holiday is a holiday participation centre in Tourism Flanders (cf. Bouwen et al. 2019) that facilitates holidays for people in Flanders that would never otherwise be able to have this experience.

In 2016 I first met the team, and together we deconstructed and unpacked the world of their work that they took for granted. We unpacked the context in which they were providing holidays for people in poverty and with disabilities.

These were questions we asked when unpacking taken-for-granted beliefs and ideas

- When we think of a holiday, what do ‘they’ say about holidays?
- Who is allowed to go on holidays in Flanders?
- What are the conditions under which people are allowed to go on a holiday in Flanders?
- What do ‘they’ say about people in poverty?
- What do ‘they’ say about people in poverty and the tourism industry?
- What do ‘they’ say about tourism in the industry?
- Who are the role players that say all of this? Who are the ‘they’?
- If you had to give these taken-for-granted beliefs and ideas a name like the title of a book, what would you call it?

These were questions we asked to unpack the influence of the taken-for-granted beliefs and ideas

- How do these taken-for-granted ideas and beliefs about who deserves a holiday influence?
  - You
  - The work that you do
  - The people that you work with
  - The teams' relationships with one another
  - The relationship to the rest of Tourism Flanders
  - The future

These were the questions we asked to name the emerging counter-narratives

- What are also emerging moments in your team and work that tells a different story than these taken-for-granted beliefs and ideas?
- What would you call these emerging moments?
- What are these emerging moments of difference saying to the taken-for-granted beliefs and ideas?

After this unpacking process, the team started referring to their context as the 'ocean of beliefs and ideas'. This generative metaphor (Marshak et al. 2015), the ocean, became a way of catching out beliefs and ideas that the team did not agree with and enabled them to unpack and ask questions about them beyond our time together.

In the past 6 years, Everyone Deserves A Holiday has been documenting the experiences of people they have facilitated holidays for, people that have provided discounts to make these holidays more affordable and people from the social sector that have supported people in going on holidays.

Recently, when I had a conversation with one of the team members, she referred to the power of their firm belief in listening to, documenting and publishing of moments that tell of a different story than the taken-for-granted ideas and beliefs of the world in which they do their work.

She also spoke about how people's lives have been transformed because they have been listened to as they expressed how they finally could tell their stories whilst somebody was interested for their story to be told and documented.

All of these narratives have been standing as evidence for an alternative possibility in an ocean of fixed beliefs and ideas about who deserves a holiday.

She further commented that now, 2 years later, the alternative/counter-narratives of their work with people have significantly shifted the ocean of beliefs and ideas, so much so that she believes that it has transformed the ocean into a place of dignity where everyone indeed deserves a holiday.

3.4 Transforming the Futures of Organisations

Thirdly, the transformational nature of the re-authoring lens and practices invite individuals, communities and organisations to take up the pen as authors and co-authors who shape the futures they want to live into individually and collectively. This notion of authorship implies that an organisation, a community and an individual are keepers and agents of the stories that are told, retold, lived, created and imagined.

To build and transform the culture of an organisation requires an awareness and understanding of the power of the storying capacity of the work-community, the power of language in the creation of the culture, the influence of power in the telling of preferred organisational culture narratives and the importance of the relationships that carry these narratives.

If the stories we tell and live shape and maintain our identities, relationships and reality, they also shape the future of an organisation. How we see ourselves, how we relate to our fellow employees on all levels and how we speak and think about the world and the place of the organisation in it can open up possibilities for the future or close them down.

The re-authoring ideas, practices, questions and conversations help individuals and organisations to steer away from opinions and analyses about 'the way things are' but rather help them to stand on the shoulders of lived moments that give them a taste of the future to be re-authored. A future that is not without histories as we know that there is never just one story. And that means that when those moments are remembered, it is as if we can remember our future. We put membership in the possibility of our future together.

If we make up stories in organisations that are not grounded in real experience and practices, or we "sell" future stories that have not been invited into the meaning-making of the community of workers, we tread on dangerous ground. Meaning cannot be forced or sanctioned; it needs an invitation to participate.

Re-authoring practices therefore transform people's relationship to the future because organisations can no longer believe that things are just the way they are. You enable organisations to fold the future into the present and remembered stories of the past, and as organisations stand as authors and co-authors who see anew, rich descriptions of new possibilities for alternative futures can emerge.

From this point of view, the future is not and cannot be cast in stone. The future in this understanding is an open book, a becoming, in which the community of workers as the keepers of the stories participate in writing and co-writing of the story. The very notion of futures of becoming assumes a multiplicity of possibilities, options and alternatives.

3.4.1 An Example

In June 2018 I had the privilege to come alongside a gathering of 130 people living in Nova Scotia, a small province on the east coast of Canada and the ancestral land of the Indigenous Mi'kmaq people. This was a grassroots gathering called How We

Thrive that had come together to build relationships and skills and to imagine how they could re-author the future of their province.

Everyone had already been together for 2 days before our session. We began by asking groups of three to consider these questions:

- Take us to a moment in the last 2 days when you saw a glimpse of the possibility of a thriving Nova Scotia. Who was there? What happened? When did it happen? What did you hear, see, feel and smell? Was there any art or nature present?
- Who would not be surprised that you are taking us to this moment and why would they not be surprised?
- What would you name this moment if you had to give it a title?

Each group then made meaning of what they heard from one another using one or more of these:

- A quote
- An insight
- A commitment
- An image

The groups were then asked to jointly write a quote, insight, commitment or image on a stickie note. One person from each group first read their 'glimpse of the future' to the whole group and then posted it onto a mural that was portrayed as an ocean. That way, the whole group could further lean into, enrich and explore the future themes that surfaced.

3.5 Transformation Through Human Dignity

Lastly, as we work with collective meaning-making through moments, deconstruct societal discourses and its influences and invite counter-narratives for alternative futures, the podium for human dignity is crucial in the invitation for these re-authoring conversations and processes to unfold respectfully whilst holding the possibility for transformation.

The re-dignifying practices, the creation of human connection and the sharing of gifts ignite the beauty and dignity of all who are present and stand central in all processes that have been discussed in the sections above.

3.5.1 Greeting and Connection

When we invite people to tell about heartfelt moments, it is important to create the context and a podium for human dignity, community and connection.

Firstly, we have to greet and 'see' one another to create human connectedness in our teams, organisations and conversations.

Examples of connecting questions:

- Why was it important to show up and say "yes" to the journey in this season of your life?
- On whose shoulders are you standing as you enter the room today? Who has made it possible for you to be here today?
- If you had to design a t-shirt that would help us understand who you are, what would it look like or say?

Our human connectedness makes room for the diversity in the room to participate without fear and in so doing trust is created.

3.5.2 Re-dignifying Practices

If we would like to create a podium for human dignity in every conversation we facilitate, the re-dignifying practices stand central as ways to be and work with people that ignite the beauty and dignity of their lives (Carlson 2017). These practices understand the societal discourses that play out in our human relatedness with one another and are therefore not mere rules or methods for better communication, they do and are much more.

These practices bring the gift of respect which comes from the Latin word 'respecere'. 'Specere' means to see and is the word that 'spectacles' come from. 'Re' means that we are challenged to look again; the word respect therefore challenges us to see again and look again beyond the labels and judgements we so easily fall into.

The re-dignifying practices provide the environment for conversations where we talk about things that really matter without thinking that we know what people mean. We create spaces where we welcome all the voices and respect the diversity of meaning and ways of seeing the world as gifts that can assist us to move forward together (Table 1).

3.5.3 The Giving and Receiving of Gifts

The giving and receiving of gifts is a very important re-dignifying practice because it enables connectedness where we are seen and see others. This practice also creates the possibility to experience our connectedness with one another in the web of stories.

Table 1 Re-dignifying practices for re-authoring conversations[a]

Avoid	You are invited to
Judging and evaluating	Be carefully curious
Assuming	Ask questions that you do not know the answer to by using the vocabulary of the narrator(s)
Fixing, solving problems, intervening and interrupting	Elevate the narrator to primary authorship
Giving advice and reframing	Listen and be open to be surprised and transformed
Giving compliments, positive judgements, applause, feedback and affirmations	Share gifts through the 'offerings of our moved hearts' (Carlson and Swart 2015–2017)

[a]Authors' own table

As we listen to the storyteller or organisation/team, we are touched, moved or struck by what we hear. We therefore share the offerings of our moved hearts with one another.

- What were the gifts you received form each person in the group?
- What were the gifts you received from the conversation?

These gifts (Block 2008) are contextual, specific, timely and created in the conversation; they can never be reproduced in the same way. As they are given, I believe these gifts are folded into the rich fabric of our 'human becoming' (Winslade 2009).

- We share gifts by saying: 'The gift I received from you in this conversation is . . .'

When we receive a gift, we are invited to accept the gift with a 'thank you' and not to diminish the gift by saying things like 'I was born like this', 'I got it from my mother', 'It is nothing special' or 'There are other people who are better at this than I am'.

When human beings share gifts with one another, they open richer descriptions of one another's identities that also help participants to understand which gifts they are already bringing to their communities or the organisation and which gifts they want to bring even more fully.

Human dignity is invited through re-dignifying practices, the creation of human connection and the sharing of gifts. These re-authoring practices bring human aliveness that invites participants to see themselves and one another anew, and as we do, transformation of our relatedness becomes possible. As we welcome all the voices and respect the diversity of meaning and ways of seeing the world as gifts, it can assist us to move forward together in a transformed relationship to all the things of the world.

4 The Last Word

The re-authoring work offers a lens and a set of practices that dares to hold the hope of transformation for individuals, communities and organisations.

St. Augustine wrote about the two beautiful daughters of hope called 'anger' and 'courage'[5] saying that nothing in our world will change unless we are angry enough about what is unjust and wrong. And equally important, nothing will change if we are just angry but don't have the courage to do something about what is wrong.

Through this article the hope of transformation is given a lens, a way of seeing and unpacking the societal context of taken-for-granted beliefs and its influence

[5]https://theunboundedspirit.com/saint-augustine-quotes/

whilst putting us back into a relation where we see the water and the air, not as fixed and fact. And in so doing, we find a place for the anger.

The second daughter of hope is courage. Re-authoring work provides a set of courageous practices that invite deep connectedness, dignity and aliveness. Through collective meaning-making grounded in significant moments of real-life experiences, a multiplicity of alternative/counter futures emerges from this work. Re-authoring work dares to transport us, not as mere spectators but as authors and co-authors of our world as we co-create moments that transform our past, present and future.

May we have enough anger and courage to dare to imagine and work towards a future and indeed re-authoring futures that would transform our organisations and our world.

References

Block, P. (2008). *Community: The structure of belonging*. San Francisco, CA: Berrett-Koehler.

Bouwen, G., Schapmans, M., & Swart, C. (2019). Re-authoring the future of travel and hospitality – An inquiring and generative re-authoring practice in Tourism. In J. Chlopczyk & C. Erlach (Eds.), *Transforming organizations*. Heidelberg: Springer.

Bushe, G. R., & Marshak, R. J. (2015a). *Dialogic organization development: The theory and practice of transformational change*. San Francisco, CA: Berrett-Koehler.

Bushe, G. R., & Marshak, R. J. (2015b). Introduction to the dialogic organization development mindset. In G. R. Bushe & R. J. Marshak (Eds.), *Dialogic organization development: The theory and practice of transformational change* (pp. 11–32). San Francisco, CA: Berrett-Koehler.

Carlson, T. (2017). *Notes for the spirit of narrative conference*. Benoni, South Africa.

Carlson, T., & Epston, D. (2017). Insider witnessing practice: Performing hope and beauty in narrative therapy. *Journal of Narrative Family Therapy, 1*, 19–38. Retrieved from www.journalnft.com

Carlson, T., & Swart, C. (2015–2017). *Conversations and correspondence*.

Epston, D., & White, M. (1990). *Narrative means to therapeutic ends*. New York: W.W. Norton.

Gumbrecht, H. U. (2004). *The production of presence: What meaning cannot convey*. Stanford, CA: Stanford University Press.

Gumbrecht, H. U. (2014). *Our broad present: Time and contemporary culture*. New York: Columbia University Press.

Lindemann Nelson, H. (2001). *Damaged identities, narrative repair*. Ithaca, NY: Cornell University Press.

Marshak, R. J., Grant, D. S., & Floris, M. (2015). Discourse and dialogic organization development. In G. R. Bushe & R. J. Marshak (Eds.), *Dialogic organization development: The theory and practice of transformational change* (pp. 77–99). San Francisco, CA: Berrett-Koehler.

Myerhoff, B. (1982). Life history among the elderly: Performance, visibility and remembering. In J. Ruby (Ed.), *A crack in the mirror: Reflexive perspectives in anthropology*. Philadelphia, PA: University of Pennsylvania Press.

Myerhoff, B. (1986). "Life, not death in Venice": Its second life. In H. E. Goldberg (Ed.), *Judaism viewed from within and from without: Anthropological studies*. Albany, NY: State University of New York Press.

Swart, C. (2013). *Re-authoring the world: The narrative lens and practices for organisations, communities and individuals*. Randburg, ZA: Knowres.

White, M. (2004). *Narrative practice and exotic lives*. Adelaide, AU: Dulwich Centre.

White, M. (2005). *Michael White workshop notes*. Published on September, 21, from www.dulwichcentre.com.au

White, M. (2007, April 1). *Trauma and narrative therapy. Part 1*. New York. [Online]. Retrieved June 16, 2016, from https://vimeo.com/34671797

Winslade, J. (2009). Tracing lines of flight: Implications of the work of Gilles Deleuze for narrative practice. *Family Process, 48*, 332–346.

Zimmerman, J. (2018). *Neuro-narrative therapy: New possibilities for emotion-filled conversations*. New York: W.W. Norton.

Chené Swart is an international narrative consultant, coach and trainer. She completed her studies in narrative therapy in 2006 and has successfully translated the work for the organisational context in the form of practices, designs, processes and workshops. Her work with individuals, businesses, and civil society organisations has given her a deep understanding into co-creating environments that serve as the ground for authorship of individual narratives and co-authorship of team and organisational narratives. Chené is the author of the book, *Re-authoring the World*, and a contributing author on Coaching from a Dialogic OD paradigm in the groundbreaking organisational handbook called *Dialogic Organization Development: The Theory and Practice of Transformational Change* published in the USA. Chené also wrote a chapter on re-authoring leadership with and within organisations that was published in *Beyond Storytelling: Narrative Ansätze und die Arbeit mit Geschichten in Organisationen*. She teaches re-authoring leadership practices at various international leadership schools and also trains organisational consultants, coaches and leaders in narrative re-authoring practices in South Africa, the USA, Russia and Belgium through apprentice journeys. At the heart of her narrative re-authoring approach is ways of working and being with people that ignite the honour, dignity and beauty of their lives. For further details you can visit her website: www.transformations.co.za.

Developing the Future Stories of Companies: Open and Closed Story Worlds

Michael Müller

Abstract

Every company has a future story, whether it knows it or not. A crucial question is: Is the company at least partly in control of this future story, or is it fate that writes the story? A second important question concerns the nature of the future story: Does a company rely on a closed or an open story setting? Closed story settings motivate employees by fear and offer few options, while open stories motivate employees by giving the work in the company a deeper meaning and offer lots of options. This paper explains the difference between both story styles and shows the process for developing successful future stories.

1 Why Future Stories?

From a theoretical point of view, there are no future stories: Stories mainly tell of events and experiences of the past—the members of a Stone Age tribe sitting around a bonfire and telling stories of what they did experience over the day hunting game and collecting berries. In our times too, everyday storytelling is about the past: what my boss said yesterday, of what a big project I was in charge with my last employer and how I met my wife. Stories about the future we mainly know from literature: Science fiction novels are set in a technically advanced future with spaceships and "beam me up, Scotty" stuff. But most science fiction novels are also written in the past tense: They tell of past events from a fictional future.

M. Müller (✉)
Institute for Applied Narratology (IANA), Stuttgart Media University, Stuttgart, Baden-Württemberg, Germany
e-mail: muellermi@hdm-stuttgart.de

© Springer Nature Switzerland AG 2019

J. Chlopczyk, C. Erlach (eds.), *Transforming Organizations*,
Management for Professionals, https://doi.org/10.1007/978-3-030-17851-2_6

But if we talk about future stories of companies, we think about stories told in a future tense about events which haven't taken place yet: In 5 years we will be number one in our market, in 3 years we will have developed a new epic product, and in 2 years we will be an agile organisation. These are strategic goals; to tell a story in addition, we would have to reveal how we will start our journey towards these goals, what challenges we will probably have to face and what obstacles to overcome. It's a story about our expectations of the future; we never can know what really will happen, if we will reach our goal or if we will fail. No one can see in the future, even if all the professional forecasters want to make us believe they can. So, future stories are per se and always fiction—stories based not on events having taken place but on wishes, hopes and forecasts. So, if these future stories are pure fiction, are they without value in an economy based on facts?

Jens Beckert, director of the Max Planck Institute for the Study of Societies in Cologne, would deny this. In his book *Imagined Futures* (Beckert 2016), he claims that "fictional expectations" about the future, i.e. stories about the future of the company and its products, are crucial to the value of the company on the financial and consumer markets. The important thing is that there is always a future story (or "fictional expectations" in the words of Beckert). If the company is active on a market at all, this story will be there, whether the company knows it or not or takes the effort to communicate it or not. If there is no story, there is no market activity and the company has failed. But if there is market activity, there are actors in whose minds are a story about the company: Somebody who is willing to invest in a company will of course have an idea about the future story of the company—if not, he couldn't be confident that his investment is a good one. And a customer of expensive goods—e.g. a washing machine—would have an idea about the future of the company in respect to getting replacement parts and services. If suddenly nobody buys the products anymore, it could be that the customers have no idea about the future story of the company and its products anymore. Maybe that is what happened to Nokia after the iPhone went on the market.

The big question for every company is: Who sets the plot for the future story? The company itself or the actors in the markets?

Of course, it is always a collaboration between the two, and no company can control its future story completely on its own. But it can formulate the basics. So it might be a good idea to invest some thought and creativity into the design of one's own future story.

2 What Is a Future Story?

Like mentioned at the beginning, future stories are not ordinary stories telling of events of the past in the past tense. Stories about the past can be factual or fictional stories. Factual stories tell of events really have taken place; fictional stories tell of events somebody has made up. Hence future stories are always fictional stories. But that doesn't mean that they don't have strong ties to reality. Pure science fiction normally can't be a trustworthy future story of a company (maybe excepting all the "make the world a better place by technology" rhetoric of Silicon Valley firms). The link to reality is normally created by forecasts, which are not only insecure but tend to lead to very one-dimensional perceptions of the future.

Of course, to link a future story to reality doesn't mean that the events described in the story will take place. Nobody can see into the future. But future stories will be linked to reality if they

(a) Do not only paint a shiny picture of a wonderful future, but tell of the steps, challenges and obstacles on the way to the future in a realistic way.
(b) Start the narration with a realistic understanding of the present state of the company.

Both may sound simple and self-evident, but a lot of future stories (or "visions" or "mission statements") of companies I know don't include those links to reality.

Both points have to do with the basic definition of "story". According to Gerald Prince, whose definition is generally accepted in narrative theory, a story has a beginning, an ending and a transformation that lead the main character from his state at the beginning to another one at the end (Prince 1973: 16 ff). An example is the following: John is lonely and sad (beginning); John falls in love with Mary (transformation); John is married and happy (ending). This transformation from the beginning to the end is crucial for an act of communication to be regarded as a "story": If there is no transformation, it's a description and not a story. So, if a company only paints a nice picture of the future, it's not a story but a description.

3 Why Do Companies Need Future Stories?

Someone may object that this doesn't matter, a description, a story, the difference may be only a scholarly one. But there is a big difference, because only with stories can employees be motivated to join the journey into the future: People want to know not only what the future paradise is like but what kind of a path they will have to take to get it. That is, as narrative psychologists claim, "... in everyday life we need things to hang together, to make sense, to have some sense of connection" (Crossley 2000: 51). Narratives are the structures we connect things to give them a meaning. Hence for employees of a company, a narrative structure, a story, is important in order for them to make sense of all the activities and projects on the way to that future. Only if it makes sense for them will they be motivated to join the voyage to the future. The lack of a story is the reason why a lot of strategies, visions, missions and change projects in companies aren't understood by the employees, and one may ask the question "are they really understood by the executives who plot them?" So, future stories are important for making sense, understanding and becoming motivated to follow the future plans of the company.

The second decisive condition for a successful future story is that it should begin with a realistic understanding of the current state of the company, because every future story has to start in the present. At first glance this realistic understanding seems to be obvious—most employees and executives will be sure to know what their company is like. But the truth is, they only know half of the current identity of their own company—they know only the official identity, consisting of organisational structures, descriptions of processes and "official" communications. What they don't know is the hidden side of the corporate identity, consisting of hidden rules, psychological imprints, beliefs and ideas about how things work in their company. To know of these hidden parts of the corporate identity is important for conducting successful change processes and for a motivating future story. To give an example, the executive board of a company is developing a future story that is supposed to explain the strategy for the next 10 years. The members of the board are convinced that their company has a collaborative, positive culture, and they begin their story with scenes outlining this positive culture. But what the employees experience in their everyday working lives is a completely different matter: They experience a very hierarchic and daunting culture, where everybody only seeks his individual perks. So, the beginning of the new future story will seem to them to be a story about a completely different company, and you can imagine how strongly they will be motivated to follow the board!

Maybe for some readers, the above case of a company where the board and the employees have completely different, almost antagonistic notions of the corporate culture may sound weird. But after more than 20 years of consulting, I can say that this is a genuine pattern. One of the reasons for that is that a lot of executives seem to be convinced that from the moment they have defined and communicated a new culture, it will become reality in everyday work. Of course, if you discuss it with them, they will agree that it will take a certain time until it is implemented. But, after all, most of them only focus on a very rational approach to change: If the employees understand what the board wants, they will immediately act on it. But only the smaller aspect of corporate culture is rational; the bigger aspect is influenced by emotions and by experiences the employees have while working. So, very often the board thinks that a new culture has been implemented, but the employees are still living in a very different kind of culture.

4 Discovering the Hidden Side of Corporate Identity

But if there is a part of the identity in a company that nobody knows, the question is: How can knowledge about it be gained? Here stories can help: The present identity of a company is always a product of the past—like the identity of individuals as well—we view ourselves and our company in the light of past experiences. For example, If employees of a company have experienced several times that projects they worked for enthusiastically are stopped by executives and all the hard labour was in vain, at a certain point, they will have the deep belief that "in our company projects never come to a successful end". If then an executive starts a new project, motivation will of course be on a low level—because they "know" that their engagement will be a waste of time. Normally in such cases, the executives don't know why the employees can't be motivated for the project, and maybe they will develop theories about the laziness of their staff. If in a company with such a mindset a future story is constructed, the employees will regard this story as a new project, and again you may imagine how motivated they will be to follow!

If the hidden identity of a company is built on events and experiences, the best way to gain knowledge about it is to look at the stories the employees tell about "how we became what we are now". The best way to collect these stories is by conducting narrative interviews with 20 or 30 employees and then analyse them, looking for common patterns and shared events beyond individual narratives.[1] Doing so, the unknown side of the corporate identity, the "company in the mind" of the employees, can be described, with all the hidden rules, beliefs and conditionings influencing the motivation of the employees and their way of getting work done.

If the whole picture of the present identity of a company—the official identity and the hidden identity—is visible, you will have a strong basis and a good starting point for a future story, a starting point, which the employees can recognise as an authentic description of their reality. On this basis you can try to tell the (fictional) story about the company's desired future.

5 Elements of a Future Story

I don't want to dive too deeply into the dramaturgy and the elements of future stories. Let me just make some short remarks about the main components of good stories. As mentioned above every story has to have:

- A beginning and an ending which differs in at least one element from the beginning
- At least one event that triggers the transformation
- A main character that can also be a group, a team or the whole company
- Conflicts or challenges that make the story interesting (Müller and Grimm 2016: 58ff; Titzmann 2013: 120)

The latter is an important point for an authentic and believable future story. If you tell your future story as though it would be an easy thing to gain, without any challenges to meet and obstacles to overcome, most people will consider your story to be a romantic dream rather than a real future story.

6 Corporate Future Stories: Open and Closed Story Settings

In his book *Save the Cat!*, Blake Snyder, an American screenwriter and creative writing teacher, has worked out a list of ten "story types", and he claims that "within these ... you can stick just about every motion picture ever made" (Snyder 2005:

[1]For more information about narrative interviews and analysing, them see Müller (2017).

24). I'm not so sure about that, but I think Blake Snyder's story types are a helpful tool to assist us to think about the genres and types of stories we are used to telling in companies. Let's take a closer look on four of Snyder's masterplots:

- *Monster in the house*: The storyline of this masterplot is based on the challenge that there is a dangerous creature in a closed room. The main character has to fight for his life, and if he fails, he dies. At the end the monster is defeated (or not) and the main character is saved (or not). A film that follows this kind of storyline is Ridley Scott's *Alien* (1979), in which an alien in the closed environment of a spaceship tries to kill the crew.
- *Institutionalised*: In stories of this type, the main character becomes part of an institution (e.g. the army, a hospital, an office). He has to decide between adapting to the rules of the institution, rebelling and escaping. Depending on this decision, the main character at the end will be successful in the institution, a dropout or dead. A referential movie of this type is *One Flew Over the Cuckoo's Nest* (1975) by Milos Forman, where the main character (Jack Nicholson) is committed to a psychiatric hospital, where he starts a rebellion against the rules.
- *Golden fleece*: Here the main character is dissatisfied with his life or the conditions he and maybe his relatives, friends and countrymen are living in, and he develops a vision, a desire for the future. He sets of to realise this vision and discovers new possibilities. At the end he has reached his goal or at least is on his way. A movie following this storyline is *The Pursuit of Happyness* (2006) by Gabriele Muccino, where Will Smith stars as a homeless salesman who fights for a better life.
- *Rites of passage*: In this type of story, the main character is in a state of dissatisfaction, whether he is aware of this or not, and then something happens that changes his state. The main character could decide for that change actively or be pushed. All coming-of-age movies follow this masterplot, an example is *The Perks of Being a Wallflower* (2012) by Stephen Chbosky, where a boy finds new friends and discovers that his beloved aunt sexually harassed him when he was a child.

6.1 Closed Story Settings

A lot of companies tell or construct their future story according to the first two masterplots, most of them using the "monster" plot: Globalisation and digital transformation are the monsters in those stories, and the company has to fight or perish. A nice example of such a monster-in-the-house future story is what Siemens CEO Joe Kaeser announced in August 2018: According to *Süddeutsche Zeitung*, he said that his company must undergo a major change because of the global trends and to protect the company from aggressive investors like those seen in the months before at thyssenkrupp (Busse 2018a, b). So we have two monsters here, global changes and aggressive investors, and to fight them the company has to change. This kind of story is dictated from outside the company: The monster acts, the company re-acts. Stories following this type are in a certain sense situated in a closed story setting: Monster-in-the house stories can have only two possible endings, either the monster is killed, or the main character dies (OK, or both, if we imagine a very black piece of storytelling).

In a similar way, stories of the "institutionalised" type provide closed story settings. Like in the monster story, there is a restricted set of endings: adaption, escape or death. These kinds of future stories are often told by companies that seem to have a very clear picture of what they are and what they do. That does sound like a good thing, and of course it can be. But it involves the danger of looking at the world only from a familiar and so far successful perspective—and not seeing what's new. The company is caged by its own story. One could imagine that Nokia told an "institutionalised" story in 2007, when Apple brought the iPhone to market. Nokia in that time was the leading provider of mobile phones worldwide, developing every year new and better phones. But these innovations were driven by a story about mobile phones (which even could take photos!), not about communication and mobile computing. They were caged by their mobile phone story. An interesting point in this story is that Nokia did have a kind of a smartphone in its product line: the Nokia Communicator, a big phone which one could flip open to reveal a screen and a keyboard on which to surf the web. Compared with the iPhone, the "communicator" wasn't successful, although you could do nearly everything with it you could do with the iPhone (at that time). Nokia marketed the communicator as a side story of the mobile phone story, while Apple told a story of a completely new device as you can see in Steve Jobs' famous presentation when introducing the iPhone (see https://www.youtube.com/watch?v=9hUIxyE2Ns8). But it's not only a question of marketing; it's also a question of the mindset of the company and the resulting future story. Is the future story of a car manufacturer about developing new cars or about the future of mobility? Is the future story of an editing house about newspapers or about communication and information?

A second problem with an "institutionalised" story is that the employees of companies with such a future story tend to tell stories about their everyday work using the same masterplot: "That's the way we always did it" and "That worked for the last 10 years, why change things?" are parts of the story you can hear in the hallways of such companies.

As we have seen, "monster in the house" and "institutionalised" are closed story settings where the plot only allows a few options for the ending. Both masterplots try to motivate employees by fear, not by providing them with a desirable vision of the future. Maybe these plots may serve for a short time in an actual crisis, but they are not expedient as a story leading the company into the future. Of course, no company would make the deliberate decision to take a "monster" story as their future story—but in fact a lot of companies talk about their future using that plot.

6.2 Open Story Settings

So, as the reader may imagine, the remaining two masterplots from our list above would be better choices for plotting a future story. "Golden fleece" and "rites of passage" provide open story setting, and they are "open" in a double meaning: Firstly, they are open because the outcome of the story isn't fixed from the beginning as a choice between two and three options like in the "monster"—and "institutionalised"—stories, and, secondly, because the kind of action or activity of the characters isn't predefined like in "monster" (fight) and "institutionalised" (adaption, rebellion or escape) stories. Although the main character in the "golden fleece" plot has a goal, and the story begins with him setting off for it, that goal isn't fixed: Maybe he discovers another, more valuable goal, or he learns that the real treasure is inside himself and so on—anything can happen. And this is true for the "rites of passage" plot, which is even more open than the "golden fleece" plot: There is no goal, but something happens that changes the life of the main character—the outcome is completely open.

Now, what does that mean for the construction of a company's future stories? Firstly it needs to develop a new attitude towards the future, not trying to gain a fixed picture of the future like the forecast-driven strategies but to hold the plot loosely: Maybe there is a goal, but it can change during the story. Maybe there is no goal but only a challenge, and anything could happen. This is an attitude of openness, an attitude that appreciates the unknown and uncertainty. And it also means that a future story is not a text written down at a certain time and is valid for the next few years but it is a process where the story comes into being while being lived and changes with every step the company takes. In other words, future story is not a task to tick but a process (Fig. 1).

The difference between "golden fleece" and "rites of passage" is that the first includes a goal (which can change), while the latter starts with a change, and the goal

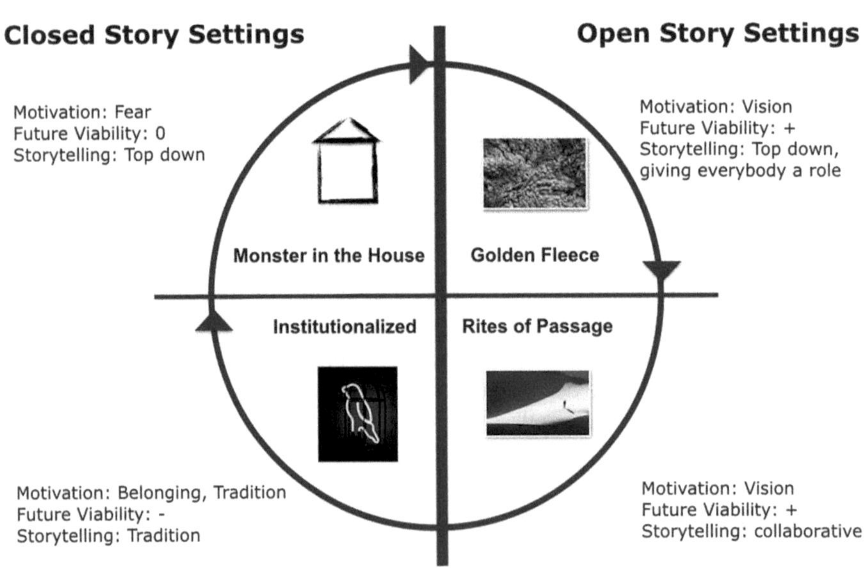

Fig. 1 Open and closed story settings (author's own figure)

or the outcome of the story is completely open. So "rites of passage" stories are even more open than "golden fleece" stories.

Let's have a—quite short—look at possible processes for developing open future stories in an organisation.

6.3 The Golden Fleece Process

The process starts with a basic storyline following the "golden fleece" masterplot, developed by the executive board or a project team in charge of the future story (we could call them a "storyrunner team"). This basic storyline includes a beginning (based on a common understanding of all aspects of the present identity of the organisation according to the descriptions above), a goal that defines the ending of the story and some events and challenges on the way to the goal.

After internally communicating this basic storyline as a first draft, it will be discussed in story circles in different departments and groups in the company; these teams are allowed to rewrite the story, developing different ways to reach the goal and maybe even change the goal.

Then the storyrunner team discusses these different storylines with representatives of the story circles, and together they develop a multi-perspective storyline (Fig. 2).

After that, the storyrunner team defines specific points of time where the story will be reviewed in the story circles and changed, if necessary. How often these story reviews should take place depends on the time allocated to reach the goal. Maybe every 6 months would be a good rhythm.

During this process the whole company or at least representatives of all important departments of the organisation are involved in the future story process and will be identified with it.

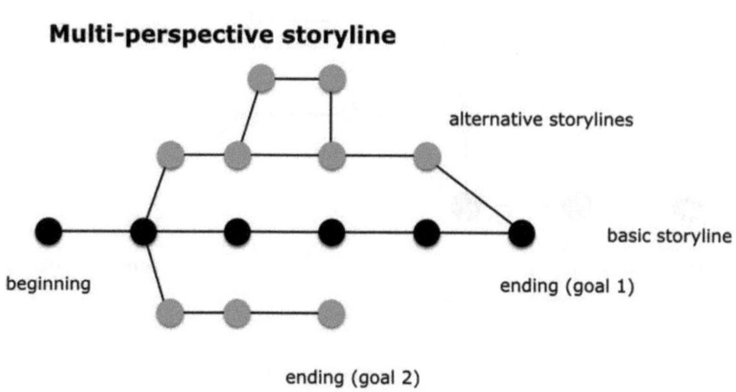

Fig. 2 The golden fleece: multi-perspective storyline (author's own figure)

6.4 The Rites of Passage Process

This process is going in a similar way as the "golden fleece" process; the main difference is that the basic storyline in the beginning is incomplete: The story told leads only to the first event that introduces a change; no final goal is defined. For example, this change can be becoming an agile company. The development of the story can happen in story circles according to the "golden fleece" process (Fig. 3).

Let me write some sentences to point out clearly the difference between a multi-perspective storyline and a fully open storyline. In the former there is a clear understanding of the goal or the outcome of the story: Jason and the Argonauts in the archaic version of the quest story know from the beginning that their journey shall lead them to the Golden Fleece. But maybe there are different paths to that goal, and maybe the goal may change while travelling. In the latter, however, there is no goal: There is only a call to change—and what will happen then is completely open.

The rites of passage process is more suitable for small companies or for teams and departments of bigger companies that want to design their own future story. For big companies and organisations, the "golden fleece" is recommended.

Of course, these two masterplots are not the only open ones (as well as the two previously mentioned closed masterplots are not the only closed plots). There may be a lot more—the four mentioned plots may serve as examples. To decide whether a future story of a company is based on an open or a closed plot, you may ask the following questions:

- Is there a restricted set of possible endings (e.g. only victory or defeat)?
- Is there a restricted set of possible elements of the storyline (e.g. only fight or flight)?

If "yes" is the answer to both questions, your future story may be based on a closed setting. As mentioned above, that is not always a bad choice—in an actual

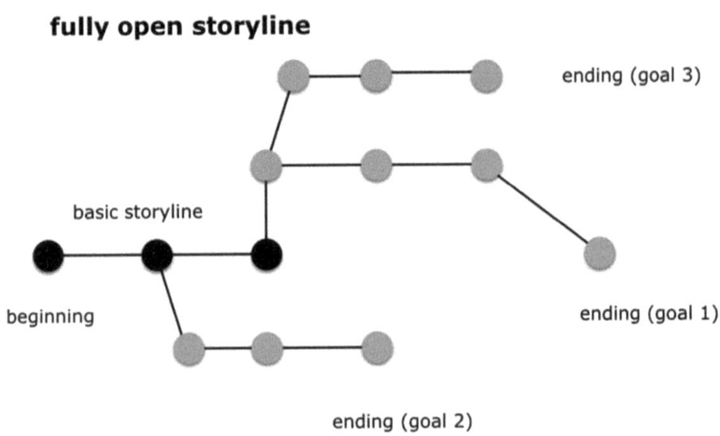

Fig. 3 Rites of passage: fully open storyline (author's own figure)

crisis or if your company provides very specific products for very specific customers to tell your story using a closed masterplot may make sense. For most of the companies in our "VUCA" world, open story settings are the better choice.

7 Frozen, Fluid and Vapourous Stories

A further question is how organisations deal with the stories they construct and tell about themselves, the basic attitude to their identity-building stories, whether they are stories about the past, the present or the future of the company. In other words, it's about the fundamental attitude of a company to its own story (worlds). The metaphor of the physical states of water—frozen, fluid or vapourous—may help us to describe different possibilities in that field.

An organisation with *frozen stories* or *a frozen story world* is careful not to allow any changes to their fixed stories. An example of this is how stories are dealt with in some religious organisations: The set of stories revealed by god or a prophet are fixed for all times, because they contain god's truth. Religions with "holy books", like Christianity or the Islam, are examples for those systems, which normally tend to be conservative. Companies with frozen story worlds are often old family-owned businesses, where for the family owner, the stories of the founders and big successes can be very important not only for the identity of the company but also for the identity of the family, and so any changes to the stories may be regarded as an assault on that identity.

At the other end of the paradigm are organisations with *vapourous story worlds*. That means that there isn't a clear understanding of a common, identity-building set of stories. Maybe every member of the organisation (or system) has their own story, or there are fragments of stories floating around, but there are no stories that all members of the system agree on. We may find vapourous story worlds in start-ups and in teams that don't know yet whether they want to be an organisation at all. That could be a group of friends who start an initiative, maybe a social one, and don't want to build up clear structures and roles (like leadership) or agree on a common basic story. This fear of clear structures and a clear story may have its origins in the wish not to become caged in an organisation that isn't easy to escape (attachment anxiety) or in an ideology of non-hierarchic and completely nonstructured collaboration. But, like vapour, organisations with vapourous story worlds tend to diffuse through lack of a clear identity.

In the middle of these two extremes are organisations with *fluid story worlds*. That does mean that there are clear identity-building stories but that they are not fixed for all times but can change, be developed and be adapted to new challenges. In a (business) world where change is standard, it's best for companies to develop fluid story worlds. It's important to keep a balance between the other two "story states", in order to keep the story world in its fluid state and not let it become frozen or vapourous. To maintain this balance, a clear core story (Müller 2010)—a definition of the narrative core of the story world and the DNA that has to be in every story told by the company—is an important tool. But in a fluid story world, even the core story

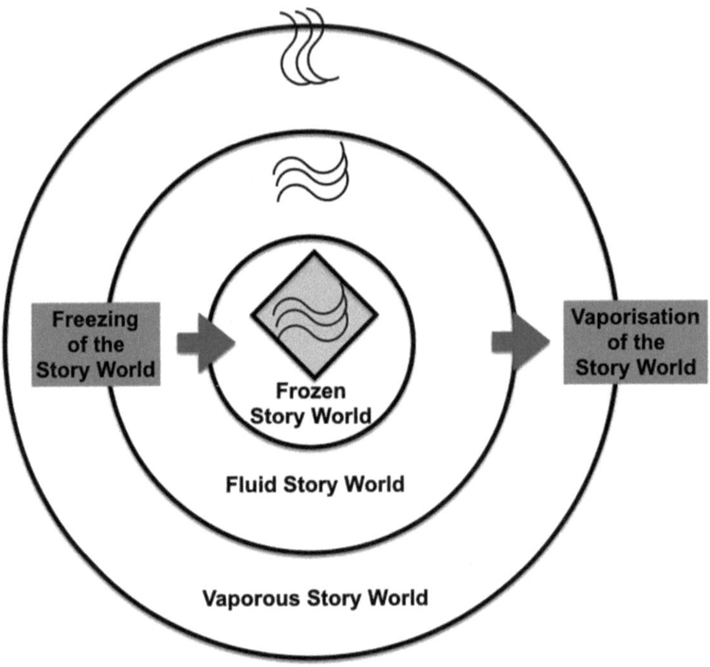

Fig. 4 Frozen, fluid and vapourous story worlds (author's own figure)

can be changed from time to time. A fluid story world is the narrative equivalent of a fluid corporate identity that keeps the core, maybe cautiously changes it, if necessary, but adapts their stories to changes in markets or cultures. Of course, a fluid story world needs an open masterplot like "golden fleece" or "rites of passage" as a basis.

Of course, the "state" of the story world of a company can change during the development of an organisation—from frozen through fluid to vapourous or vice versa. Two of these possible changes could be problematic. The first is the change from a fluid to a frozen story world. If a company recognises signs of that change, it should reflect on its ability to react to new developments in markets or in society. The second is the change from a fluid to a vapourous story world that might be a sign that the organisation's identity is dissolving (Fig. 4).

8 Collaboratively Telling the Future Story of an Organisation

In our Western storytelling tradition, we have clear roles: There is the storyteller, and there is the audience. The storyteller tells the story and the audience listens. The responsibility for the development of the plot and the narration is the storyteller's. But there are other traditions with different role models. In East African oral storytelling, the storyteller is the one who starts the narrative, and then the listeners comment, develop ideas, act as characters of the story and provide possibilities for the ongoing story (Reuster-Jahn 2016: 84).[2] That's real collaborative storytelling. In European companies we most commonly find the Western storytelling tradition—if there is active storytelling at all: The executive board or someone who is in charge of it tells the story, and the employees are the audience. In external communication, especially in "content marketing", some companies experiment with a kind of collaborative storytelling by including user-generated content in their blogs, websites and social media groups. As far as I know, there are no companies that use collaborative storytelling for developing their core story, future story, updated brand- and identity-stories, etc. Of course, to create a collaborative fluid story world using open plots, there must already be a developed structure of story circles in the company. But I think that would be a good thing, not only for motivating the employees but also to strengthen their identification with the company and to make the company more agile.

References

Beckert, J. (2016). *Imagined futures. Fictional expectations and capitalist dynamics*. Cambridge, MA: Harvard University Press.

Busse, C. (2018a). Radikalkur für Siemens. *Süddeutsche Zeitung,* 03.08.2018, 74. Jg., 31. Woche, S. 1.

Busse, C. (2018b). Ich bin zu alt, um es allen recht zu machen. *Süddeutsche Zeitung,* 03.08.2018, 74. Jg., 31. Woche, S. 18.

Crossley, M. L. (2000). *Introducing narrative psychology. Self, trauma and the construction of meaning*. Buckingham, PA: Open University Press.

Müller, M. (2010). Auf der Suche nach der Core Story: Im Kern steht immer eine Geschichte. *Wirtschaftspsychologie aktuell*, 17. Jg., Heft 3/2010, S. 58–60.

Müller, M. (2017). *Einführung in narrative Methoden der Organisationsberatung*. Heidelberg: Carl-Auer.

Müller, M., & Grimm, P. (2016). *Narrative Medienforschung. Einführung in Methodik und Anwendung*. Konstanz: UVK.

Prince, G. (1973). *A grammar of stories. An introduction.* Paris: Mouton.

Reuster-Jahn, U. (2016). Leserkommunikation bei Internet-Romanen in Tansania (Ostafrika). In P. Grimm & M. Müller (Eds.), *Erzählen im Internet, Geschichten über das Internet* (Schriftenreihe Medienethik) (Vol. 16, pp. 77–96). Stuttgart: Steiner.

Snyder, B. (2005). *Save the cat! The last book on screenwriting that you'll ever need.* Chelsea, MI: Sheridan Books.

Titzmann, M. (2013). Narrative Strukturen in semiotischen Äußerungen. In H. Krah & M. Titzmann (Eds.), *Medien und Kommunikation. Eine interdisziplinäre Einführung* (3rd ed.). Passau: Stutz.

[2]Reuster-Jahn shows in her paper how this oral tradition was brought into internet storytelling.

Michael Müller is professor for Media Analysis and Media Conception at Stuttgart Media University (University for Applied Sciences). He is teaching and researching in the areas narration, semiotics and media theory. Michael Müller studied German literature, philosophy, logics and theory of science at the University of Munich.

He began his professional career as a cultural manager with Siemens AG and as an editor with the German broadcasting company ProSiebenSAT.1. After that he was working as a consultant and coach for almost 20 years. Since then he supported companies, organisations and individuals on the basis of narrative and systemic approaches in the areas of communication and cultural development, change processes and decision-making.

Michael Müller has published numerous books and articles on the topics of organisational storytelling, semiotics, media and political narratives. He is chairman of the "Institute for Applied Narratology (IANA)" at Stuttgart Media University.

Storywork: Facilitating the Transformational Power of Story in Brand and Organizational Development

Steph K. Bachmair

Abstract

Storytelling, understood classically, refers to a one-way communication. Storywork, in contrast, is meant to be a dialogue between a teller and listener. As a dialogue storywork can become a vehicle for awareness, transformation and relationship work. Storywork integrates sensitive listening, impactful authentic telling and cocreating.

This article illustrates how story and process may interact. A story created through such interaction can impact charismatic branding and at the same time be a solid and healthy base for an organizational process of growth and transformation.

Major foci rest:

- On the iterative storywork cycle of listening (narrative research), cocreating (transformative experience) and telling (narrative strategy building)
- On archetyping to explore the organizational myth and support its expression
- On a processwork attitude and methodology to facilitate cocreative strategy building

To make theory more tangible, the article ends with cases illustrating the work on organizational lead, change and brand stories.

S. K. Bachmair (✉)
B-onfire, Hamburg, Germany
e-mail: stephanie.bachmair@b-onfire.com; https://www.b-onfire.com

© Springer Nature Switzerland AG 2019

J. Chlopczyk, C. Erlach (eds.), *Transforming Organizations*,
Management for Professionals, https://doi.org/10.1007/978-3-030-17851-2_7

1 A Story: The Watch's Suicide

A watch on the left arm, I long time felt rebellious against this German or Western European mainstream rule. It reminded me of rigidity—the negative aspect of time. I felt it constraining my free spirit in its creative flow. Over the years, I lived well without a watch on my arm.

Thirty years later, I got into a 'flirt' with a cheap golden Casio watch, a model similar to my very first silver watch in the late 1970s. Since then, life has convinced me about some advantages of being structured in our time- and action-based society and still more in my professional responsibility as an organizational consultant.

Finally, I bought it and travelled with my 'new' watch on the left arm to a Deep Democracy facilitation training[1] in Kyiv. Working on unfolding unconscious personal and group processes, we normally get slightly confused after some days, wandering between dream and reality. One afternoon, in a giggly mood, we talked and walked with some colleagues along the River Dnepr until we get to a huge bridge.

I rarely cross a bridge without pausing on it, so I ask my companions, if they would mind resting a moment in the middle of the bridge. We slowed down, paused, looked and got lost in the shimmery sun play of the water. Suddenly, with a little bang, my golden watch touched the edge of the bridge before falling freely into the depth, ending up in the river. After mentally checking the weight of my loss, I started laughing and felt relief.

Finally I understand now that I have not been in conflict with structure, time or watches but with timelessness. I still underestimate these delicate spaces, where flow rules over time. The solution or evolution is to appreciate slowing down and timelessness, the magic that happens when structure emerges—with ease—out of the flow.

2 The Storywork Cycle

2.1 Paradigm Shift: New Times, New Challenges

The dance between structure and flow is at the heart of what supports organizations to cope with the challenges of today's rapid changing surroundings. Through connecting to their own creativity and wisdom, organizations develop impactful stories: these stories are authentic, touching and transformative.

To connect storywork to the current business context, I want to refer to Gerhard Wohland. He simplifies how to understand organizations by stating that the sole goal of an organization is to solve problems. He differentiates two sets of problems: blue

[1]Special thanks here to the DDI Institute, its founders, Max and Ellen Schupbach and the faculty, my teachers, who practice and teach processwork with a special focus on leadership, community building and coaching.

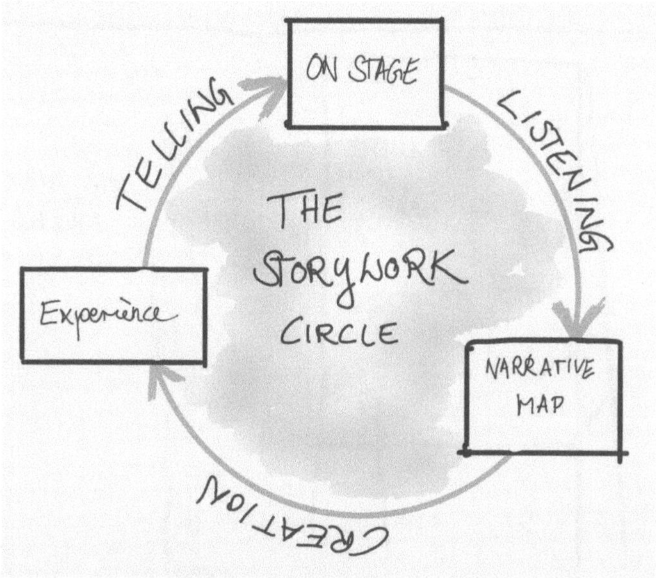

Fig. 1 The storywork cycle (author's own figure)

as complicated and red as complex problems. Whereas blue problems can be solved through knowledge and linear thinking, red problems need to be solved through talent and creativity (Wohland et al. 2012).

The new 'fast' business era causes more and more red problems. Smart long-term plans and strategies are no success guarantee anymore, as more and more surprises occur and the rules of the game continuously change. Overall organizations and leaders look for coping strategies and ways to move faster, whereas storywork invites organizations to slow down. To slow down means that people listen to each other and oneself that they aim for stories that give orientation, transform and invite cocreation.

It does not matter if I work with an organization on a brand story and a change story or with an executive on his lead story; the iterative working cycle is always the same: listening as narrative research, creating as transformative journey and telling as narrative strategy building (Fig. 1).

2.2 Story Listening as Narrative Research

Each company swims in a sea of stories. Beyond these stories is an organizational myth. This myth is a basic pattern like the DNA of the system. The myth is timeless, not easy to catch, an experience rather than a sentence. Searching for the myth is like a treasure hunt, finding it like a precious archaeological discovery. A narrative or

Fig. 2 The narrative map (author's own figure)

core story based on the myth has the potential to inspire. It is like a bonfire for a group; it creates community and makes sense. People engage (Fig. 2).

Depending on the setting, listening can have different formats. For example, stakeholder interviews focus groups or a moment portal in the workshop setting (Swart 2013; Chapter "Transforming Organisations Through the Re-authoring Lens and Practices" in this volume). The objective is to create a narrative map, illustrating the general atmosphere, different roles and tensions in the field, past stories, future dreams and facilitator's inner process. The narrative map is the base for the process design, the script for the transformative journey.

2.3 Story Creation as Collective Experience

2.3.1 Conflict as Source of Creativity and Growth

Today, most organizations focus on the telling and tend to outsource the listening or also the creative process to external consultants and/or agencies. In my approach, the working on the storyline becomes a collective, transformational process within the organization. The facilitation attitude to support this journey is quite different from the concept of expert consultancy, a creative agency or classic training. As a facilitator, I contribute my capacity for listening and for catching sparks and my ability to work with diversity and tension. In so doing, I support the unfolding of the group's own creativity.

Creativity, innovation and transformation are phenomena for which each organization aims. In fact, they emerge out of the diversity that exists in groups. Yet, many times, we fear the 'difference' rather than feeling attracted to the difference. Why?

We can summarize the causal chain behind the diversity in groups as follows: the larger the differences in groups, the greater the tension and number of tension fields. In addition, intense tension often leads to conflict. No doubt, conflict is scary. It is the most difficult part in a relationship. Also, conflict brings forth emotions. We have an ambivalent attitude to emotions. Many times we would like to have our feelings 'under control', especially in an organizational environment.

It is important to note that the avoidance of conflict might bring forth emotions such as anger and/or depression. The more we oppress conflicts, the more we might lose joy, creativity and connection.

A perhaps more sustainable attitude might be a clear 'yes to conflict'. Each conflict can be a source for creative energy and growth. If we successfully resolve or transform a conflict, it frees creative energy and might lead to a deeper connection. Understood in this way, brand development can be seen as a collective journey directly linked to organizational development. Brand development can create a deep involvement of everybody involved.

2.3.2 Some Words to Processwork Facilitation

Arnold Mindell's process-oriented psychology (in the following text called processwork) is grounded in Taoism, quantum physics and Jungian psychology. Mindell's work started with a focus on the individual therapeutic setting. Today it is also applied to large-scale socio-political conflict facilitation. In his book *Sitting in the Fire*, Mindell writes about the Taoistic influence: 'The way things are unfolding contains the basic elements necessary for solving human problems' (Mindell 1992).

What is a process? It is a flow of signals, some of them conscious, others unconscious. In Mindell's theory, the process consists of primary and secondary processes. The primary process is close to our identity, to our consciousness, whereas the secondary process consists of non-identified signals. The growth potential of the coachee, the organization or the facilitator lies in the unfolding of the secondary process. Between the primary and the secondary processes lies the so-called edge. To give an example, let us assume a very friendly company culture. The primary process is to agree, to support a leader, whereas the secondary process is to 'openly address the critic'.

It is normal that resistance builds up before one approaches or steps over an edge. Approaching or stepping over an edge might be linked to integrating non-identified parts. Individuals and organizations normally tend to shy away from what resists. Integration of the resistance, although 'counter-intuitive', can be helpful and can be a doorway that enables transformation and growth. Facilitators support the process by creating awareness of the secondary process. They catch double signals and help in crossing edges should the process lead there.

As in quantum physics, processwork considers each system a field. Within this field there are diverse voices, tendencies or roles. Some of these roles have more ease to appear. This might be because they correspond to mainstream attitudes. Other roles are more hidden, as they might be marginalized taboos or minority opinions. Those roles are called ghost roles. When these marginalized voices speak, the group normally feels relieve and can move on.

2.3.3 Facilitator's Inner Work as Added Value for the Process

Inner work is a major resource of the facilitator to bring awareness to the process. The processes within one person are also reflected in the group. This is called 'parallel process'. When you work as a facilitation team, tensions you may encounter as a team indicate what takes place in the larger field or system. Thus, as a facilitator you can process roles and tensions through inner work and bring such awareness to the group.

As an example, I amplify a current inner process. Writing on brand refinement and culture change creates a light inner tension in me. What is going on? A brand is a story, whereas culture change is a process. Let's listen to these two roles in me, the processworker (PW) and the storyteller (ST):

PW As a process-oriented facilitator, I follow process. I very much believe that working with the flow results in the best solution for everybody involved.

ST Maybe, but this book is about storytelling, where is the story in your process?

PW Everywhere, each organization tells many stories; sensitive listening helps me to understand the process. I am also convinced when you work well with the process, you can create beautiful stories.

ST What do you mean by beautiful?

PW I mean, they are congruent and authentic; they transform both teller and listener. And, to my mind, storytelling needs to be dynamic.

ST That sounds great. But my concern is that a brand is like a compass, it needs certain stability. A brand cannot be changed all the time and adapting to flow or process.

PW Maybe we can commit to a stable backbone (myth/core story) and a more fluid expression of it.

ST Not easy to understand, but this makes me curious, I want to try.... as long as an impactful story becomes visible (Fig. 3).

After the narrative mapping (listening) and the collective journey to transform tensions into collective creativity, the team and its brand(s) are ready to step on stage (storytelling). It is time to perform, prioritize content, consider format, get into dialogue with the audience and develop a brand strategy. At this point the strategy is emerging out of the flow—with ease and grace. It is now the power of a collective awareness that organizes process.

Fig. 3 My inner processworker and storyteller (author's own figure)

2.4 Storytelling as Narrative Strategy Building

After the narrative mapping (listening) and the collective journey to transform tensions into collective creativity, the team and its brand(s) are ready to step On Stage, to share the experience. It is time to perform, prioritize content, consider format, get into dialogue with the audience and develop a brand strategy. At this point the strategy is emerging out of the flow. The hope is that now the power of collective awareness organizes the process.

Such an organizing of process can happen in many ways. One way might be the focus on brand or organizational identity, which is a very useful tool to create a consistency in 'archetyping'. The work with archetypes is like a universal language to describe the quality of a brand and the experience it creates.

There are many archetypical systems derived from C.G. Jung's work. Carole Pearson developed a system of 12 archetypes to work on brand or organizational identity (Pearson and Mark 2001). In their system, each of the four groups of three archetypes is answering one basic need. In the 1960s Fritz Riemann explained that human behaviour is driven by four basic polarized needs: individuation, belonging, stability and risk mastery (Riemann 1961). Each archetype answers to human needs in a specific way (Fig. 4).

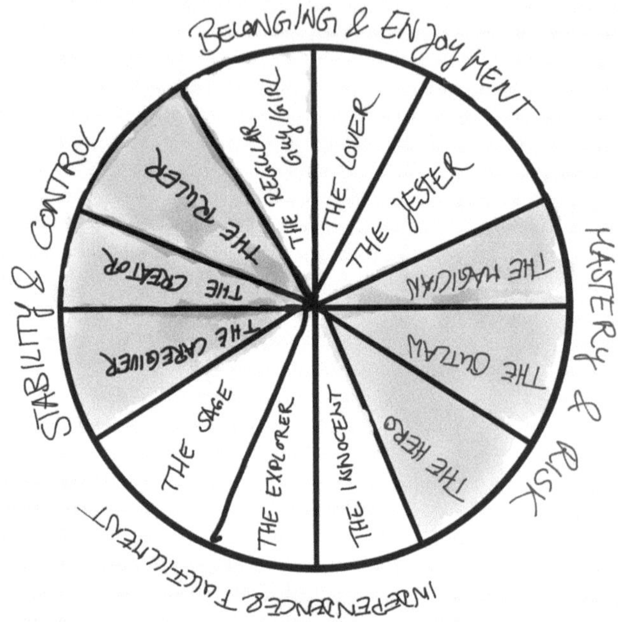

Fig. 4 Overview of 12 archetypes and the basic needs (author's own format)

Let us take the need 'belonging' as an example. There is the guy next door, who belongs through adapting and connecting; there is the lover, who belongs through attraction and seduction; and there is the jester, who belongs through entertaining and confronting others with well-packed truth.

As humans we instinctively search for mentors. Archetypes can appear in different forms like cinema heroes, therapists and teachers. Archetypes also appear in the form of brands. There are some needs derived from of our life myth or personal history; some other needs occur in certain situations or life phases (like the lover archetype can help a young adult cope with discovering sexuality).

Archetypes can bridge the deep essence level of the story level. They can help find words for the purpose, the why, and the values of the organization, the how. Properly worked through, the archetypical picture or 'Leitbild' works as a navigator, as the North Star, and may connect brand and culture. The more brand and company culture are synchronous, the stronger the organization.

Today brand and organizational leadership are often separated in terms of responsibilities and strategies. As a consequence communication with the customer and internally lived organizational values are not always congruent. Part of the idea of inside-out communication is that the brand experience starts in-house. The brand experience is expressed through the company culture so that employees become the main ambassadors of the organizational identity.

3 Storywork in Practice

3.1 Brand-Culture Fusion: A Food Retailer Walking from Purpose to Culture to Strategy

3.1.1 Narrative Research to Listen into the Organization

As stated above, my entry point into process is listening. In the case of a regional food retailer, I started to interview the main executive stakeholder. The analysis of the interview material was reflected into a narrative map, describing the current and the desired identity of the organization with a set of archetypes.

The main archetype is the 'guy next door' answering the need of belonging in a very humble, down-to-earth way. This archetype stands for solidarity, connection and pragmatism. It goes along with the metaphor of the Gallic Village, which illustrates the feeling of solidarity, the connection between people and the strong bond to a region.

During the interviews we further explored the timeline or storyline—past moments (gain/pain points) and a best possible future. It is easy to recognize that this organization is very well rooted in the present, perhaps missing a longer-term vision.

From the process of listening, a workshop design often emerges easily. It becomes a brand journey, a collective experience creating access to deeper knowledge of the organization useful for the building of a strategy.

3.1.2 Cocreation in the Management Team

'Because the people from here matter to us'. When this sentence was spoken in the workshop setting, the atmosphere suddenly changed. Here it was, the why, the purpose of the organization. A big 'wow' occurred in the room. Today nobody remembers exactly how the sentence came up, a cocreative product which emerged out of a fertile space. It felt congruent for the people involved in the process.

After this workshop with a diverse leadership team of 15 people, the sentence began to spread through the organization—effortlessly. A high dream for a marketer is the best for which one might hope. The sentence emerged so quickly that the leadership team feared not to have enough 'story' to support its quick movement. As a result, we planned another workshop with the same group of participants.

Our next step was to connect the purpose with individual stories in the leadership team. The idea was to work on a set of values, the how, and finally to discuss the gap between the desired brand perception and the status today. This gap analysis was the base for strategy work and the development of an action plan.

During this session, the leadership team came to the conclusion that this sentence—'because the people from here matter to us'—is not only meant for the consumer but needs to become an employee experience. The leadership team commits to change the focus (and our assignment) from brand strategy to a brand-culture fusion—another example of inside-out communication.

3.1.3 Telling as an Organizational Brand Journey

What started as a brand strategy assignment turned into an organizational development initiative. Over the period of half a year, 300 people (of 4000 employees) went through a workshop experience, so they could become ambassadors for culture change in their organization.

The basic structure of the individual workshop (15 in a row) was always the same. It started with a context setting, with information about the process, about attitude and the aim of the leadership team. We also outlined our facilitation approach.

The introduction is rather a frontal 'teaching', a format familiar to the participants. An important part is that at least two executives open the day by sharing their lead stories connected to the purpose sentence. After a getting to know, we go in the second important part of the day, the moment portal (Swart 2013). Participants are working in groups of five to six to share their own experiences: What moment do you remember, when was this sentence lived/not lived?

This is a door opener. It gives access to the gains and pains of the organization. Although most of the participants were not very familiar with our workshop setting, they moved easily into conversation. Connection happened, the brand sentence became alive. As facilitators we get much narrative material from our conversations. They help us understand the present topics and tensions in the group. Some of those are expressed directly; others find their way through double signals like silence, strong reactions, side stories and so forth.

In the very first workshops, we became aware that people do not dare express negative feedback. Framing this, it became obvious that the 'old' leadership attitude did not allow any critics. We worked through this with the group and fed it back to the leadership team. We found that speaking openly reduced the blockage in the group. In workshops that followed, the door for critics had opened. We now encountered a flood of outspoken criticisms. We made space for it and began to process with the group ideas about a more constructive way of feedback.

The perspective walk is another important element of the workshop day. In this exercise we visualize main stakeholders of the organization in the room. Then we ask the participants to walk through the different perspectives answering questions out of those points of view. In this way tension fields between different stakeholders become more transparent. In almost all of the workshops, we encountered a communicative 'wall' between central functions and retail markets. The feedback of participants confirms this part as a very eye-opening experience. Stepping into the shoes of the 'other' creates a deeper mutual understanding.

In the afternoon we offered a small open space. Out of previous experiences, the participants selected their hot topics. We emphasized that the topics should connect to the central expression we discovered: 'Because people from here matter to us'.

When we introduce open space principles, we encounter silence. As we explore the silence, we understand that the participants are not used to being engaged and to being asked for creative contributions. Rather, they were used to getting direct orders.

This experience of being asked made some participants curious, some sceptical and some uncomfortable and scared. Through this format, we created a small experience of a new leadership/collaboration culture of which many executives might dream.

3.2 Storywork Training as Shared Practice: A 'Universal Remedy'

Also marketeers seem to fear conflict. They often focus on presenting solutions, instead of telling stories. However, as Petra Sammer points out, nobody goes into the cinema to watch 100 minutes of solution telling. With story, time enters into the game. A story is the journey between who you are and who you can be in the future, and this can create tension.

The CMO of a pharmaceutical company decides to train the whole team in the art of storytelling. She likes the proposal to provide a 'storylab' training. The idea is that people can experience storytelling while directly working on their brand. After a first phase of listening to the organization through narrative interviews, the group is invited to work on their brand's core story. The team tells the foundation story. 150 years ago, a nun invented a remedy. The nun is without any doubt a 'caretaker' archetype.

Diving into her story, we discover the nun was much more than a caretaker. She was a very unconventional woman, without a roof over her head. After travelling through countries and healing people with her self-created remedies, she finally settled in Cologne and started producing her first remedy on a larger scale. Others started to copy her product so that she decided to ask the royal authority at that time for a certification. Through this step she received a certification stamp on her products. Her remedy was one of the first branded products in Germany, a rarely told story.

The team works further in developing a persona[2] for the brand (Uebernickel et al. 2015). The team shares that at first sight their organization appears conventional. Developing journeys for the brand character allows surprisingly unconventional aspects to appear. This confirms that the primary archetype is the caretaker and the secondary archetype 'the rebel'.

We open a group process, deepening the understanding of the secondary process by inviting the rebellious parts of the brand, the organizational system and all individuals on stage. In the afternoon, we introduce the story canvas. This is a big sheet inspired by the Business Model Canvas, which small groups use to work with each other on different—in this case story—elements (Osterwalder and Pigneur 2010) (Fig. 5).

What story does the team want to tell? Who is the audience? What is the main conflict? Why is this so important? What is the best possible outcome? How does the organization get there? To what does this organization invite the audience?

Over the 2 days, much creative material emerged, but the story creating and telling is obviously an edge for the group. Here we encounter silence, irritation and resistance. Once the group stepped over the edge, creativity starts to flow, and many

[2]The persona development as element of the design thinking process is used to work on the development of brand or target group characters in an analog way.

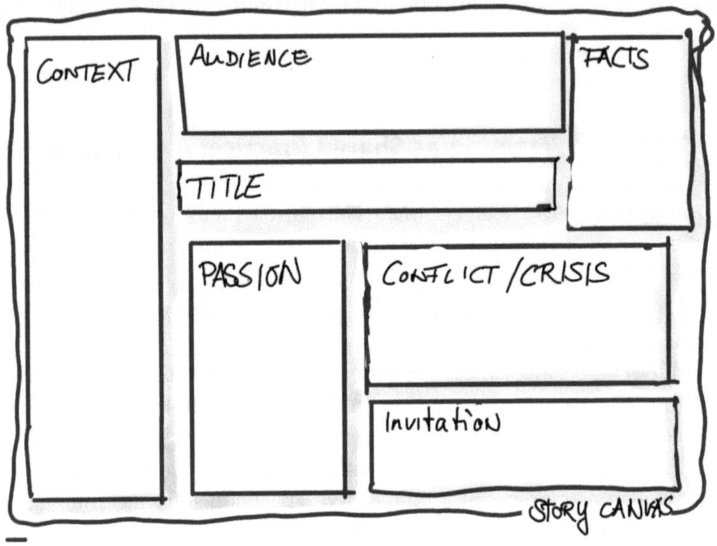

Fig. 5 The story canvas (author's own format)

diverse and colourful stories emerge. This is the perfect base from which to further explore brand strategy.

Another ghost role for this brand is spirituality. It was appearing within the storylab, but not yet the right time to integrate it. I conclude the assignment with the suggestion to integrate 'spirituality' in the upcoming strategy work.

3.3 Leading with Story: The 'Ruler' Setting the Scene for Cocreation

Working on a change story with the leader of a family-owned construction building company, we also work on archetypes. It becomes quite clear that the family foundation myth is a combination of explorer and caretaker energy, and the son is adding his impulses, a 'guy-next-door' spirit, by working on a 'building together' vision. But the organization is blocked to bring forth this vision.

There is a need to clarify structure, roles and responsibilities. The leader has to create awareness of his rank. He first needs to connect to the ruler energy, and then in a next step, he can offer a room for cocreation.

Modern organizations tend to reduce hierarchies and work on self-organization. Often they are surprised or even desperate when faced with the difficulties of collaborating on an eye-to-eye level. And the flip side of the coin: total equality is hard to ever achieve, might even be an impossibility. As Mindell states, the main source of conflict is non-awareness of rank, one's own or the other's rank. To work on lead stories also means to create awareness and transparency on rank and power (im)balances.

Brand or lead stories are to inspire fellowship; they give orientation, like a lighthouse in the fog. These stories should not be fixed and closed. Lead stories are like leading impulses brought into the room inviting people to cocreate. Like an organizational brand, a lead story also communicates the identity of the teller, his purpose and values and his tonality.

The teller needs also to be aware of what part of his story is set or branded and where is room for cocreation. Giving room for cocreation needs the ability to let go of a certain degree of ownership (control) and requires trust in the power of cocreation.

The old structure of the hero's journey is flowing from the individual into a collective story. Here leaders contribute their stake with a clear positioning, and at the same time, they create spaces for a collective journey. Tomorrow's successful leaders should communicate with awareness; ideally, they are storytellers but also listeners and facilitators.

I would like to introduce another piece of inner work, preparing a dialogue with a management executive speaking about a storywork future assignment:

Me As a facilitator, my first interest is not the result; I am following the process (ghost).
EX We will not invest in something of which we do not know the result.
Me I understand, what result do you want to achieve?
EX I want a 'change' story and people engaging in it.
Me Oh good. How will you know they engage?
EX They come up with ideas to promote the change.
Me Ok, I can sign in for this. Let me listen to your story first.

4 Try It Out: Drop Your Watches!

Ending this article, I want to summarize how storywork can support today's complex and fast-changing organizational world.

- Narrative research helps to recognize patterns and gives orientation for navigation through the unknown.
- It connects to the organizational essence, the myth and the part 'beyond identity which stays the same' irrespective of all changes.
- It creates spaces for dialogue and therefore for a collective transformation which forms a base for organizational creativity.
- It can give, through lead stories, orientation and invite for cocreation.

As many of us wear watches on the left arm, it is a challenge to give space in organizations to this kind of deep-diving storywork. Our action-based Western cultures framed by the speed of digitalization have difficulties to stand still and to recognize the creative power and knowledge of the collective. We often jump directly into telling without listening and connecting to our creativity.

Perhaps it is time to drop the watches at least for some moments and to acknowledge that the resulting inspiration, connectivity and community feelings are like ingredients for an energy drink or an empowering Ayurveda treatment. Such a stance might empower all of us—people working with organizations and brands—to success and joyfully face the speed and uncertainty of our times.

References

Mindell, A. (1992). *The leader as martial artist: An introduction to deep democracy.* Portland: Lao Tse Press.

Osterwalder, A., & Pigneur, Y. (2010). *Business model generation.* Hoboken, NJ: Wiley.

Pearson, C., & Mark, M. (2001). *The hero and the outlaw: Building extraordinary brands through the power of archetypes.* New York: Mc Graw-Hill Education.

Riemann, F. (1961). *Grundformen der Angst.* München: Ernst Reinhardt Verlag.

Swart, C. (2013). *Re-authoring the world.* Randburg: Knowres Publishing.

Uebernickel, F., Brenner, W., Pukall, B., Naef, T., & Schindlholzer, B. (2015). *Design thinking: Das Handbuch.* Frankfurt a. M.: Frankfurter Allgemeine Buch.

Wohland, G., Wiehmeyer, M., et al. (2012). *Denkwerkzeuge der Höchstleister: Warum dynamikrobuste Unternehmen Marktdruck erzeugen.* Lüneburg: Unibuch Verlag.

Steph K. Bachmair as a facilitator, storyworker and coach, supports organizations and executives in awareness, transformation and relationship work based on the work with narratives. After her studies of mathematics/international management, she worked 13 years in brand management and leadership responsibilities in fast-moving consumer goods. In 2012 she founded B-onfire, a facilitation agency with a focus on brand-/identitywork and organizational transformation. She researches, writes and teaches on storywork as methodology based on transformational storytelling and process-oriented psychology.

Keeping Your Mythos Alive: How to Nourish and Nurture a Business's Mythos Through Corporate Transformations

Silvia Zulauf

Abstract

What makes a business successful? How does it remain successful?

In order to answer this question, I have developed the MythosResearch® approach, which helps medium-sized, family-owned businesses to tap into their most important resource for making them successful: their deepest sense of purpose—their "mythos."

Mythos potential pulsates throughout a business's history, its doctrines and beliefs, and its vision of the future. A clearly defined and communicated mythos creates identification, orientation, and enthusiasm. It is therefore a magical breeding ground for a successful corporate brand.

Over time, however, a mythos may become a burden and a risk factor, as it stands in the way of new developments. The mythos then "bites back." It is therefore crucial for the leadership to become aware of the business's mythos and to realign it to the changed requirements of the market.

1 Organizational Mythos: An Introduction

1.1 Which "Mythos" Are We Talking About?

The scintillating notion of "mythos" is used in a variety of semantic fields—religious content, Greek mythology, exciting brands, and false assertions—thus creating a lot of confusion. Let's make one thing clear right from the start: in this article, "mythos" is not used in the colloquial sense of "lie" or "phenomenon," nor in the historically restrictive ancient context.

S. Zulauf (✉)
MythosResearch®, Capitol, Berlin, Germany
e-mail: sz@mythosresearch.de

© Springer Nature Switzerland AG 2019

J. Chlopczyk, C. Erlach (eds.), *Transforming Organizations*,
Management for Professionals, https://doi.org/10.1007/978-3-030-17851-2_8

Instead, "mythos" here denotes a mode of perception allowing us to experience a sense of purpose and meaning. Contrary to logical thinking, a mythos is not limited by language and its notions. In mythos mode, we perceive things in a holistic way while thinking synthetically (cf. Cassirer 1964; Langer 1992; Jamme 1999).

Members of a culture develop and use specific systems of signs and symbols as a way of talking about these perceptions. The mythical element therefore not only manifests itself as a way of perceiving but also as a way of expressing oneself. Within these processes, we can distinguish between three levels:

1. Mythical thinking as an analog way of perceiving and processing
2. Preconscious premises reflexively arising from the mythical way of processing
3. Development of (mythical) symbols to allow culture members to reflect on their perceptions and communicate them

Culture is thus primarily characterized by a prelingual, analog, and holistic way of thinking. A culture's values, premises, and actions derive from the orientation and imagination patterns thus formed (cf. Schein 2003).

Based on this perception- and symbol-based concept of mythos, a corporate culture is seen as a symbol system consisting of words, rituals, images, and mythoi helping its members to bring order to reality as they experience it. This continuous process is fuelled by the subjective perception of meaning and the desire to derive from it a collective sense of purpose. Corporate mythoi thus have the same function as their ancient models: they reduce complexity and serve to interpret the world.

1.2 The Mythos Model

The MythosModel® illustrates the complex ways the dynamics of mythical perception shapes reality. It shows that logical and mythical thinking are based on two different perception modes. Only their mutual interaction forms our image of reality (Fig. 1).

> We only know for certain what we believe in. WILHELM BUSCH (Balzer 1953)

1.2.1 What Is an Organizational Mythos?

Powerful cultures have a common crystallization point characterizing them, such as a historical mythos, a charismatic leader, an exciting product, a brand, or a powerful vision of the future.

If a company starts out with a captivating vision, a magical narrative speaking to people's minds, hearts, and souls, chances are that it will develop a powerful mythos. This is because the mythical mode of perception yearns for a sense of purpose—what is good, true, and beautiful. In people's experience, founders, events, heroes, places, visions, objects, institutions, concepts, and ideas are charged with excitement and acquire a collective meaning as they are communicated.

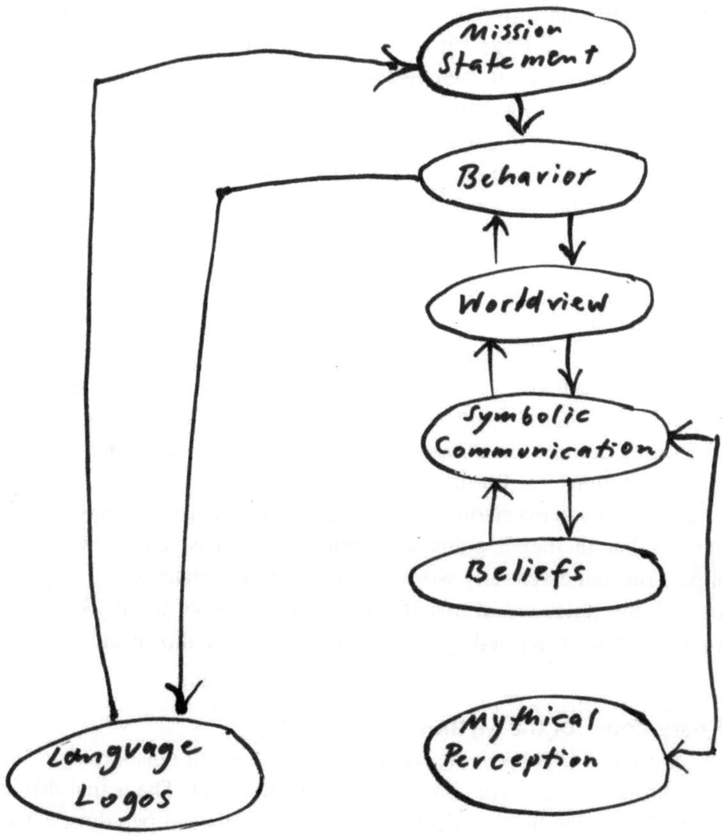

Fig. 1 Mythos Model ©Silvia Zulauf, 1992, authors' own figure

"The personal computer" (Apple), "having music moments everywhere" (Spotify), and "the free encyclopedia" (Wikipedia) were (initially) perceived as novelties. What is particularly appealing is messages that are simple while combining two seemingly disparate aspects. Robert Bosch, for instance, is a company that stands for technological innovation and social pioneering; it has remained loyal to this message. This bipolar allegiance continues to inspire the company and impact its strategic direction.

Each mythos manifests itself in objects, rituals, and patterns of symbolic language. Stories, anecdotes, legends, and proverbs implicitly convey a meaning in excess of what individual words can impart.

1.2.2 What Distinguishes a Mythos from a Narrative?

The "mythos" and "narrative" terms are of the same origin; both stand for anecdotes and tales.

The most significant difference is that a mythic story is received in a particular way. Across cultures and ages, it can implicitly convey content that speaks to us directly, independently of a factual, historical context. This is because a listener who is in mythical perception mode disregards time and history and absorbs what is said as a real-time experience (cf. Assmann 1999).

A mythos neither needs to be logical nor true. What it conveys lies not in the past and not in the future; its message speaks to us in the here and now. Typical introductions to mythical tales are:

> The story still rings in my ears...
> I see it before my eye...

Whether or not a narrative develops into a mythos ultimately depends on how people perceive it. According to Roland Barthes, everything can become a mythos: events, historical figures, concepts such as "technology" and "progress," and even places and institutions (cf. Barthes 1964, p. 85).

The reason why not everything becomes a mythos is that each new mythos takes up some familiar theme. It gains its depth and persuasiveness by invoking old cultural patterns and essentially working with mythical material.

Tales and anecdotes are ultimately secondary forms of the mythos as they are based on the premises implied by it; they point to the mythos itself.

The "Binary Code" of the Mythos

The story a mythos tells takes the form of a succession of episodes. It is, however, not about chronological events based on cause and effect. The actual driving force behind the story is the need to deal with contradictions and paradoxes. To resolve them, the mythical language operates on an enhanced level. To each conscious point, there is an unconscious counterpoint. It thus lifts its listeners to a new level of experience. Claude Levi-Strauss describes this phenomenon as the "binary code of the mythos" (cf. Levi-Strauss 1981, pp. 226ff.).

The following story told by a sales representative of Adolf Würth GmbH & Co. KG in an interview illustrates how resolving the "profit-seeking/altruism" paradox helped transform the pronounced sales orientation of the company:

> As a boy, Reinhold Würth used to pull a handcart through Künzelsau which is where the company's headquarters is today. He went from one craftsman to the next trying to sell screws. His dad died when he was still young, which by itself was very difficult for a boy who would have other things on his mind. But he went on to be the first of his industry to deliver directly to customers. I think he did it at his father's behest. It was for his dad that he turned the one-man business into a corporation with a revenue of €4.9 billion and 70,000 employees. That's the point that most touches my heart. (Zulauf, personal communication, April 2010)

A Levi Strauss-based structuralist analysis makes the binary structure of the Würth story visible (Table 1):

The persuasive power and the stability of a mythical tale are driven by these open or hidden ambivalences. Irreconcilable logical contradictions are negotiated on a

Table 1 The binary structure of the Würth story

Old town of Künzelsau	Modern Würth headquarters
Handcart	Sophisticated logistics
Lost his dad at age 19	Independent and innovative
Mourning, passivity	Ambition, activity
One-man business	Global corporation
Success for his father	4.9 billion euros revenue

Authors' own table

dialectical level, thereby overcoming intellectual paradoxes. Using a "this as well as that" and "has never been but will always be" approach, the mythical story slips through "a hole in reality's umbrella" (cf. Blumenberg 1979), tames contradictions, and creates its particular charm and dynamics in this tension field. A certain vagueness and the inclusion of supernatural elements add to its magical potential.

1.2.3 Organizational Culture and Mythos

A corporate mythos that works well is a blessing. Employees put their hearts and souls to their work; suppliers, customers, and investors are loyal; and the industry's best experts apply for jobs.

To participate in a mythos means that, on a dialogic level, opposites and contradictions are reconciled. Opposites are not analyzed but integrated. The mythos takes a position beyond the logical level, thus increasing the tolerance toward contradictions and discrepancies companies face on a daily basis, such as the one between fundamental goals and objectives and the actual operational behavior.

An organizational mythos acts as a "common denominator" in that it creates a sense of purpose, identity, orientation, and trust. It paves the way for collective action, intuition, and creativity, as well as enthusiasm and motivation, potentially leading to a self-fulfilling prophecy. Mythical stories express context and values in an inspiring way, fostering immediate action. To new employees, they communicate the priorities and principles of how to do the work. Taboos and unspoken rules are also enshrined in stories. By metaphorical transfer, they can trigger changes and preserve tradition and continuity at the same time.

These positive, culture-strengthening qualities of a mythos have a particularly dynamic impact during the founding phase and the middle phase of a company's life. They persist as long as the company's behavior and strategy are aligned to its values and fundamental beliefs.

2 Worst-Case Scenarios: When a Corporate Mythos Stands in the Way of Necessary Transformations

While a mythos is in essence quite persistent, it is not a static construct. With each act of listening, the members of a culture modify, adjust, and develop it so that it caters to their need for purpose, certainty, and orientation.

Companies are in perpetual motion. In order to survive, they need to constantly adjust to the challenges of their environments and even reinvent themselves every now and then. Changes in the marketplace, technological innovation, generation changes, and mergers have a significant impact on the corporate culture. Various primary and secondary strands, variants, and sub-mythoi can thus develop during a company's history.

While mythoi have a capacity for ignoring differences, they create cognitive dissonance and lose their power of persuasion once values, behaviors, and decisions experienced on a daily basis start to diverge too much.

A strong mythos, however, can slow down or even seriously jeopardize the development of a company. This is the case if it contains elements that do not support a necessary realignment.

All disruptive change comes with the risk of causing a deep split between the ingrained system of meaning and the new behavioral requirements. Corporate cultures often derail after a "successful" transformation when this split occurs.

Ideally, company owners and leaders have a strong cultural competence that helps them realize that corporate change requires realignment not only of its business's purpose but also of its deeply shaken system of meaning.

Corporate upheavals and changes, however, often happen unexpectedly, absorbing all available energy; in such times, the task of recognizing and cultivating a shattered corporate culture can easily take a backseat. The following examples describe the risks that characterize such transformations.

2.1 Scenario 1: Dazzled by the Mythos

Company members take refuge in their mythical self-image, ignoring the call for change. They so strongly identify with the mythos that they turn a blind eye to changing markets and conditions. This creates a huge risk that they will miss the right moment for timely adjustments. In extreme cases, people prefer the demise of their own system to revising the mythos.

Example: Leica Camera AG, a company that misjudged the digital development at the turn of the millennium.

Digital photography was regarded by the management as a passing trend which would never affect the analog luxury segment. At the Photokina in Cologne, the biggest photo tradeshow in the world, Leica representatives proudly wore lapel stickers saying, "I am a film dinosaur." Competitors however had long taken the lead, and Leica was declared as good as dead in the industry. (Cf. Nutz 2017)

Sure enough, Leica saw its returns drop by a dramatic 40% between 2000 and 2005 and suffered several crises in subsequent years. It owes its survival to an investor excited by the Leica mythos who, at the very last moment and supported by a loyal staff, made the necessary adjustments toward the market. Today, Leica

Cameras are fully digitized and well on their way—in union with the Chinese smartphone manufacturer Huawei—to recapture their place in the market.

2.2 Scenario 2: Ignoring the Mythos

The company management takes up the challenge of the market and embarks on a reorientation. They then frantically communicate new guidelines and, at best, engage a consulting agency to introduce staff members to the new values and messages on a Friday evening. Staff members' confidence, however, has been shaken; they no longer identify with the company but, instead, are overtaken by skepticism and cynicism.

A similar development, which is far from untypical, befell a Berlin company 140 years after its establishment. The large handicraft business's new management considered it necessary to introduce a new structure. However, it failed to recognize the existing mythos and to build on it; instead, it severed long-established structures and fired long-serving employees. Out of a feeling of insecurity, angry employees took to sabotage and work refusal. Within a year, product development and customer service deteriorated to such extent that the company had to file for insolvency.

While these two scenarios differ, there is a common cause: in both cases, leaders were unaware of the company's mythos; they were unable to look at it from the outside and perceive it on the meta level.

In the dynamics of the first scenario, company members were dazzled by the radiance of their mythos. Since they perceived it only on the preconscious level, they blindly fell victim to it.

In the second scenario, the new management fails to perceive the mythos and to understand its meaning. Without realizing it, the management ignored what the bearers of the culture were proud of, what they identified with, and where they put their hearts and faiths.

3 Mythos Management

The mythos often remains a blind spot even for circumspect culture managers. It is in fact easy to overlook. Not being apparent is in fact part of its communicative structure. Instead, it acts like a source of light illuminating an object while remaining invisible itself. "The narrator remains hidden; Nature herself seems to narrate" (Cf. Barthes 1964).

For company members, viewing their own mythos from the inside is barely feasible. The difficulty of recognizing a mythos is also reflected in the saying of "not seeing the wood for the trees." You need the neutral, "extra-cultural" view from the outside to be able to take in a mythos's complex and dynamic system of meaning.

Only if the management has a clear view on a company's mythos can it master these challenges:

- Align mythos and strategy in such a way that they can solve the paradox of constantly adapting to the challenges of the present future while preserving the company's origin and purpose.
- Avoid a split between a company's mythos and strategy by deliberately cultivating its culture.
- Know when a mythos should be abandoned and how the development of a new mythos can be fostered.

4 How to Work with Organizational Mythos: The MythosResearch® Approach (Fig. 2)

If you want to change or develop a mythos, you must first have a clear view on it. But how can a mythos be exposed? The MythosResearch® approach effectively helps companies to dive deep into their fundamental assumptions and beliefs. To this purpose, it uses target-oriented and qualitative one-on-one interviews all across the company, as well as seminars, field research, customer surveys, and document analyses, which also take into account official value systems, messages, philosophies, and mission statements.

Fig. 2 The MythosResearch® Approach. Illustrated by ©Helge Leiberg, 2018

4.1 Discovering the Mythos (Fig. 3)

In a MythosResearch® project, in addition to case-specific topics, key research questions include:

- Above controversial viewpoints and everyday contradictions, what are the crystallization points, fundamental beliefs, and messages shared by everybody?
- What are the impulses that led to the establishment of the company?
- What does the company see as its unique characteristic that enables it to enrich the world? What does it want to look like in the future?
- What unconscious ideas, wishes, values, and images drive people's thinking and acting?
- Are they aligned to the values and beliefs that have formed during the company's history and are manifest in the company's mission statement?
- Are these fundamental assumptions and the mission statement aligned to key stakeholders' needs?

This feedback loop helps evaluate the results of the subjective-interpretive analysis. After the stories, rituals, and object symbols have been decoded and their symbolic structures, metaphorical meanings, and emotional charges have been laid open, they are contrasted to the official mission statement to make visible value fields, contradictions, crystallization points, taboos, knots, tension fields, and power sources.

As a by-product, each MythosResearch® project provides a fund of very lively and authentic artifacts—powerful content that commissioners love to use for internal publications and external communications.

Fig. 3 The Black Box; authors' own figure

Fig. 4 The Pistol Hairdryer; archiv Springer and Jacoby (1990)

4.1.1 Symbols

Symbols are key indicators of fundamental values and beliefs. There is therefore a particular focus on identifying them and laying them open (cf. Gagliardi 1990). In the following examples, they point to the dissolution of a culture, to a product mythos, a personality mythos, and the basic character of a strong community.

The Undoing of a Mythos

The so-called "pistol hairdryer," a stick pin for deserving members of Springer & Jacoby, was formerly a highly valued status symbol. Those awarded with it wore it not only as a talisman at presentations but also after work in the trendy bars of Hamburg. Around the turn of the millennium, its meaning changed. As a relict of the 1980s, it was no longer cool. In the analysis, this change of meaning proves to be an indicator of the agency mythos's decline. While the agency expanded massively (the mythos had by now outgrown reality, becoming a pseudo-mythos), its people were no longer able to see what justified the mythos (Fig. 4).

Product Quality

A medium-sized manufacturer produces high-quality equipment. People identify strongly with their products. The "brown bread" is a powerful metaphor for quality, which can also be used for external communication purposes (Fig. 5).

Attitudes

Often a founder shapes the culture of their company far beyond their time. MythosResearch® uncovers these fundamental assumptions so that they can be used to strengthen the culture or carefully adjust it to changed requirements.

Fig. 5 Brown Bread, Zulauf (2015); designed by Manja Hellpap

Fig. 6 Each department; Zulauf (2015); drawings by ©Helge Leiberg, 2015

Here is an example: individual and group interviews with the members of a family-owned company laid bare the founder's deep-rooted message, "each department is equally important," which has ever since been lived out and passed on (Fig. 6).

4.2 Evaluate the Mythos

Everything that lives—a mythos is no less alive than the culture in which it exists—moves through the stages of becoming, existing, and passing away. A mythos that no longer fulfils its function loses power. Sometimes it is therefore inevitable to dissolve the mythical system of meaning to give way to something new. Great culture management aims to preserve its supporting aspects as long as possible by adopting a connective strategy.

After the research results have been evaluated, the mythos will be put to test:

- Does it have the messages and resources that will be a source of power in the future?
- Does it still inspire?
- Is it still sappy enough?
- Can it be aligned to current requirements?

4.3 Analyze and Transform the Mythos

A mythos cannot be socio-technically exploited; it is not possible to transform it by sheer decision or to outsource its transformation. For a mythos transformation to be successful, it must take place in a truthful and authentic way, involving each and every member of the culture.

Strong mythical systems of meaning can be primarily found in medium-sized family-owned companies. Sometimes the founder who is still in the leadership role represents the mythos, or the company is led by the second or third generation the way its founder had shaped it.

Only with top-down permission to openly deal with obstructive taboos, holy cows, outdated values, and a counterproductive self-image is it possible to evaluate and optimize a cultural system. For company owners, this deconstruction process is a huge challenge or at least demands strong self-reflecting capabilities.

The willingness of the company leadership to question themselves and their traditions is crucial for the mythos analysis and transformation to be successful. Their approval is the basis for people's confidence and willingness to strongly and openly get involved in the interviews. Only if there is transparency is it possible to take a deep look into the black box of the mythical system of meaning.

By challenging the mythos, we also challenge people's way of feeling, acting, and thinking. As with highly personal change processes, working on the foundations can evoke feelings of irritation, grief, disillusionment, and fear. One affected employee from the following case study uses a striking image to describe these feelings: "We hung with all fours in the air."

Case Study A medium-sized family-owned company has manufactured electro-acoustic equipment for 65 years. Its mostly long-term employees strongly identify with the collaborative production process and the quality products they help create. For production and economical reasons, however, the company leadership feels compelled to outsource the prefabrication of a number of component groups to Asia. This transition comes with substantial structural changes. While layoffs can be avoided, people nevertheless show feelings of repulsion, fear, and uncertainty, resulting in resistance to change and lack of motivation.

The leadership recognizes the need to take into account all parameters in order to initiate a sensitive change process potentially leading to a new self-image. They convince managers and staff to take part in a mythos analysis. As early as during the data collection process, the dynamics of the company change. As company members relate stories, uncovering their meaning, and remember episodes and traditional rituals, they start to see their company from the interviewer's external, "extra-cultural" perspective. Intensive reflection and animated conversations take place throughout the company (Fig. 7).

The results are first presented to the leadership and discussed in a workshop. Everything is put on the table: points of conflict and fields of force, taboos, nodal points, holy cows, and crystallization points. What had previously been suspected,

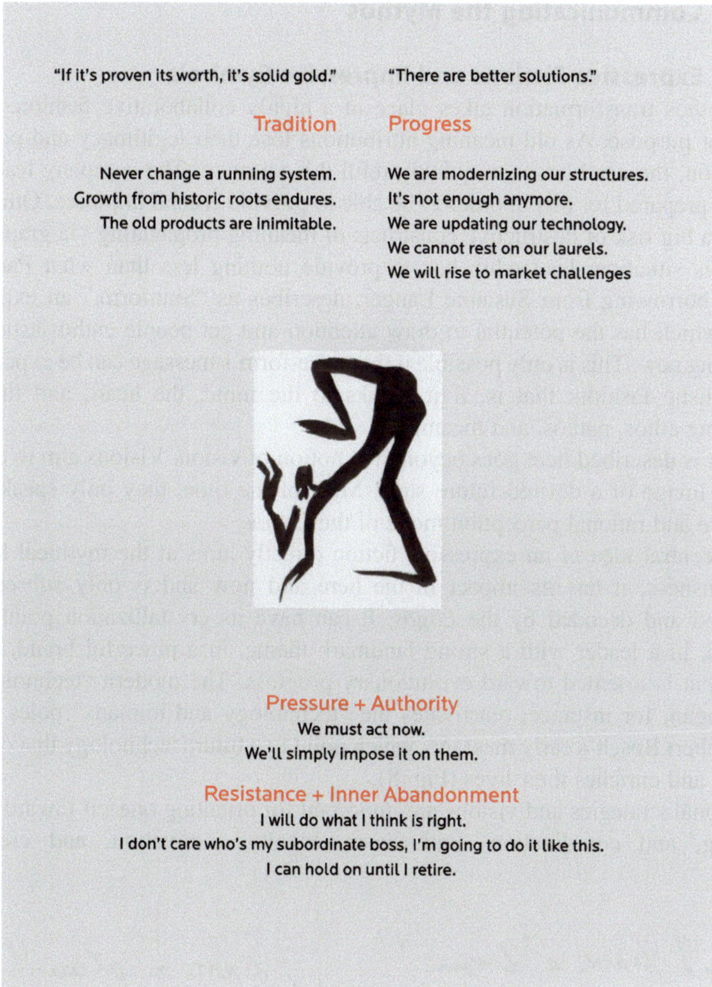

Fig. 7 Tradition/Progress, Zulauf (2015), drawing by ©Helge Leiberg, 2015

feared, hoped for, and interpreted is now visible to everybody. A common view of the present takes shape, which is an essential prerequisite for the creation of a connective strategy.

For an analysis of such depth to be successful, absolute loyalty and confidentiality in carrying out and evaluating the interviews are crucial. In a second step, of course, it is necessary to provide feedback and reflect the results back to the entire company. This requires the right filter settings and a lot of sensitivity.

As with individuals, the willingness to reorient increases if at least some of the deep-rooted fundamental assumptions can be preserved or stabilized and brought to bear on the new challenges. These fundamental assumptions should be protected. Rationalizing them would lead to their losing their implicitness and plausibility.

4.4 Communicating the Mythos

4.4.1 Expressive Fictions and Impressive Symbols

Any mythos transformation takes place in a highly collaborative fashion. People yearn for purpose. As old meaning attributions lose their legitimacy and power of persuasion, the need arises to quickly refill this vacancy. The company leadership must be prepared for this in order to be able to provide crucial impulses. Otherwise, there is a big risk of destructive constructs of meaning propagating via grapevine.

In this situation, leadership has to provide nothing less than what Paul Bate (1997), borrowing from Susanne Langer, describes as "Sinnform," an expressive fiction which has the potential to draw attention and get people enthusiastic about something new. This is only possible if the sense-form's message can be experienced in a holistic fashion: that is, if it speaks to the mind, the heart, and the soul, conveying ethos, pathos, and meaning.

What is described here goes beyond the notion of vision. Visions aim to create a specific image of a desired future state. Most of the time, they only speak to the cognitive and rational perception mode of the *Logos*.

The central idea of an expressive fiction directly aims at the mythical level of consciousness; it has its impact in the here and now and is only subsequently registered and decoded by the *Logos*. It can have its crystallization point in the tradition, in a leader with a strong landmark theme, in a powerful brand, or in a vision that is oriented toward evolutionary progress. The modern "technology for life" slogan, for instance, reactivates the "technology and humans" poles known from Robert Bosch's early message, which point to a future technology that caters to humans and enriches their lives (Fig. 8).

Rational strategies and visions are important for orienting oneself toward a goal, planning, and coordination. Enthusiasm, loyalty, motivation, and creativity,

Fig. 8 I have a dream. Drawing by ©Helge Leiberg, 2019

however, are created wherever we are susceptible to high ideals, purpose, beauty, ethos, and pathos. Only messages of this kind can germinate and take roots.

It is important to understand that a desired change of mind (or meaning) cannot be brought about and controlled by socio-technical and functionalistic means. The company leadership can at best provide impulses affecting the informal symbolic networks. In this situation, attitudes, messages, decisions, and behaviors are evaluated through continuous processes of learning and interpretation, which culture members distill symbols (mythologemes) from, wrapping them in metaphors, stories, anecdotes, aphorisms, images, objects, and rituals—thus implicitly coordinating their fundamental assumptions, worldviews, and behaviors.

If applied in a culturally sensitive and sensible way, symbols, in their capacity as the "language of the mythical perception level," help align mythical worldview with strategic direction, supporting the development of a system of meaning that company members can align their goals and energies with (Fig. 9).

Examples of an inventive use of symbolic communication include Springer & Jacoby's "The Fat Man" pamphlet, which is designed like a commercial. It was developed for employees and key customers, sharing historical and fictitious facts as well as the cornerstones of the agency's philosophy.

In a first step, stories, successes, values, and talents have been extracted from the agency culture, selected, substantiated, accentuated, and finally linked to the relevant, up-to-date message and the desired values and orientations.

It is of course vital to actually live these values, which, if communicated symbolically, can create a strong common perception of reality and a future orientation,

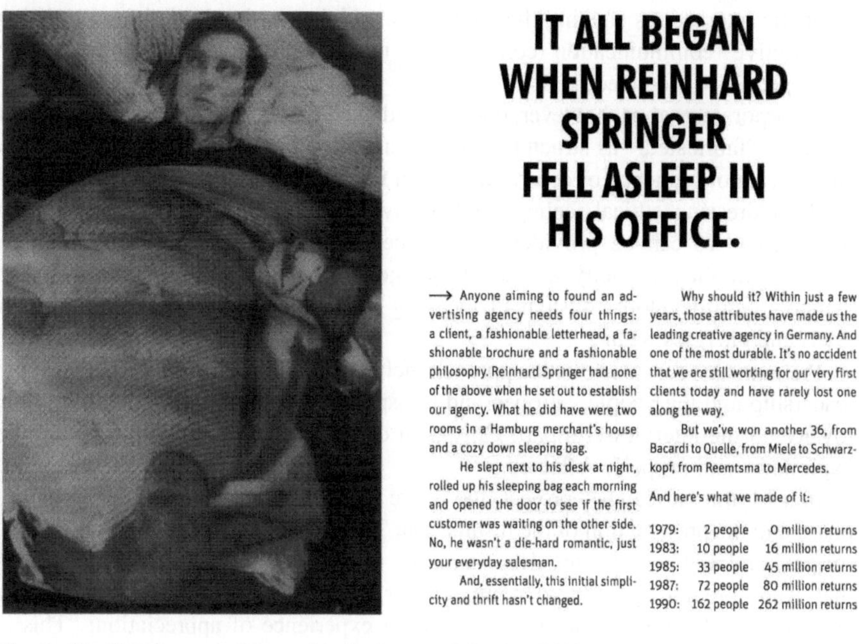

Fig. 9 The Fat Man, pamphlet, archiv Springer and Jacoby (1990)

ultimately leading to the realization of a common goal or even a self-fulfilling prophecy.

Ways to convey purpose and meaning and strengthen the feeling of togetherness include the cherishing of objects such as portraits of founder(s), the documenting of important episodes, affectionate presentation of the company's products, and cultivating rituals of appreciation and action-oriented stories and anecdotes.

5 Summary: Why Working with Mythos Is Amazing, Effective, and Fun

> Cultural sense circulates and reproduces of its own accord. There is no need to circulate or reproduce it. JAN ASSMANN (Assmann 1991, p. 26)

A corporate mythos is made from authentic material—real purpose, values, ethos, and pathos. It grows from the inside out. Once it has gained momentum, it develops a system of signs and symbols that is understood throughout the world. Such a mythos appeals to the best people, opens doors to new markets, and carries the company over cliffs and crises. Similar to the "made in Germany" label, it eventually "rubs off" on the company's products and services.

While a mythos can be a huge competitive advantage, it also comes with the risk of complacency and hubris. It is therefore important for the company leadership to take an observer's perspective, stepping out of the preconscious-mythical level of subjective sense orientation. They can then perceive (virtually from the outside) the symbolic interactions shaping the common worldview and provide impulses using "connective" communication (containing as many familiar elements as possible to allow people to reconnect).

A corporate mythos, however, doesn't lend itself to the mystification of facts, nor can it be "fabricated," as structures of meaning are an emergent phenomenon; you simply cannot influence or control them in a functionalistic way.

By addressing ethical feelings and by living values and symbolically sharing them, impulses can be provided, and processes of learning and change can be initiated. In their capacity as the "language of the mythical perception level," symbols help develop a system of meaning for company members to align their goals and energies with.

Prerequisites for this holistic approach include a relationship of trust between the leadership and the people, an open and transparent corporate culture, and absolute loyalty on the interviewer's part. Only then can the deep treasures of a culture be exploited—and properly reflected.

In a MythosResearch® project, the entire company engages in both the survey phase and the presentation of the results. The "mirroring back" of stories, anecdotes, images, and symbols creates deep impulses that release strong energies as things that were previously hidden, repressed, or vaguely surmised are now openly communicated. This also leads to an intense experience of appreciation: "This is who we are. We are unique and we are visible!"

Fig. 10 Amazing fun. Drawing by ©Helge Leiberg, 2000

A leadership endeavoring to unearth their company's deeper purpose will find promising starting points in the mythos. Against this background, it is possible, in particular, to "deepen" work on the company's strategy, vision, and brand essence. Accessing the mythos can thus be a way of guarding against short-term trends and calibrating the importance of economic interests against loyalty toward people, history, principles, and long-term goals (Fig. 10).

References

Assmann, J. (1991). *Das Fest und das Heilige* (p. 26). Gütersloher Verlagshaus: Gütersloh.

Assmann, J. (1999). *Das kulturelle Gedächtnis: Schrift, Erinnerung und politische Identität in frühen Hochkulturen* (Vol. 143). München: C.H. Beck.

Balzer, H. (1953). *Nur was wir glauben, wissen wir gewiss: Der Lebensweg des lachenden Weisen Wilhelm Busch*. Leipzig: Evangelische Verlagsanstalt.

Barthes, R. (1964). *Mythen des Alltags* (pp. 110–130). Frankfurt/M: Suhrkamp.

Bate, P. (1997). *Cultural change: Strategien zur Änderung der Unternehmenskultur*. München: Gerling Akademie.

Blumenberg, H. (1979/2001). Arbeit am Mythos. Frankfurt/M: Suhrkamp.

Cassirer, E. (1964). *Philosophie der symbolischen Formen* (Vol. I–III). Darmstadt: Wissenschaftliche Buchgesellschaft.

Gagliardi, P. (1990). *Symbols and artifacts: Views of the corporate landscape*. Berlin: Walter de Gruyter.

Jamme, C. (1999). *Gott an hat ein Gewand: Grenzen und Perspektiven philosophischer Mythos-Theorien der Gegenwart*. Hamburg: Suhrkamp.

Langer, S. K. (1992). *Philosophie auf neuem Wege. Das Symbol im Denken, im Ritus und in der Kunst*. Berlin: Fischer Taschenbuch.

Levi-Strauss, C. (1981). *Strukturale anthropologie I* (pp. 226 ff.). Frankfurt/M: Suhrkamp Taschenbuch.

Nutz, D. (2017, March 20). *Die Zeit*, 12/17.

Schein, E. H. (2003). *Organisationskultur*. Bergisch Gladbach: EHP.

Springer & Jacoby. (1990). *Der Dicke Mann*. Hamburg: In-House-Publishing.

Zulauf, S. (1997/2009). *Unternehmen und Mythos: Der unsichtbare Erfolgsfaktor* (2nd ed.). Wiesbaden: GWV Fachverlage.

Zulauf, S. (2015). *Geht's Holmberg gut, geht's allen gut*. Berlin: In-House-Publication/Holmberg GmbH & Co. KG.

Silvia Zulauf is a graduate communications specialist, systemic organizational consultant, and fiction coach. Having worked as a journalist, editor, copywriter, PR manager, and event manager, she has been an independent consultant since 2008. Her consulting approach is based on the MythosResearch® concept she developed in 1994, which regards perception, alignment, and the cultivation of a sense of purpose as key resources for creating a successful future. Working with myth is amazing, effective, and fun. The uncovering of constructs of purpose and meaning, symbols, taboos, and sources of strength is a mirror and a catalyst for the internal development, at the same time generating authentic content for external communication. It gives rise to culture-strengthening portraits such as *Sense What's Right* (Künzelsau: Swiridoff, 2015) and *Geht's Holmberg gut, geht's allen gut* (self-published, 2015). Commissioners of MythosResearch® analyses and development studies include medium-sized, family-owned companies, as well as large corporations such as Adolf Würth GmbH & Co. KG and BMW AG. Publication: *Unternehmen und Mythos—der unsichtbare Erfolgsfaktor* (Wiesbaden: Gabler, 2009, 2nd, ext. edition).

Learning Histories: Re-authoring the Future in the Mirror of the Past

Rik Peters and Karin Thier

Abstract

In this article we discuss a special kind of storytelling known as "learning histories." Developed in the 1990s in the wake of the theory of the learning organization invented at MIT, Boston, the theory and method of learning histories has found many applications worldwide. We focus first on the characteristics of learning histories vis-à-vis storytelling in general. Exploring its common basic assumptions, we will first explicate the implications of the crucial difference between storytelling and history telling focusing on the relationship between past, present, and future. Next, we will discuss the practice of deploying learning histories in an organizational and in an educational context. In this part we explore the moral dilemmas which confront learning historians when re-authoring the future by reflecting on the past. In particular we will discuss the problem of doing justice to multiperspectival evidence on the one hand and to writing an effective jointly told story on the other.

1 What Are Learning Histories?

1.1 A Short History

"Learning histories" is a method that seeks to capture the experience of people in organizations in a jointly told narrative which enables organizations to learn from their past with a view on their future. The first learning histories were developed in

R. Peters (✉)
University of Groningen, Groningen, The Netherlands
e-mail: r.g.p.peters@rug.nl

K. Thier
NARRATA Consult, Bad Bergzabern, Rheinland Pfalz, Germany
e-mail: karin.thier@narrata.de

© Springer Nature Switzerland AG 2019

J. Chlopczyk, C. Erlach (eds.), *Transforming Organizations*,
Management for Professionals, https://doi.org/10.1007/978-3-030-17851-2_9

the 1990s in the wake of the theory of organizational learning, as disseminated in Peter Senge's worldwide best seller *The Fifth Discipline* (1990). As George Roth, one of the founding fathers of learning histories at MIT, recently explained, the first idea for the method came in 1992 when an organization in a learning trajectory required to actively participate in the evaluation of the results. To underline the new relationship between researched and researchers thus established, a new name was sought to indicate the role of the researchers. At first, the researchers tried the term "capturing analyst" to stress their function to gather new insights from the stories told in the organization, but soon they changed this to "learning historian" because this was a relatively neutral term that exactly covered the function of the researchers as being appreciative of the past to look at the future (Roth 2017).

After four more years of experimenting and developing, *AutoCo Epsilon Program*, the first full-sized learning history came out in October 1996, accompanied by a full-sized *Manual for a Learning Historian* (Kleiner and Roth 1996). A year later, in 1997, Roth and Kleiner published "How to make experience your company's best teacher" in *Harvard Business Review* (Kleiner and Roth 1997). This article was one of the most important sources of inspiration for learning historians who followed the MIT pioneers both in and outside the USA. Soon after its publication, the theory and method of learning histories spread to Germany, the UK, and the Netherlands. Meanwhile, in 2000, Oxford University Press published Art Kleiner's and George Roth's *Car Launch* and *Oil Change*, two books which greatly contributed to the dissemination of learning histories in the first decade of this century (Kleiner and Roth 2000; Roth and Kleiner 2000). The method got further renowned by Karin Thier in her book *Storytelling: Eine Methode für das Change-, Marken-, Projekt- und Wissensmanagement* and by George Roth and Hilary Bradbury in an article in the *Sage Handbook on Action Research* (Thier 2006; Roth and Bradbury 2008). In the Netherlands, the theory and method of learning histories has been taught since 2004 as a Master Course at the University of Groningen which also organized an international conference on learning histories in 2017.[1] Presently, learning histories, having found their way to many countries, among which are Turkey, Pakistan, and China, can be viewed as an established research practice (Gearty and Coghlan 2018, p. 463).

Applied to a wide range of organizational fields, varying from project and knowledge management to change management and conflict management, learning histories focus on learning by collective storytelling. However, rooted in action research, they also differ in some respects from other forms of storytelling. The crucial difference lies in the importance learning historians give to learning from past experience. Typically, learning histories are based on facts, obtained by a careful

[1]International Conference *Learning Histories for Sustainable Societies*, 19–20 January 2017. All papers have been recorded and are available on https://www.rug.nl/let/organization/bestuur-afdelingen-en-medewerkers/afdelingen/afdeling-geschiedenis/learning-histories/ (last visited on 28 September 2018).

analysis of a wide variety of evidence, thus enabling organizations to reflect on their past in order to build a new future.

In order to realize this outcome, learning histories follow three imperatives: the research, the mythic, and the pragmatic (Kleiner and Roth 1996). The research imperative expresses loyalty to the "data." Data are important to make the learning history true for the readers. If the text is not true for its readers, they will not fully trust it and identify with it. "This is not us" they will say while turning away. If based on facts, learning histories will provide the readers a very concrete story of their own experiences which can be used as a starting point for a collective dialogue (Fig. 1).

The mythic imperative expresses loyalty to the story. The story is needed because mere descriptions on the basic facts will not induce the readers to learning. In order to achieve this, the learning history must "tease out" the readers by telling their stories in a new way. The learning history thus employs the many stories told in an organization to weave its own story, thus offering a new multiperspectival view on the organization's past (Kleiner and Roth 2000; Thier 2018).

The pragmatic imperative refers to loyalty to the audience. With the latter in mind, the learning historians ask how to make the story useful. How can the story best to contribute to their learning, in terms of personal growth and mutual understanding? And how can the learning history contribute to their actionable knowledge?

As the founders of learning histories stressed, it is extremely difficult to comply to all the three imperatives at once. If the research imperative is being stressed too much, the learning history may be become so dull that it bores the readers or simply puts them asleep. But if the mythic imperative predominates, the story may be rhetorically

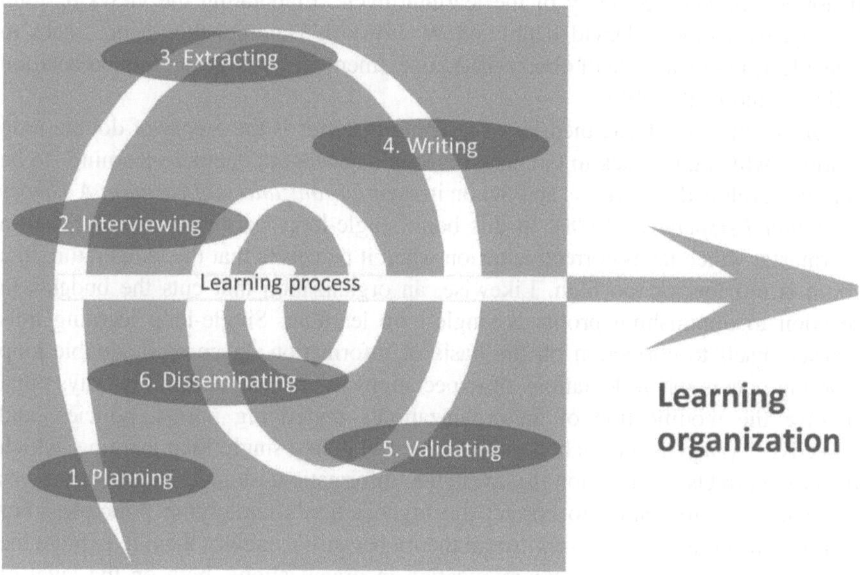

Fig. 1 The learning history process (authors' own figure)

effective, but not trustworthy. Finally, when the author focuses too much on the needs of the audience, the learning history may be become too flat, that is, too close to the reader's perspective at the cost of developing a new perspective from which they may learn. The overall quality of a learning history therefore depends on a proper balance between the three imperatives. Accordingly, learning historians must be able to do justice to the facts, to understand the individual stories of the people who work in the organization, and to address the organization as a whole. This multiperspectival view of the organization requires both empathy for the people who work in it and distance to them in order to see the organization as a whole.

1.2 The Philosophical Underpinnings

As a narrative learning histories can be seen as kind of storytelling, having its own distinctive theoretical foundation rooted in theories of organizational learning and action research. Like most forms of storytelling, learning histories share a strongly constructivist approach, but following the research imperative, they stress the evidential basis of the stories. After all, it is this basis that turns stories into histories. In contrast to many other kinds of storytelling, learning histories attempt to be true to fact, not in an old-fashioned positivist sense of assuming that there is only one true story about the organization but in a modern constructivist sense that recognizes a multiplicity of stories in organizations. The aim is not to construe one single true story about the organization, but to collect a multiplicity of stories into a jointly told story.

Employing a wide variety of theories, from ethnography to journalism, learning histories embody the theory of the learning cycle. Elaborating the views of John Dewey, Kurt Lewin, David Kolb, and W. Edwards Deming, this theory seeks to foster learning by a cycle of observation, assessment, designing, and implementation (Kleiner and Roth 1996).

One of the most basic theories of learning histories is the theory of double-loop learning which goes back to Gregory Bateson's concept of "deutero-learning" to be further developed by Argyris and Schön in their *Organizational Learning: A Theory of Action Perspective* (1978). In this book single-loop learning is compared to a thermostat which takes corrective action when it perceives that the temperature in a room is too low or too high. Likewise, an organization that cuts the budgets in reaction to diminishing profits is single-loop learning. Single-loop learning thus restricts itself to correction on the basis of information. In contrast, double-loop learning occurs when deviations of expectations are being corrected in ways "that involve the modification of an organization's underlying norms, policies, and objectives" (Argyris and Schön 1978, p. 3). So, unlike single-loop learning, which directly corrects in reaction to available information, double-learning plunges beneath this information to correct the organization's underlying principles. For learning historians this is a very useful theory because it enables them to explore the principles underlying daily communication in organizations, both on the level of individuals and on the level of the organization as a whole.

In order to foster double-loop learning, it is crucial to detect the mental models in an organization. In *The Fifth Discipline*, Senge, following Chris Argyris, defined mental models as "deeply ingrained assumptions, generalizations, or even pictures or images that influence how we understand the world and how we take action" (Senge 1990, p. 8). Since people are not always aware of the mental models underlying their thoughts and actions, it takes a special method to get them to the surface. In order to achieve this aim, learning historians often employ Chris Argyris's theory of the ladder of inference as elaborated in *The Fifth Discipline Fieldbook* (Senge 1994). There, learning historian Rick Ross gives the example of himself giving a presentation to managers. In the back of the room, he observes a manager who seems to be bored, turning his eyes away from the speaker and putting his hand to his mouth. At the end of the presentation, the manager asks for a complete report, which Ross interprets as meaning that he should move on to the next point. After this the meeting closes, and Ross leaves, disappointed and revengeful. Looking back, Ross discovered in retrospect how swiftly he had climbed "the ladder of inference" from the yawning and the remark to taking action guided by emotions on the basis of the underlying assumption that yawning means hostile disinterest (Senge 1994, pp. 242–247).

In the same vein, learning historians explore mental models. They collect stories about events in organizations, in order to reconstruct the underlying ladders of inference, focusing on the basic assumptions which constitute the mental models of the people who work in the organization. For example, civil servants in a Tax Administration will act differently when they see the tax payer as a "client" or as a "partner." Similarly, car sellers may treat customers on the basis of the mental model of "profit maximization" or a mental model of "sustainability." Mental models are also of paramount importance for the identification of the organization as a whole: it makes quite a difference whether employees see their organization as "room for dialogue" or as a "shark tank."

The ladder of inference is not only guiding learning historians' research in organizations but also their writing. As George Roth explains in *Car Launch*, the ladders of inference as exemplified in the stories of the people in the organization form the right-hand column of the learning history, whereas the learning historian's own ladder of inference forms the substance of the left column (Roth and Kleiner 2000, pp. 198–202). Importantly, the latter explains the learning historian's reasoning for the narrative, thus suggesting questions for the reader (see Fig. 2 Presentation of a learning history in two columns). These questions are crucial to invite the readers to reflect on past events in order to explicate the mental models which guided them. On the basis of ladders of inference, the learning history thus provides a truly multiperspectival view of an organization, comprising the employees, the learning historian, and the reader.

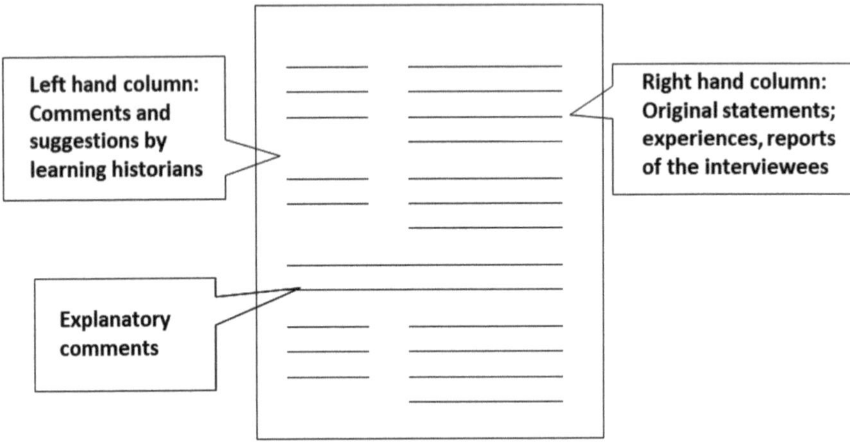

Fig. 2 Presentation of a learning history in two columns (authors' own figure)

2 How to Create and Use Learning Histories in Organizations

2.1 The Six Phases

To balance the three imperatives is one of the main challenges for learning historians. In order to meet this challenge, they follow a systematic method comprising of six phases. The "six phases form" are meant to guide for creating and working with the learning histories. Although the circumstances and thus the personal and temporal possibilities for creating learning histories can vary widely—it makes a large difference whether it is, e.g., a well-resourced research project, say, a well-budgeted mission of a company, or a rather low-budget project done by a small group of learning historians—these six phases always have to be gone through in a more or less intense way. In the following we will give a brief overview on these phases to provide the reader with an idea for what should be done to fulfill the demands of the three imperatives (Thier and Erlach 2005; Thier 2018).

1. Planning

   The main purpose of the planning phase is to build the dependable foundation for a successful procedure. Accordingly, this phase calls for a thoughtful consideration of the relevant backgrounds of the selected project or topic for the learning history, including the individuals involved and their designated roles, as well as central milestones and incidents. Additionally, the learning historians need to develop an understanding of the official (and, ideally, also the unofficial) culture of the organization and about the particularities of how the results of the storytelling method are expected to be connected with existing systems of human resources, knowledge management, and project management such as databases, handbooks, intranet, "best practice," or "lessons learned" files.

Another important element of the planning phase is to determine the (primary) target groups for the resulting experience document. To obtain this information, the team talks to different people in the organization (decision-makers, project managers) and sift through all accessible materials about the chosen topic. The planning phase is key to the success of the whole process because it sets the direction for the forthcoming learning history (Thier 2018, pp. 52–60).

2. Interviewing

   The central goal of the interview phase is to gather as much information from various perspectives as possible. This phase consists of two steps: First, the development of the interview guideline which gives the interviews direction and helps ensure that the gathered information includes all of the stories and experiences that are of particular interest to the organization. For this purpose, the guideline should already include a few central questions. Nevertheless, its role is primarily supportive, and interviewers should not merely tick off individual elements one by one. Instead, the guideline is an orientation and reminds the interviewer not to forget certain crucial topics.

   In the second step, the actual interviews are conducted. Here learning historians needs to find the right balance between covering the topics that were determined by the organization and provides the necessary space to develop narratives that go beyond the initial expectations and are based on the individual stories and anecdotes told by the employees. At the end of the second phase, the team has gathered the raw mixture for the final story: a giant "mass of data" (Kleiner and Roth 1996) from which the learning history is molded (Thier 2018, pp. 60–69).

   The interview approach of the learning history thus represents a combination of two different interview types commonly used in the qualitative social sciences: the problem-centered interview and the narrative interview. The approach is problem-centered because it addresses topics and events that were collected prior to the interview and explicitly poses related questions; the approach is narrative because it allows space for the personal stories of the interviewees (e.g., Flick 2014).

3. Extracting

   The purpose of the extraction phase is to screen and organize all information gathered during the planning and interview phases so as to arrive at the content for the story. Elements that belong together are grouped together. To ensure that the bulk of the quotes from the interviews will be evaluated in the most efficient way, the storytelling team creates suitable evaluation categories. These categories can be themes, events, or problems that are of particular interest to the learning history. They allow the team to draw a meaningful pattern based on the interviews. Subsequently, the interviews are transcribed, and content matching quotes are grouped together under the appropriate category. Often the categories evolve into a short story. The phase terminates with the "raw material" for the learning history (Thier 2018, pp. 69–76).

4. Writing

   Writing the learning history marks the beginning of the most creative part of the procedure. Now that everything is collected, arranged, and evaluated, a blend into a cohesive, interesting, and instructive story needs to be performed. Consequently, there is no general recipe for how to approach this phase: guidelines can only support the acting person to a certain extent, and different writers might end up writing very different stories based on the same material. The main guidelines in the writing process are the three imperatives: research, mythic, and practical imperative (see above) (Thier 2018, pp. 76–90).

   What all learning histories have in common is the same specific structure based on two columns (see Fig. 2). The right column recounts the story exactly as it was told by the interviewees who personally experienced the events described: it represents a narrative drawn from individual perspectives. The storytellers are usually anonymous and only distinguished by their respective job titles. The various statements, representing frequent changes of perspective by invoking different narrators, yet are interconnected. Sometimes connecting fillers are used to create a comprehensive, cohesive, and emotional story.

   The left column features comments by the writers themselves. These comments are at times provocative, and they try to encourage readers to further ponder the content and draw their own conclusions. Sometimes they also stress central ideas which might remain unclear, based solely on the original story (Kleiner and Roth 1997).

   The story can generally be presented in many different ways, and various forms of media can be employed. To ensure maximum efficiency in how employees work with their stories, readers are given a manual hinting on how to read the story before delving into the actual text. Additionally, they may receive further information about the context of the project, the interviewees, and the goals pursued by the organization that lead to the creation of the story. In combination with these appendices, the learning history becomes the final experience document which is distributed within the organization.

5. Validating

   The first draft of the story is usually distributed to all interviewees who thereby get a chance to check their statements and potentially ask for alterations or deletions/additions. Learning histories always function as mirrors to the organization they analyse. Sometimes certain contents can lead to unforeseeable consequences. Since the learning historians may not be able to predict the full magnitude of such consequences, they need to return the experience document to the employees involved one final time before it can be disseminated throughout the organization. This phase is crucial to ensure that the employees will accept the final output and that all individuals involved agree with the final story (Thier 2018, pp. 90–91).

6. Disseminating

   The learning history is now finished and replete with the lessons, tips, and suggestions of the employees who were part of the documented project. However, this should not be the end of the story and the storytelling process! To ensure a lasting benefit for the organization, the content of the story must now be discussed in more detail and questioned by the employees to make use of the documented knowledge and implement palpable improvements. The learning history becomes a treasure trove of experiences for the organization. Employees need to get ample access to this trove to make sure that the knowledge it holds is not forgotten. Ideally, as many employees as possible from various different company branches should benefit from these condensed/processed experiences. A great first step for the dissemination can be, e.g., a specific workshop during which employees that were part of the documented topics and those that are in similar situations get an opportunity to exchange their ideas and learn from each other (Thier 2018, pp. 92–95).

2.2 Areas of Application

The application areas of learning histories are manifold. They vary from project debriefing in which they help to learn from past mistakes and to identify positive experiences to the initiation of change processes where they support the development of a shared vision of the future. They also provide a good way to discover authentic stories and statements from different members of an organization which can concertedly be used for PR and marketing. The learning history approach is used both in the university context by management consultancies and by employees from companies, especially in the area of personnel and knowledge management.

Table 1 gives an overview of some of the main applications areas where learning histories surface nowadays in organizations (Thier 2018, p. 39):

Table 1 Potential applications of learning histories (authors' own table)

Knowledge management (to preserve the experiences, tips, and tricks of employees and add them to fact-based instruments)
Project debriefing (to document project experiences in a standardized way)
Documentation of important projects (to learn from past mistakes and transfer successful strategies to similar projects)
Knowledge transfer (to preserve and document the experiences of employees who leave the organization)
Analysis of organizational culture (to uncover the "real" organizational culture in the eyes of the employees)
Change processes (to develop a vision of the future that is shared by managers and employees)
Brand management (to find and strengthen the perception of a successful brand as a unique "icon")
Content management (to discover authentic stories and statements for PR and marketing)
Market research (to develop a marketing strategy that matches the emotional needs of consumers)
Quality management (as a method of the process of continuous improvement
Networks, clusters, and cooperation (to improve the "interpersonal" side of cooperation and boost mutual trust)
Conflict management (for self-reflection and to better understand the behavior of others)
Education/training (for instructing students in the application of learning histories in various organizations)

All these applications of the learning histories method have in common that they are interventions that enable organizations to reflect on their own past in order to prepare for the future. By distributing learning histories through the organization and by collectively discussing them, sustainable change can be realized since all people working in it will be involved in the reflective process. For this reason it is crucial to choose the most effective form of dissemination, varying from presentations, Socratic dialogues, learning labs, posters, large-scale meetings, articles, or books. Firmly rooted in the organizations' past, learning histories feed on themselves, thus creating an upward, future-oriented learning spiral.

3 Learning Histories in Praxis: Two Examples

3.1 Learning Histories in the Context of Organizations

Founded in 2002, the scientific consultancy network NARRATA Consult focuses on the development and the use of narrative methods in organizations. Learning histories are one of the preferred methods when it comes to knowledge transfer between project teams and leaving experts and the work with organizational culture and values in the terms of change projects. Over many years, with customers like Deutsche Post, Eckes-Granini, Heidelberger Druckmaschinen, T-Mobile, MTU Aero Engines, and Voestalpine, the learning history method was modified and adapted several times to suit the requirements of profit-oriented companies.

The main challenge when working with learning histories in a profit surrounding is that they are very time- and resource-consuming. To find the right balance between a careful execution of the method and a wise use of time and resources is one of the tasks of a learning historian. Furthermore, unlike the use in academic projects, the main goal in profit organization is not only the knowledge gain but also the benefit that the company has through the results of the learning history. This is another challenge to the implementation of the method. At the same time, learning histories in and for organizations give much room for freedom and creativity because the focus is not strict on scientific specifications of the survey and evaluation. In the end, it is not so much the clean method implementation that one focuses on but the benefit to the company.

Some peculiarities are to be considered when working with learning histories in profit-oriented organizations. Sometimes it is not clear to customers that the process of creating a learning history is also a search for the truth and that people are encouraged to talk openly about the company's culture and processes, their subjective feelings, and individual observations. The "truth" is not always what CEOs and managers want to hear, yet to find and discuss it is necessary in order to start serious change and learning processes. Therefore, it is crucial in the planning phase to discuss the explicit expectations of the organization and to clarify that the creation of a learning history always represents a journey into the unknown and that although the topics can be roughly defined with the CEO, ultimately the interviewees decide what is important and worth telling.

Due to cost and time constraints, often no full survey is possible, and a choice must be made among the participants on who will be interviewed. Because the selection of interview partners is often a very sensitive and political undertaking, the learning historians have to be careful with suggestions from customers. It should be discussed that a certain minimum and range of interview partners is needed to acquire as much as possible a multiperspectival view of the chosen subject and that difficult employees, "low in hierarchy people" like trainees or assistants, and also external partners are a very valuable resource.

"Trust" is also one of the crucial elements for the success of a learning history in organizations, especially when it comes to conduction and evaluating the interviews: trust in the organization (being allowed to speak openly), trust in the process (all input being treated confidentially, carefully, and put forward in the proper context), and trust in the learning historians and their ability to balance the demands of the management with the one of the employees. The communication about the exact procedure, the use of the statements, and, if necessary, the mediation between management and interviewees is a key role of learning historians.

During the extraction and writing phase, learning historians should pay special attention to delicate topics which could lead to trouble or discredit people, for example, when some statements personally attack a project manager. The task of a learning historian is then to find out whether this is an isolated opinion of one person or off-topic or whether the background is a private issue and, if so, to keep or delete this statement in the story. Otherwise the specific format of the document provides some options on how to deal with such issues. Instead of a quote, the delicate topic could be inserted as an explanatory comment, for example. Alternatively, all delicate statements are presented by an additionally inflicted person, as, for example, by a kind of jester, who is allowed to spell out the uncomfortable truths with a wink.

The most creative part in the learning history process is the design of the format of the final story. Depending on the pursued goal, the final learning history could look very differently. If the company intends to develop concrete recommendations and solutions for comparable processes and projects in the future (knowledge transfer), then most of the time a chronological format is chosen to help readers identify suggestions and solutions easily and transfer them to similar contexts. A more thematic form is helpful if the organization is more interested in identifying and analyzing typical problems like leadership-related questions, teamwork, appreciation, communication, culture, and values. In this case readers gain more from stories that focus on particular topics or problems (Erlach 2017; Thier 2018, p. 78). If it turns out that the content of the learning history will contain several topics about which it is almost not possible to talk and discuss openly in the company, then it should be considered whether the learning history will be presented in the form of a metaphor or a comic. With the help of fiction and humor, delicate topics can be addressed and discussed in the safe world of alienation and afterward retransmitted and solved in the real world. In Fig. 3 an example is depicted from a learning history comic who shows a typical situation for a customer who had serious problems with the integration of cooperation partners in his team. The situation shows the different expectations of employees and management which lead to serious misunderstandings during the whole project.

Fig. 3 Example of a comic from a learning history (author's own figure)

After finishing the learning history, it is very important that the organization spends sufficient time to disseminate and to work with the document, in order to give employees and management the opportunity to freely discuss their emotions, experiences, and lessons. The best format is usually a moderated open discussion. If possible, the facilitator should be an external expert with a distance to the content of the discussion, thus being able to take a neutral position on sensitive topics (Thier 2018, p. 93).

The results of learning histories are often profound and sustainable. The authentic quotes and narratives of employees remain much better in their minds than fact-orientated documents or presentations. For example, no one will forget the impressive narrative of a development team that just managed the deadline for a customer project only with massive overtime at Christmas, and surely their experiences and ideas will be listened to carefully.

3.2 Learning Histories in the Context of Education Projects

Since 2004 the Department of History at the University of Groningen offers the Masters' Course Learning Histories and Organizations.[2] In this context, more than 70 learning histories have been written for profit organizations like Philips and Atos

[2]The Masters' Course curriculum can be found here: https://www.rug.nl/ocasys/fwn/vak/show?code=LGX133M10

and for nonprofit organizations like the Dutch Tax Administration, the National Center for Employment, several ministries, provincial and city administrations, schools, etc.

For the students, being trained as historians, working in modern institutions seems odd at first, but they soon discover how they can apply their historical skills and knowledge in a completely new environment. The key skill here is to be able to understand people and situations from many perspectives, or in the system's theoretical language of the course, to be a second-order observer. Since historians normally deal with people in completely different times, they are already well acquainted with the skill of second-order observations. Moreover, historians are well versed in the medium of narratives. On the one hand, they often use narratives as source material; on the other hand, they write their own research reports as a narrative. The main challenge for history students therefore is to combine both skills in modern organization.

The research is based on a thorough analysis of the organization's documentation. As true historians, the students will first establish a solid timeline of the organization's history on the basis of the available material in archives, depositories, and increasingly also emails. Next, the researchers acquaint themselves with the content of a variety of material like mission statement and vision, year reports, the balance sheets, project documentation, etc., thus getting a first picture of the underlying mental models. On this basis, the researchers interview a carefully selected group of people in the organization. Preferably, these people work in different departments of the organization so that their stories represent different perspectives on the organization's history. In the interviews, the researchers try to view the "hot spots" on the timeline from the perspective of the interviewees. The interviewees' stories are thus of paramount importance for the learning historian own learning process.

In order to effectively elicit the interviewees' stories, the students are thoroughly trained in analyzing communication. With regard to this, students need to learn that communication is never done "in vacuo," i.e., between two people at a certain moment, but in the context of an entire organization in the course of a process. In other words, in order to understand communication from a truly multiperspectival point of view, students need to understand its relationship to the organizational system. In practice, this means that they need to expand their skills to an understanding of the organization as a communication system. For example, when a civil servant in a municipality complains about the daily work pressure in the past half year, his statement should be interpreted in the larger multiperspectival context of his colleagues, his superiors, etc. to the level of the organization as a whole, connecting all the statements to the way work is formally and informally organized over a longer period of time. Vice versa, the organization's mission statement should be connected to the meanings people in the organization attribute to it.

Like most people, students sometimes find it hard to see the part and the whole of communication. Since their hermeneutical skills are often better trained than their systemic thinking, they tend to focus too much on the individual's perspectives statements, thus neglecting the organizational perspective. A very good way to train students in seeing both the "figure and the carpet" is "circular questioning." This method, developed by the psychotherapist Mara Selvini in Il Nuovo Centro per lo Studio della Famiglia in Milan in the 1980s, explicitly views a family as a system of communications. From this it follows that "meaning" concerning an ailment within a family can only be retrieved by exploring all perspectives on it. In practice this entails that the therapist not only asks what family members think or feel about certain situations but also what their thinking, feelings, and actions do to other members of the family. These members are questioned about their reactions to each other so that a "circle of meaning" is created between them. By training in circular questioning, students realize that meaning is not restricted to individuals, but extends to groups and eventually to entire organizations.

Whereas the interviews are the most exciting phase of the learning histories trajectory, the extraction phase is often the most challenging. Confronted with lots of material, students have to get a general overview of all the information before they try to create their own perspective on it. The latter is crucial for developing the storyline of the learning history and very hard to develop because it requires to take distance from the material at hand. In practice, this means that students have to find a balance between empathy and objectivity; on the one hand, they have to understand the stories within their own perspective; on the other, they have to subsume all the stories under a single perspective. It is here that systems thinking is of paramount importance. No longer is the question "how do these employees see their reality?" but "what makes them see their reality as they see it?" This question can be answered by discovering patterns in the mental models underlying the data and the interviews and by exploring the communication which is based on it. For example, when interviews with a group of ICT developers in an organization show the recurring complaint that they are "misunderstood" by others in the organization, the learning historian can analyze the underlying assumptions of these statements, using the ladder of inference as a tool. It is on the basis of a firm grasp of the mental models underlying people's behavior and communication in organization that learning historians may help them to rewrite their future.

4 Conclusion

Since their beginnings in the 1990s, learning histories have been established as a widely recognized actions research practice. In contrast to many other forms of storytelling, learning histories use the organization's past as a mirror for re-authoring its future. Crucially, it is this link between past and future that turns stories into histories. By collecting and sharing stories in a jointly told history, learning histories enable organization to transform them in a sustainable way. Learning histories lead to sustainable transformation because, by linking the past and the future in jointly told story, they create a new time-space with which all people working in the organization can identify themselves. This identification secures both a multiperspectival approach to the organization's development and an understanding of its continuity in change. Learning histories typically do not aim at single-handed interventions, but an intensive co-creation, not at revolutionary, but at evolutionary change. After all, if we want to move forward without getting lost, we sometimes need to look backward.

References

Argyris, C., & Schön, D. (1978). *Organizational learning. A theory of action perspective*. Reading, MA: Addison Wesley.

Erlach, C. (2017). Wissenstransfer mit Geschichten. In J. Chlopczyk (Ed.), *Beyond Storytelling: Narrative Ansätze und die Arbeit mit Geschichten in Organisationen* (pp. 275–301). Berlin: Springer Gabler.

Flick, U. (2014). *An introduction to qualitative research*. London: Sage Publications.

Gearty, M. R., & Coghlan, D. (2018). The first-, second- and third-person dynamics of learning history. *Systemic Practice Action Research, 31*(5), 463–478.

Kleiner, A., & Roth, G. (1996). *Field manual for a learning historian*. Cambridge: MIT-COL and Reflection Learning Associates.

Kleiner, A., & Roth, G. (1997). How to make experience your company's best teacher. *Harvard Business Review, 5*(75), 172–177.

Kleiner, A., & Roth, G. (2000). *Oil change. Perspectives on corporate transformation*. New York: Oxford University Press.

Learning Histories for Sustainable Societies. (2017). *International Conference at University of Groningen* 19–20 January. All papers are available online: https://www.rug.nl/let/organization/bestuur-afdelingen-en-medewerkers/afdelingen/afdeling-geschiedenis/learning-histories/

Roth, G. (2017). Learning from the past for a better future. In: *Learning histories for sustainable societies*, International conference at the University of Groningen, 19 and 20 January, 2017. https://www.rug.nl/let/organization/bestuur-afdelingen-en-medewerkers/afdelingen/afdeling-geschiedenis/learning-histories/keynote%2D%2D-prof.-dr.-george-roth (last visited 28 September 2018).

Roth, G., & Bradbury, H. (2008). Learning history: An action research practice in support of actionable learning. In P. Reason & H. Bradbury (Eds.), *The Sage handbook of action research. participative inquiry and practice*. London: Sage.

Roth, G., & Kleiner, A. (2000). *Car launch. The human side of managing change*. New York: Oxford University Press.

Senge, P. M. (1990). *The fifth discipline. The art & practice of the learning organization*. New York: Doubleday.

Senge, P. M. (1994). *The fifth discipline field book. Strategies and tools for building a learning organization*. New York: Currency Doubleday.

Thier, K. (2006). *Storytelling – eine narrative Managementmethode*. Heidelberg: Springer.

Thier, K. (2018). *Storytelling in organizations: A narrative approach to change, brand, project and knowledge management*. Berlin: Springer.

Thier, K., & Erlach, C. (2005). The transfer of tacit knowledge with the method of "story telling". In G. Schreyögg & J. Koch (Eds.), *Knowledge management and narratives – organizational effectiveness through storytelling* (pp. 123–141). Berlin: Erich Schmidt Verlag.

Dr. Rik Peters is an associate professor in the Department of History at the University of Groningen. From 2004, he has been lecturing in philosophy of history, rhetoric and history in the Bachelors', and Learning Histories and Organizations in the Masters' program. For this course he has supervised more than 70 learning histories in both profit and nonprofit organizations including some larger projects for Philips, the Dutch Tax Administration, and the National Center for Employment. In 1917, he organized the first conference on learning histories, inviting scholars and practitioners from all over the world (www.rug.nl/let/learning-histories). In English, he has published a chapter on learning histories in Karin Thier, *Storytelling in Organizations*, Springer, 2018. Rik's ideas on the theory and practice of learning histories are based on his international publications in the philosophy of history and rhetoric https://www.rug.nl/staff/r.g.p.peters/.

Dr. Karin Thier is one of the founders of NARRATA Consult (www.narrata.de), a German-based consulting institute focusing on the development and applications of storytelling and narrative methods in the fields of branding, cultural change, communication, project debriefing, and knowledge management. Since 1998 she has been using learning histories as well as other narrative approaches and methods in numerous contexts in large corporations but also in medium-sized and nonprofit organizations. Presently, she works as a consultant, facilitator, trainer, and coach and has published many contributions on the topic of storytelling in organizations. Karin's main focus is on exploiting the potential of the "soul" of the company which is reflected in stories told in and about a company.

Storytelling as a Guiding Leadership Principle: A Framework for Cocreating Narratives with Leaders

Jaana Rasmussen

Abstract

Narrative competency is one of the key leadership skills to steer transformation and motivate teams. The article explains the impact of storytelling within leadership in general with an emphasis on Agile and New Work in organisations. The author shares her story framework that enables readers to develop their own leadership stories.

1 Introduction

Digital transformation is currently one of the biggest and complex tasks for companies worldwide. Technological developments such as Industry 4.0, Internet of things, cloud computing and artificial intelligence change the way we work rapidly.

Companies face changes of their own working environment both in terms of production and in new ways of teamwork and leading the generations X, Y and Z, who have different expectations towards their work and leadership than the generations before them. As different as they are, all of them expect a more collaborate way of working together beyond hierarchy. This means challenges both for human resources (how to find talents and keep them on board) and for leaders who need to adapt new ways of communication and collaboration. At the same time, corporates must still keep production running:

Leaders need to manage both day-to-day business and the sweeping organisational changes for tomorrow.

J. Rasmussen (✉)
Rasmussen Consulting, Hamburg, Germany
e-mail: jr@jaana-rasmussen.de

© Springer Nature Switzerland AG 2019

J. Chlopczyk, C. Erlach (eds.), *Transforming Organizations*,
Management for Professionals, https://doi.org/10.1007/978-3-030-17851-2_10

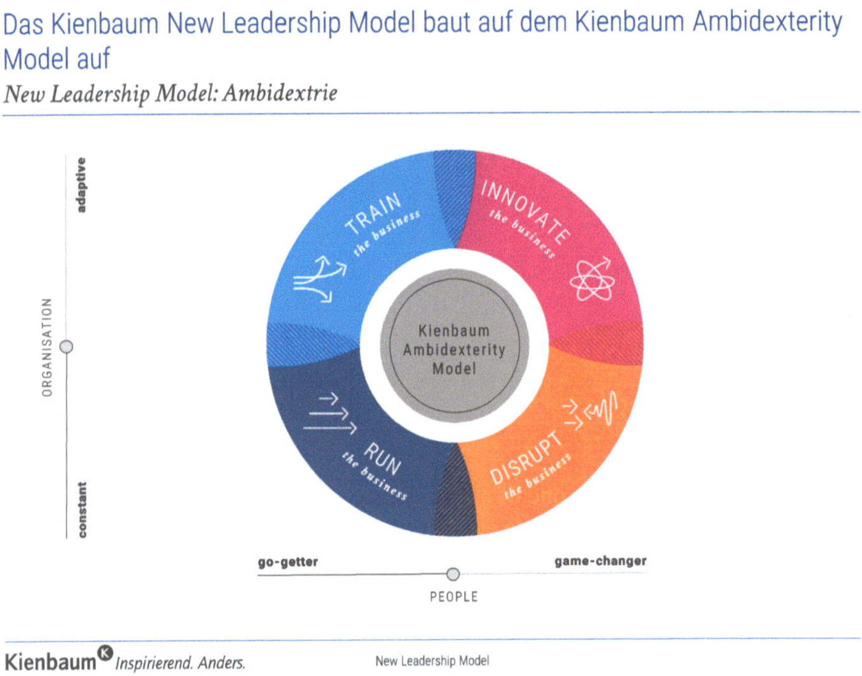

Fig. 1 Ambidexterity model

Adapting to change and simultaneously leading organisational change in the VUCA world is one of the biggest challenges leaders face today. Stephan Grabmeier from the German consultancy Kienbaum calls it "ambidexterity" (see Fig. 1), meaning doing both at the same time. Ambidexterity has its origins in the Latin words ambo, meaning both, and manus, hands (Grabmeier 2018).

Using storytelling in their communication helps leaders steer their companies through the unknown and provide trust for employees and stakeholders. As agile methods emerged and made their ways from tech companies and small start-ups to the big corporates, the ancient method of storytelling became suddenly very new and attractive.

The main application fields for storytelling within Agile and New Work currently are creating trust and buy-in for organisational change and the implementation of new ways of working together like self-organisation or scrum. As many people are rather sceptical to change within their working environment, leaders must address not only the mind but also the heart of employees to create trust and purpose within the VUCA world. Storytelling is the most effective method to reach both human minds and hearts.

2 Definition of Storytelling and Why It Can Be So Powerful as a Leadership Tool

This article follows common usage and treats the terms story and narrative as synonyms. Strategic storytelling means to communicate facts and values of an organisation to internal and external stakeholders in a systematic, narrative way.

In the following article, the impact of stories for organisational change will be analysed, followed by a list of stories every leader should be able to tell.

How storytelling works in the brain and what motivates humans to act will be outlined in part one. In the second part, I will explain my story framework based on a case study.

Don't Believe the Hype: When Everything Is Storytelling Now, What Is It Still Worth?

Storytelling has become a buzzword, mainly in marketing, public relations and advertising. Transmedia and cross-media storytelling is a huge topic in blogs, websites, newsletters and social media. What does this mean for the field of work of storytellers and story-developers?

To Infinity and Beyond! Storytelling Provides Endless Possibilities for Leaders

Coaches and consultants who work with storytelling are no longer associated with a dubious, unscientific practice and taken far more seriously than 5 years ago. DAX companies hire storytelling experts to empower their leaders with storytelling for change processes and for developing a New Work mindset. Companies like Nike and Microsoft even created a new executive position: Chief Storytelling Officer. On the downside, many unexperienced practitioners have an inadequate idea of what storytelling is and can be—this evokes misunderstandings and sometimes frustration on both sides. Storytelling is often mistaken for an elaborate tool for manipulating people, to trick them into doing something—buy a product or service they do not need or even joining an extremist organisation. Storytelling provides far more possibilities than to convince people of something or add a personal note to a corporate announcement of some kind. The possibilities are endless. To name just some, storytelling can support organisational change, executive coaching, onboarding processes and employer branding and add value and understanding to leadership learning journeys. I developed stories with leaders who needed their teams to understand complex decisions; communicate their purpose, their "why" (Sinek 2009) and their vision; and create buy-in for it. Storytelling is no hype. Storytelling is how human beings think, communicate and connect to each other. Stories are what makes us human.

Need for Soft Digital Skills Bigger than for Hard Digital Skills

Corporates expect new employees to have a different skillset than universities usually provide. In a meta-study I conducted for the association of seven universities of applied sciences called UAS7 in 2018 (Burkova and Rasmussen 2019), I found that the need for special social skills is much higher than for hard digital skills like coding. Even though the aim of the present study was only to examine the extent to which the digital transformation changed the need for digital skills in employees, the insights in the demand of specific social skills was surprising.

Overall communication skills, adaptability to change, comfort with ambiguity, collaborating with others, creative thinking, clear communication, effective reasoning and use and managing of information were among the most wanted skills.

Storytelling can help with all these skills and expectations, which will be outlined later. Stephen Denning, author of *The Leader's Guide to Storytelling* writes: "The ways in which we got things done in the 20th century are no longer working for us. Equally, the ways in which we made change happen in 20th century are also failing. The top down (...) change programs that were once deployed, no longer have the credibility to generate a genuine sense of urgency or a meaningful version of the future of which people really want to be part" (Denning 2011).

This story hype is good for story-workers and story-developers, coaches, facilitators and change-makers; at the same time, it is challenging, because it leads to even more misunderstandings than mentioned above. The main misunderstandings of storytelling are:

1. **Storytelling is a simple, emotional course of action: wrong**. The truth is that a story is a complex course of action; the emotional impact results from the value of the material, the careful choice of protagonists, knowledge of archetypes, heroes' journey and dramatic story arc by Gustav Freytag and a consequent listener orientation.
2. **Good stories are a product of phantasy, made up by marketing or public relation: no.** Good stories are of true origin, to be found everywhere. We must listen carefully to find them and be aware of the dynamics of storytelling to craft and tell them.
3. **A company can't be a story: wrong**. Every company is a story and consists of countless stories that form the corporate culture (Müller 2017). To develop a corporate story, one should start from the centre, by asking the employees about their stories with the company.
4. **The hero can be a product or a service: wrong.** In a real, meaningful story, the hero must be a human being. The antagonist can be an abstract construct, like the hectic of modern life, environmental pollution, etc. You see this misunderstanding in the very well-constructed story from Budweiser, "Lost puppy dog", where a puppy dog escapes its owner, a farmer, and gets rescued by its best friend, a horse. The story uses all five acts of Freytag's dramatic story arc (they will be shortly described later in this article), and everyone who watches it feels very attached to the puppy and hopes it will find the way home, but beyond the message that puppies are cute, and friendship is important, there is no deeper meaning in it. It would be an interesting task to retell the story with a human being as a hero.
5. **Storytelling is a tool: wrong. And right**. Wait, what? Storytelling can be used as a tool but is far more than that: The knowledge of the operation of story and the impact that storytelling and story-listening has on humans are a mindset; therefore I choose the term story-workers and story-developers for people who embrace this certain mindset.

2.1 Our Mind on Story: How Storytelling Works the Brain and Motivates Humans to Act

Oxytocin as a Secret Ingredient of Every Story

Neuroscientist Paul J. Zak has run human experiments measuring the endogenous release of oxytocin during social interactions for more than a decade. Zak discovered that the brain chemical oxytocin allows us to determine whom to trust (Zak 2014). His current research has shown that oxytocin is responsible for virtuous behaviours, working as the brain's "moral molecule". He studied oxytocin release in the laboratory as well as in field studies spanning religious rituals, folk dances and weddings (Zak 2015). He and his team have demonstrated the causal effect of oxytocin on prosocial behaviours by safely infusing synthetic oxytocin into hundreds of people's brains through their noses (Zak 2015). "Oxytocin is a powerful hormone that acts as a neurotransmitter in the human brain. It regulates social interaction and sexual reproduction, playing a role in behaviours from maternal-infant bonding and milk release to empathy and generosity. When humans hug or kiss a loved one, oxytocin levels increase; hence, oxytocin is called 'the love hormone'. Oxytocin is the hormone that underlies trust. It is also an antidote to depressive feelings" (Zak 2015). In general, oxytocin infusion increases prosocial behaviours, and Paul Zak wondered if watching movies in addition to direct personal interactions would cause measurable oxytocin release.

2.2 The Dramatic Story Arc as a Key Factor for Impact of Storytelling

The dramatic story arc is a specific arc structure of building up tension and resolving a story in the ending in five specific stages. German novelist and playwright Gustav Freytag analysed the arc structure in *Freytag's Technique of the Drama: An Exposition of Dramatic Composition and Art* (1894).

1. *Exposition*: setting the scene. The writer introduces the characters and setting, providing description and background.
2. *Rising Action*: the story builds and gets more exciting.
3. *Climax*: the moment of greatest tension in a story. This is often the most exciting event. It is the event that the rising action builds up to and that the falling action follows.
4. *Falling Action*: events happen as a result of the climax and we know that the story will soon end.
5. *Resolution*: the hero solves the main problem/conflict, or someone solves it for him or her.

The story arc is used in antique drama and in most modern narratives.

To test the five-arc structure, Paul Zak and his colleague Jorge Barraza edited a set of a short video clips about a father and his terminally ill son (Zak 2012). One version shows the father talking to the camera while his 2-year-old son, who has terminal brain cancer, plays in the background. The story has a classic dramatic arc in which the father is struggling to connect to and enjoy time with his son, all the while knowing that the child has only a few months to live. The clip concludes with the father finding the strength to stay emotionally close to his son until he dies.

The scientists also developed a video of the same father and son spending a day at the zoo. This version does not mention cancer or death, but the boy is bald (from his chemotherapy). This video lacks the tension induced by the typical story form but includes the same characters and the same information. This version served as a control story to see what the brain does when any video is being watched.

In the first study of narratives, Zak and his colleagues took blood before and after participants watched one of the two versions of the video (Zak 2015). They found that the narrative with the dramatic arc caused an increase in cortisol and oxytocin. Tellingly, the change in oxytocin had a positive correlation with participants' feeling of empathy for Ben and his father. Heightened empathy motivated participants who watched the story to offer money to a stranger who was also participating in the experiment but could not be seen or heard. The scientists connected a story to a feeling and then to a prosocial behaviour. The "flat" narrative of the boy and his father at the zoo did not increase oxytocin or cortisol, and participants did not report empathy for the story's characters (Zak 2015).

These findings suggest that emotionally engaging narratives inspire post-narrative actions—in this case, giving money to a stranger.

In further experiments, Zak and his team measured the activity of the vagus nerve, using an electrocardiogram (ECG). The vagus nerve (the longest cranial nerve, which innervates the heart and gut) is chock-full of oxytocin receptors. Using the story of the dying child again, the study confirmed that the change in oxytocin in blood correlates with changes in vagus nerve activity. Attention was measured using both heart rate and skin conductance changes from sweat on the fingers; emotional resonance was quantified using two measures of changes in the brain's relaxation response driven by the vagus nerve (Zak 2015). Zac's studies results mark a milestone in the history of strategic storytelling, because they provide scientific proof that well-crafted stories have a measurable impact on human behaviour.

3 Storytelling in Agile Leadership and Transformation

As outlined in the introduction, digital transformation, automation and artificial intelligence change the way we live and work profoundly and permanently. While the way people communicate and share information becomes more and more digital, building trust, mutual understanding and common ground with teams and customers is more important than ever. Agile and New Work require clear communication, and stories play an important role in translating complex technical systems into understandable frameworks. Let's take a quick look back to where the change began:

The origin of agile methods stems from software developers to respond to customer requirements more quickly, because the old ways of relatively linear sequential design approaches like the waterfall model were too slow to keep up with the needs of the customers and digitalisation itself. The Agile Manifesto from 2001 summed it up:

> We are uncovering better ways of developing software by doing it and helping others do it. Through this work we have come to value:
>
> Individuals and interactions over processes and tools. Working software over comprehensive documentation. Customer collaboration over contract negotiation. Responding to change over following a plan.
>
> That is, while there is value in the items on the right, we value the items on the left more.

In 1997, Steve Jobs returned to Apple after having been asked to leave the company he founded. In a town hall meeting, he said:

> You've got to start with the customer experience and work back toward the technology. (Jobs 1997)

Customer first, product and processes second. The agile mindset in one sentence by one of the masters of storytelling, Steve Jobs. By using storytelling, we put the human in the centre of the narrative above product and service, above abstract concepts and ideas.

The following paragraphs of the Agile Manifesto lay out the details of an agile mindset and the requirements of a new kind of leadership: The agile mindset "welcomes changing requirements, even late in development". Agile processes harness change for the customers competitive advantage. To work agile means to build projects around motivated individuals. The individuals should be given "the environment and support they need, and they should be trusted to get the job done".

Storytelling and story-listening to the stories of colleagues and subordinates are all about putting the human in the centre of the project and of the communication.

Sharing stories and personal perspective enables us to get insights on how a project can succeed, because we learn about difficulties that are not communicated in reports or memos. Storytelling and story-sharing nourish trust between colleagues; trust does not evolve just by asking for it.

The Agile Manifesto also claims: "The most efficient and effective method of conveying information to and within a development team is face-to-face conversation". In different agile tools and methods, sharing stories already is an essential part, in phase one of design thinking or the "user story" in scrum. In working out loud (WOL) circles, the sharing of work-related stories is also an integral part.

As agile consultant and trainer, Peter Merrick explains: "When agile doesn't seem to be working, it's almost always because of the stories/requirements. There could be other problems, but the requirement problem is how agile came about, and the agile solution does not solve the requirement problem" (Merrick 2014). Merrick points out the great need for storytellers within agile development. New Ways of working together in teams with changing leadership roles do not come easy to companies who worked within their culture of "control and command" for decades. To implement change and new methods like scrum, kanban and design thinking, people must not only learn how to use them but also let go of habits and traditional ways of organising work and communication. Stories can help with that change of mindset and culture, and by creating and telling stories of change as an inevitable driver of innovation, leaders can motivate their teams to buy in. Stories of companies, who ignored the need to change and therefore lost marked shares or even vanished, can help to show the urgent need for innovation and change in the work environment.

Uber Yourself Before You Get Kodak'ed

The tragic downfall of Kodak is still one of the best examples of a resistance-to-change story, told by countless speakers as a modern metaphor for myopia in strategy and development. Kodak underestimated the power of exponentials and collapsed nearly overnight after ignoring the disruptive impact of digital cameras. Once one of the most powerful companies in the world, "Kodak filed for bankruptcy protection in 2012, and re-emerged as a sharply smaller company in 2013" (Anthony 2016). Two months after Kodak's collapse, Instagram was bought by Facebook for 1 billion dollars.

At the same time, the start-up of Uber disrupted the taxi business with an app that enabled every car owner to become a cabdriver. During its rapid expansion, Uber has met fierce resistance from the taxi industry and government regulators.

Storytelling as the Elixir for Change Agents

James Kalbach, Head of Customer Success at MURAL, says: "The signs are there: we're witnessing a shift in business of Copernican proportions: today, customers don't revolve around the business; rather, the businesses must figure out how they fit into the lives of their customers. This requires a new mindset" (Kalbach 2017). Many organisational design strategies suffer from the same myopia as the conventional behaviour change strategies—being overly focused on the rational mind and forgetting to account for the two other critical elements, the emotional mind and the path of change.

In their book *Switch: How to Change Things When Change is Hard,* Dan and Chip Heath point out that change can be successfully implemented, when leaders or change agents address both: the rational mind and the emotional mind. The Heath brothers call them "the Rider and the Elephant". The rider refers to our rational brain; the elephant refers to our emotional brain. The book focuses on change of behaviour, and the key thesis is that most behaviour change efforts fail because they are focused only at the rational mind—the rider. Stephen Denning shares a similar perspective: He calls it the "Marriage of analysis and narrative", meaning that "Management is among the last disciplines to recognize the central significance of narrative to the issues that it deals with" (Denning 2011).

By creating stories of change and designing a path of what a new working environment looks like, storytelling tames the elephant and steers him towards the new direction.

Storytelling Is an Essential Leadership Tool

According to Ludmila Mládková from the University of Economics in Prague, storytelling is one of the most efficient methods to improve and intensify influence of leaders on their followers: "When used properly, it helps the leader to explain his ideas to his constituents, to share his knowledge with them, to build shared vision and settle conflicts peacefully. Storytelling is the tool that addresses people's emotions—not their rational mind. It has the potential to overcome barriers people build to protect themselves against the external world and new ideas" (Mládková 2013).

The potential to overcome barriers is the main reason why storytelling is both popular and successful in transformational processes: Through well-crafted stories, leaders and change agents can address people's fears and thereby overcome resistance to change. Storytelling is actually the opposite to convincing someone by facts and figures; it is re-authoring the whole situation by telling a story why the company needs to change and also telling a story about what happens when the company will not change.

4 Narrative Competence and Five Narratives Every Leader Should Be Able to Tell to Move Organisations

Every story with a strategic purpose has certain elements that the story-developer chooses wisely in order to craft a strong, meaningful narrative:

- A reason to be told, a core story, a learning: A message that offers the story-listeners a new perspective, an important information or a change of beliefs (see leadership stories at the end of this chapter).
- A problem or a challenge that the main character/the protagonist needs to overcome. The challenge can be an abstract one or a real person, an antagonist.
- Every story needs a plot. A clear development: A beginning, an escalation and an end.
- A specific structure, for example, the dramatic story arc (Freytag 1863) or the hero's journey (Campbell 1949).
- Every story needs certain characters: A protagonist and an antagonist, often also a sidekick, a mentor and others, that tell us something about the main character.
- The protagonist must grow in terms of character and mindset within the story. He or she also develops new skills that enable them to face the challenges.
- Use of archetypes within the protagonists (and within the core message) of the story.
- A strong use of visual language and haptics.
- Listener-oriented language.

Leaders can develop their storytelling skills by learning and practising as often as possible and, secondly, by developing a portfolio of stories for different occasions.

A story does not have to be crafted perfectly with all the elements mentioned above to have an impact on the listener. The elements help to build a story, but also stories that are imperfect can spark action in an organisation. There are certain basic narratives that every leader should be able to tell (Lampert 2015): Stephen Denning, author of *The Leader's Guide to Storytelling*, argues that "different narrative patterns are useful for the different purposes of leadership. Knowing which pattern is suitable for which task is a key to the effective use of storytelling" (Denning 2011):

> In my work with leaders, the stories we create together mostly follow one of these patterns:
>
> The *who I am* story
> The *who we are* story
> The *what we have learned* story
> The *why are we changing* story
> The *how to change perspective and grow from it* story

Pattern 1: The *Who I Am* Story
As shown before, the task of leaders nowadays is not only to deliver results but also to "connect authentically with the hearts and minds of others in order to motivate and inspire them towards a desired outcome" (Kavanagh 2018).

Some leaders may tend to tell typical hero's stories about themselves. This is not what a true leadership story should look like; modern leaders should speak openly about what they have learned from failure and even show vulnerability. I use the hero's journey with my clients to get to understand life as a series of challenges we must overcome. These challenges let us grow as human beings and as leaders.

As Carol Lampert says, "A well-crafted who I am story helps people believe in you by answering these important questions" (Lampert 2011):

- How and why did you get to be a leader?
- What are your strengths? What are your limitations?
- What have you learned along the way?
- What do you stand for?
- Why do you stand for those things?

An impressive and famous example of a *who I am story* is Steve Jobs' Stanford speech from 2005 (Jobs 2005). He speaks about his personal leadership journey in three different stories from his life.

One of his key messages is that people should love what they do: "Getting fired was the best thing that could ever happened to me…I'm convinced that the only thing that kept me going was that I loved what I did. You've got to find what you love".

Pattern 2: The *Who We Are* Story
The follow-up to the who I am story is the story of the organisation: The next step, according to Lampert, is "to help the organization embrace who they are and who they are capable of becoming". What are the underlying values of the team? Is there

a shared purpose within the company? Why would people want to be a part of it? A well-crafted *who we are* story answers these questions and helps to create the conditions where people *want* to participate in their organisation. Addressing the basic human need to belong and to be part of something bigger than ourselves, the "who we are story" should be told repeatedly in team meetings, within employer branding and the onboarding process. It does not have to be the exact same story, rather a variation of stories with the same core story.

A bright and shiny example is Michelle Obama's "If they go low, we go high" speech from 2016.

Pattern 3: The *What We Have Learned* Story

Strategic organisational storytelling was invented by a team of researchers in the Massachusetts Institute of Technology to save implicit knowledge in organisations when experts leave. In organisations with a high rate of change in management, one way to keep intellectual capital is to get very good at telling the *what have we learned* story.

This story provides context for current decision-making and tells the founding story of the organisation. It helps acculturate new employees and passes knowledge on from one generation of leader to the next.

Pattern 4: The *Why Are We Changing* Story

The *why are we changing* story is the most important narrative for change agents in the VUCA world. Most change processes fail because of a lack of trust and buy-in of the team. Strong stories can help to create trust and alignment in times of change, when change is inevitable.

According to Lampert, the *why are we changing* story answers the questions people always have during times of complexity and transformation:

- *What the heck is going on?*
- *Why do we need to change? Things have been fine the way they are.*
- *What will happen if we don't change?*
- *How will the change help us make more money, improve our relationships or improve our health?*

This type of story helps convince people that change is no threat to the company but essential to survival.

Storytelling expert and organisational consultant Stephen Denning provides a strong example of a *why are we changing* story:

In the mid-1990s, Denning was working for the World Bank.

> In June 1995, a health worker in a tiny town in Zambia went to the website of the Centre for Disease Control (CDC) and got the answer to a question about the treatment of malaria. Remember that this was in Zambia, one of the poorest countries in the world and it was in a tiny place six hundred kilometres from the capital city. But the most striking thing about this picture, at least for us, is that the World Bank isn't in it. Despite our know-how on all kinds of poverty-related issues, that knowledge isn't available to the millions of people could use it. Imagine if it were. Think what an organisation we could become! (Denning 2000)

The story helped World Bank staff and managers to envision a different kind of future for the organisation. It is also important that teams listen to these kinds of stories together and repeatedly, because the same areas in the brain gets activated in storyteller and story-listener and this creates a connection as a team with shared goals, vision and purpose. Storytelling is as close to magic as we will get.

Pattern 5: The *How to Change Perspective and Grow from It* Story
A core competency for a leader is the ability to dream, to set vision and to create strategy. People and communities can achieve great things when they understand what success looks like, which is why the *how change perspective and grow from it* story is perhaps the most important in a leader's portfolio.

In 1977 when Bill Gates first said that he wants his company to put a computer on every desk in every home, most people thought he was crazy. What would the average person do with a computer? Computers were for hobbyists. But his vision became a reality, in great part, because he articulated his story clearly, consistently and with passion.

One of the masterpieces of commercial storytelling and an example of Pattern 5 is *1984*, the television commercial that introduced the Apple Macintosh personal computer aired on January 22, 1984, during a break in the third quarter of the telecast of Super Bowl XVIII by CBS: "'1984' used an unnamed heroine to represent the coming of the Macintosh (indicated by her white tank top with a stylized line drawing of Apple's Macintosh computer on it) as a means of saving humanity from 'conformity' (Big Brother). These images were an allusion to George Orwell's noted novel, Nineteen Eighty-Four, which described a dystopian future ruled by a televised 'Big Brother'" (Wikipedia 2018).

In hindsight, the success of the personal computer seems like a highly predictable scenario. What about a present view on technologies as artificial intelligence, virtual reality or blockchain? Leaders need to decide today on future technologies and convince their teams, boards and investors what to focus on. Storytelling is the best way to envision a possible future and rally the troops for the right decisions to create this future together. The video that Apple had directed by Ridley Scott in 1983 to launch their operating system in 1984 is a breath-taking example of a story that moves people to see the known world in a new context and make them believe there is something that will make their life better. Its tagline, "Why 1984 Won't Be Like 1984", plays on George Orwell's dystopian novel and reassures viewers that Apple's new technology would be used for freedom, not control.

5 The Story Framework: How to Support Leaders with Narrative Stories

I work as a systemic consultant and facilitator in leadership trainings and coaching and transformational processes. Within this environment I created a framework to use storytelling in different scenarios.

Through the story framework, clients learn to develop stories strategically and tell them to a defined group. I developed the framework to enable my clients to craft stories fast and test their impact in an early stage in a group or with just me as a listener. I use it both in sessions with a single client or with groups.

Before I introduce the framework, the client or the participants have come to know the following principles of storytelling:

1. Gustav Freytag's dramatic story arc
2. The hero's journey by Joseph Campbell
3. The impact of J.G. Jung's archetypes
4. Effect of storytelling on the brain

5.1 Approach and Case Study

The client or participants receive both canvases and I explain the principle of the story canvas as follows:

The business model canvas was developed originally to speed up the development of a business plan. The story canvas (see Fig. 2) works similarly.

We begin by deciding the purpose of the story, the reason it should be told. Usually the reason is one of the five narratives mentioned above. Another possibility is to develop a story, which is about personal values and attitudes in a job interview. This story is then used when a question like "tell us something about yourself" or

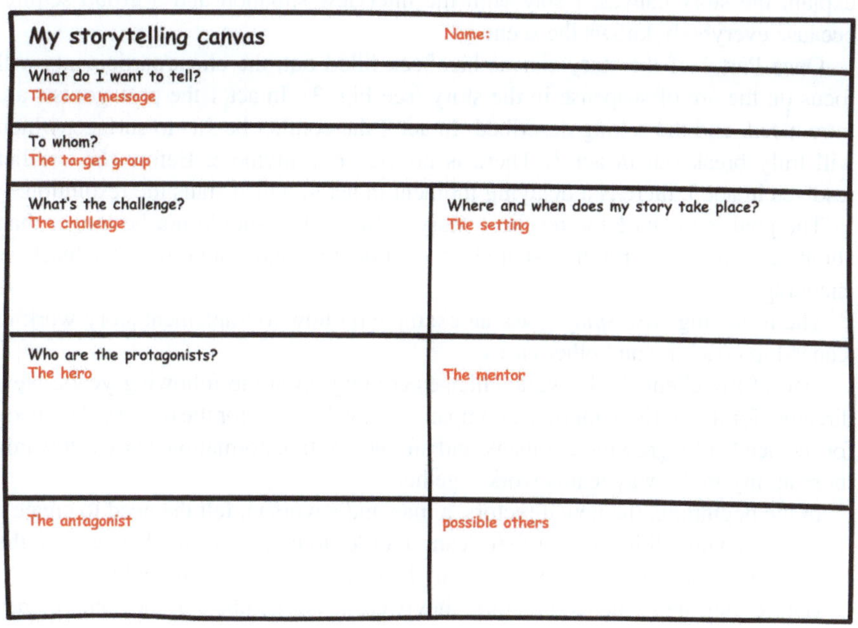

Fig. 2 My storytelling canvas (Source: Rasmussen Consulting)

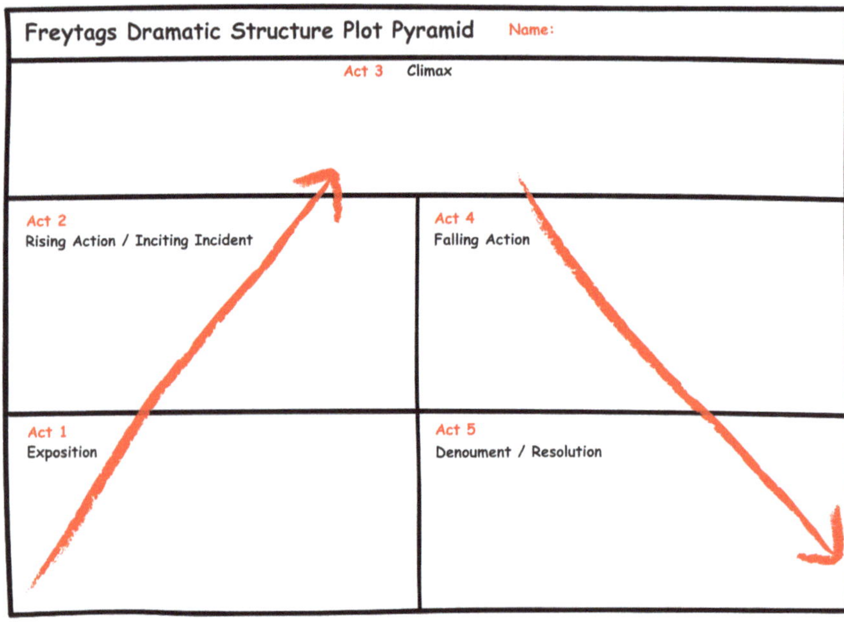

Fig. 3 Freytag's dramatic structure plot pyramid (Source: Rasmussen Consulting)

"what was a serious professional challenge" or a similar question is asked. To explain the story canvas, I stay with the interview situation and a group setting, because everybody knows the scene.

Once Part 1 of the story canvas has been filled out, the client/participants will focus on the arc of suspense in the story (see Fig. 3). In act 1 the protagonists are introduced, and the setting described. In act 2 the conflict begins to surface, which will truly break out in act 3: There is no way out anymore. Before the conflict resolves in act 5, there is a delaying moment in act 4, which stalls the resolution.

The goal is to share the resulting story at the end; it should not be longer than about 2–4 min. Everything shared is confidential and supportive feedback is encouraged.

The following *case study* gives an example on how to implement story-work in leadership coaching and other cases.

One of my clients had several changes coming up in the following years: New directors for the Berlin Unit of the company, a new location for the office tailor-made for the needs of a growing company and an internal transformation process towards more agility in the way teams work together.

In the beginning, the new directors, a man and a woman, felt the need to create a story they could tell in front of their team in order to communicate their values, the direction that the company would take in the following months and why.

Before their new role as directors, they were team members at the same hierarchical level as their colleagues, who were now to become their subordinates. Both

Fig. 4 A hero's journey (Source: Rasmussen Consulting)

had the feeling they needed a narrative to mark the changes that were to follow and to speak about their leadership with tangible values.

I interviewed them individually and started by asking questions about their career so far, childhood, their parents and their experiences at school and university. When some answer or even certain keywords evoked an association, I asked more deeply and motivated the client to bring back memories of how the situation felt, who was there with them and what the location looked like and smelled and details about daytime and weather.

When I felt there was enough material, I reorganised the memories in the 12 steps of the hero's journey by John Campbell together with the client. By that, we cocreated the client's personal hero's journey (Fig. 4).

With the personal hero's journey as framework, we cocreated stories for the different challenges the team would face through the year: As the clients announced their new role at a team retreat, they used large parts of their hero's journey for their *who am I* am story. The woman, who immigrated from Ukraine in the 1990s, choose the story of her first days in a small town in Bavaria. As she had already worked in a company in Ukraine and earned enough to pay for her own flat, she had to start all over again to study at a German University, to start her career. She described how helpless and lonely she felt when she could hardly communicate with her fellow students and how humiliating it was to live in a refugee camp in the beginning. It took a while to encourage her to share this story, but when she did, her colleagues learned a lot about her personal values: She works very hard and has respect for those who do, too. She strongly believes that women can become whatever they want to, when they work hard enough and do not let themselves be hindered by any circumstances. She already championed women in her company wherever she could. Through the story process, she became even more aware of her tendency to micromanage her subordinates sometimes and the reasons for that. As a result, she talked about this side of her personality at the team retreat. By that, she showed self-reflection and the ability to embrace her weaknesses as part of her personality—two very important leadership skills.

The male director shared one story that was very emotional. His parents fled from East to West Berlin a few months before the wall was built that divided Germany for 27 years. It was a cold winter night, and his father has been interrogated by the "Stasi" two times within days. The agents demanded personal information about his colleagues. His father, a deeply religious man, felt he could no longer stay in a country that asked him to spy on his neighbours and fellow workers. He also knew that he would be put to prison when he resisted the Stasi and his wife, expecting their second child soon, would be left alone without any income. One dark, December night, the small family of father, mother and little child left their home and walked over the last unmanned border at Bernauer Straße. It was snowing lightly, and the family had only their clothes and a small handbag, because carrying more baggage could have risen suspicion.

The client told the story as if he had been there, as if he himself had felt the snow on his skin and sensed the fear of his parents about being taken into custody and never seeing each other again. The funny thing is he could not possibly have been there; he was born a couple of years later when the family lived in West Berlin. When I told him that I misunderstood him and believed at first that he himself crossed the Bernauer Straße (where nowadays the Mauermuseum tells stories like his), he said: "It FEELS as if I have been there! When I was younger, I even believed I was there though my mother told me, I was not".

This is the power of story: Our memories are not fixed like a picture or a film that we rewatch endlessly, and that remains the same; our memories change by the level of intensity and the way we share stories repeatedly.

So, what happened with these precious memories? Let's take a closer look what that story contains and why it was an ideal material for a leadership story:

The male client has lived in Berlin most of his life, and his new role was to develop the Berlin unit, so the story had to be about Berlin. This is the first layer of the story.

Like his fathers, the client's values are based on Christian belief and human dignity. The story communicates these values strongly without even mentioning the client's religious beliefs.

The story is a hero's journey. The hero is the father, who left all his belonging behind to start again with nothing, because he knew he could not betray his colleagues and his beliefs. By not talking about himself but choosing a story of his family, where his father was the main protagonist, my client communicated one of his characteristics: He is a very humble person and is able to praise others for their achievements. He does not have to put himself in the centre of a story because he does not need to. These are very modern leadership characteristics. Finally, the story is a deeply religious one—homeless couple, mother pregnant, with no belongings at all, looking for a shelter in a foreign country: It is the story we all know, the story of the birth of Jesus. Also, the female leader's story referred to basic human desires: Her story also was about coming as a refugee in a new country and having to start again from nothing. It reflected the basic human desire to get help by other humans at new beginnings and to be respected for great personal efforts in the end. Both stories also contain the American "you can make it if you really want" narratives that we all know and embrace.

As the team retreat was to take place mid-December, it was no surprise that people would be touched by it, even if they were not religious. I prepared my clients that things could become quite emotional when they would tell their stories, and so it happened. Everybody had tears in their eyes, and it was the most intense moment the team shared so far.

Storytelling served to define my client's values and ethics by working with the hero's journey and communicate them in a narrative way. Practised regularly, storytelling can become a guiding leadership mindset.

6 Conclusion

Using Storytelling Requires Caution with People's Memories and Identity
Using storytelling and story-listening with clients presupposes certain skills. The story-developer needs to be aware that remembering events of the past can be very emotional and even re-traumatising; sometimes clients feel rather sensitive about the memories that come up. To be able to create a safe environment, it requires coaching skills and a very clear knowledge of the story-developers role and its limitations. If painful memories emerge, the story-developer needs to be able to react appropriately.

Even if clients do not dive deeply into their personal history, developing their own leadership stories makes them reflect on their values und priorities in work as well as in life. It is very common that this initiates an inner process. The story-developer should be skilled in both coaching and providing follow-up coaching sessions and creating an atmosphere within the group, where sharing stories leads to deeper connection and everybody feels safe.

If these requirements are met, the story framework is a very powerful tool for leaders to reflect on their own journey and values and develop strong narratives that let teams and organisations flourish.

References

"1984" Advert by Apple. (1984). Accessed December 10, 2018, from https://de.wikipedia.org/wiki/1984_(Werbespot)

Anthony, S. D. (2016). Accessed December 10, 2018, from https://hbr.org/2016/07/kodaks-downfall-wasnt-about-technology
Beck, K., Beedle, M., van Bennekum, A., Cockburn, A., Cunningham, W., Fowler, M., Grenning, J., Martin, R. C., Highsmith, J., Hunt, A., Jeffries, R., Kern, J., Marick, B., Mellor, S., Schwaber, K., Sutherland, J., & Thomas, D. (2001). *Agile Manifesto*. Accessed December 10, 2018, from https://www.agilealliance.org/
Burkova, O., & Rasmussen, J. (2019). Digitale Kompetenzen aus Arbeitgebersicht. *Studie* (2018), UAS7. Accessed from http://uas7.org/index.php
Campbell, J. (1949). *The hero with the 1000 faces*. Novato, CA: New World Library.
Denning, S. (2000). *The Springboard: How storytelling ignites action in knowledge-era organizations*. Oxford: Butterworth Heinemann.
Denning, S. (2011). *The leaders guide to storytelling*. San Francisco: Jossey-Bass, Wiley Imprint.
Freytag, G. (1863). *Die Technik des Dramas*. Berlin: Autorenhaus Verlag.
Grabmeier, S. (2018). *Ambidextrie als Organisationsprinzip- Innovationen und Kerngeschäft verbinden*. Accessed December 10, 2018, from https://grabmeier.kienbaum.com/2018/03/03/ambidextrie-als-organisationsprinzip-innovationen-und-kerngeschaeft-verbinden/
Jobs, S. (1997). Accessed December 10, 2018, from https://www.youtube.com/watch?v=FF-tKLISfPE
Jobs, S. (2005). Accessed December 10, 2018, from https://www.businessinsider.de/steve-jobs-stanford-commencement-speech-full-transcript-video-2016-10?r=US&IR=T
Kalbach, J. (2017) *Rapid techniques for mapping experiences*. https://www.oreilly.com/learning/rapid-techniques-for-mapping-experiences-report
Kavanagh, P. (2018). *The Definition of Leadership presence*. Accessed December 10, 2018, from https://info.arielgroup.com/blog/the-definition-of-leadership-presence-an-interview-with-ariel-ceo-sean-kavanagh
Lampert. (2011). http://www.arielgroup.com/five-narratives-that-move-organizations/2019
Lampert, Carol in Ariel Group. (2015). Accessed December 10, 2018, from https://info.arielgroup.com/blog/five-narratives-that-move-organizations/
Merrick, P. (2014). Accessed December 10, 2018, from https://medium.com/agile-storytelling/agile-teams-need-storytellers-c375521ada04
Mládková, L. (2013). Leadership and storytelling; 2nd International conference on leadership, technology and innovation management. *Procedia – Social and Behavioural Sciences, 75*, 83–90.
Müller, M. (2017). *Einführung in narrative Methoden der Organisationsberatung*. Heidelberg: Carl-Auer Verlag.
Sinek, S. (2009). *Start with why*. London: Penguin Group.
Wikipedia. (2018). Accessed April 30, 2019, from https://en.wikipedia.org/wiki/1984_(advertisement)
Zak, P. J. (2012). *The moral molecule: The source of love and prosperity*. Dutton.
Zak, P. J. (2015). Why inspiring stories make us react: The neuroscience of narrative. *Cerebrum, 2*.
Zak, P. J. (2014). Accessed December 10, 2018, from https://www.ted.com/talks/paul_zak_trust_morality_and_oxytocin

Jaana Rasmussen is a systemic consultant, facilitator and ECHA coach. From 2009, she has been lecturing in Storytelling, Fundraising and Management at the Department of Cultural and Media Management at the Hamburg University for Music and Theatre. From 2014 she has been lecturing Talent Research and Development at the Department of Business and Social Sciences at Hamburg University for Applied Sciences. She worked in different management positions before she became a freelance consultant and lecturer. In 2017, she specialised in story development with executives and companies and narrative methods for transformational processes. Jaana has published several articles on storytelling, fundraising and talent development and conducted a study on mandatory digital skills for university graduates.

We Become What We Talk About: How Experimenting with Dialogue Can Change an Organization's Culture

Jeffer London, John B. McGuire, and Filipa Santos

Abstract

To change the culture of an organization, it is important to get people talking about the behaviors that they experience and that they want to experience in the future. Organizational behavior is based on personal beliefs. These beliefs may be invisible to individuals and those around them. Storytelling can make beliefs visible and expose the behaviors that make an organization's culture. People's stories and conversations are microcosms of what is happening at an organization-wide level. Programs that encourage the exchange of views shift the way people think, feel, and act at work. We can change an organization one dialogue at a time.

This case illustrates how one organization, a large governmental bureaucracy, transformed itself by sharing stories and perspectives. Their stress was causing unhealthy reactions ranging from complacency to sabotage to burnout. As a public institution, they could not make financial and structural changes, but they could address the human element.

The leaders decided to run "Dialogue Experiments," a series of simple and effective dialogues to shift people's mind-set. Together, the organization found its own way forward. The staff revitalized their vision, found engagement, built

Jeffer London, John B. McGuire, and Filipa Santos work with the Center for Creative Leadership. CCL® is a top-ranked global provider of executive education that develops better leaders through its exclusive focus on leadership education and research. CCL helps organizations worldwide, in both private and nonprofit sectors, build their leadership capacity and make a true, sustainable difference.

J. London (✉) · F. Santos
Center for Creative Leadership, Brussels, Belgium
e-mail: Londonj@ccl.org; SantosF@ccl.org

J. B. McGuire
Center for Creative Leadership, Colorado Springs, CO, USA
e-mail: McGuireJ@ccl.org

© Springer Nature Switzerland AG 2019

J. Chlopczyk, C. Erlach (eds.), *Transforming Organizations*,
Management for Professionals, https://doi.org/10.1007/978-3-030-17851-2_11

collective leadership, and resolved the fundamental issues that were stifling the group.

This chapter explains how to set up Dialogue Experiments to get your own people talking, showing how these conversations can bring about positive change.

1 Introduction: We Become What We Talk About

Change the conversation, and you change the organization. This is a story about an organization that changed itself. Faced with challenges that could not be solved by exerting external pressure, they turned inward to understand the roots of their dilemma. They brought about transformation through the sharing of reflections, stories, and dialogue. Their collective leadership is an example that proves how change happens one conversation at a time.

The organization found positive business results: efficiencies, synergies, motivation, and teamwork—better services that guaranteed a healthy future. The path to these results was made of a 1000 little personal breakthroughs—each of which felt like a triumph for humanity. In this story of how one group approached transforming their organization are the concepts for you to keep in mind if you want to transform your own.

The following pages explain how people in the case ran "Dialogue Experiments" as a testing ground to improve the way they talked with one another. These experiments were about their culture, as well as objectives, collaboration, performance, and impact. These experiments were part of the research for a project called "Stimulating Conversation: How to Get People Talking" (London 2018). This case and the body of research highlight the importance of putting foundations in place, so the rest of the chapter explains the following concepts that make this type of transformation possible:

- *Invitation*: How to initiate group forum work and get people to join in?
- *Safe space*: How to create an environment that allows for personal sharing?
- *Perspectives*: How to ensure you have representation from the entire community?
- *Possibility*: How to set conditions that encourage positivity and appreciation?
- *Questions*: How to shape the central question to bring optimal dialogue?
- *Facilitation*: How to identify, develop, or bring in facilitative group leaders?
- *Leadership*: How to collectively build direction, alignment, and commitment?

Before we get into the "How to" areas, imagine you were asked to make change happen in this organization.

2 Transforming an Organization: One Dialogue at a Time

2.1 The Crisis

The people involved worked in a large governmental bureaucracy. Faced with rising demands and diminishing resources, they were under pressure. Many were complacent, some resorted to sabotage, and others burned out. They clearly needed to change. As a public institution, they could not easily make financial and structural changes; their only option was to address the human element. However, some members of the staff leaned toward denial and avoidance and did not welcome the prospect of dealing with the issues in a group forum.

2.2 A New Leader Brought In

The main character in this case, who we will call Peter, does not see himself as the star of this story—he would say that the transformation was thanks to the people involved. His previous roles in the institution had involved major reorganizations. Peter was clearly put here to implement change. Peter had what he called "Scandinavian common sense"—a way of looking at situations that was emotionally detached but still very humane. He had a track record of simplifying, reorienting, and downsizing other divisions of the organization.

His new management team was disjointed and could not agree on a way forward. The leaders had differing opinions on what had led to their situation, what was going on, and what should be done. What they shared was the pressure they felt from politicians and the public, who perceived their staff's performance as poor.

While Peter was respected in his previous divisions, his new team was skeptical about an outsider coming in to fix what they could not. What his new team did not realize was that Peter would evoke in them an exceptional sense of empowerment and vision. Peter deeply believed that people had positive intentions and that they wanted to do good. He believed in people's capacity and potential and noticed that the staff members were simply stuck in their behaviors and trapped in a bureaucracy that they did not believe in. Peter thought if they had a better option, the staff would take it.

2.3 Facilitating Positive Dialogue

Over the years, Peter had worked with an external facilitator, through whom he had an understanding of Appreciative Inquiry (Friedman 2011) and of the importance of having all voices at the table. Now Peter invited his management team, along with the facilitator, for a positive discussion about the possibilities for them and their organization.

Don't Say the Word "Change". At the meeting that launched what later became a transformation, the word "change" was in every sentence. "We need to change... I have been appointed director to make a change... Our stakeholders demand change. . . People have to change. . . They need to change their mentality. . ." A long wish list of changes. The background narrative was clear: we are no good; this is not working; this is not a worthy endeavor. This narrative was responsible for high absenteeism, a culture of blame, defensiveness, and dwindling motivation.

Noticing the prevalence of the word "change" and the lack of any mention of what was working well was the first "Aha Moment" for this small group. When the conversation moved to what was working well, what could be salvaged, and what could be built upon, the group found energy and a sense of possibility—it was the second "Aha Moment" in just an hour. The group imagined other people in the organization also feeling a sense of possibility if the conversations shifted from "we need to change what is bad" to "we need to build on what is good."

2.4 A Tentative Step Forward

The management team discussed the proposition of bringing the entire organization into dialogue. This felt too risky for them. They did not want to have what one member called "a giant complaining session." They were ready, however, to *run a small dialogue experiment*. They had felt the value of exchanging stories about what was working well and what they wanted to see working well—and wanted to find out if what was true for them was also true for others.

While Peter had experienced and appreciated the Dialogue Experiments in his previous roles, his new team wanted to know: *What is a Dialogue Experiment?*

2.5 Dialogue Experiments: Enabling Transformation

Peter and his core management team decided to organize a 2-day strategic retreat for their extended management team—department heads, deputies, specialist roles—24 people in total. Together with an external facilitator, they did six Dialogue Experiments—one in the planning process, four as the event itself, and one as a follow-up debriefing session.

2.5.1 Experiment 1: Building the Foundation

Between the initial meeting and the first planning session, many of the members had contacted people in Peter's old division. The positive echoes of the Dialogue Experiments there were reassuring, and the group got into the rhythm quickly.

That first planning session included discussion about how to create an environment where people felt free to express themselves and open their hearts to listen to others. Their own office space was charged with negativity and full of distractions, so they decided to hold the strategic retreat offsite, in a venue that held significant meaning for the heritage of the institution.

2.5.2 Experiments 2–5: The Strategic Retreat

A month later, the group united at a historic home surrounded by forests. It was the same place where their predecessors had designed the institution that they were now running. The agenda was built on the results of their first Dialogue Experiment and infused with the emblematic heritage of the site—this was a place where ideas had been born and ideals had been turned into the organization that they now needed to transform.

Given the group's history of tension, disagreement, and rivalry, the facilitator worked with the group to create a psychological contract about the behavior they wanted to adhere to. There was special attention to debriefing each section of the event with the same three questions: *what was helping? What was hindering? What were they learning?* This pattern of reflection was a turning point for the group. What Peter and the facilitator hoped would happen by the end of day 2 was already achieved in the first morning: they were engaged and ready to move on together.

The rest of the time flew by. There were blowups and shutdowns, but there was also compassion and resolution. In the end, the group had a shared understanding of the situation, had internalized the need to transform the mind-set and processes of their institution, and were all onboard to make it happen.

2.5.3 Experiment 6: Reviewing Progress and the Path Ahead

In the debriefing, it became clear that all the pent-up frustration had become debilitating; and the key to changing that was the sense of *experimentation*. If Peter had come with proclamations and directives, the team would have rejected them. But by exploring subjects as an experiment, with no foregone conclusions, people felt included, empowered, and responsible.

In Peter's previous divisions, as in most companies, the Dialogue Experiments were done at all levels of the organization—with a focus on organizational culture and the entire system of people working together. In this case, getting direction, alignment, and commitment among the top leadership community was enough to make a significant difference. Beyond the constructive dialogue and renewed energy, this team was able to put mechanisms in place to refresh their vision, break down silos, and offer better service to their stakeholders.

3 About Dialogue Experiments

3.1 Conversation Is Transformation

If you have ever thought "this organization needs to change," you are not alone. Most of us want change, but we also know the folkloric statistics about how 70% of "change initiatives" fail. This bleak outlook on the failure to change was declared in Hammer and Champy's book, *Reengineering the Corporation*; while unsubstantiated, it still resonates. Having witnessed many of these initiatives go from hopeful optimism to bitter regret, the lingering questions about the few successful projects are: *Why?* and *How will my project be successful?*

One observation is that failed projects are often dominated by top-down directives and status reports about compliance, while successful projects are characterized by authentic conversations and grassroots engagement.

While planning tools have gotten increasingly sophisticated, the most fundamental tool, talking, gets little attention. This is strange because when things go wrong, people don't blame the plan, they blame poor communication, lack of engagement, and mixed messages—in simpler words, we didn't talk.

Of course, this phenomenon does not apply only to the office. In any social situation, people may feel shocked or disappointed if they have not been consulted or involved in a decision.

From this observation, a hypothesis was born: *dialogue is essential for engagement.*

The Dialogue Experiments were set up to explore how to get people talking.

3.2 What Is a Dialogue Experiment?

A Dialogue Experiment is a testing ground for groups who want to improve their dialogue and engagement. These group exercises bring people together around topics (purpose, intentions, challenges, conflicts, collaboration, citizenship, their work, the future, each other) and have them exchange with one another in a number of ways (reflection, visualization, conversation, feedback, storytelling). Groups typically do a series of experiments, and after each one, they ask themselves three questions:

- *What has helped us be in conversation? And why is that important?* (Working Well)
- *What hindered, diminished, or blocked our conversation? And why is that important?* (Area to Explore)
- *What have we learned about stimulating conversation? And why is that important?* (Personal Learning)

The answers to these questions are shared among the participants, and over time, the group has a body of collective intelligence about what helps, hinders, and encourages dialogue. These insights and resources are available through the research project called *Stimulating Conversation: How to Get People Talking* (London 2018). As many groups around the world have been doing these experiments, a considerable package of insights and tips has been generated. This knowledge supports groups who are doing their first experiments to have better conversations, faster.

Into this atmosphere of positive dialogue, challenging topics may be introduced. Groups have tackled all types of topics—from *How can we build bridges in our community?* to *How can we sell more to our clients?* to *How can we create a brighter future together?* Often, the experiments are dedicated to a big question facing the group (Figs. 1, 2, and 3).

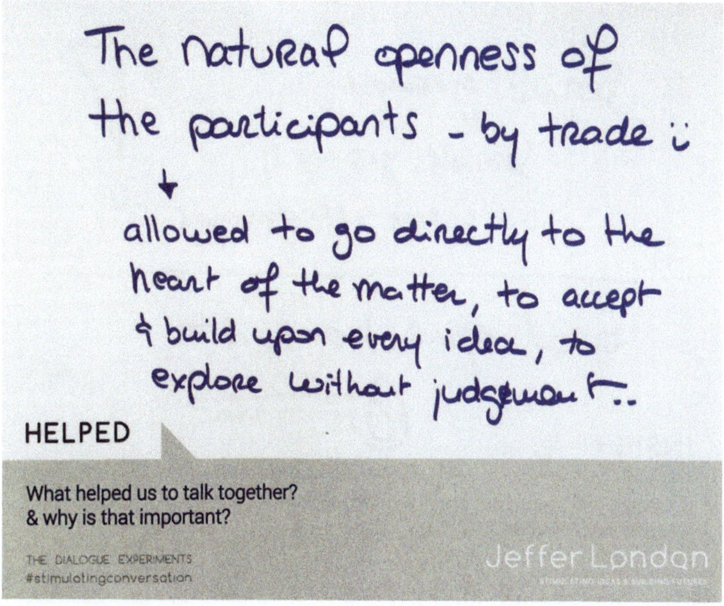

Fig. 1 One of the participant cards about what was "working well" in their Dialogue Experiment (Picture taken by the author)

Fig. 2 One of the participant cards about "areas to explore" based on their Dialogue Experiment (Picture taken by the author)

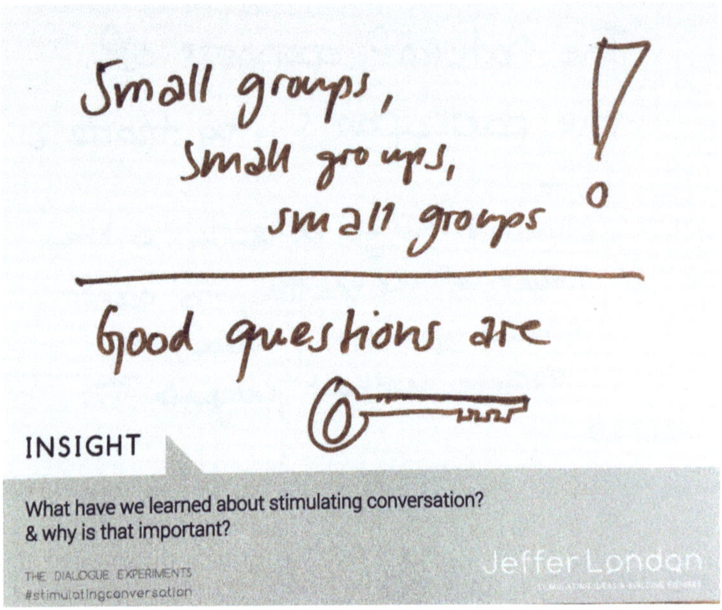

Fig. 3 One of the participant cards about "personal learning" from their Dialogue Experiment (Picture taken by the author)

3.3 Results of the Experiments

Included. Valued. Progress. Empowered. Listened to. Shared leadership. Making a difference. No longer afraid. Feeling part of something bigger. These are the testimonials of participants of the Dialogue Experiments. For groups who have overcome conversational challenges, the outcome is much more than a temporary feel-good moment. As one participant expressed: "The weight of avoiding [this topic] has been lifted and I feel we can be honest about where we are going as a team and an organization."

For organizations faced with significant and complicated pressure to change, the Dialogue Experiments have been a simple way to understand the issues and each other and to decide how to move forward together (Fig. 4).

Fig. 4 A group experiencing a Dialogue Experiment at the Berlin Change Days (Picture courtesy of Jeffer London)

3.4 Preparing to Run a Dialogue Experiment

There have been all types of experiments, ranging from an hour to 2 days in length and with topics that may be light or serious, simple, or complex.

Box 1 Typical Flow of a Dialogue Experiment

- Shape your question, ideally with a couple of peers.
- Select a convivial space, set a time, and start preparing.
- Create your invitation, and invite 10–40 people.
- Welcome the group, set the tone, explain the intention.
- Remind people about the debriefing outputs of the previous sessions.
- Facilitate a series of designed social interaction activities (see below).
- Debrief the session (see below).
- Share the results.
- Repeat 3–10 times, with a couple weeks between sessions.

3.5 Designing a Dialogue Experiment

Experiments have been run by people with all levels of facilitation skill. Experienced facilitators, with their skill in making complex flows run smoothly, can sometimes be a disadvantage—as their will not be many noticeable mistakes in the process.

Many of the best experiments were run by "normal people" without much experience in running workshops, who kept things simple but showed an authentic desire to explore group dialogue. Generally debriefing is on the participant experience, not the facilitation process.

Box 2 Some Possibilities for Designing the Social Interactions in the Experiment

- The instructions can be as simple as "get into groups of three and discuss the question."
- Run it World Café style (Brown and Isaacs 2005), discussing the same topic twice, in different groups of four.
- Offer a sequence of three topics, mixing the groups each time [(1) In pairs, on: Why was it important for you to join this conversation today? (2) In triads, on: How is this topic impacting you? (3) In quartets, on: What would you like to see happen next on this topic?] Follow each discussion with a few words from each group on the outcomes.
- Elicit stories, asking people to pair up and each tell the other a 7-min story, followed by a couple minutes of response: What is it about the story that struck the listener? Set the topic in advance; it can be about business (Tell me a story about how your work has changed in the new structure) or something personal (Tell me a story about how your parents' culture shaped your own behavior).
- Use a formula to frame a series of stacking conversations. For example, five 15–45 min rounds of Appreciative Inquiry: *Definition*: How would you define our situation? *Discovery*: How do you see our situation today? *Dream*: How do your dreams for the future look? *Design*: How would you design the way forward? *Destiny*: How does the future feel when we fulfill our dreams? This may take from 2 h to all day, but allowing people to discuss, share, and mix with each other allows the group to really get in touch with the subject and the context (Stavros and Torres 2018).
- Other tried and true formulae include Design Thinking (Brown 2009), Thiagi Frame Games (Thiagarajan 2006), Divergence and Convergence (Orland-Barak 2007), and the many Liberating Structures (Lipmanowicz and McCandless 2014).
- Often the experiments evolve over time, with the early ones exploring the definition of the problem, then moving on to options, and finally plans, execution, and evaluation.

People can get nervous about designing these sessions and about participating in them. Generally, these concerns are unfounded, as the sessions are almost always a learning experience. In fact, some of the sessions that were reported as disasters were the ones that offered the best debriefs. Either way, over time, the sequence of sessions builds competence and confidence across the group.

Table 1 Debriefing questions and process[a]

Debriefing a dialogue experiment: three question cards, written on in sequence		
Working well	Areas to explore	Personal learning
What has helped us be in conversation? And why is that important?	What hindered, diminished, or blocked our conversation? And why is that important?	What have we learned about stimulating conversation? And why is that important?

[a]You can download debriefing cards at #stimulatingconversation or create your own branded version

3.6 Debriefing the Dialogue Experiment with Feedback Cards

At the end of each experiment, it is important to have a proper debrief. In fact, the effort is senseless without this closing. Different groups have tried variations, but it works best when you use the standard three question cards. This way you can compare your results with many other groups (Table 1).

3.7 Debriefing a Dialogue Experiment

Allow 20 min of debriefing following a 70–80-min session. Here are the steps to follow:

- Have the group sit in a circle so they can see each other and feel part of a community.
- Put baskets of felt-tip pens and three stacks of the printed question cards in the middle. (Print more than enough.)
- Allow 9 min (3×3) to reflect and write on each card.
- As people complete the cards, have them lay them in the middle of the circle.
- Ask volunteers to tidy up the cards so everyone can see them.
- Request participants to summarize and read the main themes—one for each set of cards. Let people draw their own conclusions.
- Take a photo of each set. If there is a card that is emblematic of the theme, take a photo of that one too.
- Share the photos with the group, and use them as the entry point for the next session.

3.8 Story-Based Dialogue Experiments

The essence of the Dialogue Experiments is testing out ways to express, listen, and create together. When we get groups to share their story, we learn about their values, their choices, and the way they experience the world. These topics can be hard to talk about head-on, but when we listen to others' stories we enter into their view of the world.

For organizations with transformational aspirations, sharing stories about the way we interact together can illuminate the macrocosm of our workplaces through the microcosms of individual stories.

Stories have surfaced in many of the Dialogue Experiments. Here are some ways you can encourage storytelling in your groups:

- *Opening the session*: *Once upon a time…* is a magical way to launch an event. Stories evoke listening, and archetypical settings, characters, and plots can quickly set the scene for the type of dialogue you want to stimulate.
- *Sharing of experiences*: When we ask people to pair up and listen to each other's story, we bring humanity into people's rushed worlds. Slowing down by sharing stories and our gratitude for the stories establishes intimacy and respect—essential ingredients for any conversations that follow.
- *Story sessions*: You may want to dedicate entire sessions to the creation and sharing of stories. In this case, you may want to adjust the way you debrief the session. This can be straightforward: *What has helped you hear the stories? What got in the way of your listening? What did you learn through the stories?* Or more poetic, inviting celestial views on each story: *What has the SUN found illuminated in this story? What has the MOON seen reflected in this story? What do the STARS predict for the future of this story?*
- *Testimonials*: After hours of dialogue in large groups, it can be hard to encapsulate the many views covered. Asking a couple people in the group to observe while they participate and to share a story at the end can offer powerful meaning-making for the group and a useful communication to people beyond the group.
- *Ripple effect stories*: When emblematic stories surface in your session, capture them and create ways for that story to be heard beyond the session. Videos, illustrated stories, and road shows are all ways to let wider populations understand their shared story through one well-told story.

4 Foundations of the Dialogue Experiments

Conversation and storytelling are integral to the human experience. We all know how to converse and tell a story, yet when groups get together in workplaces and communities, the pressures of time, of performance, or of others' reactions can limit our expression and our listening. Here are some ways that you can encourage people to speak with one another.

4.1 *Invitation*: How to Initiate Group Forum Work and Get People to Join In

Put some thought into your invitation. Whether you are inviting a colleague for lunch or a team to talk, the way you invite them will influence the event. When we feel that someone really wants to hear from us—that they truly care about our point of view—conversation can easily follow. People love to talk about their own lives, but for most, listening to other people's problems is boring. Your invitation needs to present an opportunity.

Balance intrigue with information. To get people to sign up, your invitation should make them curious and excited, like a movie poster or trailer. Create anticipation with a catchy title that shows the spirit of the event you want to have. Besides the practical details about when and where it will happen, mention anything they should start thinking about in advance—such as the question that will be discussed.

4.2 *Safe Space*: How to Create the Environment That Allows for Personal Sharing

We need space for dialogue: mental space, physical space, emotional space, and temporal space. If we don't have the time or energy to talk with people, it simply won't happen. If you think back to the great conversations you have had, you can recognize certain elements that helped those conversations to happen—you made time for it, you were very present with the others, and you felt it was important. These conditions for conversation can be recreated—and the space made will become the vessel for your conversations.

Certain places just say "let's talk." Coffee shops with communal tables, campfires, garden benches, and face-to-face sofas—these places invite us into conversation. Other places, like work cubicles and theater seats, tell us "keep to yourself." From our earliest memories, sitting in a circle has meant dialogue. For our prehistoric elders, self-help groups, and kindergarteners, the circle has represented inclusion and sharing. In the circle, we are equals, as there are no better or worse seats. In the circle, we each have a voice and can be seen by all. When we are more than a few people getting together to talk, forming a circle is a symbolic first step that echoes our heritage of talking in the round.

4.3 *Perspectives*: How to Ensure You Have Representation from the Entire Community

Be sure to include a diversity of people in your initial experiments. Having a variety of perspectives is critical, as it illustrates how we all see the world differently, exposes our blind spots, and lets us practice in a real-life situation. When groups are too like-minded, we forget how important it is to make fewer assumptions and more inquiries when trying to truly understand others' viewpoints. The challenge is to be comfortable with the discomfort of listening to different perspectives while facilitating a process that engages with a wide base of people. Bringing groups of people together to work on a problem does not guarantee effective collaboration, but it does provide the perfect opportunity to experiment with how to make collaboration work. To tap the collective intelligence that successful collaboration brings, design your dialogue environments to include the full spectrum of your people (Pea 2004).

The solutions to complex challenges are easier for teams who can build bridges across wide-ranging boundaries that exist beyond the cultural lens (Ernst and Campbell 2011). Combining the brainpower of all employees, instead of relying on a few senior thinkers, brings organizations benefits in productivity, creativity, and coordination (Wanous and Youtz 1986).

Box 3 Boundary Spanning: Creating a Common Language

The world, communities, and businesses are often separated by boundaries of expertise and function. Partners, vendors, customers, and stakeholders are constantly bumping against demographic and geographic boundaries. *Boundary Spanning Leadership* is a research-based model based on three strategies that can support leaders, groups, and organizations to span boundaries effectively (Ernst and Chrobot-Mason 2011).

1. *Manage Boundaries*: The first step is to create or strengthen the boundaries. Use the power of differentiation (e.g., clarifying role, purpose, areas of expertise) in order to build safety and knowledge across boundaries.
2. *Forge Common Ground*: Discover what is shared, and bring the groups together to achieve a larger purpose, to build trust, engagement, and shared ownership across boundaries (creating a shared vision and unified force).
3. *Discover New Frontiers*: Where groups collide, intersect, and link, a new organism is created: one that integrates differentiated expertise, experience, and resources, yet is driven by a common vision to support innovation and transformation.

Six practices are embedded within the three overarching strategies: buffering, reflecting, connecting, mobilizing, weaving, and transforming. Dialogue Experiments offer an environment for bridging communities and collaboration among previously divided groups.

4.4 *Possibility*: How to Set Conditions That Encourage Positivity and Appreciation

The Dialogue Experiments work best when you adopt the belief that we can positively affect people by asking questions and listening in an appreciative manner. This approach, called Appreciative Inquiry, fosters positive change and dramatically improves the outcomes of our conversations. By focusing on what we want to happen instead of what we want to avoid, and asking questions to deepen understanding and increase possibilities, we expand creativity, improve productivity, and unleash potential, at work and home (Stavros and Torres 2018). As you become more aware of how dialogue is handled, both in your personal circles and across your organization, take note of the tone, vocabulary, and degree to which it is affirming and empowering.

Everything looks better with a bit of sunshine, but sometimes we have to imagine our own sunshine. As Desmond Tutu said, "Hope is being able to see that there is light despite all of the darkness" (Tutu 2004). Help yourself see the possibility of conversation by shedding some light on what could be. We can all have better conversations. The first step is to start noticing which conversations feel rewarding and empowering; then we have to see how the elements that led to that positivity can be used explicitly. When we learn to be attentive to these elements, our conversations begin to improve. Whether you want to have better conversations about passions, problems, or perspectives, you can influence the underlying patterns that bring about successful dialogue.

Box 4 Appreciative Inquiry

Appreciative Inquiry is an affirming and uplifting pattern of asking questions that helps people to build on the past and envision the future by discussing the positive aspects of the present situation. The cycle invites conversation on:

- Where would be the best place to go in this conversation? (Destination)
- What is positive about where we are now? (Discovery)
- What would you like to see improving in the future? (Dream)
- How shall we make this dream come true? (Design)
- How will we be when we are in this new wonderful world? (Destiny)

The basic idea is then to build—or rebuild—perspectives and dynamics around what works, rather than trying to fix what doesn't. This positive focus makes for inspired conversations that foster relationships and synergy.

4.5 *Questions*: How to Shape the Question to Bring Optimal Dialogue

At the center of most conversations, there is a question. What's happening? Where are we going? Why do you feel that way? When we have a good question, conversation just happens. By improving the questions we ask, we evoke curiosity, encourage exploration, and stimulate conversation. Asking questions is not just a chance to hear other people's views, it is an affirmation that we believe in others' potential. The better the questions we ask, the better the conversations we have. What question would you like to explore?

When inviting a large group of people to investigate a subject, we can make better use of their time by refining and then announcing the questions in advance. That way, they'll have time to think about it, and they can jump into conversation as soon as they arrive. You may invite a few members of the group to define the question in a focus group as part of the planning process. This can be an insightful experience that lets people explore the context and connect to the question. The challenge is that it takes a lot of time and may go in unexpected directions. If you would like to let the group shape the discussion questions, you can start with an icebreaker question like "Which question attracted you to this event?" Questions can also reorient a group midway through an event, for example, "What questions are now becoming important?" You can also reenergize a group with "What do you need now, to make this conversation come alive?" Finally, at the end of the session, you can ask: "What question would you like to think about for a few weeks, before we reconvene?"

Box 5 Shaping the Question that Will Bring Conversation

Here are some of the questions to ask yourself while shaping your question into a conversation starter:

- Is this question relevant to the real life and real work of the people who will be exploring it?
- Is this a genuine question—a question to which we really don't know the answer and are genuinely open to?
- What "work" do I want this question to do? (What conversation, meanings, and feelings may this question evoke for people?)
- Is this question likely to invite fresh thinking/feeling? Is it familiar enough to be relevant and unique enough to be special?
- What assumptions or beliefs are embedded in the way this question is constructed? Are my or others' views biasing the responses that will follow?
- Will this question generate hope, imagination, engagement, action, and new possibilities? Or will it a focus on old stale issues?
- Does this question leave room for new and different questions to be raised as the initial question is explored?

4.6 *Facilitation*: How to Identify, Develop, or Bring in Facilitative Group Leaders

The better the facilitation, the better the outcomes. Talented facilitators can work with you to design the process, run the sessions, and create an atmosphere for dialogue. Ideally, you will find facilitators within your organization, but often groups opt for bringing in an external professional facilitator. Whether you are looking to do it yourself, find a colleague, or bring someone in, be mindful of the core competencies needed.

Support the emergence of "Facilitative Leaders" by noticing, nurturing, and nudging people who have the ability to facilitate dialogue. You can use the skills and behaviors promoted by the International Association of Facilitators (IAF 2018) as a benchmark. Ultimately, you want these skills to be inside your organization, the instincts for better dialogue to be in all your staff—the debriefing of the Dialogue Experiments will help with this, but it is also important to celebrate these skills and hold them up as model behavior for others.

The International Association of Facilitators[1] promotes six competencies that facilitators need in order to be successful. Go to their website to understand facilitator qualities, to see what to expect from a facilitator, or to find a facilitator near you.

- Create collaborative client relationships.
- Plan appropriate group processes.
- Create and sustain a participatory environment.
- Guide group to appropriate and useful outcomes.
- Build and maintain professional knowledge.
- Model positive professional attitude.

4.7 *Leadership*: How to Collectively Build Direction, Alignment, and Commitment

As you think about your organizational transformation, and the role Dialogue Experiments can play, think about your leadership as a shared activity. Instead of putting the entire weight of leadership on yourself or individual managers, it's important to examine how the whole system is involved in making leadership happen (McCauley 2018). For example, the exchanges between employees and their managers, the interactions among peer managers or team members, the quality of relationships throughout the organization, the actions of teams and committees, and the use of existing organizational structures and processes can all impact whether leadership happens or not.

Rather than thinking about leaders and followers, consider a team of collective leadership. Teams are more motivated when they define their common goal together and co-create their approach to get there. By encouraging a systemic and collective view, you can start talking about the factors that have influenced the organization to become what it is. Dialogue brings out in the open the hidden assumptions and beliefs that can control an organization and prevent any meaningful change (McGuire and Palus 2015). Years of valuing hierarchy, status, authority, and control—even implicitly—can lead to assumptions and behaviors that are out of date, unnecessary, unhelpful, and at odds with stated goals and strategic direction. As you look at organizational transformation, it is important to think about your wide network of people, your leadership culture, who all have a hand in leading change.

In the whole system perspective, leadership happens in the interactions and exchanges among people with shared work. Leadership can be happening within teams, work groups, task forces, divisions, communities, and whole organizations. Leadership can be happening across teams, levels, and functions. Regardless of the group, for leadership to happen, the interactions and exchanges among people have to create:

[1] See iaf-world.org for more information.

- *Direction*: Agreement on what the collective is trying to achieve together
- *Alignment*: Effective coordination and integration of the different aspects of the work so that it fits together in service of the shared direction
- *Commitment*: People who are making the success of the collective (not just their individual success) a personal priority

These three outcomes—DAC for short—make it possible for individuals to work together willingly and effectively to realize organizational achievements. So when we say making leadership happen, we mean making direction, alignment, and commitment happen. In fact, we think the only way to know if leadership has happened is to look for the presence of these three outcomes (McGuire and Palus 2015).

4.8 Designing a Dialogue Experiment

If you have change in mind for your organization, think about who you could bring together to discuss your intentions. Review the foundations above, which support the dialogue-based initiatives, and then start small. Here are the basic requirements for customizing the Dialogue Experiment to your context—be creative!

- *The question*: What question will ignite conversation and sense of possibility?
- *The invitation*: How will you elicit curiosity and desire to be in conversation?
- *The atmosphere*: How will you open the session and frame the conversation?
- *The activity*: How much time will you allow, and what will you do with that time?
- *The harvest*: How will you handle debriefing and the sharing of results?

Finally, remember to keep track of the preparation, actions, and results in a journal. These projects work best over time, but as we progress, it is easy to forget where we started. It is helpful for the participants if you can have them recall the path they have taken together, complete with the moments of trepidation and excitement, trials and breakthroughs, and challenges and achievements—as well as the progress they have made toward a place where they know what helps, hinders, and encourages dialogue.

5 Transforming Your Organization

Dialogue is a key to organizational transformation, but for it to work, the dialogue has to be real. People easily spot inauthenticity and manipulation. If the dialogue is authentic, people will feel free to put the organization into question, and this may move your project in an unexpected direction. It is important that you enter into the journey as an investigation.

5.1 Let Yourself Be Transformed

When new managers arrive and want to change everything, people can have that "here we go again" feeling—does the new manager not know people have been working on this issue? Recognizing the issues, and getting people talking about them, is important. To make these conversations real, one must enter them open to being transformed.

As you discuss your organization, try to limit your assumptions, understand the many views on the subject, and accept that it might be you who needs to change. By being open and able to shift your own behavior, you invite others to do the same and enable a much better dialogue. While the conversation may be unpredictable, it is much more likely to lead to lasting transformation.

5.2 Work on It Collectively

Transformation is not something you do *to* people; it is something you do *with* people. Build a team with collective leadership who can take a whole system perspective on the organization. To have the ripple effect needed, you will need critical mass. Invest time in your core team—facilitative leadership takes more time, but sometimes we need to slow down to move faster.

Ensure you have representation of the different parts of your organizational system in your team. Look not only for functional leads but also for people who reflect the diversity of views in your organization. Including a variety of voices in the project from the start will help you later, as people start noticing who is involved and who they can turn to, to get involved.

Finally, think about bringing in a facilitator. We have seen many projects driven by determined leaders who did value dialogue, but whose staff saw them as distant, cold, or tough. Having a soft hand as partner can bring more inclusion and intimacy.

5.3 Do Your Own Experiment

The spirit of experimentation sets the tone for curiosity and possibility. People are rightfully skeptical of initiatives designed to change things; experiments carry less risk. Steer clear of edicts and opt for experiments.

What Peter and his organization experienced was truly a transformation, but it started with a simple experiment among a few people—an experiment you can do too. Shape a question that you think your organization needs to discuss, and invite a few people to talk about it.

After an hour or so, ask your group to reflect on and share insights on the three questions:

- What helped you get into conversation, and why is that important?
- What hindered your conversation, and why is that important?

- What did you learn about being in conversation, and why is that important?

Summarize your insights and apply what you learned to your next get-together. It is that simple: *you become what you talk about.*

References

Brown, T. (2009). *Change by design: How design thinking transforms organizations and inspires innovation*. New York: HarperBusiness.

Ernst, C., & Campbell, M. (2011). *Boundary spanning leadership (CCL Organizational Leadership Whitepaper Series)*. Retrieved from http://www.ccl.org/leadership/pdf/research/BoundarySpanningLeadership.pdf.

Ernst, C., & Chrobot-Mason, D. (2011). *Boundary spanning leadership: Six practices for solving problems, driving innovation, and transforming organizations*. New York: McGraw Hill.

Friedman, R. (2011). The use of appreciative inquiry in organisational change. *Evaluation Journal of Australasia, 11*(1), 20–25.

IAF. (2018). *Core competencies of facilitation*. Retrieved from https://www.iaf-world.org, https://www.iaf-world.org/site/professional/core-competencies.

Isaacs, J. B. (2005). *The world Café: Shaping our futures through conversations that matter*. San Francisco: Berrett-Koehler.

Lipmanowicz, H., & McCandless, K. (2014). *The surprising power of liberating structures: Simple rules to unleash a culture of innovation*. Seattle, WA: Liberating Structures Press.

London, J. (2018). *Stimulating conversation*. Retrieved from http://jeffer-london.com/, http://jeffer-london.com/#.

McCauley, C. (2018). *Making leadership happen with direction, alignment, and commitment*. Retrieved from https://www.ccl.org/, https://www.ccl.org/articles/white-papers/making-leadership-happen-alignment/.

McGuire, J. B., & Palus, C. J. (2015). Toward interdependent leadership culture: Transformation in KONE Americas. Retrieved from https://www.ccl.org/articles/white-papers/toward-interdependent-leadership-culture-transformation-in-kone-americas/.

McGuire, J. B., & Rhodes, G. (2009). *Transforming your leadership culture*. Hoboken, NJ: Wiley.

Orland-Barak, L. (2007). Convergent, divergent and parallel dialogues: Knowledge construction in professional conversations. *Teachers and Teaching, 12*, 13–31.

Pea, R. D. (2004). The social and technological dimensions of scaffolding and related theoretical concepts for learning, education and human activity. *The Journal of the Learning Sciences, 13* (3), 423–451.

Stavros, J. M., & Torres, C. (2018). *Conversations worth having: Using appreciative inquiry to fuel productive and meaningful engagement*. Oakland, CA: Berrett-Koehler.

Thiagarajan, S. (2006). *Thiagi's 100 favorite games*. San Francisco, CA: Pfeiffer.

Tutu, D. (2004). *God has a dream: A vision of hope for our time*. New York: Doubleday.

Wanous, J. P., & Youtz, M. A. (1986). Solution diversity and the quality of group decisions. *Academy of Management Journal, 29*(1), 149–159.

Jeffer London facilitates dialogue among people working together. From the lunchroom to the boardroom, he brings people together to discuss how to produce shared results in a satisfying manner. He runs a research project called "Stimulating Conversation: How to Get People Talking." Besides his advisory role at CCL®, he sits on the board of the International Association of Facilitators.

John B. McGuire is consultant, author, and speaker focused on advancing leadership in an interdependent world. He is a senior fellow at CCL® where he leads the transformation practice. He is the author of *Transforming Your Leadership Culture* (2009, Jossey Bass) and numerous articles on mediated dialogue, interdependent leadership, change, and transformation.

Filipa Santos works at the interconnection of technology and people with a focus on the future and emotions. She designs learning and organizational development programs at CCL® where she supports clients to be agile, grow, and thrive. With a background in clinical psychology and a curiosity about the diversity of humanity, she develops programs that help organizations shape the human side of their strategy.

“Disruptive Story-Work” as an Intervention for Organizational Transformation

Yannis Angelis

Abstract

As most organizations strive for a sustainable growth in an era of constant disruption, some of them fall into a paradoxical mythology, the one that they are capable of keeping control and ensure safety for their business as they grow toward the future, the same way they did in the past. It is inevitable that a different approach is needed to detach themselves from the paradox that this mythology provokes and move toward a new narrative which reflects the multidirectional forces of the environment that they operate. In this chapter, such a supportive approach is deployed. It consists of a serious game concept combined with a first-person story development, where disruptive interventions are used as ignitions and catalysts for the individual and collective future stories to emerge. Additionally, it addresses the needs and curiosities of the key players to take a courageous and influential role in the future stories that they create inconsiderably of any blueprint that may exist. This happens also independently of the level of disruption that occurs in the system that they operate. The outcome of this approach is characterized by a high level of emotional engagement and connection among the various members of the organization. In this sense, it becomes the starting point of one being transformed in the present accordingly, and start sensing already that the desired future turns out to be more conceivable to occur.

In a paradigm from the corporate learning domain, the abovementioned concepts and methodology have been used and are explained in detail in this chapter. This case study taps into the idea of safely experiencing a disruption in a story-based setting, which inspires people to reveal their creative self fearlessly and liberate their potential for the creation of new future narratives in their area of expertise. The implementation of the “Disruptive Story-Work” method has

Y. Angelis (✉)
Beyond Storytelling Partners, Bad Homburg, Germany
e-mail: yannis.angelis@beyondstorytelling.com

© Springer Nature Switzerland AG 2019

J. Chlopczyk, C. Erlach (eds.), *Transforming Organizations*,
Management for Professionals, https://doi.org/10.1007/978-3-030-17851-2_12

shown that the newly crafted narratives have a transformational effect. Thus, they could be effectively used as the core elements for a strategic approach toward a desired future for the organization as long as the individual stories are respected and woven into the projected future.

1 Introduction

Story is "a thing that does" rather than "a thing that is."[1]

What future could be more challenging than the future that doesn't include me? In a highly polarized social and political landscape where diversity is currently challenged, what is the story which illustrates the richness of my identity? In a disrupted future, where I am said to be replaced by cleverer than me machines, how will I be transformed? On an individual level, these are burning questions, which reflect the existing narrative of the world we live in as it is portrayed and communicated by science, technology, and foresight research and as it is amplified by the media.

People are influenced and carry these concerns in their everyday work. At the same time, they find themselves in a constantly changing environment, which challenges them to adapt and adjust accordingly. Eventually, we know that organizations are transformed when their people are transformed. Now the core question that arises is "how do we support people in organizations to find their transformational path towards a desired future, which includes and involves them in the design and realization process of it?"

The "Disruptive Story-Work" is a road map for igniting the journey and reaching this point of mutual transformation of organizations and their people. It is a methodology that benefits organizations, communities of practice, and individuals by supporting the co-creation of the desired future no matter the level of disruption that takes place at anytime through this journey. The core characteristic of the method is that it takes into consideration the current disruptive domain that people operate in. It exaggerates it in a safe enough environment that a serious game framework provides, and then it bolsters people to craft their personal stories and roles in a disruptive future. Working with future personal stories, considering and "embracing" the disruptive environment that these will exist in, induces an inclusive transformational modality, where one becomes capable of shaping their positive role and imagining their life in service to something larger than themselves at that distant time.

[1]Quote by **Brian Boyd** an Irish author and professor of literature at the University of Auckland, New Zealand.

2 Terminology and Hermeneutics

2.1 Disruption and Its Nuances

Real disruption is a wound to the integrity of an identity.[2]

Most people when they hear the word "disruption" they contract and feel a kind of discomfort. They even may move to a place of fear due to the unknown consequences and the harshness that the word introduces. That makes sense when we think of its definition as "...an interruption in the usual way that a system, process, or event works."[3]

If we break it down to its components, the word disruption consists of two parts: dis + ruption. Both components carry a kind of strong negative flavor. The first component "dis" comes from the Ancient Greek prefix (δυσ-), and when added to the front of any word, it induces a bad condition or capacity of the second component, which comes after.[4] It is such a strong prefix that even if the second component is a word with a positive notion, it totally nullifies it (e.g., harmony-disharmony). When the second component also has a negative notion, then the prefix "dis-" intensifies it. This is what happens with "ruption," a word of Latin origin from the fifteenth century, which is defined as a breaking or bursting open.[5]

What is it that renders disruption as a major factor today in the organizational parlance and reality as well? Disruption really works in a level beyond change. This is the level of transformation, which is deeper and vitally related to the identity, the core values, and the culture of an individual and an organization. This is a complicated matter to deal with in an organizational system. Change is situational and relates mainly to the external environment, or to what can be seen. Transformation is psychological and can be understood as an inner reorientation or as what can be deeply felt and supports us to incorporate the change that takes place in the environment. This is the level where disruption affects and challenges individuals and systems to grow or vanish. It does that in a radical, acute, and emerging way. In a healthy growing environment, it creates the space and issues an invitation for a profound intentional transformation rather than a superficial adaptive change. This kind of transformation gets softened as and when it progresses through the development of personal future stories crafted in present time. The intentional transformation can ignite those stories because it carries the flame of people's vision and mission. These stories open the possibilities for oneself to reorient themselves, their goals,

---

[2]Quote by **Nik Beeson**, a Canadian change navigator and co-founder of the "Toronto Change Days" conference.

[3]Definition of "disruption" from the Cambridge Business English Dictionary © Cambridge University Press.

[4]https://en.wiktionary.org/wiki/%CE%B4%CF%85%CF%83-

[5]https://www.thefreedictionary.com/Ruption

and their business via an innovative detour. The old identity is dying and a new one becomes ready to emerge.

2.2 Story-Work and Its Variables

Story is the human operating system.[6]

"Story-Work" literally means "working with stories." It goes beyond storytelling. It approaches stories from a holistic point of view as an opportunity for creating a field for an intentional change. The similarity to disruption is that it also works deeper at the level of transformation. Several experts in this area have integrated "Story-Work" in their offer and profession, weaving a rich tapestry of various slightly different but complementary approaches and meanings. Shawn Callahan defines it as the combination of three story-related attributes: storytelling, story-listening, and story-triggering. All three play a role in discovering an insight and influencing a decision-maker to act (Callahan 2016a). He also considers it "as a core competency" to forge genuine relationships and develop the ability to understand and work with emotion in organizations that want to be agile and adaptive (Callahan 2016b).

Chené Swart, in her excellent book *Re-authoring the world: The narrative lens and practices for organizations, communities, and individuals* refer to it "as a way of being." It frames it as the essential work which supports us moving from dominant problem-saturated narratives[7] to alternative ones as we comb through "...moments and relationships in our history where that problem narrative was not true, was not the whole truth or was not present. Those different moments and relationships become the seeds for exploring the alternative narrative" (Swart 2013).

Yannis Angelis has developed "Story-Work" mainly as part of an instructional design model for corporate learning (the "Lov-e & Car-e-osity™" model) to inspire participatory processes to take place for best leveraging the informal learning inside an organization. The "Story-Work" process is metaphorically renamed as "Story-Odyssey™," and it includes story-witnessing, story-listening, story-harvesting, collective story creation, and lead storytelling. It is an invitation to a series of wanderings filled with notable experiences and hardships in service of a story-based transformation process where various organizational actors are involved (Angelis 2017a). Stephanie Bachmair distinguishes it from classical storytelling, which has the focus on sending a message, by defining "Story-Work" as a dialogue. "The narrative becomes a vehicle for working on awareness, transformation, and relationship. "Story-Work" is the sensitive listening, powerful authentic telling, and creating together" (Bachmair 2017). Lastly, Mary Alice Arthur translates "Story-

[6]Quote by **Mary Alice Arthur**, a story activist and host for organizational and social change.

[7]Dominant problem-saturated narratives as defined by Chené Swart (2013) are narratives in which the person is seen as the problem, the reason for the problem, and the cause of the problem.

Work" to Story Activism which means "...working with stories for positive systemic shift and to use critical intelligence on pertinent issues. ...creating spaces where the right story can take people to the next life-giving future that they're longing for" (Arthur 2015).

All the approaches mentioned above have two things in common: firstly, "Story-Work" goes beyond storytelling and includes it, and, secondly, they consider "story" carrying such an unwavering power so that when working with it, it induces an essential transformation impact both on individual and organizational/social layers.

2.3 Disruptive Story-Work

If you want to be an agent of disruption, first become its subject[8]

"Disruptive Story-Work" goes beyond "Story-Work" and disruption by weaving them together. It delves into the amplifying nature of a synergy leveraging the effect that both have on a transformational process. In this sense, the impact and the quality of the transformation are intensified.

The core attribute of this method is a process which invites and accommodates the generation of disruptive future scenarios by prompting several disturbances to the system that one examines. These disturbances may cause more complexity and even also reach a point of challenging the existence of the system in examination itself, as they may provoke the total elimination of many of its elements! What follows next is the triggering of personal stories and their integration into the created scenarios. In this way, the new individual and collective stories become the catalyst for the transformation of the organization no matter the kind and the intensity of the disruption, which has initially challenged them. The whole process along with respective paradigms is unfolded in the next pages of this chapter.

Evidently, apart from the implementation of the "Disruptive Story-Work" as a method to support the transformation of organizations and their strategic plans, there are already existing narratives around disruption which are affecting the way that organizations move toward the future.

3 Organizational Narratives Around Disruption and Related Metaphors

As organizations walk the path toward their future, they carry with them some heavy baggage like the one of permanent success and vigorous growth. Thus, for some of them, it becomes challenging to be receptive to new alerting messages especially when these come from a world, which is unmapped and yet unknown as the disruptive world is. They also struggle to become agile toward any change needed

[8]Quote by **Whitney Johnson**, author of the book *Disrupt Yourself*.

to take place or is desired in this new environment. In most cases, they are high jacked by something familiar, which has been "tested" before and creates a kind of safety. The paradox that is taking place here is the belief that an organization can grow safely in a disruptive environment the way it did it in the past. The existing outdated narrative in this kind of organizations is expressed as "never change a winning horse in the middle of the race." And the metaphor that takes precedence over the mind-set of the whole organization is still of "the one who runs to win the race."

However, disruption breaks down the door of such organizations and reaches their heart in an unprecedented way. As a consequence, it forces the existing narrative and metaphor to change, no matter the time that it may take for that. The latest years, according to my experience, especially in the area of "for profit" organizations, three common narratives of disruption seem to be in a prominent position. The first one is *a fear-inducing narrative* which has two non-desirable consequences:

(a) It forces the organization to try to maintain the status quo and avoid any kind of reflection on the signs of the future that already appear in the present, so as to act accordingly. Most of the times, the underlying pattern of this risk-avoidance attitude is a desire for safety.

    The late British philosopher Alan Watts used a great metaphor to draw how such a condition is really ineffective: "To hold your breath is to lose your breath." Also, Otto Scharmer, a senior lecturer at MIT, names this kind of response to disruption as "muddling through" and "downloading" (Scharmer 2017).

(b) It provokes the design of adaptive strategies in a careless way toward the future. Adaptive change sounds like "I do it because everybody else does it so it must be OK to do it as well." The metaphor which visualizes this attitude is of an avalanche with fermented hands coming out of it trying to manipulate a steady direction as rolling fast down the hill.

The second is *a propitiating narrative*, which aims to weave itself into positive and desired organizational processes like innovation and transformation. This has led the corporate and lately the "start-up" world to an overuse or even misuse of "disruption" as a term attempting to provide a narrative of a positive rapid-induced change that may lead to an innovation mind-set. In this case, what it is mostly experienced as a result is disruption becoming another "airy-fairy" buzzword in this corporate narrative. What is named innovation in the organizational setting, it actually is an "improvement" of existing functions and products. The metaphor depicted here is of a growing giant but with legs made of old dried clay. Both the narratives mentioned above are dictated by a "disruptee"[9] mind-set.

[9]Disruptee: the one who is disrupted.

The third disruptive narrative is *governed by a disruptor*[10] *mind-set.* In this case, an intentional approach to future strategy, with agile characteristics, a culture of curiosity, and a "lean-into" the unknown mind-set are the driving forces for a conjectural, however, desired future. The metaphor illustrating this moving-forward narrative is the mirror image of a face on the surface of a lake, artistically transfigured by the ripples caused by the person's finger touching the water.

There is a fourth disruptive narrative met mostly in the social domain, however also in an organizational one, and it's worth mentioning. Otto Scharmer names this as a "moving backward response" (Scharmer 2017). A current example is the story behind the phrase "Let's make America great again" as it is told and felt by a big part of the US society, means the story of going back to past structures and behaviors to feel great as a citizen of my country. This seems to be a *problematic narrative,*[11] and it is mainly invented as a form of social control. Even the word "again," the way it is used here, implies a hidden blame; somebody is responsible that we are not anymore "great." However, if we think of "story" as an intervention, we know that depending on the mind-set and the inner state of the storyteller, the meaning that the listeners make out of the story varies, even if the story remains the same (Angelis 2018). So, could we imagine how different would have been the impact of "Make America great again" if an *alternative narrative*[12] that fosters the interconnection, shapes the identity, and enhances the pride of a nation through diversity would have informed the creation and experience of that story?

Reflecting on those mentioned above, it becomes evident and inevitable that in our era, disruption is shaping the current organizational narrative in many ways, and it can reform the culture and identity of the organization accordingly. At the same time, it ignites and catalyzes the new story which wants to emerge, making it able to "bury down" the old one as it affects a routinely functioning identity and a well-established culture in several ways. It also challenges organizations to find new approaches, to set new goals, to inspire their people, and to include them in the co-creation of the new future story of the organization. An issue that could emerge here is that "...most of the time the goals are too aspirational, too far in the future, too platitudinous and that just creates a seedbed for continued illusion or delusion or both. ... where you can take actions that create stories you first need to understand the context, in particular, you need to understand the dispositional state of the system and the likely energy cost of attempting change" (Snowden 2018). As long as this happens, it might better serve a new story that carries the energy and values of people's mission and dream for the future, toward unmapped disruptive territories in a, respectively, fast pace. A recent example of this at its best is the "Working Out

[10]Disruptor: the one who disrupts.

[11]Problematic narratives are at the core of the narrative practice as it is informed by the work of **Michael White** and **David Epston**, originators of narrative therapy.

[12]Alternative narratives are at the core of the narrative practice as it is informed by the work of **Michael White** and **David Epston**, originators of narrative therapy.

Loud," a concept of building relationships through narration and social collaboration.[13]

The "Disruptive Story-Work" method considers and reforms appreciatively all the abovementioned disruptive narratives. By introducing a serious game working frame, it detaches them from their rigid connection to the present and expands their limited meaning and container. Continuing after with the "I-stories" approach, it provides the individuals and the communities a safe enough space to reflect, work upon, and "re-author"[14] those stories that will guide them toward a desired luminous future. Whereby "re-authoring" is meant that "...when an individual or a community takes back the pen in the active participation and writing as authors of their lives, they are actually re-authoring their lives in alternative, preferred ways that grow from their gifts, skills, values, hopes, and dreams" (Swart 2013).

4 The "Disruptive Story-Work" Method in Praxis

Any useful statement about the future should at first seem ridiculous.[15]

4.1 Description and Operational Context

This chapter elaborates on the design and structure of the method as it is implemented in the format of an interactive workshop in an organizational context, where the mandate is to support the transformation of existing structures and processes of a function inside the organization toward the desired future. Corporate learning is used here as an example, but the method can be applied in any organizational function or societal context. Any group of people working in organizations or being closely related to them can experience the method as long as the main goal remains to design a desirable future that includes them, even if this has to take place in a disruptive and complex environment. In the next paragraphs, I use the term "actors" to describe these people because the method not only inspires them to re-author their future lives but it allows for immediate implementation of what has been experienced and learned during the workshop starting acting already in the present, in their everyday work.

[13]The WOL concept has been developed by John Stepper and is described in his book *Working Out Loud: For a Better Career and Life* http://workingoutloud.com/en/the-book/.

[14]"Re-author" is a term in narrative therapy that was introduced by **Chené Swart** (2013) into the organizational field.

[15]Quote by **James Allen Dator**, professor, and director of the Hawaii Research Center for Futures Studies, Department of Political Science, University of Hawaii at Manoa.

4.2 The Design

The "Disruptive Story-Work" method combines basically a serious game concept with a storytelling and story-building approach. It invites the various organizational actors, to form small working groups. Then, through a highly interactive process, actors are addressed to not only explore challenges and opportunities around the future of corporate learning but to support inventing it through several disruptive interventions.

The first step is to work with disruptive scenarios where the actors are taking over various roles different and distant from the current ones of their professional life. In this sense, as there are no such competencies in the room, the participants become creative and playful in a noncompetitive safe enough space. The task that they have to work upon is something that any know-how skills and competencies are not expected or requested. For example, the Learning and Development managers are given the roles of airplane designers or building constructors and work on respective mini-cases. They are introduced gradually and smoothly to the process, and they become able to liberate their creative self and deal fearlessly with the disruptive scenarios.

In the next step, the actors are introduced to the serious game arena. A serious game goes beyond entertainment and fun and is designed for training and development in areas like education, business, science, and much more. Serious games are a subgenre of serious storytelling, which is "...storytelling outside the context of entertainment, where the narration progresses as a sequence of patterns impressive in quality, relates to a serious context, and it's a matter of thoughtful process" (Lugmayr et al. 2017).

In the "Disruptive Story-Work" method, the working ground is a serious table-game. Table 1 shows its core features.

Let's examine these features and their functions in detail.

(a) The set of cards representing the elements of the system that we aim to explore its future is the core item of the game. They demonstrate the knowledge we have about the system that we want to intervene on, disruptively. In our case study, the system is the corporate learning, and its elements are referring, for example, to what type of learning we explore, what kind of content is referring to, what are

Table 1 Features of the serious table-game, as part of the "Disruptive Story-Work" method (author's own table)

Serious table-game features	Function
A set of system element cards	To define and distinguish the elements of the system for exploration
A set of disruptive interventions cards	To "disturb" the system's elements
Actors' roles	To enhance the creative process of building future scenarios using the game cards

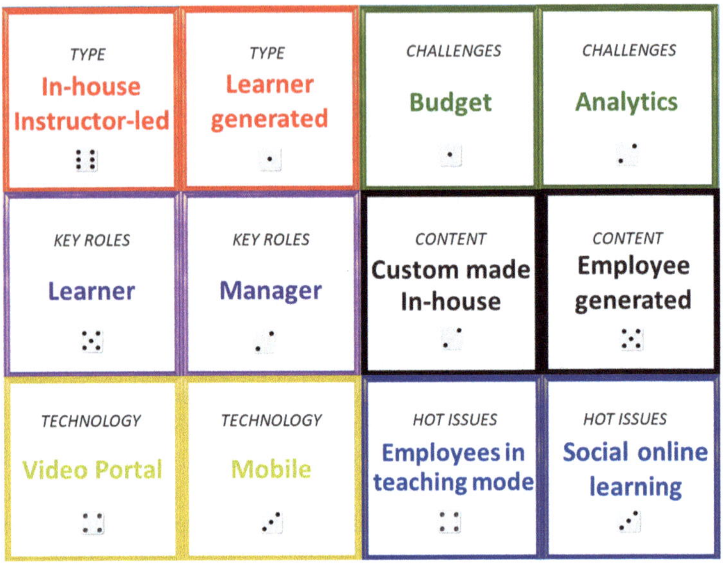

Fig. 1 A sample of a set of system element cards as used in a corporate learning case study (author's own figure)

the hot issues, who are the key roles in this system, what is the supporting technology, and what are the current challenges. Other system elements could be the provider of the learning solutions, the sponsor who is covering the costs, and much more. They are all printed on hard paper cards with a color definition. Some of these cards referring to the system of corporate learning are shown in Fig. 1.

(b) The set of disruptive intervention cards are used to disturb the system's elements.[16] Each card represents a disruptive action, which will "hit" the various system's elements, one at a time, via a random process with the help of a pair of dices. Some of these interventions and the respective actions that the actors have to perform are shown in Table 2.

(c) Actors are also addressed to take various game roles in their working groups to support the creative process. Three specific game roles take place. For the reader who is familiar with the concept of archetypes, these roles also represent 3 of the 12 basic archetype figures.[17] See Table 3.

[16]The basic idea of this game has been developed by Cornelia Daheim in Future Impacts (https://future-impacts.de/en/about/).

[17]Archetypes represent fundamental human motifs of our experience as we evolved; consequentially, they evoke deep emotions. The psychologist Carl Gustav Jung defined 12 primary types that symbolize basic human motivations: ruler, creator/artist, sage, innocent, explorer, rebel, hero, wizard, jester, everyman, lover, and caregiver.

Table 2 Various disruptive interventions and the respective actions as part of the "Disruptive Story-Work" method (author's own table)

Disruptive interventions	Scenario development basis
Replace	Replacing an element of the system not necessarily with something that it already exists
Reconcile	Find ways so that two contradictory situations or beliefs related to an element could now exist and work together
Rocket	The element progresses extremely fast toward ultimate success
Redirect	Keep the element but find ways to guide it to another direction which could still support the system
Resurrect	Bring back to use an attribute of an element that had disappeared or ended
Collapse	The element collapses and it doesn't exist anymore
Rebel	Fight against the authority that the element may represent
Resource	To provide the element with something supportive

Table 3 Actors' roles, archetypes, and respective functions performed (author's own table)

The role	Description of the role	The archetype
The disruptor	Looking at a situation from an entirely different perspective than is the norm. Visionary, brilliant, and taking absolutely nothing for granted. Challenging every assumption and fundamental principle and strategies even those that may appear to work well within the current horizon	The creator
The challenger	Challenging the scenarios created by the other members in the group overturning what seems not to work as a new scenario. Their bravery can give rise and bring into focus alternative better scenarios	The rebel
The spy	Visiting the other groups and "borrowing" ideas from their scenarios, bringing them back to their own group for discussion, analysis, and potential adaptation	The sage

Now let's describe briefly how the game starts and evolves in its different steps.

1. Playing: With the use of dices, a disruptive intervention "hits" an element of the system. This is the starting point of the future scenario building as a consequence of what kind of disruption has hit the system. Actors working as groups and performing their game roles are creating future scenarios, which contain metaphors, fictional elements, and illustrative imaginaries. What becomes impressive at this stage is the emergence of entirely unprecedented working cases due to the combination of a system element and a disruptive intervention at random. There have been examples where actors were addressed to work creatively in cases, which would seem today so alien, like the collapse of managers, the crash of the L&D departments, the reinvention of budget, the

rocket of employees in a teaching mode, or even the collapse of the learners. This opens up a field for the creation of future scenarios, which would have been very difficult to articulate via a cognitive process based just on trends and current practices.

2. Mapping: After actors come up with and harvest several innovative future scenarios, they are asked to map them regarding how possible is it for these scenarios to be reenacted in the future and if so what the level of their impact is expected to be. A harvesting wall is an arena for this process. The outcome of the mapping process indicates the most possible and most impactful scenarios.
3. First-person stories: During this last step, the actors imagine and build their future personal stories inspired by the selected future scenarios. For this, the "I-stories" approach is proposed as the appropriate methodology, and it will be explained further in the next pages.

Additionally, in the next paragraphs, we will dive deeper into the philosophy and transformational impact of the method and explore the correlation of an individual story and a futuristic scenario.

5 The Transformative Benefits of the "Disruptive Story-Work" Method

5.1 Processes of Transformation

There are several behavioral responses evoked by the method which affect and influence actors toward a transformational outcome.

The first response that takes place is about *getting familiar with disruption as an intervention*, as led by the actors' initiatives in the system's environment. For this to be effective as a transformational process, the first thing needed is a safe enough space for the actors to operate, like the one that an experiment or a workshop concept offers. Secondly, actors need to take over and perform several disruptive roles in order to develop future scenarios starting with the ones that are distant to their current professional roles. In the corporate learning example that we introduce here, the L&D experts start working together as airplane designers. It is the co-creation of "... a learning experience by designing and guiding an experiment that is risky ...in terms of trying out new behavior but conducted in a safe environment, thereby enabling to garner new perspectives on the issue" (Siminovitch and Van Eron 2006). The introduction of a strategic serious game allows actors to deploy their collaborative skills playfully and enter a less rational or cognitive planned behavior in the exploration of the disruptive tasks that they work with. What is experienced in these workshops is that when people play they enter a state of effortless concentration and flow where it tends to become respectfully easy to deal with the disruptive scenarios that are emerging during the game process (Angelis 2017b).

As actors gradually liberate themselves from a cognitive procedure at the moment, the following behavioral response is that *through playfulness, they start becoming really creative* producing brand-new ideas, scenarios, and future stories, which may even sometime seem quite revolutionary. A serious game as a process enables a safe environment for people to experience and "play" with disruption. The actors' creative self blossoms in various moments throughout the process, starting slowly at the beginning and evolving up to the end where they have to create and tell the story about the outcome of their work. Actors mentioned that their creative self is mostly felt when they start taking pleasure in the process in the "Here and Now" rather than only taking pleasure and focus on the outcome about the future they want to create.

The next behavioral response is birthed when *physical actions are introduced to support actors embody the disruptive interventions*. This is an essential step in the process as it enhances the acceptance of disruption as an inevitable and sometimes desired intervention. An example from the organizational field referring to the implementation of the method is described in the next paragraph in order to explain better this response.

The Global Learning & Development (L&D) managers and experts of an international chemical enterprise are participating in a respective workshop with the goal to define the strategic action plan for the transformation of the L&D in their company in 2025. The "Disruptive Story Work" is used as a method to support their goal. The participants are playing the serious game with enthusiasm and they have already come up with interesting scenarios. They follow the process where a disruptive intervention card "hits" an element card and ignites the creation of the respective future scenario. One of these disruptive intervention cards, which I intentionally give to the participants to use sometime in the middle of the game and not from the beginning, has a particular effect. After picking up this particular game card, they are asked to move away from their chairs and table and go to a specific quiet place which has been created for them for this part of the game. They lean back into sofas and armchairs, take a minute of silence, breathing in and out, take one more minute for reflection and finally let their imagination to fly for the scenario they have to build. This intervention becomes very effective as it is a combination of brainstorming and body-storming techniques. At this particular moment, we have a very peculiar process outcome as one of the participants nicely described: "...we became able to disrupt the disruption!"

This progressive experience of several behavioral responses is already giving birth to and sustains a transformational process. This is guiding the actors to the last phase of the method, the generation of the personal stories which will be integrated into the disruptive scenarios related to the future of the organization or of the system under examination.

5.2 The "I-Stories" Approach and Its Benefits

A day will come when the story inside you will want to breathe on its own.[18]

[18]Quote by **Sarah Noffke**, an American author.

The "I-stories" is the part of the method that comes after having created and mapped the future scenarios at the end of the serious game process. The "I-stories" are applied as follows:

Each of the key actors is asked to come up with their imagined personal story inspired by the co-created future scenarios. They pick the scenarios that resonate the most with them, and they build and narrate a first-person story. The story needs to answer questions like:

- Who am I going to be in this future time that the scenario describes?
- What will be my life and professional role?
- In which way I will be influencing the environment at that particular time?
- Where do I see in this future my dreams, values, and passion?
- What purpose will I be serving and what issues will I be trying to solve?

This set of questions invites actors to an episodic future thought[19] journey, which helps them make sense of a future in which they belong and they contribute. A future projection without a story seems to have no meaning. When during the next step, they start sharing these stories, they are entering a territory of collective sensemaking of an organizational future which includes them. Because sensemaking makes sense when "you are part of the story." This is essential for a future strategic planning, and it accommodates a decision-making process.

What expands the value of the "I-stories" is that the more attractive, intimate, and meaning-making these stories are, the more these will energize actors to take respective action in the present. These actions in the "here and now" create moments to be recorded and used in a future time. So, actors start creating the desired future now and the transformation of the individual and the organization is on its way! The next step is to start combining these stories in a collectively created foresight scenario, which could also be part of the strategic plan of the organization at least for the respective system that it was examined through the serious game process. These scenarios become fundamentally important for the overall organizational narrative because they envelop the actors' stories. Only when people can locate themselves inside the story of the organization that they work for, they will be willing to participate in its present and future narrative (Margolis 2009).

There is a paradox regarding the pairing of scenario and story: when we think of a scenario as the result of a foresight research and recording, it is a kind of "story" illustrating possible events or predictions more likely to take place in the future. At the same time "The Story" with a capital "S" means the integration of the individual narrative is most of the times missing from it. The "I-stories" approach comes to close this gap. It breathes life into what seemingly is perceived as dry and soulless foresight reports and scenarios, and it gives people a visceral sense of the future. Moreover, in the case of the "Disruptive Story-Work," the actors are going through a

[19]Episodic future thought is the ability to simulate specific personal episodes that may potentially occur in the future (Szpunar 2010).

transformation after they have first gone through a creative fearless process of developing these scenario cases.

Another exciting aspect of the method is that since the re-authored futures[20] are enriched by the creative spirit of the role-plays/archetypes that were introduced during the serious game, they may reveal a nostalgia for unlived lives, unexplored identities, and roads not taken. As children, we have the opportunity to play at other roles; as adults, we often find ourselves confined by the ones we have been assigned or the ones we have chosen. Yet we remain forever curious; what other stories could I have been part of? (Bauman 2017). The "I-stories" opens that space for the unmet and left behind life possibilities to be transformed through stories in the service of a luminous future. In this way, the process could also work as an indirect invitation to the past memories that can be woven into the future story. Neuroscience research has revealed striking similarities between remembering the past and imagining or simulating the future, including the finding that a common brain network underlies both memory and imagination (Schacter et al. 2012).

The actors, by having already reached a level of trust in the process during the previous stages, they become able to work with the "I-stories", making it easier to avoid any *used future*, which is defined as someone else's future or the one based on an old mind-set about the future (Inayatullah 2008). In contrast, it opens a possibility of moving toward a *disowned future* which may make them feel uncomfortable in the beginning because it contains roles that they don't own in the present or because it seems too disruptive to their current identity. However, it is crucial for shaping the desired future. The "I-stories" offers the space to meet and become familiar with the disowned futures by supporting the creation and further evaluation of *alternative futures* as it addresses people to include their first-person stories and test them thoroughly. Ella Saltmarshe nicely depicts that "...We can use story to create immersive scenarios of the future that engage people on an emotional and intellectual level. This work can make the possible feel more probable, bring new perspectives that challenge the goals and mindsets of a system, and enable the transformation of rules and processes" (Saltmarshe 2018). In general, as people become part of the future that they are creating, they may also develop a caring attitude toward it, which could be translated to a more conscious approach to the desired future already through their present initiatives and actions.

Elaborating more on the disowned futures, neuroscience findings show that our brain is wired to see our far future self as a stranger, one that we don't like. First-person thinking, as it happens in the "I-stories," connects us to our future self because the brain fires up faster, with more flexibility (Abraham et al. 2008), making more connections. It is like creating a future memory which is easier to remember after (Benoit et al. 2014). The core question which is explored is: How will the future transform me and my organization? The metaphorical image which could define the new dominant narrative is: I am experiencing my future life in a virtual reality

[20]Re-authored futures are the new scenarios that derived by the integration of the individual stories into the organizational disruptive scenarios.

chamber where the protagonist is a stronger and better version of me. The more I practice it, the more familiar it gets. This is a way that our future is transforming us now.

5.3 The Parallel Process Phenomenon

No sneeze is ever free of the leaf that fell on the other side of the hill.[21]

All the abovementioned take place in a present environment, introducing a transformative process for the actors. At the same time, they may have an impact on the actors' behaviors in the future more likely in a way as they have been experienced at a present time. The scientific background of this assumption comes from the theory and research on Gestalt[22] psychology and therapy.

Gestalt practitioners and theorists have elaborated on the *parallel process phenomenon* to diagnose aspects of the relationship between different interrelated systems, like the one of a therapist and a client, a client and his/her working environment, and a therapist and her/his supervisor. "Studies of parallel process…show that what happens in one system has an impact on another…" (Davies 1997).

In the case of the "Disruptive Story-Work" method, two interrelated systems are taken into consideration:

A. The actors and the process they follow all through the workshop
B. The actors and the work they (will) perform every day in their working environment

In regard to the parallel process phenomenon via interrelated systems, what is happening in system A (actors in the workshop environment) may likely have an impact on an interrelated system B (actors in their working environment in real life) in the same way as experienced in system A. So when actors are invited or even challenged to reach an effective level of creativity, experience the creation of disruptive scenarios, and then include their personal stories in them, it is more likely that they will reenact those learned attitudes in their everyday tasks and duties in the same way. Further on, they will be able to even reform their present using several disruptive interventions and imagined stories as an attitude learned during the workshop experimentation (Angelis 2017a). The more they work with that, the more they learn to *take advantage of the unanticipated changes or crises of the*

---

[21]Quote by **Norman Mailer** (1923–2007), an American novelist and political activist.

[22]Gestalt therapy is a form of experiential psychology that focuses on elements of the here and now. It takes a holistic approach to healing and personal growth. What we experience as we develop and how we adapt to that experience come into the present as unresolved problems. The purpose of Gestalt therapy is to teach people to work through and complete these unsolved problems. People learn to follow their ongoing process and to experience, accept, and appreciate their complete selves fully (Sinay 1997).

experimenting environment as opportunities to review and decide how to respond to these changes in the real world. This opens a field of new narratives to be created.

6 Epilogue

> Each time you change an "it" and a noun, to an "I" and a verb, you get a 0.0001% of your potential back.[23]

In the above pages, a methodology which combines Story-Work and Disruption as catalysts for organizational transformation has been described. The combination of sophisticated tools like the serious table-game and the "I-stories" take the various organizational actors into a transformational journey, which furthermore becomes the vehicle for the transformation of the organization.

Actors perform under a flow of creativity in the service of the creation of future scenarios and later on first-person stories, which are woven into the organizational strategic plans. A disruptive mind-set "is also learned" and assimilated better as everything takes place in a safe-enough environment as a workshop where several roles are tested could be. Then what is learned can be reenacted in a real context situation in a, respectively, free-flowing way.

Though it was not possible to include in detail all elements of the "Disruptive Story-Work" methodology within this chapter, we eventually managed to demonstrate clearly the backbone of the process and its beneficial effect for the individuals and the organization. So, what are the overall learning points and benefits that the various actors obtain as they participate in this process? In a nutshell:

(a) They learn the importance of "slowing down" as a process for enhanced creative thinking.
(b) They level up their creativity and imagination.
(c) They realize that creative foresight work becomes fun and thus more attractive for an engaging outcome.
(d) They learn how to transform seemingly challenging disruptive scenarios to positive ones by fueling them with their optimistic personal future stories.
(e) They become more collaborative as several given roles enable them to "work" in a safe noncompetitive environment.
(f) They experience oral storytelling as a vehicle from the individual to the collective, from the personal to the community.

The "Disruptive Story-Work" constitutes a gate opener for learning to think and act in an innovative way. Embodying disruption as an intervention for change guides various actors toward a path of responding rather than reacting to various incidences

[23]Quote from **Fritz Perls**, a German-born psychiatrist and psychotherapist, who has developed along with his wife, Laura Perls, in the 1940s a form of psychotherapy called "Gestalt therapy."

in complex and fuzzy organizational environment. Re-authoring the future of a system inside such an organization, in the form of co-created future scenarios, which envelop the actors' first-person stories, becomes a fearless, transformative, and strategically important process for the organization.

Note *The author's use of "they" acknowledges gender fluidity and non-binary descriptions of gender.*

References

Abraham, A., Schubotz, R., & von Cramon, D. (2008). Thinking about the future versus the past in personal and non-personal contexts. *Brain Research, 1233*, 106–119.

Angelis, Y. (2017a). E-learning with impact: The role of narrative structures and methods in designing and delivering E-learning in a corporate environment. In J. Chlopczyk (Ed.), *Beyond storytelling* (pp. 303–332). Germany: Springer Gabler.

Angelis, Y. (2017b). *Introducing disruption as an intervention to co-create the future of corporate learning*. Retrieved October 18, 2018, from https://www.linkedin.com/pulse/introducing-disruption-intervention-co-create-future-learning-yannis/.

Angelis, Y. (2018). The magic of working with stories. In W. Tonninger, J. Chlopczyk, & Beyond Storytelling Team (Eds.), *Re-authoring futures. Con-texts* (pp. 124–127). Austria: Almblitz.

Arthur, M. A. (2015). *Taking back the power of your story*. TEDx talk at Kiel University. Retrieved May 11, 2018, from https://www.youtube.com/watch?v=ilMwoEdqMTs.

Bachmair, S. (2017). StoryWork – mit narrativer Arbeit Führungsund Organisationskultur transformieren. In J. Chlopczyk (Ed.), *Beyond storytelling* (pp. 81–107). Wiesbaden: Springer Gabler.

Bauman, Z. (2017). *Retrotopia*. Cambridge: Polity Press.

Benoit, R., Szpunara, K., & Schactera, D. (2014). Ventromedial prefrontal cortex supports affective future simulation by integrating distributed knowledge. *Proceedings of the National Academy of Sciences of the United States of America, 111*(46), 16550–16555. https://doi.org/10.1073/pnas.1419274111.

Callahan, S. (2016a). *The role of stories in data storytelling*. Retrieved February 17, 2018, from https://www.anecdote.com/2016/08/stories-data-storytelling/.

Callahan, S. (2016b). *Putting stories to work: Mastering business storytelling*. Melbourne: Pepperberg Press.

Davies, R. (1997). Parallel processes in organizational consulting. *The British Gestalt Journal, 6*(2), 114–117.

Inayatullah, S. (2008). Six pillars: Futures thinking for transforming. *Foresight, 10*(1), 4–21. https://doi.org/10.1108/14636680810855991.

Lugmayr, A., Suhonen, J., Sutinen, E., et al. (2017). Serious storytelling – a first definition and review. In *Multimedia Tools and Applications* (Vol. 76, p. 15707). New York: Springer Science & Business Media. https://doi.org/10.1007/s11042-016-3865-5.

Margolis, M. (2009). *Believe me: A storytelling manifesto for change-makers and innovators*. New York: Get Storied Press.

Saltmarshe, E. (2018). *Using stories to change systems*. Retrieved May 25, 2018, from https://ssir.org/articles/entry/using_story_to_change_systems.

Schacter, D. L., Addis, D. R., et al. (2012). The future of memory: Remembering, imagining, and the brain. *Neuron, 76*(4), 677–694. https://doi.org/10.1016/J.NEURON.2012.11.001.

Scharmer, O. (2017). *Trump and transforming capitalism: Making our movement see itself*. Retrieved June 12, 2018, from https://www.huffingtonpost.com/entry/trump-and-transforming-capitalism-making-our-movement_us_5a06ef9ce4b0f1dc729a6b39.

Siminovitch, D., & Van Eron, A. M. (2006). The pragmatics of magic: The work of gestalt coaching. *OD Practitioner, 38*(1), 50–55.
Sinay, S. (1997). *Gestalt for beginners*. New York: Writers and Readers Publishing.
Snowden, D. (2018). *Context in narrative work*. Retrieved September 24, 2018, from http://cognitive-edge.com/blog/context-in-narrative-work/.
Swart, C. (2013). Re-authoring the world: The narrative lens and practices for organizations, communities, and individuals. Randburg: Knowres Publishing.
Szpunar, K. K. (2010). Episodic future thought: An emerging concept. *Perspectives on Psychological Science, 5*(2), 142–162. https://doi.org/10.1177/1745691610362350.

Yannis Angelis is a story practitioner, an organizational development and change trainer, and a narrative futurist. Yannis' work is informed by the principles of Gestalt psychology, narrative therapy, theory U, and the Art of Hosting. He facilitates teams on storytelling, collaboration, learning strategies, innovation, and future making in a disruptive world. He designs and hosts events on organizational change and personal transformation. He also coaches individuals on their career path toward a luminous future. He is the co-author of the *Beyond Storytelling*, a book which demonstrates how to work with stories in organizations and communities and as an individual. He has designed the "Lov-e & Car-e-osity™" model, a participatory process mainly for e-learning development. The model leverages principles and tools from Gestalt therapy, positive psychology, behavioral economics, theory U, gamification, and Story-Work with informal learning.

We Are All Chimeras: Promoting Unity, Diversity, and Ingenuity Through Metaphorical Storytelling

Brooke Hessler and E. D. Woodworth

Abstract

Using a mythological creature, the Chimera, and organizational metaphor analysis to guide the process of crafting stories, we focus this chapter on how professionals can, and do, envision themselves and their organizations as multifaceted or hybrid organisms—reflecting on their past, present, and future possibilities. The aim is to find the value of diversity of particular communities while also promoting collective, collaborative identities. This chapter and workshops on this topic have been inspired by Gareth Morgan's *Imaginization* and a case study at an art and design college where students, faculty, and staff adopted as the school mascot the Chimera: a fantastic beast from Greek mythology that has come to mean any dazzling, seemingly impossible, or ingenious combination of things.

From this beginning, we imagine what could be possible if we embraced the Chimera as a personal icon. In today's world full of possibility, with the opportunity to craft multiple personae on- and off-line, we choose to playfully explore characteristics that might seem too risky for everyday life. The more we exercise our ingenuity to create alternative versions of ourselves, the more we are able to reach beyond our ordinary limitations and expectations—to envision new stories and new futures.

B. Hessler (✉)
California College of the Arts, San Francisco, CA, USA
e-mail: bhessler@cca.edu

E. D. Woodworth (✉)
Air War College at Air University, Maxwell Air Force Base, AL, USA
e-mail: ewoodwor@aum.edu

© Springer Nature Switzerland AG 2019

J. Chlopczyk, C. Erlach (eds.), *Transforming Organizations*,
Management for Professionals, https://doi.org/10.1007/978-3-030-17851-2_13

1 The You We Cannot See: A Metaphorical Thought Experiment

If you had to choose, would you describe yourself as a dragon or a honeybee, and why? This may sound like a party game or an arbitrary question, but what if your whole life depended on the answer?

Perhaps it does.

Both creatures can fly: one swoops and soars; the other dances and dips. Both are reputedly fierce if provoked, defending their territories. The dragon is typically viewed as magical and majestic, long-lived, solitary, and destructive; the honeybee is visible mainly as a drone, short-lived, and communal, a builder and pollinator, but it might also be a queen. In popular culture, the dragon and the honeybee are portrayed as both dangerous and endangered; both inspire art and poetry, fear and lore. If you had to identify with just one, which would it be?

When we pose this sort of question to workshop participants, most make a quick intuitive choice and then, on further reflection, begin to resist seeing themselves as just one or the other. Because the more we contemplate the characteristics of a creature, the more complicated that creature becomes.

The characteristics we see in ourselves can greatly influence how we interact with others in work and in life. They affect the expectations we set for ourselves and our organizations. These characteristics can give us resilience in the face of professional upheaval; they can be sources of self-awareness and continuous self-improvement.

The simple exercise of imagining yourself as a dragon or a honeybee is likely to have sparked associations in your mind, instances where you behaved as one or the other. Perhaps in rejecting both images (or in combining them), you were able to identify a pattern in your personal or professional life.

What do we learn from this exercise? That behind every metaphor is a story about who we are and what we wish to be.

In this chapter we introduce a process called strategic metaphorical storytelling, an approach that helps people reimagine, rethink, and re-author their futures by reflecting critically, creatively, and even playfully about their professional identities. We begin with a brief overview of the strand of metaphor theory that most directly influences our approach: the organizational metaphor theorizing and methodologies developed by Gareth Morgan and by the researchers and practitioners who have challenged, enriched, and applied it worldwide over the past 30 years to engage the storied experiences of organizational life.

We connect this narrative work to the storytelling of classical mythology, where gods and monsters express metaphorical truths about the heroic journeying of the human experience. One mythical monster, the chimera, deserves special attention as a dynamic model of the possibilities and perils of pursuing an unconventional and multifarious life. We trace this creature's narrative history from ancient Greece to contemporary blockbuster films to show how its cultural significance has been hidden in plain sight: few may be familiar with the term chimera, yet it turns up everywhere from young adult novels to scholarly articles on transgender posthumanism.

To discuss how the chimera has been used in organizational storytelling, we share a case study from California College of the Arts, where a college mascot is being transformed into a vehicle for promoting unity, diversity, and ingenuity during a period of dramatic institutional change. Finally, to demonstrate how the chimera can inspire reflection and dialogue in your own professional context, we share the basic framework, method, and tools of our strategic metaphor workshop, a makerspace-style approach that invites each participant to invent their own unique chimera and explore how its story can help them compose the next chapter of their professional odyssey.

2 Metaphorical Storytelling in Organizations

Visualize your workplace. If you had to choose, would you describe your working group as more of a team or a troupe, a band, or a crew? How about your organization: is it more of a zoo or a circus or a well-oiled machine? These are the kinds of reflections made famous by management researcher Gareth Morgan, whose book *Images of Organization* (Morgan 1986) spawned a movement in organizational behavior theory and scholarship based on the power of metaphor.

Simply put, a metaphor is a way of seeing something in terms of something else. Scholars in cognitive psychology, philosophy, and sociolinguistics have taught us that metaphors profoundly influence the way we conceive of the world as well as the ways we communicate about it. In particular, George Lakoff and Mark Johnson, in their seminal work *Metaphors We Live By* (Lakoff and Johnson 1980), demonstrate that we can learn much about ourselves and our communities by studying the assumptions behind our everyday metaphorical concepts, such as LIFE IS A JOURNEY or ARGUMENT IS WAR or LOVE IS A GAME.

Likewise, within our professional environments, familiar metaphorical concepts like A CAREER IS A LADDER or A BUSINESS UNIT IS A TEAM or even A MANAGER IS A LEADER communicate and shape expectations that may or may not fit with our current experiences or aspirations. Gareth Morgan advocates applying metaphor as a flexible lens for highlighting and discussing salient aspects of these interactive spaces. In other words, organizational metaphor theory is about recognizing and deploying metaphor to delve into an organization's structures and characteristics, with the understanding that metaphor gives us a shared vocabulary and framework for storytelling, inquiry, and intervention. Any given organization can be viewed productively in terms of many different metaphors; the aim isn't to limit our view to just one lens but rather to skillfully apply each lens to bring "complementary and competing insights" into focus (Morgan, *Images*, 1986, p. 6). So, your working group might be productively viewed as both a team and as a circus; your role may be viewed as coach or captain today and lion tamer or tightrope walker tomorrow.

To more systematically apply metaphorical lenses to organizations, Morgan initially proposed eight key images: the organization as a machine, the organization as a living organism, the organization as a brain, the organization as a culture, the organization as a political system, the organization as a psychic prison, the organization as a locus or condition of flux and transformation, and the organization as an instrument of domination (Morgan 1986). Over the years, numerous scholars of organizational development, communication, management, and sociology have continued, challenged, and extended his work (see, e.g., Grant and Oswick 1996; Ortenblad et al. 2016, 2017). Some have generated new metaphors through evaluation and critique, conceptual development, imagination and fantasy-focused approaches, and/or empirically focused research and observation. For example, Jonathan Pinto uses the metaphor of the Icehotel to explore how an organization can be paradoxically always changing and different yet also the same (2016). Morgan continues to encourage such innovations, reminding managers and researchers that a diverse toolbox of metaphors is best. After all, if you only have a hammer, everything looks like a nail (1997, p. 263).

In his later work, *Imaginization*, Morgan aims at a broader audience of professionals and equips readers for another shift in focus: from the organization to the individuals who comprise or depend on it. The book begins with a comic-style illustration of a pig surrounded by characters meant to represent a butcher, an artist, a wolf, a farmer, a veterinarian, a philosopher, a cleric, and a small child. Morgan's question is: What is the pig? (1997, p. 3). Each character represents a very different relationship and set of assumptions regarding the animal. Likewise, we might adopt the pig's point of view and imagine the extent to which each character represents a threat, a playmate, a healer, and so on.

Just as metaphors can influence our assumptions about one another, they can shape our assumptions about ourselves. Morgan explains that "people and organizations tend to get trapped by the images that they hold of themselves ... genuine change requires an ability to see and challenge these self-images in some way" (1997, p. 288).

In many ways, our development of strategic metaphorical storytelling is influenced by the image of Morgan's pig confronting multiple perceptions and self-perceptions. Another influence is classical mythology, where an animal is never just one thing: a monkey is also a god, a crane is a queen, and a horse is a centaur or hippogriff. This last image is the focus of our workshops: the magical creature who emerges from human imagination to communicate our hopes and fears. Creatures that reveal their diversity in unexpected ways are both awesome and frightening. Today they are called chimera, named for an ancient mythical beast.

3 The Power of the Chimera: Its Origin and Ubiquity in Metaphorical Storytelling

As with all metaphors, exploring the context of the chimera helps us appreciate its power and persistent influence. In Greek mythology the chimera is typically a combination of a lion, a goat, and a serpent. Representations of the chimera have been found on pottery, in mosaics, in jewelry, and in sculpture. One of the most beautiful is the *Chimera of Arezzo*, an Etruscan bronze from about 400 BCE. Scholars

Fig. 1 The Etruscan Chimera of Arezzo (Photograph by Carole Raddato (2015). Creative Commons BY-SA 2.0) https://de.wikipedia.org/wiki/Chim%C3%A4re_von_Arezzo#/media/File:The_Chimera_of_Arezzo,_c._400_BC,_found_in_Arezzo,_an_ancient_Etruscan_and_Roman_city_in_Tuscany,_Museo_Archeologico_Nazionale,_Florence_(22636282885).jpg

trace this mythical beast from Greek colonies established in Southern Italy from the eighth century BCE (Fig. 1).

The *Chimera of Arezzo* has the body and head of a lion. A goat's head emerges from mid-bank with a long neck; the goat has a slight beard but substantial horns. Sharp barbs run down the back from the goat head and neck to the rear of the body, where the tail is a serpent with its head at the end. This chimera is in agony; it's been wounded in the neck of the goat, and the ribs and haunch of the lion body. The serpent, the goat, and the lion all seem to writhe in pain. The lion's mouth is wide in a silent scream. The goat's head flails. The serpent's mouth is biting or grabbing one of the goat's horns. Its body is crouched down to protect its belly, but the sense of the bronze is that there could be some fight left in this creature.

According to this narrative, the chimera is ultimately defeated by the hero Bellerophon, riding the winged horse deity Pegasus. We know of his grand endeavor from sculptures and other visual texts left to us but also from Homer's *Iliad*, in a story-within-a-story told by Bellerophon's ancestor Glaucus to Diomedes (Fagles 1998, pp. 199–203).

The notion of the chimera doesn't cease to leave a cultural trace with the Etruscans or the Greeks or the later Italians, but it continues to appear in illuminated manuscripts in the Middle Ages, often transforming to meet the needs of those storytellers. Demons are often depicted with chimeric bodies, feet of a goat, head of a lion/goat, wings, and serpents for tails. Manticores, a similar creature to the chimera, but from Persian myth, appear in modern culture as part of Harry Potter's world in *Fantastic Beasts and Where to Find Them*, which explains "The Manticore is a highly dangerous Greek beast with the head of a man, the body of a lion and the tail of a scorpion. As dangerous as the Chimaera, and as rare, the Manticore is reputed to croon softly as it devours its prey. Manticore skin repels almost all known charms and the sting causes instant death" (Rowling 2001, p. 28).

In another young adult verse, author Rick Riordan creates a scene with a chimera in the first book of the Percy Jackson and the Olympians series: *The Lightening Thief* (2006, pp. 197–211). Percy, the protagonist, meets a woman and her Chihuahua who turn out to be Echidna and her child, the chimera of myth. Of course, Percy must do battle with the chimera to protect innocents. Percy escapes but not without a poisoning bite from the serpent tail. (He lives and appears in many more books by Riordan.)

A modern film appropriation of the chimera metaphor comes through the *Mission Impossible* franchise. In *Mission Impossible:2* (2000), the Impossible Mission Force agent, Ethan Hunt, must hunt down the seller of a deadly virus called Chimera. The cure is called Bellerophon. Naturally, Agent Hunt wins managing to secure Bellerophon which defeats the Chimera.

Transitioning from fiction to nonfiction, chimera is also a term used by writers to denigrate innovative science by smearing research with that monstrous metaphor. The use of the word can be enough to suggest that research is wrong-headed and evil, tainted by the unnaturalness of such a Frankenstein's monster. But that's not the whole story. It's also a term used to understand difference and possibility: chimerism in modern science refers to any living thing that is composed of cells from two or more organisms. Scientists continue to learn from naturally occurring instances of chimerism. For example, Rachael Rettner, in a 2016 "Live Science" article for *Scientific American* writes about research on humans with more than one set of DNA markers, like those who absorb a twin in utero, pregnant women, and those who undergo bone marrow transplants. She acknowledges the negative use of chimera as applied to human/animal experiments. Words change with time and become "good" and/or "bad" depending on their context and utility. Some words live on, past their inception, to end up meaning the exact opposite, but not chimera. It has come to mean both its monstrous past, reckless science, and the current possible life-changing science of saving lives.

Developments in technology have brought us another category of chimera, the cyborg—a combination of human and machine. In an era when most of us depend intimately on technology, posthumanist scholar Donna Haraway argues, "we are all chimeras, theorized and fabricated hybrids of machine and organism" (1991). As such, we are all monsters, creatures living in ways that are "unnatural"—which calls into question the role or idea of the monster itself. This shifting perspective on the chimeric self has inspired and empowered artists, activists, and other seekers of social justice to reframe discourse about our innate, inevitable, and intentional diversity and the "monsters" in our midst. As transgender scholar Sam Doran observes, "There is a great deal of power in owning one's whole identity, a power which risks dilution in narrative consolidation" (2016). Seeing ourselves as chimera can foster self-awareness or self-authorship; presenting our chimeric identities to the world can be a step toward personal and social transformation.

4 Case Study: We Are Chimera/I Am Chimera-Made—Organizational Metaphor Storytelling in an Art and Design College

Our inspiration for the strategic use of the chimera for professional and organizational reflection comes from California College of the Arts (CCA), an art and design college in the San Francisco Bay Area of California. When viewed through the lens of organizational metaphor analysis, a college is particularly interesting because its stakeholders include both people who currently work, study, and collaborate with it, as well as other groups, such as alumni: graduates of the college who remain invested in its reputation, culture, and identity. The focal point of our study is the college mascot, an image keenly tied to the experiences and identity branding of students (past and present), as well as to faculty and staff, and to prospective students through, for example, marketing campaigns and community events featuring the mascot. To keep this discussion within a manageable scope, we will offer a brief history of CCA and its use of the Chimera as its mascot and then concentrate on the recent developments that appear to be most pertinent to the topic of re-authoring futures through organizational storytelling.

The college was founded as California College of Arts and Crafts (CCAC) in 1907 by German cabinetmaker Frederick Meyer, who was inspired by the Arts and Crafts movement to educate students in a studio environment that would prepare them to deeply know the history, craft, and social significance of art while training them as sophisticated designers, illustrators, and makers in a wide field of endeavor. Over time, the curriculum grew to encompass studio practices ranging from ceramics to creative writing, from digital animation to glassblowing, as well as critical visual studies, community arts activism, and so on. The campus was situated on the east side of the San Francisco Bay, primarily occupying a park-like estate in the city of Oakland. In the 1980s it began offering courses in architecture and design on a second campus in San Francisco, which is on the west side of the Bay. The institution continued to evolve in ways that reflected its geographical and economic ties to San Francisco, Silicon Valley, and the global market for design professionals. In 2003, California College of Arts and Crafts (CCAC) changed its name to California College of the Arts (CCA), and by 2006 the college's leadership announced their intention to begin the process of unifying the two campuses, moving all programs from the verdant enclave in Oakland to a new urban builtscape in San Francisco.

As of the time of this case study (2017–2018), CCA exists as two campuses with two distinct personalities, divided by the San Francisco Bay. The move to San Francisco is scheduled to be completed by 2021. The physical upheaval of the campuses is a bold decision that remains controversial to some stakeholders within various groups (alumni, faculty, staff, students, and citizens close to the Oakland campus). In many ways, particularly to those passionate about the craft heritage of the school and its local legacies, Oakland and CCAC represent an identity quite different from San Francisco and CCA.

The community is further fragmented by its day-to-day logistics. Every day, many students spend hours in buses and trains traveling across the Bay from one campus to the other, perhaps having morning classes in one city and then afternoon or evening classes or studio work in another. Additionally, the student population has become more diverse every year; nearly 40% are international students. The organization's challenge is to bring a sense of stability amid the fluctuation and to cultivate an identity that can be meaningful to everyone, one that honors the past and future of the college and one that fosters unity while valuing diversity. An important component of this cultural challenge is the college mascot and its presence in campus life.

Perhaps it is fitting that, in the way of such mythical creatures, the chimera mascot's origin is a bit of a mystery at CCA. It seems to have arisen in the college consciousness by the 1980s, showing up in artworks and campus lore, becoming the title of a literary magazine that some say was inspired by the gargoyle chimeras of Notre Dame Cathedral featured in the photography of Vilem Kriz (1948), a noted surrealist and beloved CCA instructor. The Notre Dame chimeras are metaphysical guardian demons, beautiful and grotesque. CCA students were inspired by the dual nature of these creatures and for decades created various interpretations of the chimera as totem, as informal mascot, as character study, and so on. In 2006, CCA's Student Life Organization amplified students' desire to cultivate a sense of school pride by officially adopting the chimera as the college's mascot (Seko 2017). Students were invited to create their own versions of the creature while also developing a common chimera mascot logo for use campus-wide.

An early phase of this purposeful use of the chimera for organizational storytelling was aimed at giving students a common way to articulate their shared values as a community. Known as the "We Are Chimera" campaign, organizers—including both college staff and student leaders—used banners featuring multiple definitions of the term, along with phonetic symbols to help everyone pronounce it the same way.

The next phase, the "I Am Chimera" campaign, encouraged everyone to come up with their own definitions. Students, faculty, and staff were photographed for individual posters featuring their image, the heading "I am Chimera because I am ..." and a caption of their own choosing; for example, "I am Chimera because I am unconventional" or "I am Chimera because I am a believer that differences are our beauty."

The most recent phase of the campaign, "Chimera Made," is intended to encourage storytelling about how the CCA experience shapes the individuals who study, work, and create there. Everyone who comes to CCA is changed and enriched, by the community. Additionally, this campaign highlights the shared identity of the "maker"—whether one's work is printing or architecture, interaction design, or textiles, all are makers. In this way, the campaign attempts to support the interdependence and equality of artists and designers across all disciplines, whether long-established or comparatively new to the institutional culture.

The current campaign is still under development and involves special attention to the symbolic and physical process of campus unification. First-year undergraduate students entering in Fall 2018 are beginning their experience shuttling between the

Fig. 2 Chimera self-portrait by CCA student Jordan Barbosa (2018). (Used with permission)

two campuses but will graduate from a campus that exists only in San Francisco. To help students creatively explore this change, the Student Life Organization has begun to experiment with a day-long orientation journey that ritualistically begins on the Oakland campus and invites them to join a team of their peers on a scavenger hunt as they trek across the Bay together, taking photographs, sharing experiences, and finding a random artifact along the way that they will ultimately contribute to a sculpture of a chimera—collaboratively and uniquely constructed by hand on the San Francisco campus, alongside their new peers.

Observing this organizational metaphor work-in-progress, some persistent challenges appear to remain: the creature is unfamiliar to newcomers and difficult to explain; also, since a chimera can be a combination of anything, it is harder to imagine vividly as a shared common symbol. Yet these are also the special strengths of the chimera—particularly for an artistic community: the chimera is mysterious and esoteric, a creature that requires a kind of initiation into the community in order to understand, and its ever-changing nature can be perceived as an open invitation to imagine new possibilities. The chimera is the ideal mascot for people empowered to reinvent themselves, their community, and their world (see, e.g., Fig. 2).

The CCA campaign became our inspiration for reinventing a professional development workshop that we had created years ago, based on the classic Hero's Journey archetypes in the writings on comparative mythology by Joseph Campbell, particularly *The Hero with a Thousand Faces* (2008). While the heroes found in world myths can be a rich resource for personal reflection and goal setting, we saw in the chimera a much more complex and flexible protagonist. The chimera's nature as potentially monstrous or misunderstood makes it more relatable as a symbol of human vulnerability and taps the all-too-familiar experience of feeling like an outsider—as someone who does not belong. Composing oneself as a chimera is a way to confront those dimensions constructively and dialogically. We began piloting the workshop with professionals outside our current academic institutions while also drawing upon its methods in our work with undergraduate and graduate students reflecting on their cultural identities and career paths.

5 Chimeric Thinking in Practice: A Strategic Metaphorical Storytelling Workshop

When we create the environment for a workshop on chimeric thinking, our goals are twofold: (1) to empower individuals to seek new ways of naming who they are through the metaphor of the chimera and (2) to help groups define and visualize the multiple dimensions of their organization through the metaphor of the chimera.

Much like Gareth Morgan in *Imaginization*, we encourage the exploration of metaphor to imagine how we are as individuals and then how we fit into a larger group. Unlike Morgan, we scaffold our workshops on a single category of metaphor, the animal/chimera, as a way to more quickly engage participants in the process of creative reflection on their individual and organizational experiences. While our approach and materials are intentionally simple and playful, professional developers and education/cognition scholars will recognize our use of makerspace pedagogy: fostering an environment of hands-on learning in a collaborative environment where participants are asked to literally make objects of their experience—constructing three-dimensional objects and multimodal stories as a way to shift thinking into an open and shared space where it can be viewed from multiple perspectives, altered, hacked, or reconfigured, to generate new iterations and insights (see, e.g., Schrock 2014; Kurti et al. 2014; Oliver 2016). The method and tools are flexible and adaptable as short, 90-minute immersions or as full-day retreats. In Box 1 and 2 we share the outline of each approach, which we distribute to "train the trainer" participants interested in developing their own workshops.

We begin with a short icebreaker, using cards featuring illustrations of mythical and real creatures, to help participants begin to think metaphorically. Each person is given two cards. They are asked to pick the card they most connect with: for example, beaver or oyster, wolf or dragon, octopus or mouse, and griffin or lamb. We then ask them to articulate why they picked one over the other. What characteristics made them choose as they did? Why not the other?

A few volunteers talk briefly about their choices. Conversation ensues. We discuss how such an exercise allows us the freedom to explore and explain aspects

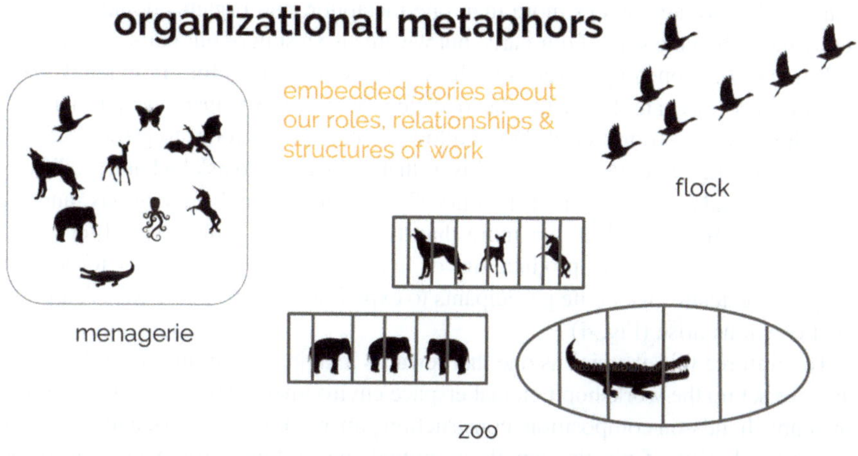

Fig. 3 Sample workshop slide prompting organizational metaphor discussion. (Authors' own figure: Hessler 2017a, b)

of our true nature as individuals and, if extended out to our organization, aspects of our true nature as members of an organization. We can extend this activity by doing the same with the animal cards and participants, picking one over the other regarding their organization. This strategy behind this process is deceptively simple: through metaphor, we can illuminate that which words often fail to express.

As we identify ourselves with the animals, we create a kind of menagerie in the room—a collection of unique creatures, bonded in one space for further study. We invite participants to notice our casual use of that term, "menagerie," asking them to consider what if instead of the metaphor "menagerie," we organized ourselves into a "flock"? What would be the consequence of that? A "flock" is typically a metaphor for groups of birds, so some of us—those of us whose creatures are not birds or winged creatures—might feel left out. When we see a flock, it's more likely to be an assembly of the same kind of bird, too. If we were to call ourselves a flock, we might be implying we are all "birds of a feather who flock together"—highlighting our similarities rather than our differences. In contrast, if we were to organize ourselves by saying, "this place is a zoo," depending on our cultural context, we might be emphasizing our welcoming and diverse gathering (more like the menagerie), or we might be emphasizing that while we are diverse, we are confined or constrained. Perhaps similar creatures or stereotyped creatures are all grouped together for show (like elephants), or perhaps individuals with intriguing but dangerous ideas are displayed but isolated (like snakes). How we name who we are and how we are part of a group, metaphorically, have meaning well past the figurative and influence the literal (Fig. 3).

Returning to the individual creatures, we find that, while it is an interesting game to see ourselves in terms of a specific animal—highlighting a strength or weakness, for example—in fact, we are more complex than any one metaphor can encompass.

Individually, we are always more than one metaphor, and organizationally, we are surely more than the sum of our parts, but we are also a sum of our parts—a chimera.

But as the opening exercise shows us constraints for individuals and organizations, we are left with the question, why choose just one animal, one metaphor? We say, don't do it. Don't allow the constraints room to grow.

The chimera, rather than asking "this or that," allows us to ask "what if. . .?" Why not two animals—the wolf and the butterfly, the dragon and the octopus, and the elephant and the bee? Why not more than two? Why not a dragon/wolf/octopus? Drawing upon the playful productivity of improvisational comedians, storytellers, and jazz musicians, we invite participants to experiment with "Yes, and . . ." and see what creations arise (Fig. 4).

To reinforce this exercise as one that rewards imagination, intuition, and creative play, we set up the workshop in a makerspace environment, with plenty of materials for simple hands-on composition: construction paper, colored pencils, and so on. We also bring dozens of plastic stencils in animal shapes that participants can use to quickly draw experimental combinations of creatures. This "flash assemblage" technique is a pedagogical strategy for helping participants avoid the pitfalls of overthinking and self-criticism (Hessler 2011). We urge everyone to "make now, think later."

The following images show the kinds of chimera made under these circumstances, during a short workshop at the Beyond Storytelling Conference in Hamburg, Germany (2018) (Fig. 5).

The samples illustrate how even when common characteristics are selected (such as wings to fly), participants assemble them in unique ways that reflect or define something important about themselves. Working within a limited timeframe and with shared resources, constraints can become liberating as individuals grab what's closest to hand and interpret the exercise in their own way. Notice how the maker of the "dragonflying dolphin" added words to describe motivational and aspirational

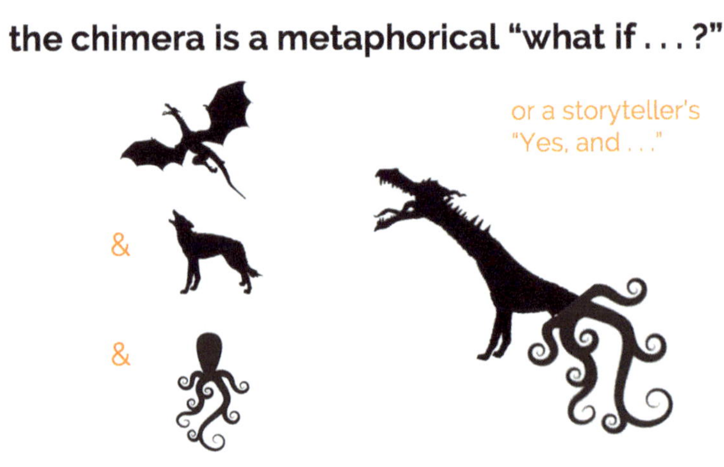

Fig. 4 Sample workshop slide introducing personalized chimera building. (Authors' own figure: Hessler 2017a, b)

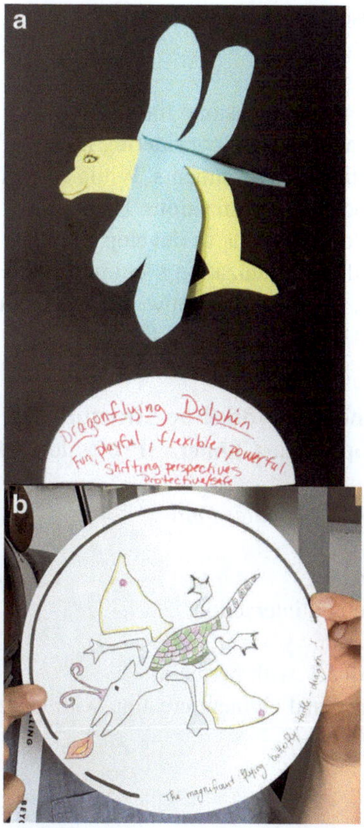

Fig. 5 (**a**) and (**b**) "Dragonflying dolphin" and "Butterfly-Turtle-Dragon": chimeras made as flash assemblage creations. (Authors' own figures: Woodworth (2017))

characteristics. Some of the makers used the templates to draw, some used the templates to cut out and paste, and some added additional elements of their own invention. Some pasted their new creations onto black card stock. Some created their chimera on plain white paper and connected the parts through ink and pencil only.

In longer workshops, following their quick creation of individual chimeras, participants are given time to pause and reflect on what they made and what attributes arose as important. Next, they transition to discussions about what these fantastic creatures (versions of themselves) need to survive or thrive.

We also facilitate flash storytelling exercises with the chimera with prompts like these:

- Spend a few minutes pondering your chimera, and then write about a time when you felt like this creature—or wished you could have.
- Imagine your chimera has been cast as a superhero in a film: what are the special powers that result from this chimera's unique combination of features? How

might the chimera use them to fight for good? What hidden weakness might disarm your chimera?

The chimera can become a touchstone for developing a personal or professional development plan, or as an avatar for considering how you function within working groups or other organizational environments. While an individual can be, metaphorically, a chimera, so too can organizations be chimeric and made up of many chimeras. Participants work in teams to develop thinking around the animals they might put together for their organization's chimera. After creating or comparing organizational chimeras, they consider how their individual chimeras fit into the collective.

Box 1: 90-Minute Chimera Workshop Structure and Materials

90-Minute Workshop: Your Chimera (Professional Development Focus)

Workshop structure: *90 minutes total*

- 10-minute introduction
- 20-minute practice and interaction
- 30–40-minute creation
- 10–20-minute feedback with partners
- 10–20-minute share final chimera creation with large group

In the workshop:

- 12 participants
- 2 facilitators
- 1 session recorder

Workshop supplies:

- 40+ animal templates
- 1 ream of black paper
- 1 ream of white paper
- Multiple sheets colored and/or patterned paper
- 5–6 pairs of scissors
- 7–8 glue sticks
- 2–3 rolls of tape
- 1 dozen black fine-tip markers
- 1 dozen sharpened pencils
- White boards or large adhesive paper for group reflection and chimera galleries

Box 2: 1-Day: Metaphorical Storytelling Workshop

1-Day: Metaphorical Storytelling Workshop

Morning: 9 am–12 pm (individual focus)

The morning session is an extended version of the "Your Chimera" immersion described in Box 1, with more time assigned to introduction, practice exercises, and creation of individual chimeras and more time allowed for deeper conversations during the chimera-sharing:

- 15-minute introduction
- 25-minute practice and interaction with shared results
- 55-minute creation
- 15-minute break (could be taken at any point mid-way through)
- 35-minute feedback with partners within small groups or across small groups
- 35-minute share final chimera creation with large group, posting them to the informal gallery

Lunch break: 12–1:15 pm

Afternoon: 1:15–4:30 (organizational focus)

This session uses the "menagerie" created by the participants, viewing the chimeras as avatars for themselves within the organization. Participants are invited to co-create narratives or visual metaphors to reflect on group configurations and to co-create an actual and/or aspirational chimera to portray the organization itself—all to spark storytelling and strategic reflection on the shared future they might co-author for this place and its people. Approximate timeframes are given for a sample afternoon's sequence of activities.

- 15-minute reflection—thriving within an organization
- 25-minute small group breakout session: configurations and collective metaphors
- 55-minute small group co-creations: organization as a chimera (real and aspirational)
- 15-minute break
- 35-minute comparisons and discussion across small groups
- 35-minute all-group reflection and next steps
- 15-minute individual reflection

The lessons learned so far—from our workshops and from observing the processes underway at CCA—reinforce the importance that individuals be nurtured as unique characters, able to author their own stories even as they contribute to the larger narrative of an organization. Even at institutions like where a diverse, chimeric culture is explicitly promoted, the institutionalization itself can be perceived as a "bureaucratization of the imaginative" that imposes its own limits and hierarchies, privileging some metaphors over others (Burke 1959, p. 225). Ultimately, the goal of any strategic metaphorical storytelling workshop is to spark reflection, reflexivity, and dialogue. No chimera should be fossilized; it should be nurtured as a living, breathing, ever-changing being—the kind of being each person can uniquely bring to their daily life, workplace, and community.

6 Conclusion: Promoting Chimeric Thinking

At a time when virtual reality technologies and video games give us the opportunity to adopt alternative personas, including animal forms, we can choose to playfully explore characteristics that might seem too risky for everyday life. We can simulate the experience of soaring with eagles or vanquishing a foe with fiery breath. We can imagine ourselves transcending human form, adopting a persona that may even feel truer to ourselves than the physical body or conventional social role we've adopted so far. The more we exercise our ingenuity to create alternative versions of ourselves, the more we are able to reach beyond our ordinary limitations and expectations—to envision new stories and new futures.

Viewed another way, the chimera confronts us with what it means to be human—at our best and worst—and enables us to imagine a story beyond the workaday person we appear to be.

The magic of making a chimera, no matter its form, is the magic of storytelling itself; doing it once inspires you to do it again and again, and it helps you become more curious about the people around you: what might their chimeras be, and why?

Likewise, cultivating a chimeric mindset is quite similar to cultivating the mindset of a storyworker (Lambert and Hessler 2018, pp. 86–89):

- **Everything is interesting.** Valuing diverse or chimeric ways of being means *expecting the unexpected* in the people, organizations, and places that surround you.
- **Reflection is critical.** Identifying with metaphorical creatures is intuitive, playful work that can take us to deep places within our memories, fears, and aspirations and help us forge profound connections with others.
- **Learning is social.** Although chimeric reflection can be done solo, in the privacy of our own home or workspace, it is most potent as a starting point for dialogue and co-creation, a way to share, exchange, and listen to stories.
- **Telling stories makes you a better storyteller.** Chimeras remind us that we are all many different things. Composing your chimera and telling its story are a brave, creative performance that can help you articulate aspects of your personality that might otherwise remain hidden. This storytelling may be practice for re-branding yourself or clarifying your goals; it might also be the precursor to

making another chimera that emphasizes other important traits, giving you more stories to write and tell, refining your own story, and seeing where it can take you.

- **Every story matters.** Chimeras remind us to remain compassionate and curious about the multifaceted people we encounter every day and the organizations we/they have created to make a difference in the world. Chimeric thinking is never only about ourselves; it is never only about making and telling. Above all, it is about radical listening.

So as curious, chimeric thinkers, we ask you: As you read this essay, did you find yourself tempted to imagine the chimera you would be? What animals did you choose, and why? What if your whole life depended on the answer to that question?

It very well may.

References

Barbosa, J. (2018). *Chimera self portrait*. Illustration.

Burke, K. (1959). *Attitudes toward history. 1937*. Berkeley: University of California Press.

Campbell, J. (2008). *The hero with a thousand faces. 1949*. Novato, CA: New World Library.

Doran, S. (2016). We are all chimeras: Transgender embodiment as cyborg hybridity. *Rag Queen Periodical*. Retrieved November 2, 2016, from https://www.ragqueenperiodical.com/single-post/2016/11We-are-All-Chimeras-Transgender-Embodiment-as-Cyborg-Hybridity

Grant, D., & Oswick, C. (1996). *Metaphor and organizations*. London: Sage.

Haraway, D. (1991). *Simians, cyborgs, and women: The reinvention of nature*. New York: Routledge.

Hessler, B. (2011, April 6). Assemblage art: Living and learning "third mind" through 3D composition. In *Conference on college composition and communication*. Atlanta, GA.

Hessler, B. (2017a). *Sample workshop slide introducing personalized chimera-building*. Illustration.

Hessler, B. (2017b). *Sample workshop slide prompting organizational metaphor discussion*. Illustration.

Homer. (1998). *The Iliad* (pp. 199–203) (Robert Fagles, Trans.), Penguin (Estimated origins, 10th century BCE), Book 6, Lines 137–282.

Kriz, V. (1948). *Paris*. Photograph. J. Paul Getty Museum. Retrieved from http://www.getty.edu/art/collection/objects/221400/vilem-kriz-paris-american-1948/

Kurti, R. S., Kurti, D., & Fleming, L. (2014). The philosophy of educational makerspaces. *Teacher Librarian, 41*, 8.

Lakoff, G., & Johnson, M. (1980). *Metaphors we live by*. Chicago, IL: University of Chicago.

Lambert, J., & Hessler, B. (2018). *Digital storytelling: Capturing lives, creating community* (5th ed.). New York: Routledge.

Morgan, G. (1986). *Images of organization*. Beverly Hills, CA: Sage.

Morgan, G. (1997). *Imaginization*. San Francisco, CA: Berrett-Koehler.

Oliver, K. M. (2016, March). Professional development considerations for makerspace leaders, Part One: Addressing "what?" and "why?" *TechTrends, 60*, 160–166.

Ortenblad, A., Putnam, L. L., & Trehan, K. (2016). Beyond Morgan's eight metaphors: Adding to and developing organization theory. *Human Relations, 69*(4), 875–889.

Ortenblad, A., Trehan, K., & Putnam, L. L. (2017). *Exploring Morgan's metaphors: Theory, research and practice in organizational studies*. Thousand Oaks, CA: Sage.

Pinto, J. (2016). 'Wow! That's so cool!' The icehotel as organizational trope. *Human Relations, 69* (4), 891–914.

Raddato, C. (2015). *The Etruscan chimera of Arezzo*. Photograph. Retrieved from https://de.wikipedia.org/wiki/Chim%C3%A4re_von_Arezzo#/media/File:The_Chimera_of_Arezzo,_c._400_BC,_found_in_Arezzo,_an_ancient_Etruscan_and_Roman_city_in_Tuscany,_Museo_Archeologico_Nazionale,_Florence_(22636282885).jpg

Rettner, R. (2016). 3 human chimeras that already exist. *Scientific American*. Live Science. Retrieved from https://www.scientificamerican.com/article/3-human-chimeras-that-already-exist/

Riordan, R. (2006). *The lightening thief*. White Plains: Disney-Hyperion.

Rowling, J. K. (2001). *Fantastic beasts and where to find them*. New York: Bloomsbury.

Schrock, A. R. (2014). Education in disguise: Culture of a hacker and maker space. *InterActions: UCLA Journal of Education and Information Studies*, *10*(1). https://escholarship.org/uc/item/0js1n1qg

Seko, N. (2017, December 11). *Personal interview*.

Woodworth, E. D. (2017). *Chimera collages*. Photograph.

Dr. Brooke Hessler is an award-winning educator and Fellow of the DaVinci Institute for academic innovation. She co-founded the Virtual Archives Project, a 12-year transformative learning partnership that trained college students in primary research and multimedia storytelling through hands-on work with museum artifacts. Her scholarship on pedagogy and story-work has appeared in Community Literacy Journal and in Digital Storytelling in Higher Education: International Perspectives (Palgrave 2017), among other journals and collections. After serving 14 years as Carrithers Chair of Writing and Composition at Oklahoma City University, Brooke followed her bliss to the San Francisco Bay Area, where she now teaches writing, digital storytelling, and Yoga for Mindful Learning to artists and designers at California College of the Arts.

Dr. Elizabeth Woodworth is an Associate Professor of Strategic Communication in the Department of Leadership and Warfighting at the Air War College, part of the USAF's Air University at Maxwell Air Force Base. For 10 years, she was on faculty at Auburn University at Montgomery where she was an Honors Associate Professor and the University's Distinguished Teaching Professor, 2015–2018. Elizabeth has been teaching since 1992—courses on multimodal writing, the nineteenth-century, British literature, the detective novel, rhetoric, writing pedagogy, and now, strategic communication. Elizabeth has published on K-university education, writing studies, Victorian poetry and drama, and open education. Since 1988, she has written and published works of creative nonfiction, poetry, and short stories.

How to Look Up When You're Facedown: The Rising Strong Process in Organizations

Katarina Veselko

> *When you are in the middle of a story it isn't a story at all, but only a confusion; a dark roaring, a blindness, a wreckage of shattered glass and splintered wood; like a house in a whirlwind, or else a boat crushed by the icebergs or swept over the rapids, and all aboard powerless to stop it. It's only afterwards that it becomes anything like a story at all. When you are telling it, to yourself or to someone else.*
>
> Margaret Atwood, Alias Grace, 1996 (345–346)

Abstract

We are storytelling animals—story-making is natural to us. This chapter is less about telling business stories and more about living them. Are we as good at living the stories as we are telling them? Do we live the stories we tell and do we tell the stories we live?

This article deals with the less popular part of our business stories—falls and failures. It leans heavily on Brené Brown's work around the Rising Strong™ process, which is a storytelling approach to getting through adversity.

Storytelling is so natural to human brain that it can't be avoided. If we don't actively engage in creating stories that serve us, our brain still makes up stories that are meant to protect us, but very often fail us. Following the pattern of the Hero's Journey, we explore how and why our business stories often try to disregard the hardest part of the process. We take apart the outdated idea that our business lives are somehow less emotional than our private lives. Rising Strong is a story-based process of dealing with falls and failures in private and business lives. Dealing with facedown moments and rising from them are essentially emotional and spiritual practice, no matter where the fall happens. Diving

K. Veselko (✉)
O. K. Consulting, Ljubljana, Slovenia
e-mail: katarina.veselko@okconsulting.si

© Springer Nature Switzerland AG 2019
J. Chlopczyk, C. Erlach (eds.), *Transforming Organizations*,
Management for Professionals, https://doi.org/10.1007/978-3-030-17851-2_14

into the emotional struggle midst-fall, we can explore the narratives our minds create when they lack information and discover the dangers of these stories for our future. This is far from easy, because the Rising Strong is a deeply vulnerable process. There are many challenges we need to overcome to get engaged with our stories, as both our nature and our corporate culture play against letting ourselves being vulnerable.

We follow the Rising Strong process through all three stages, the reckoning, the rumble, and the revolution, using smaller- and larger-scale real business examples of the process at work. In the reckoning, we point out the important questions to ask ourselves to begin the healing process. In the rumble, we present the "shitty first draft," a method of exploration of difficult situations; and we touch upon the most common rumbling topics in the work place. The revolution is the final stage, and this is where our futures are rewritten and organizations are transformed. This is where the story we want to write comes to life.

1 Storytelling: A Trap or a Salvation in Transformation?

Organizational transformation is the most sensitive time for all of its employees. It's unknown, it's vulnerable, and it's uncertain. Humans as storytelling animals will make up stories in any environment, especially in one where we don't know what exactly is going on. Story creation was our evolutionary advantage in the past, where our world was small, mostly familiar, and quite predictable, while most unknown and unexpected things were dangerous. Story creation is in essence recognizing a pattern in events around us and making sense of them in a way that can predict the future. Whether our ancestors encountered circular natural phenomena, such as weather changes, life cycles, or a starry sky, seeking patterns increased their chances of survival and the feeling of control and influence. However, our remarkable pattern recognition ability often leads us to wrong conclusions. When the world is simple, a lot of these stories can be useful, even when they are not true—if only they predict the future. It was important for our ancestors to know that the sun will rise every day and that the seasons will change every year, even though the stories they told about the reasons why were all wrong. These stories worked—because the sun did rise every day and the seasons did change.

In today's business world, however, predictability is severely limited. We live in an environment where changes are fast, times are uncertain, and the future is unknown. In such an environment, the stories our brain automatically creates cease to be helpful—they lead us to wrong conclusions which lead to bad business decisions. Story-making is dangerous in a world where there are few repeatable patterns—it leads us to believe we know the future when we actually don't. It influences our actions in the present. We behave as if what we have made up is true—and thus we cannot learn.

Stories are in our neurology and biochemistry. We cannot stop ourselves from making up narratives, not in our everyday lives and even less so in business. Therefore it is important that we own and work with our stories. If we don't own our story, our story owns us (Brown 2013)—and in a business environment, that can lead to disastrous results. Story-based approaches to change management use this power instead of trying to deny or avoid it. In this article we will dive into story-making in situations where our most dangerous stories are born—failures and falls—and use a story-based Rising Strong process to disentangle facts from fiction and learn to write a narrative that supports the change we wish to achieve.

2 The Left-Out Story of Business Failure

Steve Jobs was fired by his own company. Abraham Lincoln became a president after a long series of failure after failure. The Beatles were rejected by a record company, because "Guitar groups are on their way out." J. K. Rowling kept sending Harry Potter to publishers who didn't even bother to open the book. Michael Jordan missed more than 9000 shots. We have all heard at least some of these stories and know how they ended: the stories of failure which turned into a great success.

Inspirational quotes usually skip the most important part of the story: the art, science, and skill of getting back up. We know about the fall. And we know about the success. But very little do we know about how it made them feel to be down, what it meant to Michael Jordan to miss a shot when a game depended on him, how Steve Jobs felt when the board of directors decided to boot him, or what it was that let Abraham Lincoln recover over and over. What we fail to notice and talk about is the moment on the floor, when we're face down in the mud, wounded and sore, heartbroken, and grief-stricken, that painful moment before we get back up and dust ourselves off to try again. This is exactly what is at the core of Rising Strong—the path from our fall to our rise, both as emotional humans and as business professionals.

2.1 The Hero's Journey

All stories, whether our current business stories or ancient legends, spring from the same source—the human brain. As Campbell (2007) collected myths and legends from different cultures all over the world, his own pattern recognition ability let him realize that all of these stories were essentially the same. They had different heroes, different environments, different challenges, and different endings, but the underlying structure of these stories was the same across cultures and remains the same in everyday stories we make up. That is why the Rising Strong follows the same three-act structure of the beginning (setup), the middle (confrontation), and the end (resolution): the reckoning, the rumble, and the revolution.

Every story begins with a protagonist—maybe a young hobbit, a bored office worker, or a lion cub—living their normal life in the known, familiar world in a small hobbit village, an office, or the wide savannah. This peaceful existence gets kicked out of balance by an inciting incident, something Campbell calls "the call to adventure." That might take different forms: the discovery of a magic ring, a strange

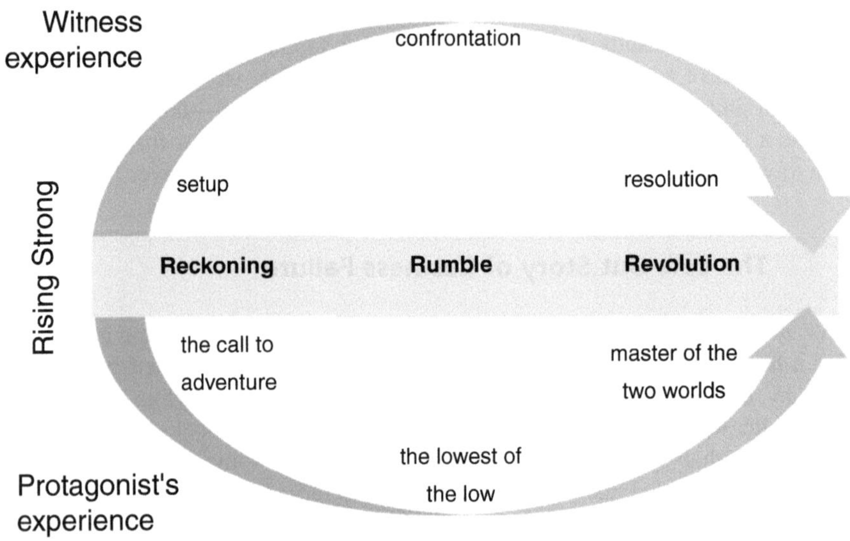

Fig. 1 The Rising Strong process and the story arc. (Author's own figure)

man offering "the blue pill or the red pill," or witnessing a father's violent death under a stampede. The protagonist then leaves the certainty of their safe home environment. Sometimes they willingly follow their curiosity, but often they are forcefully thrown into the adventure, crossing the threshold. They venture into the unknown beyond the point of no return. In this new, unknown world, they are faced with a series of tests and adversities, and also falls and failures. Oftentimes they are tempted to leave the quest, searching for easy solutions and refusing to change and let go of their ego—like Simba, finding a "hakuna matata" life with his friends, denying his lion nature. This then leads to the lowest of the low, a defeat in which transformation becomes inevitable—Simba hanging from a cliff at his evil uncle's claws, Frodo departing on his own, and Neo meeting the Oracle and finding out he's not the One. This is the point in the story where the hero gets the opportunity to truly become the hero, where they learn the most, reach out for help to their mentor, and ultimately need to abandon the ego and find a new power within to endure the crisis. This is the climax of the story, the true initiation of the hero, who needs to learn that all they need is already within. For us enjoying the story, this is the best part. For the person living the story, this is the worst part (see Fig. 1; witness experience vs. protagonist experience). After this great trial, the hero achieves greater understanding, through which he is transformed and finally able to fulfill the great quest. With this revolutionary experience, the hero returns to their world (sometimes not without resistance and temptation to stay where such success had been achieved) as the master of two worlds. Enriched and empowered by the experience, they begin a new life of freedom, balancing between fear and courage, inner and outer world, and past and future.

The stories which follow this plotline are good, credible, meaningful stories. They portray the way life works—we enjoy these stories because we recognize our own struggles and pains along with the desire to rise from them. They acknowledge the fact that when we want to rise, we need to change. As simple as it sounds, it isn't easy. The magic of the ancient myths and modern film plots is that they show us our heroes midst struggle. These stories inspire us because the hero is "just" a human before they rise to their challenge and overcome the pain.

It's interesting to notice, though, that when we listen to business success stories, they are usually not told like fictional stories we enjoy reading and watching (even though in reality, they very probably took a similar path). They lack exactly what makes the stories interesting: they lack the struggle.

2.2 Why Are Business Success Stories so Boring?

Every story has a beginning, middle, and end—the call to adventure, the journey with the ordeal, and the return. In business "success" stories, we often leave out the most important part of the journey—the ordeal and the striving—because it's vulnerable and unpleasant. We jump straight to the "we kept trying and finally succeeded," because emotions and failure are still mostly a taboo.

Failure, mistakes, and falls used to be strictly forbidden in the business vocabulary. Even though there has never been a time without failure, there had certainly been a time when failure, especially in business, was shameful and therefore hidden. It is very natural for us to try and avoid failure in all areas of life, not only business. Only children can afford to fail (and learn) because somebody always has their back—but not serious businesspeople. Therefore, even when admitting to having been through tough times, the "failure to success" stories seem to skip the most important (and the most interesting) part of the story—the fall and the way back up. Even in telling the story, we are prone to omitting the difficult, painful parts of our journey.

We can link our proneness to avoid failure to the nature of the human brain. We are wired for survival, not for quality of living. When our brain was developing, the most important task of a Homo sapiens was to find food and avoid becoming food (Sinek 2014). In the Paleolithic era, the world was a very dangerous place—food wasn't available at the supermarkets but had to be gathered or caught. We were not living in safely built houses, but in whatever shelter nature offered. The average lifespan was around 30 years, and people were mostly dying due to disease, violence, or hunger (Harari 2016). It was an environment in which failure and mistakes very often had a very severe consequence: death (either of an individual or of an entire tribe). Therefore, our brain is naturally developed to try to avoid failure. Our automatic stress responses of fight, freeze, or fight serve us very well in life-threatening situations. Even though they tend to be quite unproductive in our working lives, our body perceives threat and responds with a flush of adrenaline and cortisol to prepare us for the demanded action. When this threat comes in the shape of an unhappy boss, a promising client, or an approaching deadline, fleeing or fighting might not be the best option. Still, avoiding failure is a survival strategy in an environment in which we do not feel safe—and many business environments do not fulfill our primal need for safety. Our leaders, instead of being the protectors of our tribe, often seem like a more powerful opponent. Our coworkers, instead of our allies, become our competitors in the battle for the survival of the fittest (Sinek 2014).

Our scarcity culture also supports the failure avoidance. The society has invented the perfect mechanism to keep people from doing mistakes that might endanger the whole community: shame (Brown 2007). Shaming others who bring us to danger and excluding them from the group help keep the group safe. If in the business environment failure is seen as danger and needs to be prevented, shame around failure does a very good job at keeping people in line, not taking risks or stepping into uncertainty. Shame is an emotion that is extremely painful, as it dehumanizes us and keeps us disconnected and lonely (Cyrulnik 2012). Unless we find a safe place in which our shame can be met with empathy, we will stay small, hide, and pretend (Brown 2013). When our businesses are not safe environments which offer protection and an empathetic response to failure, and mistakes and falls are met with judgment, criticism and blame, two things emerge. Firstly, we try to compensate the feelings of shame by proving, perfecting, pleasing, and performing: we work extremely hard for success which will ultimately hide our inadequacy (Cyrulnik 2012). Secondly, when we inevitably do fail, we hide it, blame others, and avoid accountability (Brown 2013). Failure, falls, mistakes, and adversities remain unspoken in environments that do not offer the safety to accept and work through them; and business environments unfortunately rarely do that.

In recent years failure is viewed as the inevitable part of every successful business and mistakes as the inevitable part of the process. So much so, actually, that fake news and false data are circling the Internet, pointing to the great failures of great people. Not just that the most successful people we know have failed—we even make up stories of their failures to make them more inspiring. As we fact-check some of the statements in the beginning of this chapter, most turn out to be half-truths. But even though the facts might be wrong, the moral stands—failure is inevitable. Setbacks and falls are essential parts of the path to success.

2.3 The Messy Middle

The middle of the story, the part we leave out, is what makes or breaks the company, the team, or the individual facing a difficult situation. This is the part of the story that requires the protagonist to change and jump into the discomfort of vulnerability. If Simba, Neo, and Frodo gave up when they got to the most difficult part of their journeys, if they had refused to change and transform, we would not be telling their stories. The same goes for Steve Jobs, Albert Einstein, and Michael Jackson. How we get out of the struggle defines us. It requires rebirth, a transformation.

We call this point in the story "climax," the highest point of the story arc. At the same time, that is emotionally the lowest point for the person living the story. When we are in the middle of the story, it never seems like a story. It seems like a mess. It is full of confusion, uncertainty, emotional exposure, and often pain and fear. Mostly, we don't think when we're midst struggle—"This will make a great story one day." We are just trying to survive. This is the point in which a consultant usually enters the story of a company—we enter not as the heroes but as mentors and guides, offering the protagonist (the individual, the company, the organization) support in accepting the challenge. As Campbell (2007) writes, the usual hero adventure begins with someone from whom something has been taken, or who feels there is something lacking. It always begins with a loss, a struggle, something that has become undone. In the organizations, that can be anything from a failed project, a change in policy, or just a conflict between two coworkers. The hero of the monomyth (Campbell 2007) then begins a series of challenges, through which she needs to grow and develop. Leaders in organizations try everything they know to solve the problem—which often means doing more of the same and trying every comfortable way to get out of the situation (Brown 2015). In stories of fiction, this is the part of the story we enjoy most—seeing a character be tested and fail, following their falls, feeling with them through adversity and pain, and finally watching them face their demons and rise (Campbell 2007). We connect to these stories because they feel like home—we know the falls and the struggles and wish to rise like these heroes rise. And yet, we'd like to avoid and skip the hard parts of the story, especially in organizations, because falling hurts and pain is uncomfortable.

Organizations, like any system, are constantly balancing two forces—one trying to maintain the status quo and the other pushing for change (Cummings and Worley 2009). When the inciting incident happens in the organization, it brings these forces out of balance. The first step of the organization is usually to try to return to the status quo. Campbell would call that "rejecting the call" (2007)—but calls for change in the business world can never be rejected for long without it causing serious damage in the future. Rejection of the call is really the decision that we want to stay the same and hold on to our current beliefs, systems, and ways of conduct. It is not the beginning of an adventure, but its denial and a return into a continuous cycle of what has always been done. Instead of embarking on a journey into a different future, we keep to our traditional organizational culture.

Rejecting the call is often a side product of the norms and rules, the taken-for-granted beliefs around what it means to "stay professional" in an organizational context (Swart 2013). Every organization, even every industry, holds a specific set of norms that underpin what people in certain roles should and should not feel or express (Fineman 2000). These often play a part in the decision to avoid situations that might trigger an emotional response—which all transformative processes, challenges, and failures are. In business, the aim is often to try and stay "objective" (and not emotional) and to discuss the "facts" (and not the feelings or identities informed by stories we make up about the situation); but in reality, the stories, feelings, and our sense of self are where the transformation truly happens (Stone et al. 2010). If we leave out the messy middle, it's impossible to rise after a fall (Brown 2015).

2.4 Tough Emotions and the Professional Attitude

Emotions, until the last two decades, were largely regarded as feminine, private, and irrational and outside the domain of the public, masculinized, rational world of work (Fineman 2000). This now seems to have changed. However, the management teams around the world still seem to be mostly male, and thus this cultural conserve (the taken-for-granted beliefs) is changing more slowly in practice than it is in ideology. What now comes up is the balance between rationality and emotionality. There is a myth of rationality built around the belief in expertise, objectivity in making decisions, and the requirement that managers approach problem-solving objectively (Hatcher 2008). The corporate character should be committed to efficiency, instrumentality, and rationality. This is now unsettled by the messy and unpredictable postmodern business environment which required a different attitude.

Emotional intelligence is thus seen as a key—and emotions have earned their entrance into the business world, but only if and when they are bounded, managed, and controlled. The same principles that measure rational thinking (i.e., IQ) are employed in discussing and measuring the emotional intelligence (EQ); we use hard science to measure soft phenomena, because we realize that soft skills have hard consequences (Hatcher 2008). However, as Brené Brown (2015) writes, it is impossible to engineer a vulnerable, emotional process into a one-size-fits-all formula. Numbers and facts are not telling us enough about making the best use of our emotional experience at work—and this is where storywork comes in.

3 The Rising Strong Process

Every job and every project also brings adversity, failures, and tough times in the process. These events are often deeply painful; at the least they are uncomfortable and at worst they can even be traumatic. On the other hand, they might be a trigger of a great transformation for the organization if they are well processed and invite a revolution. Introducing big changes and organizational transformation always unsettles the status quo and thus makes everyone more vulnerable. In situations like this, we need to manage uncertainty, risk, and emotional exposure. Most of us are not taught how to deal with pain (but we are taught how to avoid it, bounce it, deny it, or hide it), and we bring our nonoptimal dealing strategies into organizations—which usually makes the situation worse, disables the learning process, and stalls or completely stops the transformation.

The Rising Strong process offers a clear structure to getting back up after a fall. It is a research-based resilience practice, developed by Brené Brown, aimed at individuals and groups that enter the arena and suddenly find themselves facedown. It is an approach that guides us through re-authoring our stories and into creating a lasting transformation both for ourselves as individuals and for the whole organizations.

The stages of the Rising Strong process are based on the structure of a story—the beginning, the middle, and the end (Table 1). They work the same in small-scale and

Table 1 The Hero's Journey and the Rising Strong process in comparison

The Hero's Journey	**ACT I—beginning**	**ACT II—middle**	**ACT III—end**
	The call	**The ordeal**	**The return**
	The character faces or is confronted by a challenge and accepts that challenge. The rules of the world are established It ends with an "inciting incident"	The character looks for every comfortable way to solve the problem. By the climax, they learn what it's really going to take to solve the problem This act includes "the lowest of the low"	The character needs to prove they have learned the lesson, usually showing a willingness to prove this at all costs. This is about redemption—an enlightened character knowing what to do to resolve a conflict
Rising Strong	**Reckoning**	**Rumble**	**Revolution**
	Walking into our story	**Owning our story**	**Process becomes practice**
	Recognize emotion, and get curious about our feelings and how they connect with the way we think and behave	Get honest about the stories we are making up about our struggle, and then challenge these confabulations and assumptions to determine what is the truth, what is self-protection, and what needs to change if we want to lead more wholehearted lives	Write a new ending to our story based on the key learnings from our rumble, and use this new, braver story to change how we engage with the world and to ultimately transform the way we live, love, parent, and lead

Content from Rising Strong by Brené Brown (2015)

large-scale situations, in business, and in private lives. The stages are predictable and learnable and can be utilized right away.

3.1 Rising Strong and the Hero's Journey

As we make up stories anyway, it makes sense to focus on actively taking part in the creation of stories we really want to create. Brené Brown talks about owning our story, Chene Swart talks about re-authoring, and other narrative approaches might have different names for it—but they all call for active participation in the creation of our lives. In the beginning, there is no story. It's just a situation that brings us out of balance. What Joseph Campbell called "the call" is only the first step: the reckoning requires us to (1) recognize the call (recognize emotions) and (2) take the call (get curious). The call in our lives most often comes in the form of a strong emotional reaction to something that happens to us. When we reckon and take the call, we set out on a journey. The journey in the Rising Strong is usually a symbolical one, most of which might happen in our own minds, or in a company, in deep, honest conversations about our most vulnerable work experiences. Brown (2015) calls this part of the process the rumble. It is where we struggle with our idea of who we are and what we believe, explore the first story we made up, and start exploring alternative narratives. The end of the journey, the return of the master of the two worlds, is called a revolution. In the final act, we write the new ending to our story which transforms the way we live, lead, and connect from that moment on. Both the individual and the company have undergone change that is irreversible and that hopefully leads into a brighter and a more aware future.

3.2 The Reckoning

In navigation, reckoning means calculating your position based on where you've been and what factors influenced your movement. In the process of Rising Strong, it's finding out where we are emotionally and how we got there.

When something happens that triggers us, we first need to recognize we have been triggered and get curious about it.

3.2.1 Recognizing Emotion

Reckoning requires us to first realize something emotional is going on. Even though emotional reaction is a whole cycle of experience that includes thoughts, feelings, and actions, most often what we notice first is our bodily response. We get tight, and hot, we sweat, and or our heart starts racing. And then—especially in business—we "pull ourselves together," shake it off, and pretend it never happened. We need to learn (or relearn) what our body is telling us when we catch ourselves clenching our fists, biting our nails, or munching on carbs. In part, these patterns of behavior, bodily reactions, and action tendencies are universal, i.e., the tendency to move away in fear, etc. (Bloch and Lemingnan 1992); and in part we develop our own typical emotional reactions. At work we often quickly conceal these first signs—and so miss out on opportunities to learn. Not recognizing emotion and getting engaged with it also have direct consequence in conversations: we use more shields and disconnection strategies to keep ourselves safe (Brown 2015), and the unprocessed emotions leak or burst into the conversation and contaminate our behavior, make it difficult to listen, and harm our self-esteem (Stone et al. 2010).

Box 1: A Personal Rising Strong Story

The best way to shed some light to the process is to share my own story—it is the only story in which I also deeply know the background and the inner dialogue that played out.

I am about to start a workshop, jumping in for a coworker who got sick. Exiting the restroom, a conversation in the hallway makes me stop mid-step. A participant of the workshop is talking to our secretary in an angry tone. "I have to listen to HER again? Had I known it will not be HIM delivering, I would have canceled." I retreat back into the toilet. I feel warmth wash over my face,

(continued)

Box 1 (continued)
my heart races, my palms are sweating, and my mind is racing in a conflicting internal dialogue.

I just want to hide. Who the hell does she think she is??! I'll prove she's wrong about me, I'm every bit as good as my coworker. I'm working my ass off and that pretentious b**** can't appreciate quality! But what if she's right, they'll find out I don't know what I'm talking about... I'm unlikable...

What is going on? I am triggered. This is the reckoning. I breathe out, give myself permission to not try to win her over, and start the workshop, doing my best not to focus too much on her crossed arms and bored expression.

In the break, I write down my thoughts. This is the rumble. In my SFD, it's easy to find judgments that are not based on facts: she doesn't appreciate quality, she doesn't know, she's pretentions, etc. Underneath the anger hides a dangerous identity story—what if I really am not competent or likable enough? The leap from "I'm not good enough" to "I'm better than her" happens so fast that within seconds the original (and more painful) narrative had been pushed into subconsciousness.

What about the revolution? In reality, I don't even know exactly what her complaint was about; all I heard was that she expected somebody else and was disappointed he wasn't here. I am perfectly capable of running the workshop. But unless I rumble, I get stuck with my first story which can only lead to a shame shit-storm; and as a facilitator that is the last place I want to take the group. I am good enough—and I need to facilitate from a place of worthiness.

3.2.2 Getting Curious

Then comes the second, equally crucial step of the reckoning: getting curious. This is as simple as asking "What is going on?" and yet it's hard—because we are story-making animals. It's hard to ask questions when we think we know the answers—and our brain is much better at providing answers (though not necessarily accurate) than staying with the questions. Curiosity requires us to stay with the "not knowing," while our brain is wired to create a story out of the limited data points we have available. Curiosity is vulnerable (Brown 2015). When we feel triggered and threatened, we actually need to work against our default mechanism of story-making and consciously choose staying in the uncertainty to engage with curiosity.

Getting curious about emotion is especially hard because the "sea we swim in," the taken-for-granted beliefs about emotions, views them as a sign of weakness, frivolous, or even dangerous. These beliefs are so integrated in our lives and our thinking that we consider them as truth, "just the way things are" (Swart 2013).

Both our nature and our nurture support offloading emotions instead of getting engaged. This is the rejection of the call, our way to try and avoid the adventure. Yet, getting engaged is the only way to find our way into transforming the future.

3.2.3 Offloading Hurt

People don't like to hurt. We are deeply motivated to minimize our discomfort, even if that might hurt other people or bring more trouble in the long run. Campbell (2007) calls this "the rejection of the call" or "denial." We want to stay as we are and hold on to what we believe to be true. We try to offload our pain using well practiced strategies we have learned growing up—passing it on to somebody else, pushing it down, masking it, etc. We see ourselves as the victim of the story and wait for salvation; but this can only bring misery (Campbell 2007). Repeating the same patterns, we keep ending up in the same known scenario (Steward and Joines 1987). As long as we remain passive victims, we are never free to shape our futures. Once we know our patterns, offloading hurt strategies are easily recognized and can be replaced with effective reckoning strategies: breathing deeply, staying mindful, and giving ourselves permission to feel (Brown 2015).

3.2.4 Reckoning as a Community

In an organizational environment, we often need to reckon as a community. When trust is established, a single person who first realizes something is happening can invite others into the reckoning. Tension in the room, avoidant or (passive) aggressive behaviors, defensiveness, or a sudden change in tone can all be signs that something is up. We can expect the need to reckon anytime there is conflict in the team, a failure, a disappointment, a rejection, a sudden change (especially coming from the outside), a departure of a team member or the arrival of a new one, or even a successful end of a big project. A courageous individual who begins to reckon might be able to invite others into the process by practicing vulnerability even when trust is not stable. Courage is contagious. It can be spread by small acts of ordinary courage (such as speaking up), until the critical mass is on board with the process—and transformation becomes inevitable.

3.3 The Rumble

The rumble is the hard part of the story—it's where we face the story we tell ourselves and discover the anomalies in it. This is the journey through which the protagonist becomes the hero—the author of their destiny. We need to capture the first story we make up in writing, challenge its assumptions and ask ourselves what more we need to know.

Emotion is a clear sign that something matters to us (Milivojević 2008), and hence it is important to figure out what is happening. Most often, our brain will provide us with an explanation for a situation before we even realize we've been searching for one. The problem with this explanation, though, is that even though it might satisfy our need to know, it is very rarely accurate, and it most often contributes to deepening the problem we're facing (Brown 2015).

When we're vulnerable and triggered, these stories flourish. That means that in every difficult situation at work (and beyond), there are usually several different stories from the people involved; and each has parts that were made up—unchecked assumptions, conspiracies, and confabulations. We believe our stories to be true—and so does everyone else. The rumble is the part of the Rising Strong process that lets us disentangle these stories and create a better understanding of what matters.

3.3.1 The SFD

The SFD stands for "shitty first draft (Brown 2015)." What Campbell discovered exploring ancient myths also holds true of our most everyday stories—they all are a result of our evolutionary need to figure things out and explain the world to ourselves. The first step of the journey is capturing that first survival story we make up as soon as something happens: writing down our first response, first thoughts, feelings, actions, and desires (unedited, honest, direct, and possibly unsharable).

When we let these stories go unexamined, they influence how we feel and what we think of ourselves and inform our behavior. Capturing that first story lets us explore what this situation is really about and why it matters so much to us (Stone et al. 2010).

3.3.2 Conspiracies and Confabulations

When we write these stories down, we make it possible to catch the problem narratives (Swart 2013), our assumptions, the conspiracies, and confabulations. Conspiracies are stories that explain what happened with limited data points and answer the question of who is to blame and who we should fear. Confabulation is a lie told honestly—when we lack information, we make it up to fill in the story, and we believe our explanations (Brown 2015). The reason all cultures have stories about creation of the world and men is that humans always require an explanation for why things are the way they are (Campbell 2007).

When we dive a bit deeper into our stories, we might find ourselves facing some of our go-to narratives about our identities, about our flawed selves. These often lie underneath our initial response and in the work environment most often go unspoken. Some of the most common identity stories are (Stone et al. 2010; Brown 2015):

1. "I am not competent/creative/smart/... enough."
2. "I am not a good enough person."
3. "I am not worthy of love and belonging."

These show up at work as much as they do in our private lives; however, at work they are often more difficult to address and remain hidden—but they trigger our shields and armory, because they make us feel vulnerable and even ashamed. In myths we often find characters who stay in denial of their confabulations—a tragic hero, for example, is brought to their miserable end by their unacknowledged flaws (Campbell 2007). If we want to turn a tragedy into a revolution, we must face these flaws and accept our humanity. That is why, in nearly all of our stories, a rumble with shame and vulnerability is inevitable (Brown 2015). In a process of an organizational transformation, the most common rumble topic is trust. Trusting relationships and a circle of safety needs to be established before a team or an organization can dive into the vulnerable process of facing the challenges together (Sinek 2014).

3.3.3 The Rumble as a Shared Effort

When an organization goes through change, there will be many different SFDs emerging from each employee. As Tolstoy writes in the beginning of Ana Karenina—"All happy families are alike, each unhappy family is unhappy in their own way." Organizations face different struggles, and individuals in organizations might have to go through different rumbles. However, working with many different teams and individuals, I have come to realize that the revolutionary results of these rumbling are very often very alike and touch upon our common humanity.

In an organizational setting, the rumble will often involve having difficult conversations (Brown 2018). To successfully rumble as a team, trust needs to be established and nurtured at all times. It helps when everyone is on board with the process and willing to let go of their own stories as the one and only truth. The situation is usually more complex because it includes a multitude of truths, stories, experiences, and knowledges—but the process remains the same. When a community rumbles, each individual in this community also goes through their own rumble, asking uncomfortable questions and committing to uncomfortable learning. It can be done within minutes, or it can take months—but every team needs to go through the messy middle of the story to create true transformation for the future.

3.4 The Revolution

> When we deny our stories, they define us.
> When we run from struggle, we are never free.
> So we turn toward the truth and look it in the eye.
> /. . ./ We are the authors of our lives.
> We write our own daring endings.
> [Brené Brown, Rising Strong, 2015 (267)]

The final stage of the Hero's Journey is the return. The hero became the master of the two worlds and brings the elixir back to the world from which he first ventured out. After the rumble process, we are transformed, and when we return to our "normal working life," we think, feel, and act differently and thus create different futures.

Transformation can be slow, incremental, and evolutionary; but it can also be a deep and groundbreaking revolution with no going back. Rising Strong can be a series of incremental changes in small, everyday stories—but when the process becomes practice, it is revolutionary (Brown 2015). When this process becomes part of an organizational culture and a way of engaging with the world for a critical mass of employees, it ignites a revolutionary transformation. It changes us, it changes the people around us, and it changes our whole work environment (Brown 2018). Courage is contagious, and because the rising process is a courageous way of dealing with our falls, that becomes contagious, too. Seeing others go through a transformation and rise, we want to join them in this journey. Through falling, engaging with our vulnerability, and finally getting back up transformed, we give others permission to do the same. Moving from the initial narrative that is black and white, clear and certain, into our new learning and the alternative story we wish to live by is what makes the process come to life.

Box 2: A Rising Strong Story from a Client: Lala Inc.

The inciting incident for Lala Inc. was the fact that they received unsatisfactory results to an employee survey which showed that a remotely located team has a trust issue with the management. This triggered them; it was the reckoning. They responded to the call and became curious: we planned a rumble meeting in which both the frustrated employees and the management team could explore their stories of how they see this relationship.

After some much needed container building and creating a safe space to share, we found out that the biggest issue the remote team saw was a lack of accountability. They felt that whenever something goes wrong, there is a lot of finger-pointing and fault-seeking. They fear making mistakes (and being punished) and feel that the management is reluctant to admit when they are wrong.

Many of these behaviors played out in real time. People were reluctant to share and give feedback. I asked what lies behind the silence. After a minute or so, they began speaking: they were afraid they might offend somebody, they've tried to speak openly before, but that only triggered defensiveness and just can't be bothered anymore; they don't want to be the "bad guy." Since the trust was too fragile for such a vulnerable conversation, each of them rumbled with their story individually. Even though work in this case was "side-by-side" rather than communal, it still sparked a series of small revolutions, and many of them came to the same conclusions.

I was quite inspired by the learnings that came out of the rumble process around trust with Lala Inc.

"We are all doing the best we can. We all have the same goal. We are different and do things differently. We are willing to accept (and give) constructive feedback. We are all human. We desire to speak out. We believe change is possible and wish to contribute."

This was just the first of many rumbles they will need to go through if they wish to bring all this to life and truly change the culture, but it triggered a process of transformation.

3.4.1 Revolutionary Transformation of the Business World

A multitude of stories in our organizations is inevitable. People will always make up explanations for what is happening. If we don't take authorship of these stories, they will turn dark and harm us both as individuals and as organizations. Our protective imagination makes up stories that are meant to drive our survival, and these stories often fail us. They either overlook our flaws, fears, shame, or anything that might require us to change; or they make them seem impossible to overcome—and that only stalls our learning process. However, when we can use our amazing ability of story creation to rewrite our futures in a way that is helpful for our organizations, the stories become our most valuable ally.

The process of Rising Strong in an organization can happen on an individual level and anyone who follows it will walk out changed. Sometimes this will only be a small piece of a puzzle, and sometimes it will be a deeply profound transformation of the way we engage with life and work. When we rumble as a community, we can achieve results that influence not only our company but also everyone we work with, our clients, stakeholders, and our business partners. Through re-authoring the story of one leader, one team, one department, and one company, we can eventually transform a whole industry and, finally, the business world as a whole. We can write the ending of this story. We can re-create our cultures to more closely relate to our values. We can rehumanize the corporate world by bringing conscious story-making back into the way the web of meaning around how we do business.

We must own our toughest stories so that we can learn and grow and transform. It's hard, but when it becomes part of organizational cultures, it unleashes innovation, creativity, and the drive to change into who we truly desire to be. It doesn't always feel comfortable, but courage rarely does.

4 Summary

Every business endeavor will definitely also include adversity, falls, and failures. These situations trigger our cognitive protection mechanisms of meaning making—in the shortest possible time with the information we have available, we make up a story that offers straightforward answers to survival questions: "Who's good? Who's bad? What's safe? What's dangerous?" However, the answers we get are mostly neither true nor helpful. If we are to actively transform our organizations into who we wish to become, we need to engage in the oftentimes messy process of story creation. We need to learn to look up when we are facedown.

The Rising Strong offers a step-by-step process which is both natural and deeply challenging. It is natural to us humans because it follows the same structure as all stories—it has a beginning, the middle, and the end, like all myths and stories throughout history. However, it is also challenging, because it requires us to engage in the vulnerability of change, stay curious in the uncertainty of the learning process and let go of what we believe to be true to write a new ending to our story. Within organizations, individuals and teams need to learn to trust themselves, each other, and the process and overcome some of common taken-for-granted beliefs and norms that guide our business lives. Rising Strong is an emotional and spiritual practice, and as long as emotions and our inextricable human connection to each other and to something greater than us are taboo in the business environment, true transformation cannot happen. And yet, if we make it part of the company culture to engage in the process of reckoning, rumble, and the revolution, meaningful and lasting transformation becomes inevitable.

References

Atwood, M. (1996). *Alias Grace* (pp. 345–346). London: Bloomsbury.
Bloch, S., & Lemingnan, M. (1992). Precise respiratory-posturo-facial patterns are related to specific basic emotions. *Bewegen & Hulpverlening, 1*, 31–40.
Brown, B. (2007). *I thought it was just me (but it isn't): Making the journey from "what will people think?" to "i am enough"* (Kindle edition). Retrieved from https://www.amazon.com/
Brown, B. (2013). *Daring greatly: How the courage to be vulnerable transforms the way we live, love, parent, and lead* (Kindle edition). Retrieved from https://www.amazon.com/
Brown, B. (2015). *Rising strong* (Kindle edition). Retrieved from https://www.amazon.com/
Brown, B. (2018). *Dare to Lead: Brave work, tough conversations, whole hearts*. New York: Random House.
Campbell, J. (2007). *Junak tisočerih obrazov*. Nova Gorica: Eno.
Cummings, T., & Worley, C. (2009). *Organization development and change* (9th ed.). Retrieved from http://www.mcs.gov.kh/wp-content/uploads/2017/07/Organization-Development-and-Change.pdf
Cyrulnik, B. (2012). *Sram: Če povem, bom umrl*. Ljubljana: Modrijan.
Fineman, S. (2000). Emotional arenas revisited. In S. Fineman (Ed.), *Emotion in organizations* (2nd ed., pp. 1–24). London: Sage.
Harari, Y. N. (2016). *Homo Deus: A brief history of tomorrow*. New York: HarperCollins.
Hatcher, C. (2008). Becoming a successful corporate character and the role of emotional management. In S. Fineman (Ed.), *The emotional organization* (pp. 153–166). Oxford: Blackwell.
Milivojević, Z. (2008). *Emocije*. Novi Sad: Psihopolis Inštitut.
Sinek, S. (2014). *Leaders eat last: Why some teams pull together and others don't*. London: Portfolio Penguin Books.
Steward, I., & Joines, V. (1987). *TA today: A new introduction to transactional analysis*. Chapel Hill: Lifespace Publishing.
Stone, D., Patton, B., & Heen, S. (2010). *Difficult conversations: How to discuss what matters Most* (Kindle edition). Retrieved from https://www.amazon.com/
Swart, C. (2013). *Re-authoring the world*. Randburg: Knowres Publishers.

Katarina Veselko leads a double storytelling career: she is an organizational psychologist and a theater improviser. Both through her work in organizations and teaching (also performing) improvisational theater, she strives to bring her core values into practice: courage, inspiration, and integrity. As a trainer, facilitator, and a coach in a small Slovenian consultancy O. K. Consulting, she supports leaders and teams in their development. Currently, her main focus revolves around leading organizations into a more modern organizational culture through deepening trust and spreading courage by exploring and changing the different narratives the teams live by. Her background lies in transactional analysis (TA counselor), neurolinguistic programming (NLP Coach), psychodrama, and both Daring Way™ and Dare to Lead™ [CDTLF (Certified Dare to Lead Facilitator) and CDWF (Certified Daring Way Facilitator)]. When she is not deepening her skills and knowledge in diverse educational programs, she spends her free time practicing and teaching improvisational theater, dancing, writing, and free climbing.

Re-authoring the Future of Travel and Hospitality: An Inquiring and Generative Re-authoring Practice in Tourism Flanders

Griet Bouwen, Marianne Schapmans, and Chené Swart

Abstract

In this chapter we tell the story of a future in travel and hospitality that is being re-authored as we speak. This story is currently unfolding in the governmental office of Tourism Flanders (Visit Flanders) and its Holiday Participation Centre. Appreciative inquiry, generative journalism and the re-authoring work collaborated to facilitate transformational ways of seeing and being that reignited the dignity of all who participate in creating possibilities for people to travel and to host travellers. Together we will explore the practices of listening, writing and sharing of real-life stories that re-author the future of travel. Re-authoring (You can read more about the origins and further developments in re-authoring ideas and practices in chapter "Transforming Organisations Through the Re-authoring Lens and Practices" written by Chené Swart.) the future of travel and hospitality is an exciting movement that will inspire you, spark your imagination for the

This chapter has been translated and adapted from various published documents: *Connect Your Story* manual, Re-authoring Futures Con-Texts and several articles published on www.verbindjeverhaal.be. A prior version of this chapter has been published on www.connectyourstory.org and www.iedereenverdientvakantie.be under the title, Re-authoring the Future of Travel and Hospitality: An Unfolding Practice in Tourism Flanders. Re-used here with permission from the authors, Griet Bouwen, Marianne Schapmans and Chené Swart.

G. Bouwen (✉)
Nieuwmakers, Bilzen, Limburg, Belgium
e-mail: griet@nieuwmakers.be

M. Schapmans
Holiday Participation Centre, Visit Flanders, Brussels, Flanders, Belgium
e-mail: marianne.schapmans@iedereenverdientvakantie.be

C. Swart
TRANSFORMATIONS, Pretoria, Gauteng, South Africa
e-mail: chene@transformations.co.za

© Springer Nature Switzerland AG 2019

J. Chlopczyk, C. Erlach (eds.), *Transforming Organizations*,
Management for Professionals, https://doi.org/10.1007/978-3-030-17851-2_15

futures you would like to re-author, give you the tools and practices to embark on your own journey and also show you how you can be part of this movement.

1 Introduction: Why Working with Stories in Travelling and Hospitality?

Roman emperor Marcus Aurelius wrote in his *Meditations* that it is not death that people should fear but that they should fear never beginning to live. This experience of being fully alive can overwhelm us when we travel. Immersing ourselves in the sounds, smells and tastes of new places sharpen our senses, and, in a way, they remind us vividly that what we feel is pure, pure life!

When we travel, we move away from the domestic life. We put on a new set of eyes, ears and a sensitive skin for what surrounds us.

This is what we hear when we invite people to talk about their holiday experiences. We've listened to more than 1500 stories, and almost each one is telling about the 'new set of eyes' people seem to get during travelling and hosting. They talk about moments they felt connected to their family again and about the amazement of standing in front of a remarkable painting of an old Flemish Master. People tell us about shifting thoughts, building resilience and finding friends. We think about the multiple stories about youngsters who enjoy a break in a group holiday for the first time in their life or stories about a reconnection with nature that stays in someone's life forever afterwards. We'll never forget the story about a woman who suffered depression and learnt on a holiday that silence can also be light and white instead of heavy and black.

The stories we listen to, speak about what Heidegger would call 'Spielraum' (Brown 2013): a time and place where we as human beings can consider the life we lead and the possible changes that can be made. Because people are meaning-making beings, we are, from time to time, faced with the question of what an authentic life could be for us, Heidegger says. Because of our vision on working with stories, we would add to the philosopher's vision that we are not only meaning-makers but also story makers (White 2007). We connect experiences and make stories that hold conclusions about who we are, what our life is about and how the world is.

So, let's dig a bit deeper into this idea of story-making and meaning-making. Could it help to season our everyday lives with the spices and flavours of our travel experiences? Alain de Botton, an English philosopher, said that tourism can grant people an understanding of what life might be about outside the constraints of work and the struggle for survival (Brown 2013). We think he has a good point, and we like to add this question: what if travelling has a partner that joins the ride, namely, reflection?

In surveys on transformational tourism, it became clear that reflection is a spark for transformation. People who journal, take time to think about their adventures or have deep conversations about it report more often that travelling changes their life. This is where the narrative work comes alongside Heidegger's Spielraum.

If we host a Spielraum where people are asked to reflect on moments whilst travelling, hosting or even contributing to travelling opportunities for others, we create a space for deeper thoughts and surprising insights. And there is more: if we document these stories, we add another layer of meaning to people's experiences. As we pour our energy into this dedicated work of writing stories, we can share them in a larger context: a network of travellers and travel facilitators, a broader public of policy makers and public opinion. Then, something can start to shift. Then, these experiences tell stories about tourism way beyond its economic value.

By finding stories, listening carefully to people's experiences, exploring insights, documenting and sharing stories in networks, we slowly shift towards a broadened image on what travelling and hosting really means to people and communities. We move away from a dominant economic vision on tourism. We move into a vision that reveals the possible contribution of tourism and travelling to wellbeing, sustainability and becoming fully alive. And, most of all, we connect people around this topic and inspire them to deepen their actions in creating opportunities for others to enjoy the benefits of a holiday.

That is what we have discovered in an ongoing experiment at the Holiday Participation Centre in Flanders. In the following pages, we dive deeper into our 6 years of practice with story work around travel and hospitality in this network. But first, let's introduce you to this unique network.

2 The Holiday Participation Centre in Flanders: Why and How?

Societal challenges such as poverty, integration, social exclusion, loneliness, inclusion, ageing and health care are often so complex that one organization or policy domain cannot tackle them on their own. These are complex issues that require the knowledge and effort of a whole society. An invigorating holiday or a pleasant day trip with the family is not a miraculous solution to get out of poverty or social isolation, but it is a step in the right direction and part of the answer. A holiday creates space in the lives of people who are often faced with severe difficulties.

Poverty has a huge impact on people's leisure time. The EU-SILC survey of the FPS Economy shows that one in four Belgians cannot afford a week's vacation. In Brussels this figure goes up to 40% (Minnaert and Schapmans 2009). People who struggle to make ends meet feel compelled to focus on their basic needs. There is usually no money or energy left to enjoy life, and people in these circumstances quickly get the feeling that they cannot keep up. Even their children have little opportunities to enjoy the benefits of participating in leisure and social activities such as sports, culture or youth work.

Because of exclusion, people in poverty have less opportunities to build a social network and therefore have a limited amount of contacts to draw on. They are ashamed, shut themselves off and end up in a negative spiral. As a society we have to offer opportunities also to experience enjoyable things. By making a vacation possible, we are giving a space to breathe again, the courage to carry on and a sense of equality and freedom. This is an important gift for the future of people who are often faced with challenging difficulties.

2.1 The Holiday Participation Centre Facilitates a Unique Collaboration

In 2001, Tourism Flanders decided to take action in preventing social exclusion and established the Holiday Participation Centre. This new Holiday Participation Centre started with their ambitious mission to bring people in poverty out of their homes and the daily grind of their lives. They set up a public-private partnership and asked operators of tourist attractions and holiday accommodation to offer discounts. In addition, social organizations were encouraged to invite people to make use of the offer, to provide appropriate guidance and to ensure that the discount only reaches people who live below the poverty line. Transport companies were also asked to provide their social rates.

It is now 17 years later, and the Holiday Participation Centre is facilitating a network of more than 2400 partners, consisting of 660 tourism entrepreneurs and 1750 social organizations. This network thrives under the shared mission 'Everyone Deserves A holiday'. Thanks to their powerful cooperation, every year more than 150,000 people in poverty can go on day trips or short holiday breaks in Flanders.

This network 'Everyone Deserves A Holiday' is the result of a unique collaboration wherein all the partners have committed themselves with full conviction. But this kind of fertile network does not fall from the sky and neither can it be sustained without support. It needs a motivator and inspirator to keep the work going. Tourism Flanders, through their Holiday Participation Centre, has taken on the role of a connector that coordinates the commitments and efforts of all partners in the network.

2.2 Lifting Cooperation Above a Win-Win Logic

How do you align all of these partners? And how do you ensure that this network remains solution-oriented and ambitious? Working together is extremely captivating and enriching, but it is not easy. When numerous different perspectives of people and organizations come together, it becomes a risk that one logic threatens to take over and then the diversity gets lost or the cooperation breaks up through disagreements.

Supported by the Holiday Participation Centre, the network Everyone Deserves A Holiday has managed to write a new story together and to formulate a shared ambition. There is room for everyone's expertise, ideas and logic.

The classical thinking in win-win relationships has been abandoned because in these double-win relationships, cooperation revolves around the following idea: I do something for you, you do something for me and we both win or are better off. The network thrives through a vision on a triple-win relationship. In this triple-win relationship, another dimension is added: when we work together, something new is created that is greater than our separate interests. The effects of this triple-win relationship become wider and broader, and more people become involved. The joint forces are bundled together without having one direct benefit for either the partners but for the broader social context.

The glue in this network is the attention for appreciative practices, appreciating what partners do and showing who the partners are without forcing anyone to cooperate. Participation in this network is voluntary. It's about listening carefully and being as helpful as possible, looking for connections and looking for what is needed.

The Holiday Participation Centre team supports the efforts of all partners in the network, links their initiatives, links questions and solutions with one another, preserves the big picture and fumes the flames of energy. They create opportunities where people can discover one another's expertise, can learn together and set up partnerships. They communicate widely about the efforts of all partners and the results that can therefore be achieved.

As a result of this appreciative triple-win relationship thinking, new holiday opportunities are developed for different target groups. Other results are a deepened awareness (and willingness to take specific actions) in the partner organizations around lowering barriers for people who live in poverty, people with disabilities, etc.

2.3 Story Work in the Holiday Participation Centre

An important tool in connecting, supporting and communicating in the network 'Everyone Deserves A Holiday', is story work. With a continuous stream of stories (two stories per week, shared via www.verbindjeverhaal.be and social media), the network keeps drawing attention to initiatives, evolutions and people with passion who help to promote the right to a holiday.

Through the collecting and sharing of stories, the immeasurable is made visible. These stories are not an end product but rather an infectious spark that creates new possibilities for the narrator, the network and the wider audience that reads these stories. They show what lives in the network and also show new insights. They bring about energy and connection. The stories of vacationers and the integrated experiences of partners give concrete handles in discussions with policy makers.

Authentic stories have special power. They confirm the right of human experiences to exist; they connect, clarify, enthuse and bring things into motion. They make tangible what cannot be expressed in numbers. They give complex themes a face and make them comprehensible, human and real. Without the small stories, there would be no bigger story.

How does the network, Everyone Deserves A Holiday, work with stories? How did this work come about? Where do we stand now and in which direction has the story work evolved?

3 Methodologies Underpinning the Story Work in the Holiday Participation Centre

In 2011 during the annual large-scale network meeting, called the Forum, important questions emerged: 'How do we manage to keep the network connected throughout the year? How do we bring everyone's hopes, ideas and initiatives to the surface so that we can reap the benefits together?'

As a way towards finding answers to these questions, the Holiday Participation Centre of Tourism Flanders started experimenting with stories in 2012. After all, the large network of tourism entrepreneurs, social organizations and people who, despite limitations (financial, social, physical), found their way to a vacation was bursting with stories. Since that moment, a dedicated story maker listens to vacationers, volunteers and professionals by asking open and curious questions about holiday experiences, ideas and dreams. She helps people making meaning about their experiences and gives them a platform where their stories can shine and inspire others.

Within 6 years, more than 500 stories were collected about holiday experiences. We bring the stories together on www.verbindjeverhaal.be and share them via social media, print and newsletters. We read the stories in public and use them in publications. The collection of stories continues to grow and offers a wonderful insight into hundreds of experiences about holidays and the meanings that people give to their holidays. In 2017, another 1000 anecdotes—the smallest stories—were added to the collection, through a large listening exercise with voluntary listeners. Together these stories tell an alternative story about how—close to home—the experience of holidays for people living in poverty contributes to a dignified existence.

The methodical roots of the story work at Everyone Deserves A Holiday lies with appreciative inquiry (AI), a philosophy and methodology that is mainly used in organizational development. With the application of AI, the story work became—from its first beginnings—focussed on finding strengths, hopes and possibilities that are (or could become) alive in the network. For the concrete application of AI to find and share stories with a view of strengthening connections and innovative capacity in the network, we found inspiration at the Canadian Axiom News. They developed a specific form of journalistic work, which they called generative journalism. Generative journalism added a journalism approach to our AI practice and a methodological frame to invite, write and share stories in the network. From the beginning, both visions and methodical processes formed the basis for the approach to start the story work. A few years later, the ideas and practices of the re-authoring work were added as it brought the gifts of human connectedness, practices of dignity and a lens to see the context in which people experience their holiday and/or contribution to lowering thresholds for people with less holiday opportunities. In the following sections, we will explain how these three approaches support our story work.

3.1 Appreciative Inquiry

Appreciative inquiry (AI) is a way of looking at people and groups from the perspective of what works well. AI is primarily a process, an activity of inquiry, discovery and development. The origin of this work is in Cleveland, Ohio, at Case Western Reserve University and the founders include Suresh Srivastva, David Cooperrider, Ronald Fry and Frank Barrett (Bouwen 2010). Appreciative inquiry is essentially an activity that people undertake together to bring about change in themselves and in the groups of which they are a part.

3.1.1 AI Principles

Six principles underpin the approach and inspire the story work at Everyone Disserves A Holiday:

Principle 1: Outspokenly Choosing the Perspective of Strengths

The basis for development lies in discovering and appreciating what is already good. Seeing the past and present as a source of possibility rather than problems is providing recognition and safety to step into adventures of change. The appreciative glance is a choice: we can ask every person, in every situation, any question and go on an inquiry. What you discover depends on the questions you ask. If you look for deficits, then you will find what you are looking for. If you seek strengths, then strengths will come to the forefront.

Principle 2: Stories Create Coherence

A story is a coherent set of events and experiences that are meaningful to the narrator. Stories tell about what someone did, what it felt like, who was there, what others did and what influences played a role in the background. A story creates coherence, so that the content of what people think, find, fear or hope can stand in a new and fuller light.

Principle 3: People Grow in Relationship with One Another

Our practice shows that choosing for an appreciative perspective contributes in an astonishing way to high-quality relationships among one another. Appreciation is an activity between people. It is about recognizing the best that is already there, between people and in the world around us. The effect: people feel recognized and valued. What is good becomes clear and possibilities become visible. This is a stepping stone to strong relationships in which dialogue and cooperation can germinate.

Principle 4: The Future Pulls Us Forward

Attractive and credible visions of the future move people into action. Striving for something attractive inspires us much more than getting rid of something that is annoying. Prospect, hope, joy and inspiration give people energy to make plans and to move into action.

Principle 5: Words Create Reality

People shape reality by giving words to it. Talking to each other is about the exchanging of words which gradually originates into meaning. Talking with each other therefore also means making something together: a collective image of reality. 'Our' reality originates when together we find agreement and together we give meaning to our words and what we see. The choice of our words gives more direction than we usually realize. If we use positive and enlivened language, our conversations become vibrant, rooted in the concrete existence which is hope filled.

Principle 6: A Question Sets the Change in Motion

A question is an intervention that focuses attention. Attention sets development in motion. In fact, attention is energy that, as a seed, directs our thoughts and actions. That is why it is so important to formulate our questions with care and to take into account the principles mentioned above. Good questions seek strength, elicit stories and are formulated in positive, enlivened and attractive language.

3.1.2 Appreciative Inquiry as Methodical Process

The methodology of appreciative inquiry consists of a cycle of four steps, called the '4-D circle': discovering (what is already strong today), dreaming (what does the future look like if it is built on strengths), designing (which path can we follow then) and destiny (how are we going to do that and what is needed for this). The process always revolves around a core theme. We also use these steps in our conversations with storytellers.

As an example, let's give you an idea of what an AI questionnaire could look like. The core theme mostly is linked to curiosities in the network, or themes the Holiday Participation Centre wants to understand and develop. Questions help us through the AI conversation.

An example of a core theme we want to understand more about: how can we increase the healing effects of holiday?

Step 1: Discovery. Tell me about a time where you returned from a holiday and felt healthy, energized or stronger than before. Tell me about what you felt. Tell me about the holiday. What happened? Who was there with you? What did you do, and what did others do? What in this holiday made you experience this energy, strength or health? What was the specific quality of it?

Step 2: Dream. Now close your eyes. Imagine it is a couple of years later, and the things that help you feel energized, healthy and strong on a holiday are now in reach for everyone. Imagine you go on a holiday again, in an environment that energizes and heals you and other people. What do you see? Who is there? What is happening? What do people do differently than today? What do you do differently than today? What is the magic shift?

Step 3: Design. Now, with all this imagined, what do you think is essential in this imagination? What is really needed to move into this direction? In other words, which of the qualities you have mentioned are core to this story? And what do you think needs to be done, by whom and in what way?

Step 4: Destiny. What are first things that can be done to move in this direction? What can you do? Is there someone who can be of any help in this? And what do you need then?

3.2 Generative Journalism

Generative journalism is an extraordinary interpretation of journalism, developed by Peter Pula, CEO of Canadian Axiom News. He invites the journalistic world to intentionally take responsibility for what we create with what we call 'news'. After an encounter with Peter Pula at the AI World Conference in Ghent, Belgium, in 2012. Marianne and Griet quickly began to implement his ideas as they wanted to give this way of working a chance in the network Everyone Deserve A Holiday.

For the Axiom News[1] team, a news item is not the end result of a journalistic process alone but a stepping stone to the future. News that is published always does 'something': it affects people, in whatever way. It focuses attention, and what gets a lot of attention, will grow faster than what gets less attention. Making news is therefore never without obligation. Every news item has the potential to affect something, both in the 'subject' of the news and its readers. Peter Pula therefore calls this work 'generative journalism': it has the potential to generate next steps towards a future we hope for.

News can cause movement in the direction that we want. Through the publishing of an abundance of personal and practical stories, generative journalism shows what is already present when it comes to strengths, talent and passion and how, from this place, an attractive future can emerge. Readers discover what is already working and how they can also get moving. The source of the news—the person being interviewed—experiences recognition and encouragement.

Each news item is the result of an appreciative inquiring contact between a journalist and a person from the stakeholder network who knows and/or does or wants to do something interesting. Together with the person, it is a search that looks for the essence of what he/she does, wants to do or knows. It is a search for hope and pride and the promise that lurks in the experience waiting to also inspire and activate others.

3.2.1 What Is the Contribution that Generative News Makes?

All stakeholders get a voice in the bigger picture. With this, inclusive and co-creative organizing of the network Everyone Deserves A Holiday comes closer. People in and around both the Holiday Participation Centre and the network Everyone Deserves A Holiday also start moving in the direction of their common shared images of the desired future.

We've seen vacationers becoming more closely connected to the network, even taking up a role as a volunteer after their story was seen and shared in the network. We've heard professional partners talking about new collaborations that grew out of

[1]You can read more about Axiom News on their website: www.axiomnews.com.

shared stories. We've experienced how the team members of the Holiday Participation Centre became closely connected to the mission, the contributions of the network partners and the difference their works makes in the lives of people struggling with poverty or disability. And we experience that generative journalism builds more public understanding about the importance of holidays, not only for the so-called hardworking middle class but for everyone.

Generative news inspires, encourages creativity and motivates the discovery and utilization of opportunities. Consciousness, understanding and appreciation for people who take initiative, grows. Gradually, all stakeholders discover opportunities and cultivate pride, connection and mutual support.

3.3 Re-authoring Work[2]

In 2015, the narrative approach came by to enrich our story practice. Chené Swart, a South African narrative expert, came alongside the developing practice. Chené Swart discovered how narrative ideas and practices can contribute to the work with communities and organizations and wrote a book called *Re-Authoring the World: The Narrative Lens and Practices for Organizations, Communities and Individuals*. Her ideas held the promise of understanding more about the unfolding work and effects we saw. Indeed, something magical was happening in the process of listening to and documenting authentic, often alternative stories of ordinary people. The narrative work helped in understanding the effects of this work on a deeper level. In this discovery, the re-authoring work added more philosophical and methodical foundations to the work that was unfolding.

3.3.1 What Is Re-authoring Work?

At the end of the 1970s, two social workers, Michael White from Australia and David Epston from New Zealand, met and started thinking and working together on what was initially called re-authoring therapy and is now better known as narrative therapy (Epston and White 1990). In this regard they were inspired by the work of Barbara Myerhoff (1986:145) who wrote about people as 'authors of themselves'. Re-authoring work creates a context in which people can once again give meaning to significant moments in their lives: moments that are often seen as an exception, unimportant or too ordinary. These meaningful moments are then woven into their lives in a way that creates new possibilities for conclusions about identity, relationships and the future.

How does re-authoring work see people? The re-authoring work sees people as meaning-makers and story makers of significant moments in their lives. Moments are seen as the smallest unit of experience (Zimmerman 2018). Because we give meaning to our experiences, moments are strung together into a story. These stories are very powerful, since they shape and maintain the identity, relationships, lives, history, future and reality of people.

[2]See Chap. 5 for further reflection of re-authoring practices.

Re-authoring ideas see identity as socially co-constructed by the context, cultural background, relationships and history of each person. Therefore, a person cannot be seen as a fixed identity, and this work always unpacks the extent to which people's identity conclusions fit in with the hopes and dreams for their lives.

Our identity is thus formed within a social context, in which generally accepted ideas present themselves as facts and truths about our lives. In this respect we can see narrative therapy as work in the field of social justice, because it is always aware of the dominant contextual ideas and their influence on people. The same applies to power relations that creep into conversations. This work stands next to people who experience injustice and does not work from a position of 'knowing about' or 'making decisions for' others.

As a result of this *dignified view* of people, a person is never seen as the problem. But the problem is the problem. People are therefore in a relationship to problem moments in their lives. The problem never has the last word, because there are always alternative moments that stand in contrast with problem moments in people's lives. This view, and the nature of the questions we ask, brings important relationships and moments in the lives of people back into their stories. This enables people to live again from the 'forgotten' dreams, skills and values of their lives.

Re-authoring practices consist of the externalization of problems, a transformative questioning and listening attitude, an appreciation for the creation of documents about the identity of a person, the use of the vocabulary of the person we are listening to, a focus on unique moments and alternative stories and finally the deconstruction of power.

What does re-authoring work do? This way of listening to stories enables listeners to ignite the beauty, dignity and honour of the narrator again. Both the narrator and the listener are therefore 'transported' to new insights, new experiences and new connections.

Re-authoring work strengthens our work with stories. We started working with the vision and practices of the re-authoring work, laying it as an extra foundation for our work with stories. Our conversations with storytellers continued to deepen, and we witnessed more than once a process in which people discovered new layers of meaning and possibilities in their stories.

4 Emerging Insights in 6 Years of Dedicated Story Work

From the end of 2012 up to and including 2015, we experimented with appreciative inquiry and generative journalism in the network Everyone Deserves A Holiday. In the beginning we published three stories every week, which we mainly wrote after telephone conversations with storytellers. Gradually we discovered that in face-to-face meetings with storytellers, a valuable depth was achieved, and we chose to continue further on this path. The meetings became more intense, and the stories became richer. From 2014 we published two stories per week. We further deepened the practice of listening, writing and sharing story by story. We especially discovered the power of a good conversation and were touched by how working with stories gives people the experience of being seen and how encouragement comes from publishing their authentic stories. Which effects did we gradually determine?

4.1 What Were the Effects that We Saw?

The team at VISITFLANDERS experiences a deeper connection with the mission of their work when they are surrounded by real-life stories from people who—despite their confrontation with limitations—experience a holiday. The team members discovered story after story to what and whom they are dedicating their work. Each story gives them insight into the effects of holidays on the lives of people in poverty, on their relationships with family and friends and on their experience of connectedness with society—precisely because they have access to holidays. Every new story is an opportunity for the team to be inspired and motivated again, because the stories whisper about values and hopes for the future. The valuable collection of stories also gives direction to the team in their work to make holidays even more accessible to everyone.

Professionals in the network, Everyone Deserves A Holiday, tourism entrepreneurs, community workers, social workers and policy makers can discover which projects, ideas, hopes and dreams are alive in the network. Whilst reading the stories from colleagues and vacationers, they find inspiration for their work. They discover with whom they can collaborate and how other network partners can strengthen their work. When holiday makers talk about their dreams for the future and their wishes for the society at large, they reconnect with their passions and with what drives them. This gives energy and fuels the fire. Then we see people acting on the basis of what they told as their hopes and ambitions.

Each story enriches our understanding of the essential meaning of holidays. It is an enlivening way to do an inquiry, a form of inquiry that is not 'outside' the field but stands in the midst of it. This way of inquiry does not only look 'at' the field but also develops this field of work: because every in-depth conversation with people, every written and shared story, influences the reality and what can become possible in that reality.

Every story is the result of relations between a narrator and a listener wherein dignity can be confirmed or restored. By embracing the re-authoring approach from 2015, we see a story-based work that not only focuses on communication and connection in the network, not only offers learning and cooperation opportunities, but also builds towards a world in which human dignity is restored. And yes, perhaps the most important outcome is that people—often people who feel excluded in society—have been seen and have seen themselves anew. They have been recognized, accepted and seen in their experiences, wisdom and hope. These people have experienced that they indeed have a voice. In this way, the story work contributes to the 're-dignifying' (Carlson 2017) of people.

4.2 Building Towards Dignity and How?

Firstly, we do not invent or make up stories. We go out and look for real-life experiences of people. We are not looking for '*the* big story' nor for exceptional achievements or experiences. We simply make contact and discover the richness in the real life of real people. We have a good, in-depth conversation with people in poverty, people that are differently abled, volunteers and professionals. We talk about who they are, about their lives, about their holiday experiences and their dreams for the future. We do not shy away from difficult stories. When we hear these kinds of stories, we try to find the desire and the strength behind the difficulties. We want to understand how holiday experiences offer people strength and strategies to cope with and overcome what is difficult in their lives. Our conversations are warm, thoughtful, encouraging and affirming of what is.

Secondly, the story worker writes the story. She/he brings structure into these life experiences and puts a spotlight on the underlying meaning. Then she/he sends the first text to the storyteller with the question: Is it a true reflection? Does this story tell about what is really meaningful to you? Does it tell it in a way that is respectful and suitable to be made visible in the network? In this phase people discover that their story has worth in the world, that they are valued as a person with meaningful experiences, hopes and dreams. A written story is also a document that holds an appreciating mirror up for people. To see their words, doubts, hopes and experiences on paper, written by someone who listened to them, is often a powerful experience that deeply anchors their hope and brings people to insight and action.

Thirdly, we publish the story and distribute it in the network. The experience that my story is worth sharing, that it is authentic and beautiful, that it contains exactly the words that I want to use, that my narrated story is structured in a meaningful way: that is, a deep, powerful experience. People then start to share their story in their own networks. We see people starting to act on the basis of what they told as their hopes and ambitions. We see people being 'seen' by their environment that their way of being is better understood and that they receive empathy, understanding and often even help.

Fourthly, we realize that this is work of dignity and re-dignifying. This is 're-authoring' work. Our work helps people to 'rewrite' their experiences, with more depth and a broader sense of meaning and preferred conclusions, moving away from thin and superficial holiday stories to colourful experiences full of values, strengths, hopes and possibilities. We believe that through this kind of story work, people become more aware of the richness of their personal experiences. We see how the eyes of people start to shine when they discover new experiences and insights that ultimately influence their choices and the visions of their life. Through this process of listening to stories, documenting and sharing, a treasure chest of rich identity conclusions opens up. Storytellers become more aware of who they are as a person, how they are connected to others and what gifts they have to offer to the world.

This work is extraordinary, valuable and humanizing. In 2017 we therefore decided to give this work an extra push. We wanted to deepen, spread and invite other people to become part of this work of dignity and re-dignifying. This work became *Storyweaving*. From 2018 we invited Storyweavers to cooperate with us on the international level in the re-authoring of travel and hospitality. That's why we came up with the *Connect Your Story* project.

5 The Birth of Storyweaving: A Dedicated Dignifying Practice

In our practice of finding, enriching and sharing stories for the past 6 years, we learnt that story work is *patient*: it is important, but almost never urgent. Without people who are devoted to finding, listening to and sharing stories, this work is hardly ever launched, because it requires attention and time, which is scarce in our working environments. That is why we appointed a dedicated story maker, whose assignment is to give the stories in the network all the space they need. But what do we call such a person whose dedication goes to the dignity practice of finding, enriching, documenting and sharing stories? The usual terms such as 'journalist', 'author', 'writer' or 'storyteller' fell short of a sufficient description. Moreover, we place the conclusive authorship not so much with the writer but with the narrator of the story. A storyteller is the person who tells his or her story. He or she is and stays the owner of the story.

In 2017, we started calling the listener-documenter a *storyweaver*: someone who carefully helps to weave every story that has been listened to into the life of the storytellers and the network in which this story resounds. A storyweaver understands the powerful impact of stories and the context from where these stories originate. She, or he, creates spaces in which people can take up the pen again and be the 'primary authors' (White 2005:9) who shape their own stories. A storyweaver is carefully curious about people. A storyweaver wants to learn from the stories people tell about who they are, what they experience, what they believe in and how they view the world. A storyweaver helps stories to be born and weaves them into the lives of narrators and the community. These stories can show alternatives, encourage others and create new opportunities.

This work is important in our world today, because the wisdom and knowledge of ordinary people—usually without status and without a voice—is often not seen and is not heard. Stories that are not heard do not resound and are not included in decisions: in communities, organizations and society at large. The more stories we discover and document, the more diversity will be recorded in these stories, and as a result the story of our world and our reality can become richer. And the richer our understanding of reality becomes, the more we can inspire towards transformation. In this way, storyweavers collectively participate in weaving an alternative world, in which the lives of people who are connected stand in the centre. Where the lives and voices of all people are equal in shaping and transforming our world.

5.1 Ways of Doing and Being as a Storyweaver

5.1.1 An Already Moved Heart (Carlson and Swart 2015–2017)

When we as storyweavers want to create the space where the dignity of the narrator can show up in the conversation, it is important that we come to the conversation with an 'already moved heart'. A heart that is already moved and ready to be touched, a heart that is already open to the beauty, dignity and aliveness that we will meet. Such an already moved heart focuses on love, respect, compassion and the firm belief to always hold on to hope in the conversation.

5.1.2 Creating the Atmosphere

Storyweavers create an atmosphere in which people can tell about moments that are of great significance to them. In this atmosphere we build a platform for human dignity, relationships and community. We create atmosphere by being attentive to the right place, the right time and a wealth of deep connections.

5.1.3 Focus on Connection

An appropriate atmosphere for a good conversation starts when we greet each other and connect before we dive into the content (Block 2008). Greeting and connection means that we are being attentive to who is with us. Who is this person? In which community does she/he live? We are inspired by a greeting that is customary to the Zulu people who greet with the words: 'Sawubona'. That means I see you. 'You' means much more than what we usually mean in individualistic societies. With 'Sawubona' we also see each other in the richness of our history, our soil and our relationships (Swart 2013:18).

5.1.4 Asking Transporting Questions

We greet, connect and invite stories through questions. In our questions, we pay attention to the identity of the other person, the community of the other person and their relationship with the world. Transporting questions are surprising, they make people think and remember and help people find words for what might not have been so clear to them.

5.1.5 Embodied Knowings (Carlson and Swart 2015–2017)

When we tell our stories—and are listened to—new insights, understanding, images, connections and possibilities are created and become visible. These discoveries touch and move us. We then reflect on the movement that we see and feel. The knowledges that emerge from these reflections originate from experiences and deep connection and can be described as 'embodied knowledge'.

5.1.6 The Exchanging of Gifts (Block 2008)

In working with stories, we pay attention to giving 'gifts' back and forth. The listener tells what touches him or her in listening to the stories of the other person. And he/she invites the narrator to do the same. Gifts are not compliments, or positive judgements. A gift tells about how our hearts have been touched and moved by listening to the story of the other.

5.1.7 Re-dignifying Practices[3]

In order to make every conversation a podium of human dignity, the 're-dignifying practices' are central. These practices give the 'storytelling rights' (Madigan 2011:16) back to the people we listen to.

The re-dignifying practices go back to the original Latin meaning of the word 'respect'. The word for respect originates from the words to 'look at' (specere) and 'looking back at' (re-specere). Looking back or seeing again means seeing without judgement and presumed knowledge of the other, which has often become a generally accepted practice.

The re-dignifying practices consist of being carefully curious (instead of judgements), asking questions to which you do not know the answers (rather than assuming), using the narrator's language in your questions (instead of giving advice), being open to be transformed (instead of wanting to solve things) and giving gifts.

In a world where people are often bombarded with questions and interrogations, and in which questions are asked that have a 'right' answer in mind, the re-dignifying practices help to restore the balance. Storyweavers are not parents, teachers, recruitment agents, journalists or researchers who have a correct answer in mind. The re-dignifying practices help us to take nothing for granted, to not fill in words for the other person and, on the contrary, to always keep the narrator's authorship at the centre.

6 Wild Dream for the Future: Let's Connect Stories!

2012 now lies more than 6 years behind us. What started out as an experiment grew into a core practice in the network Everyone Deserves A Holiday. Gradually we have broadened our experiments to the edge of the Flemish network. Our first-generation storyweavers have attended several conferences where academics and professionals from the international community around tourism and leisure have gathered. At these conferences we have also listened to stories about holiday experiences and how

[3]In many conversations Tom Carlson and I (Chené) shared between 2015 and 2017, Tom spoke about the re-dignification of the other. Over the years I have referred to practices of respect in various ways, but since my conversations with Tom, I have come to call these practices re-dignifying practices.

we can make holidays accessible for people who have fewer opportunities to go on a holiday.

This work has been welcomed with much enthusiasm. People who told us their stories said how valuable it was for them to remember through the telling why they are so passionate about their work in the tourism industry. The work stood out at the UNWTO, the World Tourism Organization of the United Nations. Tourism Flanders was invited to think about the start-up of an international collection of stories. Administrator General of Tourism Flanders, Peter De Wilde, responded enthusiastically and supportively. Former Secretary General of UNWTO, Taleb Rifai, accepted the patronage of the project and launched the start of the international stories collection *Connectyourstory.org* in Ghent, Belgium in 2018.

The goal of Connect Your Story is to stimulate conversations about the value of travelling in the lives of travellers, hosts and communities. *Connect Your Story* wants to gather stories about how tourism contributes to the world in a positive way. How travel connects people to each other, to place and to the world. Each conversation is simultaneously an opportunity to enrich worldwide stories about travel, to deepen our understanding of the essential values of tourism and to weave an alternative narrative for the sector 'tourism', based on the stories of 'ordinary' people, whose voices often remain unheard.

The more we remember and share our stories about travelling and being hospitable, the more we experience the benefits of those adventures. The more we experience those benefits, the more we can commit ourselves to giving people opportunities who would have fewer opportunities without our commitment. Through remembering and sharing our stories, we become more committed to opening our world to ourselves and to others: as a traveller, host or as a professional and volunteer in the tourism sector.

At the core of Connect Your Story is a community of 'storyweavers'. With *Connect Your Story* we want to build an international community of people who want to collect stories on a voluntary basis about how travel contributes to a dignified life for inhabitants of our planet. They receive training in the art of storyweaving wherein they will stimulate conversations, listen carefully, document and further tell the stories they have heard. They will weave thousands of stories into a pattern that tells about dedicated people who contribute to the possibility that tourism can turn the world into a place where the dignity of all life is central.

Connect Your Story wants to honour and encourage the hopes and initiatives of people. It wants to raise awareness about the contribution that tourism can make to the welfare of people, to prosperity, peace and cooperation. It will spread ideas and opportunities throughout the international tourism sector. It will connect people and bring citizens' initiatives into the limelight. It also wants to become a valuable resource of meanings in action research. Everyone who is filled with enthusiasm upon hearing this idea is welcome to join this effort!

7 Conclusion: Restoring the Dignity of Life Through Story Work

Imagine for a moment that you live and work in an organization or network where the future is built on the hope and willingness of all its members; that you feel connected to the whole at all times; that strengths are seen, by everyone; that opportunities continuously pop up and people are excited to make things happen; that your organization contributes to restoring the dignity of life in your (local) community; and that you are showered in stories of how the lives of people change through your work in the organization. This is exactly what we experience in our story work at the Holiday Participation Centre in Flanders. So, to end this contribution, we dive into this final important question: what does this narrative work add to our specific context and the larger network of Everyone Deserves A Holiday?

7.1 An Organizational View: The Future Lies in Networks

We believe that the future of successful professional cooperation lies in a particular form of how people organize themselves. Professionals and volunteers are already attracted to dedicating their efforts in structures that act as networks. Typical in networks are the non-hierarchical way of organizing and the triple-win philosophy. In a network, contributors are connected to the mission and to each other in equal relationships that honour the contribution of each participant to the whole.

7.2 Basic 'Data' in Networks Are Stories

The more all members are aware of purpose, possibilities and results, the more a network establishes its mission in broadening circles of influence.

Maybe the most important basic building blocks of networks are stories, because stories carry the language and images of life. In a (organizational) world that is entrenched with an alienating vocabulary of data, industrial language and even war-language, we long for stories about people experiencing real hope and establishing prosperity in each other's lives. Real-life stories speak to us about moments, images, enlivened language, metaphors, feelings, gifts and future opportunities.

7.3 Establishing Dignity Through Lived Stories

We are bombarded with stories nowadays, and to us it seems that stories have become a method for gaining influence in the lives of people. Leaders are trained to tell their influential organizational story. Brands try selling their goods with stories. Stories are shaped to direct human behaviour that aligns with what influencers want: directions that create feelings of being deprived if you do not have a particular device or experience. We admit this breaks our heart.

Because for us, stories carry and ignite our human existence and relationships with all of life. We see ourselves in the mirror of our stories. We connect with others through stories. We learn through stories. We envision the future through stories. We find meaning in our stories. We are seen and encouraged through our stories.

7.4 The Pace of Patience

Working with dignity is respecting the pace of life. No flower or any beautiful landscape is ever created through shortcuts. Networks are expressions of shared lives and have a life of its own. We cannot subject life to our own eagerness for quick results without offering life to death. So, patient commitment is a core attitude for leadership and story work in networks. Just like profound re-authoring work is, every story deserves our full attention and commitment.

7.5 We Can Make a Shift, Together

This is the hope we hold dear for the network 'Everyone Deserves A Holiday' in Flanders and the international *Connect Your Story* project: giving people the opportunities to tell their stories, so that they can connect their travel and hosting experiences with the hopes that surfaced in these moments and that they can draw meaning from these experiences for their life and for the world.

Then, after a long time of finding, documenting, sharing and connecting stories, we wake up in a new world. This is exactly what happens right now in the world of the Holiday Participation Centre.

That is why we want to broaden our work and created *Connect Your Story*. And that is why we invite you to become part of this adventure.

References

Block, P. (2008). *Community: The structure of belonging*. San Francisco, CA: Berrett-Koehler.

Bouwen, G. (2010). *Leiden naar talent en bezieling. Energie van mensen verbinden tot teamkracht*. Leuven: Lannoo Campus.

Brown, L. (2013). Tourism, a catalyst for existential authenticity. *Annals of Tourism Research, 40*, 176–190. https://doi.org/10.1016/j.annals.2012.08.004.

Carlson, T. (2017). Notes for the spirit of narrative conference. Benoni, South Africa.

Carlson, T., & Swart, C. (2015–2017). *Online conversations and correspondence*.

Epston, D., & White, M. (1990). *Narrative means to therapeutic ends*. New York: W.W. Norton.

Madigan, S. (2011). *Narrative therapy*. Washington, DC: American Psychological Association.

Minnaert, L., & Schapmans, M. (2009). Tourism as a form of social intervention: The holiday participation centre in Flanders. *Journal of Social Intervention: Theory and Practice, 18*(3), 42–61.

Myerhoff, B. (1986). "Life, not death in Venice": Its second life. In H. E. Goldberg (Ed.), *Judaism viewed from within and from without: Anthropological studies*. Albany, NY: State University of New York Press.

Swart, C. (2013). *Re-authoring the world: The narrative lens and practices for organisations, communities and individuals*. Randburg, ZA: Knowres.

White, M. (2005, September 21). Michael White workshop notes published on www.dulwichcentre.com.au

White, M. (2007). *Trauma and narrative therapy part 1*. Retrieved from https://vimeo.com/34671797

Zimmerman, J. (2018). *Neuro-narrative therapy: New possibilities for emotion-filled conversations*. New York: W.W. Norton.

Griet Bouwen is the author of two books around appreciative inquiry and coaching and AI and change towards humanization in organizations. Currently, she runs her small business Nieuwmakers, where she uses story work to lift up and connect people and their ideas, and, in that way, she shows visions of strengths and possibilities that are/become alive in organizations and networks. She's the co-creator of the *Connect Your Story* platform and co-organizer of re-authoring workshops, a re-authoring learning journey in Flanders and currently on a learning journey into practices of story harvesting and documentation.

Marianne Schapmans is running the Holiday Participation Centre in Tourism Flanders, which aims to strengthen the lives of people in poverty via a holiday experience. She is currently launching the *Connect Your Story* project, in partnership with the World Tourism Organization (UN), and is the ignitor of many change processes in her organization and network. In her work, she adapts the ideas of appreciative inquiry and re-authoring work.

Chené Swart is an international narrative consultant, coach and trainer. She is author of the book *Re-authoring the World* and contributed chapters on *Coaching from a Dialogic OD Paradigm* and *Re-authoring Leadership With and Within Organizations*. Chené is based in South Africa and is deeply involved in the project with tourism and travel. She offers training in re-authoring work in Flanders, Denmark, South Africa and other parts of the world. She is committed to ways of working and being with people that ignite the honour, dignity and beauty of their lives.

Re-authoring Careers: Changing the Narratives Around Work for Individuals and Its Impact on Organizations and Society

Marieke Genard

Abstract

This chapter describes the process of making career choices utilizing stories. It shows how a coachee finds the tools to navigate in different contexts and situations to approach his personal goals. The chapter starts by introducing the holistic vision for looking at a person. The career plan is part of his whole life. This is best captured by the ikigai principles. In the second and main part, the seven-step process is described and illustrated by two cases. Stories of his past make clear what already works and what needs more attention. On the other hand, future stories help the coachee envision where to find the horizon he wants to approach. By knowing the right words to express his future needs, the coachee can look at the labor market, find the most suitable place, or design the path to get there. In the last part, we look at the impact on organizations and society. The Flemish government now provides funding for individuals' career coaching to support people in their quest before developing a burnout, losing their job, or becoming unemployed. When individuals, supported by a coa, bring up important topics in the working environment, they make waves in the water, and the coaching can affect whole teams and organizations.

1 Diving, Swimming, or Floating in the Water? Introduction and Vision

The nature of our work with individuals is to empower them to accept that which calls to them. The metaphor of the swimmer helps us to reveal the coachee in his needs and actions as well as the context of the water. Personal drive will make some people dive, others swim faster, while others might feel the need to float.

M. Genard (✉)
Werk met Zin, Antwerpen, Belgium
e-mail: marieke@werkmetzin.be

© Springer Nature Switzerland AG 2019

J. Chlopczyk, C. Erlach (eds.), *Transforming Organizations*,
Management for Professionals, https://doi.org/10.1007/978-3-030-17851-2_16

1.1 Making Sense of Work

In this article I want to dive with the reader into the practice of using stories in career coaching.

The approach of re-authoring careers by working with stories is of great value to me because it seems to succeed with very different people, no matter what their background, studies, sector, or level of responsibility.[1] One day a professor walked out of my coaching room, and a cleaning lady entered just after. In both sessions, I used the same coaching method I will describe in this article. This approach was successful for both, despite their backgrounds and needs. It helped them make the choices which brought them closer to themselves and offered focus to their search on the labor market.

People can describe *why* they are taking the next steps toward their new goal. In a time when so many people work in "bullshit jobs,"[2] they lose the sense of work. Graeber says "People want to feel they are transforming the world around them in a way that makes some kind a positive difference."

The words we use to describe our present or future work create the world we are moving toward. In our language, the word *carrière (career)* refers to the image of climbing up, status, respect, and money.[3] The Dutch word *loopbaan* refers to the more holistic view: worth and values we[4] strive for during our working life. When talking about career coaching in this article, we aim for a holistic approach where we see people as a human beings or, even better, as "human becomings" (Swart 2013) while seeking harmony between his personal and professional goals.

The word *work-life balance* seems to indicate that there is only one way or the other: we work or we live. We prefer to look for a balance, best defined in the Japanese word *ikigai*[5], where four different approaches come together in harmony at the juncture of personal and societal needs (Fig. 1).

In this process, we are constantly looking for words to describe our world. *Finding the right words* for each individual quest(ion) leads us to the answers we are looking for. As soon as the person can specify the goals he is working toward and can see the horizon he wants to reach, he will be able to communicate with others about his future. To know the "why" of your personal goals is the first necessary step in reaching the "how" and "what" (Sinek 2009). In this way, the person can look for understanding, connect with supporters, and maybe find co-creators if they see a common horizon ahead.

---

[1]When writing about a person, I might use "he," but this can be applied to M/F/X.

[2]Graeber, anthropologist, at the School of Economics in London, did his research on useless jobs.

[3]The word "progress" is always part of the descriptions. The verb "career" refers to "rush, blast, shift." The etymology refers to Latin word "carrus," wheeled vehicle.

[4]When using "we," I refer to Werk met Zin, our cooperative coaching company. We share this vision with 27 coaches. When describing my personal coaching practice, I use "I," since we all work with our own methods and tools.

[5]Ikigai, a Japanese word to find a long and happy life.

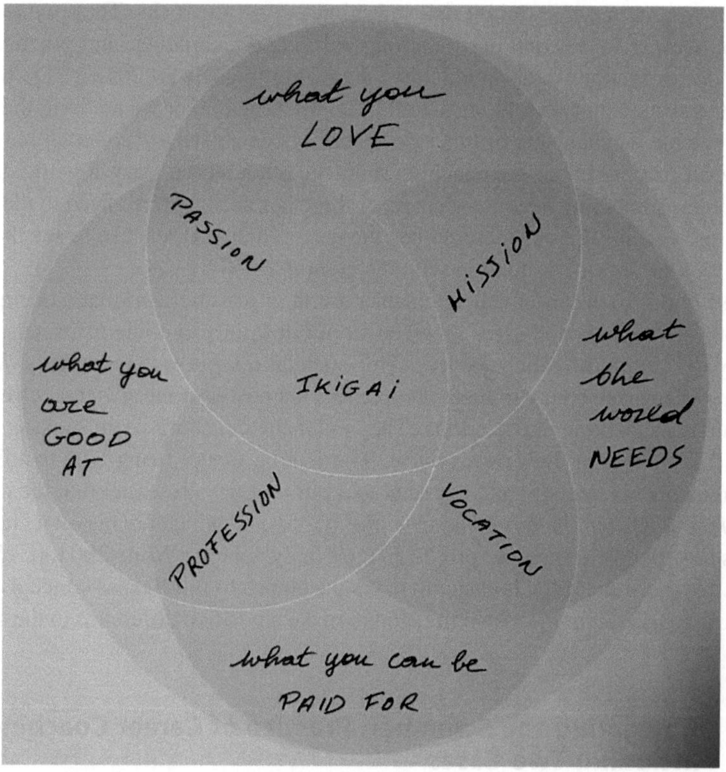

Fig. 1 Ikigai. Author's drawing based on Ikigai Wikimedia Commons

1.2 The Swimmer

As a swimmer, the working person (here: the coachee) is moving in his context or working environment. This environment can be a big lake, where the water is deep and calm. It can be a wild river, where the swimmer is dragged by the current, or it can be a small puddle, where he can barely move, or a stormy sea with high waves.

Together with the swimmer, we try to find out where he wants to go, and *we look for the navigation tools*. He can choose to swim faster, with or against the current, or he can just try to reach the coast as soon as possible and switch to a more suitable pool of water. That new water might require new swimming techniques.

When the swimmer knows where he wants to go and he sees the horizon in front of him, he will be more willing and eager to *learn the new technique*. Therefore, we help the swimmer to see the horizon clearly and to find out the nature of the water he is in. We support him in his search to identify the distance it takes to get to the shore and what competences he needs to develop to approach his goal.

Sometimes the swimmer needs to let himself *float with the current* for some time, to regain the energy to start moving again. But those who only let themselves float with the current or waves might risk smashing against the rocks. Those who choose to *swim against the current* need a strong will, good techniques, and practice.

But do we see the water in which we are swimming (Swart 2013)?[6] Do we truly notice the system and society we are all living in? The longer we are in it, the harder it is to see the mechanisms of this environment because *we are so much part of it.*

When a coachee enters the coaching room, he often feels uneasy at work: one way or the other, something needs to change, or there is a need to look ahead to the future. The career coach is an outsider and has the task to help the coachee to see the water and to look at the work situation with different eyes.

The (working) environment is much more than just the workplace or organization; it is also beliefs and ideas received from our family, a circle of friends, a city, country, or culture in which we live. This societal discourse entails many *different expectations* we are trying to meet. People feel the power of the societal current drag them along with these expectations. They enter the coaching room looking for the courage to transform their own course. The feeling of not being able to fulfill the "requirements" is stressful and can lead to a burnout. It is essential that the coachee sees *which ideas and beliefs come from the system* and which are his own choice, as well as how people refuse and protest in their daily actions (White 2004, p. 154). By seeing this more clearly, it is easier to make the choice to fulfill these concepts or not, to choose to transform their own life, and to make a positive difference to the society.

2 Navigating the Swimmer: Practice of Career Coaching Including Two Cases

This chapter is divided into three phases where the reader is guided through the seven steps of my coaching practice.

2.1 Why Do You Want to Swim? The Starting Point

Career coaching is preferably used as a *preventive* measure. As soon as people start feeling uneasy in their working situation and feel they have a need to reflect, they are ripe for coaching. When used preventively, coachee and coach are advantaged in thinking more freely of future stories, as there is no great pressure to start moving immediately. The career plan can be realized step by step. Therefore, the measurable effects of the coaching sometimes take place long after the coaching sessions.

[6] Swart Chené (in *Transformation through deconstructing societal discourses*, her chapter in this book) describes this water as "the ocean," the societal system, and culturally assumed taken-for-granted beliefs and ideas that have been constructed over time that surrounds and influences us. These beliefs and ideas or contexts are often referred to as "the way things are."

But the reality shows us that people often only ask for a coach when they *feel the urge* to do something about their work and when the situation has already escalated or is almost unbearable. When both parties are in conflict and barely manage to talk to each other, or when burnout strikes the coachee, or when the employer is about to fire the coachee, in the heat of the struggle, their needs might be different.

Many *initial questions* turn out to have *underlying questions*, e.g., a conflict with the boss might lead to the conclusion that the coachee and organization have different values. Coach and coachee might therefore redefine the initial question during the process of career coaching. The kind of questions we ask determines the answers we will get. Therefore, carefully formulating and redefining the question is part of the process.

2.1.1 Step 1: Asking the Question

This is the moment to introduce the story of two coachees, *two different cases*: *Mike* and *Martha*. I will describe their processes from the first meeting until the point when they make their choices.

Both cases in this article have started with Coffee & Coach[7], which is an introduction session to the 4 hours of a Career Cheque.[8]

Case 1: Mike, 28 Years Old, Works as a Nurse at a Psychiatric Center

A humble and shy young man walked up to my table. This was my first impression of Mike when he came to Coffee & Coach. He immediately told me that it was an enormous step for him to come and ask for help. He had crashed last summer because of work and had been out for a few weeks. Since then he had made a fresh start with a new employer but could feel the signs of a second crash approaching.

Mike realized he needed some support in his decision-making and had concluded that the sector he was working for, namely, in psychiatric centers with quite demanding and difficult patients, was not his environment. The permanent understaffing and lack of decent organization made him sad and angry. He felt he should make a radical career switch but had no clue where to aim.

[7]We offer "Coffee & Coach," a free introduction talk in a coffee house, to reduce the threshold for people who doubt if a coach can help them in their search.

[8]A career cheque is funded by the state, for the cost of 40 € the individual can get 4 hours of coaching. See Sect. 3.1 empowering the working individual how and why the state is funding career coaching.

Case 2: Martha, 39 Years Old Is a Team Leader in a Social Community Service

When Martha met me at Coffee & Coach, her questions consisted of various components: she was not sure if her present job fit her, and she had doubts about the organization as well as about her own leadership qualities. Should she eventually conclude that she didn't fit at her current job, she indicated she would like to explore other options and opportunities. Martha studied anthropology, is a mother of two young children, and works 4 days a week. She seems to have managed the combination until doubts about her work started to have an impact on her sleep.

I asked Martha to tell me the story of a situation when those doubts arose. We concluded that leadership styles and values, which seem to be very different between Martha and her boss, will be an important focus of the coaching.

2.2 Dive into the Stories and Re-author Careers

Here we take the reader along in the first steps of the *process of making choices*. Stories play a vital role in this process and make a good starting point. They help us to get a clear image about what gives energy, what puts people in motion, and what makes them strive to take their very personal journey. Will it be with or against the current? Only when they know what their goal is do we look at the job market, to see what kind of environment this person could flourish in.

At the end of the first meeting, the coachee gets "homework" to prepare for the next session. I ask them to think about three stories and tell me about them in the next session. Stories of very specific *moments which gave them energy*, moments they were doing something that made them forget time, moments[9] that made them feel competent and powerful, and stories of flow that gave them the kind of feeling they want more of in their life, whether these moments occurred in their working or private life, recently, or in the past.

2.2.1 Step 2: Telling Past Stories

Telling stories is very essential to enable the coachee to revive the enthusiasm he once experienced. At the end of this second session, the coachee will have the first feeling of a clear direction. This is the beginning of a process that will make them feel competent again and make them believe (again) in their own capacity.

Before getting into the stories, I also ask them how it felt to collect them. Here very different processes occur. There is no "right" or "wrong." The stories the coachee chose will be relevant to work on.

[9]More on the importance of moments can be found in the chapter in this book by Chené Swart.

Mike

Mike's present working context received a lot of attention in our sessions because of the sense of urgency. It was necessary to talk about it in this coaching session, before we could start working on his plans for the future. His mood puts the coaching room in a grayish fog, which I tried to clear by asking him for his stories.

The stories Mike told showed me—as a coach—another Mike, engaged and creative in his job and a careful and cheerful friend in his free time. In those few moments at his work when he had time to devote his full attention to a patient in need, he managed to establish a good connection. He could see his own contribution to the positive evolution of the patient, and he was proud of the outcome. Mike also felt the same energy when he could bring a group of patients together and, by playing a game, have an interesting group conversation. But Mike is more than just a working person. In his leisure time, he loved handicrafts, bringing friends together and setting the atmosphere for a festive evening.

While he was talking, I could see his eyes shining, a big smile appeared on his face, and from time to time, he lost himself staring in the void of those memories. He had to admit that there was a lot of passion at the core of his job, but the unfortunate circumstances of the context prevented him from doing what he was good at.

Martha

The stories Martha chose showed me a very creative and adventurous person who loves to have very personal contact with people from various backgrounds. The stories referred to travel experiences as well as working with the target group of the social center. While telling the stories, Martha concluded that in her present role, she rarely has personal contact with her target group. She remarks that she is not able to deliver quality because of the lack of time. She has three different teams to manage, which fragments her work into many small pieces.

While the coachee is telling the three stories, I do not intervene, unless there are questions for clarification. I do this to get a better impression of the context, the people involved, and the role of the coachee. The only questions are those meant to enliven the stories, to *live in the presence*[10] *of the experience*. I am not leading the coachee to certain conclusions in this stage, but sometimes when the people

[10]In the apprentice journey, Chené Swart introduced the flow between living in the presence of stories versus meaning making.

themselves come up with a summary, they see the similarity in their stories. It is only in the next step that we will actively search for those similarities.

2.2.2 Step 3: Defining Ingredients

In this phase I take the coachee from those very specific moments (presence) to a more abstract level, where we define words to give meaning. We start looking for the key concepts that reveal positive energy (Bouwen and Meeus 2007, p. 49). What *ingredients* do the coachee see coming back in his moments? Those can be interests, competences, verbs, values, contextual aspects, etc.

In this phase the coachee looks—with a little help from the coach—for the right words. The coach *collects the words* on a flipchart, not in a list but as individual entities (in random order and place). The words should be formulated in a positive sense; this means we avoid the word "no" or "lack of." This is not easy for a coachee who comes to a session already frustrated.

When we have written down about five words on the flipchart, I ask, "Imagine a situation where all those things are present (I sum up the words) in your work and/or private life: is this sufficient for you? Or are you still missing something?". Mostly we continue looking for more words defining the coachee's energy sources.

I repeat the same question, over and over again, until the coachee is happy with all the words written on the flipchart. Most of the time, we have between six and ten words on the flipchart.

Mike

After listening to his stories, I asked him to look at those different situations and find some terms they have in common. This is how we started story weaving, finding the connections as a thread in his stories. I wrote these words on a flipchart in a random order: "helping others," "to puzzle/riddle," "appreciation," "creativity," and "working with hands". He grew speechless and looked at me.

"Imagine, you are working in a job where you find all these ingredients. Would this be the perfect place for you? Or is there still something missing?"

"A team! I really need colleagues to share my concerns and experiences."

I added the word "team" and repeated my question the same way as before. After some thinking we completed the word cloud with "coaching" and "organizing."

By the end of this session, we had a flipchart with eight different words, describing the best context, interests, competences, and qualities of Mike. These are the main ingredients he is looking for in his future work.

Martha

When looking at Martha's stories, she was quick to come up with the words "development," "working together," "appreciation," "being useful," and "people." After looking at what she misses now, we translated the "lack of time" into "delivering quality," which is what she needs the time for. The lack of contact with the target group she translated into "empathizing" and the word "translating" also appeared on the flipchart. When she looked at the eight words on the flipchart, she took a deep breath. "This is me" she said, "this is exactly what I need to be happy in my job and life."

To close this coaching session, I explain the next two steps to prepare as homework, so we can talk about them in the following meeting:

- Elaborate on these "basic ingredients" in a dreamcatcher.
- Start dreaming and thinking about a future story.

2.2.3 Step 4: Weaving the Web

The *dreamcatcher*[11] is an exercise to go more deeply into the basic ingredients or energy sources by weaving a web of associations as to what those words mean to the coachee. The model I use is a "dreamcatcher," where all the main ingredients come together in the center. That is where "the dream" can emerge without needing to give it a name at this stage. It is the exact mixture of those ingredients, well enough defined and personalized, that makes clear what the coachee is looking for in his future life. For example, "team" is only a word. It might appear on many dreamcatchers for all kinds of different people. In weaving the web, it becomes more and more clear what the coachee needs in a team.

Mike

For Mike the word "team" means support, listening to each other, telling stories, openness, and taking the lead. When adding these words, the web becomes a very personal interpretation.

The web grows with these associations, from about 8 words to almost 40. Sometimes we see the same word coming back in another association. This is comforting, as it proves the solidness of the web and makes sure different things are connected. In Mike's web we see "listening" being repeated, as well as "appreciation." Could this say something about what he is missing right now?

(continued)

[11]This tool has grown in my practice but was originally inspired by an existing exercise (Struik 2008, p. 20).

Stories of energy provide us with necessary words, but this does not mean we have to ignore the tough times. Mike is suffering from his present work so much that there is the need to tell these stories as well, even though he is quite convinced he will quit this job very soon. Considering that problems are signs of needs, we can reverse the thinking on what might come out of his frustrations, namely, "the lack of, etc." In this way we find words like "structure," "problem-solving," and "time for personal contact." Mike works in shifts and has late working hours, which have a negative impact on his private life and friendships. Since he knows these are important for his well-being, he adds them to the web (see further on Fig. 3, dreamcatcher Mike).

Martha

In her dreamcatcher (Fig. 2), Martha discovers many ingredients she sees represented in her work. But at the same time, it also clarifies that her actual function, being a leader of three different teams, makes it impossible to find all her energy sources in the job. The culture of her employer, and especially of her boss, contradicts certain values she needs. The clear question arises: is it possible to achieve them with this employer or does she need to look for a new one?

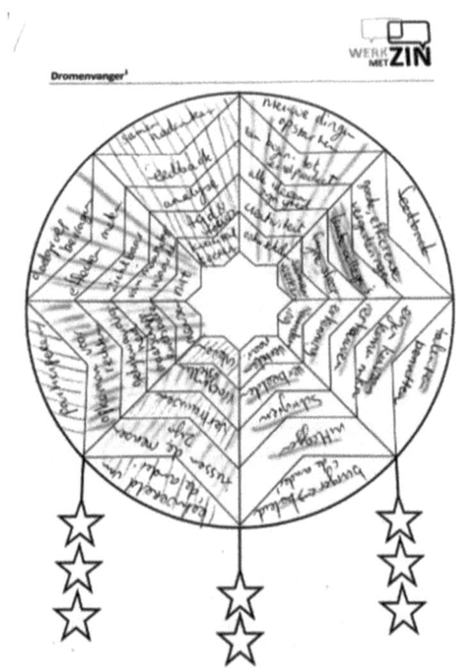

Fig. 2 Dreamcatcher Martha: in the center Martha wrote, "development," "working together," "appreciation," "being useful," "people," "delivering quality," "empathizing," and "quality." Each of those terms generates associations. For example, "development," "creativity," "all ideas are good," "from start till end product," and "starting up new initiatives." Author's own figure

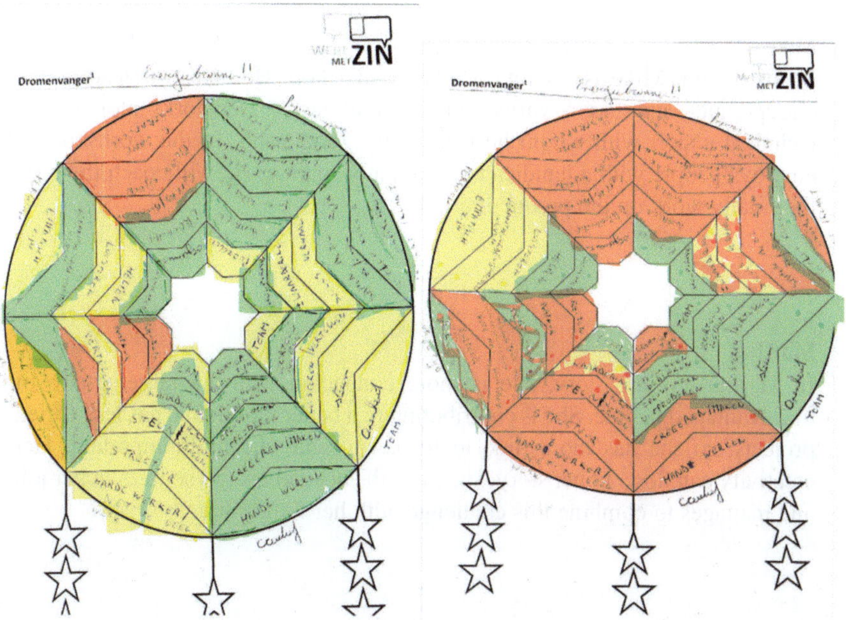

Fig. 3 Dreamcatcher Mike compares two different contexts. He used the colors of the stoplight to indicate if he would find in this option his energy sources. The words on the dreamcatcher are the same. The context of the two jobs he is comparing is different. That makes a different color effect: *Green* stands for YES, it is present in this context/job opportunity. *Yellow* (or orange) stands for MAYBE or A LITTLE. *Red* stands for NO; this source of energy will not get the needed space in this context/job. Author's own figures

2.2.4 Step 5: Telling the Future Story: Daring to Dream

In the next step, the coachee is asked to start dreaming. "Fly" with one's head in the clouds and let his imagination flow. The energy sources, or the full dreamcatcher web, can serve as an inspiration; they will be the ingredients of the future story. We do this with "the miracle question."

We ask the coachee to imagine he wakes up in 3 years' time, and *the miracle has happened, he is living the dream*. What does a (working) day look like? What does he do that day? From waking up until going to bed, he is asked to describe the full day in detail. This also includes work-life balance. Who does he work with? What does he do? Where does he work? He should let his imagination flow like water, dare to dream, and not let reality hold him back ("this will not be realistic").

We have noticed that dreaming a future story is not an easy task for many of our coachees. It is hard to let go into the imagination. But the dreamcatcher can help them to formulate the desired future.

Mike
In his dream, Mike is running a bike repair shop. He takes the lead as the entrepreneur and has a variety of different tasks. He works alongside a technical expert with whom he has a very good bond. In the workshop he employs people with a handicap on the labor market. He will coach them on their daily work on the production line.

Martha
In Martha's future story, she is more connected with the target group of disadvantaged people. She is contributing to a better world. She has less varied projects, so she has more time to focus on what she finds important. Her creativity can flow. In her story, she finds the needed energy sources in her job and manages to combine this challenge with her family life.

2.2.5 Step 6: From Here to There: Facing Reality

Dreaming of a better future helps people see the horizon toward which they want to start swimming. But this future might look far away. In the next step, the coach helps the coachee with a reality check.

We look at the present: where do we stand now? How can we look at the horizon and *take the first strokes toward swimming in the desired direction*? By dividing up the distance with buoys (rest places) or even a shore on which to rest in-between, the far away horizon becomes more "reachable." We must be aware that there is a distance to cover and that it will take effort to reach the goal. We must take care that, if we start swimming, every stroke brings us to the right direction and that we do not take a side route that would take us in another direction or let us drift with the current and end up somewhere else.

The dreamcatcher can be used as a compass to help us to navigate. Each of the opportunities passing by can be weighed against this web. A job vacancy the coachee selects either does or doesn't fit when placed against the mold. To measure this fit, I propose a very visual way of working with colors. The three colors of a traffic light can be used to mark each of the words in the web:

- Green if the ingredient could be present in the new opportunity
- Red if it is clearly nonexistent
- Orange in case of doubt or only partly present

This method shows very clearly where this path would lead and what does and what doesn't match with the coachee's dream.

If the coachee starts by analyzing his present working situation, it represents a visual template to compare future options. Each option might have its weak spots, orange, or red words, but the future should be attractive enough to take the risk and change jobs. When applying for another job, the colored web of that situation should be "greener" than the present work is. We only take the step to change if it would bring us closer to the final future story. That could be by getting to know a new sector, learning new competences, or even start studying again.

Mike

Mike is young and idealistic, but he has enough awareness of reality to not dive into taking big risks. He knows he must get to know the social economy sector as well as the technical part of bike repairing. Therefore, he looked at the labor market for vacancies leading to the next step of his career.

When he picked a vacancy of a coach/instructor in social economy, Mike discovered a good match and applied for the job. As a comparison, we did the same exercise with his present job and saw much more red appearing (see Fig. 3). Another option was to work in a supermarket with more routine work, meaning he would switch off his mind for some time. This last option would not bring him any closer to his dream; also, it would lack many of the ingredients of his web. Conclusion: this part of the labor market would fall out of his future focus.

In this usage of the tool, we are comparing a present (well known) situation, to a future path (unknown, but assumed on the bases of gathered information). The only way to get to know more of this future and how much it would fit his personal growth path is to investigate, ask, inform, read, and possibly try it for some time.

In Mike's case, a jump into the unknown is not taking inordinate risks. He is young enough to learn from this step, to get into another job, and, if needed, to switch again. He has no family or responsibilities other than to himself. He is both experienced and young enough to be attractive to an employer and thereby gain the chance to grow in his function.

2.3 Changing the Course of the River or Floating with the Water: Results and Effects for the Individual

This process can go quickly or take a long time, depending on the situation. On the one hand, we see small changes can make huge differences: job crafting and looking at the old realities with fresh eyes. But sometimes we also see very big changes: new job, new sector, back to school, or starting their own business.

A coachee, according to his needs, can choose to accept the situation as it is; sometimes they even realize it is not that bad at all. In these cases, they might look again at their work situation, having now identified the aspects they need to work on. They might choose to enjoy floating with the water, or they might have the faith that they can be part of the changes in the working environment.

2.3.1 Step 7: Starting to Swim—Heading Toward the Future

This is how we *take the first steps* in clearing out the future perspective of careers. For some people this is sufficient, and they will move on without the need of a coach to support them. Others still like to have the coach standing by their side while taking their first steps into their future stories. The coach could provide support in preparing their talks, in applying for jobs, or in writing their CV and motivation letters. Most of the time, one Career Cheque (4 h) can be enough to bring the coachee far enough so that he can see a future plan clearly. The second phase (check) can be used to realize the plan. We will not focus on this next stage in this article, as it exceeds the scope of this story and diverges in a very broad range of approaches.

Mike

In our fourth coaching session, it looked like Mike was absolutely convinced he must leave his present job as soon as possible. His internal complaints led to his superiors exhibiting a lack of trust in him, and they acknowledged this in the last team meeting. They suggested they would take steps, without clarifying what those would be. Mike hoped they would decide to fire him, so he could be free to spend his energy looking for another job.

He was happy though; his colleagues took his word and defended him. He needed to feel he was appreciated, even when deciding to leave. They praised his work with the patients, his willingness to share his experiences with newcomers, and his hard work and clear insights. This support was essential for Mike's self-confidence. Looking at his dreamcatcher again, it was one of the positive ingredients which was confirmed: a team with support and trust for each other. Alas, the superiors mainly got to see his anger and frustration and did not see enough of his qualities.

Mike finished this series of coaching sessions by writing his personal development plan. He is looking forward to a future as a social entrepreneur. That is the horizon he will aim for. First, he will take the steps in-between, to get to know the social economy sector. After working hours, he will enroll in a course in bike repair to get a grip on the technical part of the work, not to become the technician but to understand the craftsmanship well enough to be able to run the company.

Mike believes he can go on with implementing his plan, without the need for further coaching. He promises he will come back as soon as he feels he is ready for the next step. He says my support has empowered him to feel confident again and make a clear plan with realistic next steps.

Martha

Since Martha still believes she could realize her dream with her employer, she dares to dream of the perfect balance in her job as a team leader. Together we unfolded the expectations of "leadership" from different angles: the expectations she has herself, her manager has, the board has, her team has, and those of the target group. We used the method to "unpack" the reality.[12] This picture of all the different expectations makes clear that she will have to make choices. She'll bring in her personal values in order to make clear which expectations she wants to work on. Only when this is clear will she be ready to start communicating her wishes to her employer. She will present her vision on her personal future within the organization. Only if she feels the employer is willing to go along with her needs will she go for this job.

In the first discussion with her manager, she received very positive reactions and felt the openness to work with her on a new future.

This is where the first Career Cheque ended. Martha decided to ask her employer for coaching in the workplace. The employer agreed; even while writing this article, we are about to start the continuation of this coaching but now paid by the employer and within the triangle of coach-coachee-manager. Martha believes the changes are needed and realistic. It might involve a change of the work culture in the organizations, but she found some supporters inside, and together they are willing to work on changing the course of the river.

These changes don't always look spectacular, and they might even seem trivial. But every step counts and brings them closer to the goal.

Our short- and long-term evaluations show that after the coaching takes place, people take a fresh look at their situation and see this as a positive result. Coachees learn to appreciate what already is, to discuss and change what they are missing, and to take responsibility of their own career by taking concrete steps. A long-term and a short-term plan to work on their future goals helps them to re-author their career.

This is how past and future stories can re-author careers.

3 Waves in the Water and Changing the Waterway: Career Paths in Society and Organizations

3.1 Empowering the Working Individual: How and Why the State Is Funding Career Coaching

In a program begun in 2013, the Flemish *government is funding individuals* with coaching Career Cheques. A person who works can buy a check for 40 euros, worth 4 h of coaching to help reflect on their working life. During a pilot project

[12]Chené Swart notes from the apprentice journey *Re-Authoring the World.*

(2004–2013) funded by the European Social Fund, research proved that career coaching (where the employer is not involved) for the working person is successful on various aspects (Verbruggen and Sels 2009, pp. 28–61).[13] The Career Cheques are available to everyone who works (be it as an employee or self-employed), renewable every 6 years. The individual is entitled to two checks of 4 hours of coaching by a recognized career center.

Four years after the launch of the Career Cheques, the number of participants has grown quickly: 63,721 individuals have used at least one check. 20,847 of them used a second check (VDAB 2017, p. 12). The government decided to create an *open market for career centers*, and the rise in recognized coaches (individuals as well as within organizations) has been spectacular. Between 2013 and 2017, the number of recognized centers grew from about 50 to 232. There are now almost 3000 locations where people can meet a coach. The numbers are still growing. This means it has become a very *competitive sector*. The need to raise quality standards is high.

3.2 The Effect on Organizations

The Career Cheque is *the private right of every working individual* and can be used totally separate from the working environment. This means that many employers are not aware of the fact that their employees are in career coaching. If an employer wants to encourage an employee to use his checks, he cannot force it. The choice to use a Career Cheque is totally individual and is part of the coachees' privacy.

Still, it is possible that *employers encourage* their staff to reflect on their careers. They can provide support by informing people of their right or even sponsor the 40 € per check. The employee, though, must be aware he is using his right and his checks and will have to wait 6 years to use this right again.

When the individual follows career coaching, the effect can be positive for everyone at the workplace. Setting things in motion makes waves which also affect the rest of the workforce. And what about burnout prevention by starting career coaching in time? And what if conflicts can be discussed and solved? The coach can provide support in *finding the words to talk about what really matters*. Even when the coachee decides to leave the organization, it has an impact, because he either gives up fighting for his aims or because he concluded this organization is not the right place for him (anymore). The departure of someone could solve an ongoing conflict. Or the employer might be shaken awake by the departure of his staff and decide to work on enacting better working conditions.

[13]The aspects are satisfaction with the service, better self-knowledge, better insight in the labor market, clear career goals, higher self-confidence, lifelong learning, etc.

3.3 The Effect on Society

Burnout has become such a common problem that it affects more than the working environment only. Career coaching can help to *prevent burnout*. But unfortunately, many people crash before they take the first step to begin career coaching. After the worst physical phase of burnout has been worked on by a doctor and maybe by a therapist or psychologist, a new *perspective on the reintegration in working life* is needed. This is where the career coach comes into the picture.

People suffering from a burnout often end up on long-term sick leave. Their absence makes waves in the workplace and could make the burden heavier for co-workers. It also has a great impact on the Federal states' budget of sick allowance. The effect is great as well on the private lives of these individuals: partners, children, and other family members who are confronted with the effects of a long-term dropout.

Another impact of career coaching on society is the start of a lot of *entrepreneurial* plans and projects. When people conclude their goal is to be undertaken outside of an existing structure or organization, they develop their own project. This start-up might later grow into a company employing others. In this way coachees have an effect on the (local) economy and can even *create employment.*

4 Conclusion

Throughout the course of these seven steps in career coaching, the coachee will find personal words to describe his future, not through tests and checklists trying to fit his personality into existing categories but by utilizing stories to help find his unique framework to focus on. The web of words he creates is about more than only work, it is about the meaning he wants to give to his life. With these words, the individual finds the power to start swimming, either with or against the current, and thus re-author his career and transform the world around him by contributing to it from a position of personal strength.

References

Bouwen, G., & Meeus, M. (2007). *Vuurwerkt, met Talent Toekomst Maken*. Leuven: Lannoo Campus.

Sinek, S. (2009). *Start with why: How great leaders inspire everyone to take action*, Portfolio.

Struik, A. (2008). *52 Vonken, Ruimte om te Stralen*. Leidschendam: Quist.

Swart, C. (2013). *Re-authoring the world, the narrative lens and practices for organisations, communities and individuals*. Randburg: Knowres Publishing.

VDAB. (2017). *Monitoring van de loopbaancheque, 4 jaar na lancering*. Brussels: VDAB.

Verbruggen, M., & Sels, L. (2009). *Loopbaanbegeleiding in Vlaanderen, de instroom in en effecten van loopbaanbegeleiding onder de loep genomen*. Leuven: WSE report, Steunpunt Werk & Sociale Economie, KULeuven.

White, M. (2004). *Narrative practise and exotic lives: Resurrecting diversity in everyday life*. Adelaide: Dulwich Centre Publications.

Marieke Genard works as founder-coordinator in Werk met Zin ("Werk met Zin" has two meanings in the Dutch language: "make sense of work" and "enjoy working."), a cooperation of 27 coaches and trainers working all over the Flemish region in Belgium. During her studies of Slavonic Languages and Cultures in the early 1990s, Marieke supported the development of new youth organizations in Central and Eastern Europe just after the fall of the Berlin wall and the collapse of the Soviet Union. Organizational development connected with individual growth has been the thread in her work. She combines field research and entrepreneurship with her coaching practices. Since 2004 she learned the craft as a career coach for individuals. Stories have been a part of her life since her childhood. Storytelling as a method entered her coaching work after getting to know appreciative inquiry (AI) in 2010. She became an accredited AI practitioner. From then on, she coached over 500 clients finding her with different questions and needs. More recently, she dove deeper into narrative ideas and practices through an apprentice journey with Chené Swart called Re-Authoring the World. She works with the approach both in teams and organizations as well as in her own cooperation.

The Magic of a New Beginning: A Personnel Development Department Reinvents Itself the Future of HR. Current Developments and a Methodological Approach to Narrative Transformation of HR Identity

Melanie Gabert

Abstract

We are in an ever-changing working world. Employees need to develop to meet new requirements, which require a constant effort to develop their own identity. Stories, to which one has an easy access to, are an effective tool for dealing with constant change. In addition, they are ideally suited for importing knowledge, motivation, and inspiration. This not only presents personnel development with new challenges but also with its own new role model and a changed professional identity. Storytelling can help to rewrite your own story as well as for a whole department. What this might look like in practice is described in the following chapter.

1 Introduction or "Just Because It Is Labeled Agility, It Does Not Mean Is Agile"

Recently in personnel development of a large medium-sized company, which has added the still very young but increasingly popular method of "design thinking" to the training program, I thought, "Great!". The new methods that stimulate greater agility and self-organized work are currently finding their way not only into global corporations but also into small- to medium-sized companies. However, I was still involved in devaluing the somewhat different understanding of this agile method in the department. Apart from the offer of new, modern, and agile working methods, carried out by external speakers, the new way of working in the department itself had

M. Gabert (✉)
Adult Education, Kolping Bildungswerk Württemberg e.V., Stuttgart, Baden-Württemberg, Germany
e-mail: melanie.gabert@kbw-gruppe.de

© Springer Nature Switzerland AG 2019

J. Chlopczyk, C. Erlach (eds.), *Transforming Organizations*,
Management for Professionals, https://doi.org/10.1007/978-3-030-17851-2_17

not yet sunk in, at least not permeated. Valuation-free brainstorming was a challenge for the long-standing staff of the personnel development. Discussions were held at endlessly long meetings, with detailed minutes being drafted. Corrections were read by a small circle of attending confidants before the minutes were sent. An enormous investment in time and effort. Agility, simply being miles away. The HR director was open to these new working methods. The team was not present yet and was simply forgotten in all of the company's implementation efforts. And even the boss had not completely internalized the subject. By no means an isolated case. Often the personnel development receives tasks to put forth, or they should suddenly lead topics in the enterprise without having even clearly understood the topic themselves. A difficult and unrealistic undertaking, if there is not enough knowledge and competence, attitude and passion for the new cause. In addition to this problem, scarce human or monetary resources or overburdening with new skill requirements for the workplace is difficult to cope with. It is the personnel developers who should prepare the employees for the requirements of tomorrow.

New work requirements lead to new competencies for the entire workforce. Personnel development is first of all a pioneer, then an initiator, companion, and further educator. These changing roles that human resource developers are accepting create a new self-image, a new identity to support the rewriting of their own story.

This chapter deals first with the change of the working world and competencies required in the future. It shows the new role and identity of HR developers and exemplifies how storytelling can describe their own professional role in a workshop. A final glossary shows HR developers or HR development consultants the various ways of storytelling and story listening in the context of the 70:20:10 model for their practical work.

2 New Demands in the Working World Result in New Roles of HR Developers

Increasing digitalization and mechanizations mean enormous changes for companies. Who wants to still be in the front row tomorrow has to be fast, flexible, and agile. Companies need to prepare their employees for these changes, not temporarily but continuously and for a lifetime. Old predominantly hierarchical structures, processes, and tools have had their day. Self-organized and responsible work becomes standard. With the new demands on the working procedures, each employee also changes the way of learning. "We need to teach people what they really need: critical thinking, basic technology literacy, data analytics, learning abilities, working independently, and entrepreneurial skills," according to the results of the International Delphi Study of the Millennium Project "2050: The Future of Work" (Daheim and Wintermann 2016). Above all, it's about a pleasurable change and a flexible-open mind-set. How open this is can be seen again and again in practice. I often hear from HR developers that there are other, more important issues to deal with than storytelling. As a result, cite, "not even e-learning is properly used" but rather pure classical seminar management is pursued. Personnel development is more than just the offering of rhetoric courses and team development seminars. Storytelling should not be seen as an additional task with so often already scarce human resources but much more as a company-enriching, accompanying method. Above all the entrepreneurial benefit must be in the foreground. A strategic relationship to the company goals must be present. "Although there are plenty of concepts, know-how and tools, success so far has been modest. This is primarily due to the experience and competence of the personnel developers: Apart from the exchange of door titles and business cards, hardly anything has changed in the mindset and behavior of the personnel development departments. Where 'strategic personnel development' is written, it is still mainly education and further education" (Wirl 2011). So it is no longer just about the mere transfer of knowledge or behavioral change but rather about the development of a changed mind-set, which includes lifelong learning and open-mindedness toward changes, in order to be able to cope with the already increasing demands of today but also of the future.

The Institute for the Future (IFTF) for the University of Phoenix Research Institute (2011) has identified the six drivers of change that have already had a significant impact on the professional environment and will continue to have in the future:

- Increased life expectancy
- Computerization/digitalization
- Intelligent machines/artificial intelligence
- New media
- Superstructured organization
- Global networking

With these changes, employees are increasingly asked to perform self-organized, to think entrepreneurially, to decide faster, to bear responsibility, to acquire new knowledge independently, to work interdisciplinarily and interculturally, and to adapt flexibly to the most current work requirements. As a result, the tasks of the personnel development also change (Fig. 1).

Personnel development has a stronger than ever requirement to meet the demands of the new working world and to work on the mind-set of employees. "Training will have to evolve constantly to become a learning organization that can adapt quickly to change. Digitalization makes it possible to reach employees quickly, cost-effectively, anywhere and in any time zone. The main tasks are to make training more enjoyable and to offer fun and playful competition in addition to pure learning content" (Sons 2016). In doing so, the competencies required in the company are worked out and analyzed with regard to target achievement. How can the entrepreneurial spirit of a single employee be strengthened, and how can agility and creativity be promoted?

The publisher of the magazine "Training", Christoph Wirl cites Wayne Gretzky, the world's best hockey player of this time: "Most players are pretty good, but they go where the puck is. I go where the puck will be." To bring the team or at least the

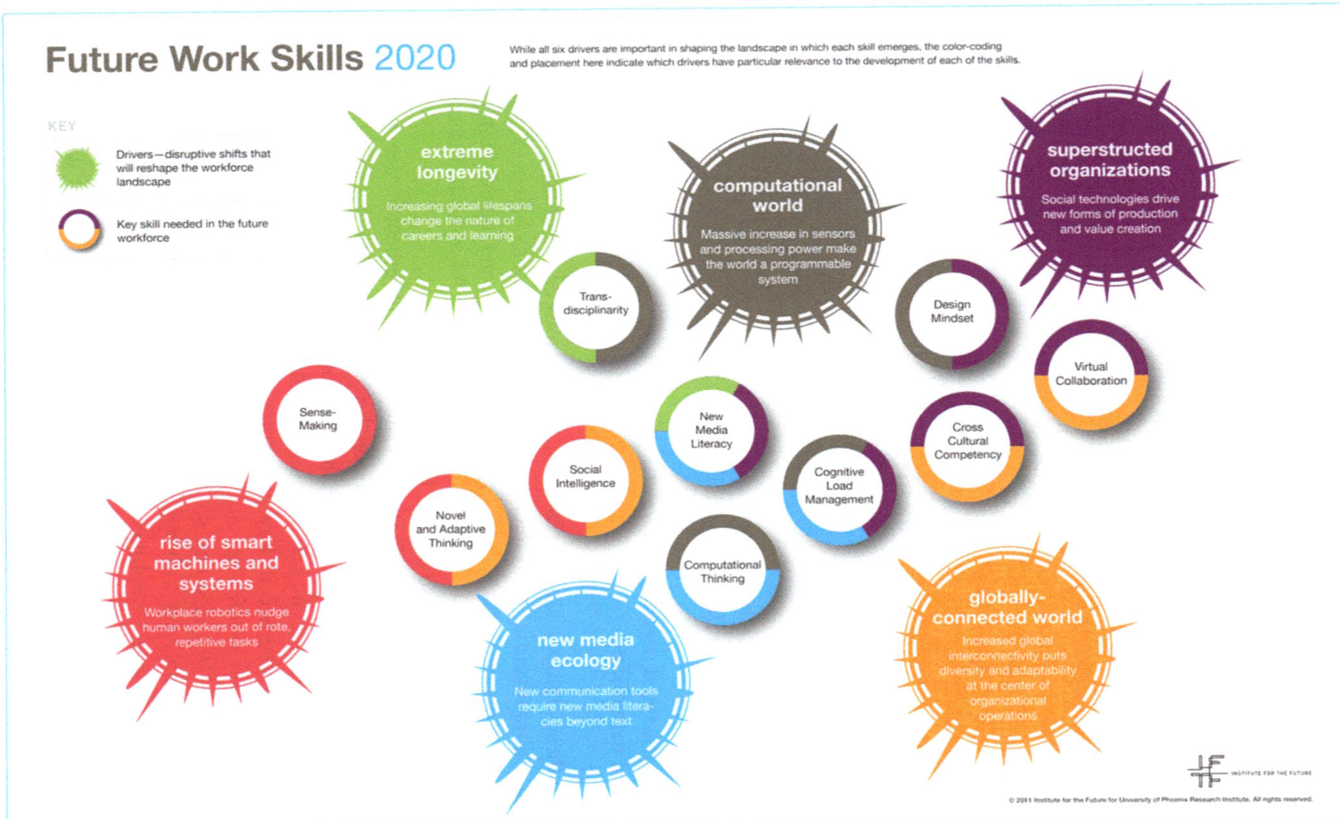

Fig. 1 Future Work Skills 2020 with kind permission of Institute for the Future. URL: http://www.iftf.org/futureworkskills/

executives there should be top priority.[1] "The ability to persuade others should be strengthened" (Schwuchow 2016), with this communication skills are becoming more important (Zink et al. 2016). An effective method of convincing and communicating is stories which, through their power and magic, emotionally touch people, influence, and eventually convince them.

3 The Changed Working Area of the Personnel Developer in the 70:20:10 Model

Large-scale studies by the Center for Creative Leadership in North Carolina have already shown in the 1990s that employees acquire most of their professional skills in the workplace and not in the seminar room. The 70:20:10 model developed from these findings by Morgan McCall, Robert Eichinger, and Michael Lombardo represents three different levels of learning, all of which occur in companies but are not put into practice everywhere:

- Experience-based learning
- Learning from others
- Formal learning

According to this, 70% learn the most at work, in doing (learning by doing), followed by learning from others (20%), for example, through coaching or mentoring. The smallest 10% share is acquired in formal learning, which includes attending seminars and reading specialist literature. This shows the extremely heterogeneous field of work of a personnel developer, which in practice, however, is often restricted to pure seminar management, i.e., the smallest area of learning. It also demonstrates the diversity and need for action. "Because successfully [ambidextrous] companies offer their employees sufficient holistic learning experiences based on the 70:20:10 model" in order to address the different learning methods of a business (Koch 2015).

The HR developer not only takes on the role of initiator of various educational formats, but also sees himself as a supporter and process companion. The use of stories on all three levels can be very helpful (see glossary).

[1]Leadership development: Younger generations are increasingly placing the question of meaning at the center of their professional activity. Work has to make sense, and the big picture needs to be understood. It is not the hard facts that convince but background knowledge, which is transmitted through stories. As a result, executives are increasingly required to use stories in their daily work, which needs to be sensitized in further education, and the ability to tell stories must be strengthened. For those who can tell and convince in an exciting and eventful way, but, of course, contextually and accurately, they have already won in meetings, in presentations, in negotiation talks, and so on. Communicative expressions are to be promoted. In addition to teaching narrative structures, knowledge of hero's journey and Co., practical training with feedback options should be the focus of the seminar or workshop. Ideally with video recording of each participant and subsequent joint evaluation.

However, before the HR developer turns his department around and redesigns educational offers based on the 70:20:10 model, it's all about his own role and identification with the new tasks. How the personal as well as departmental identity can be rewritten is shown in the following example.

4 The Role and Identity of the Personnel Development: A Workshop

Monday morning in a former sugar factory, 12 personnel developers, including the boss, meet for the further development of the departmental profile in a rebuilt and revitalized old factory. The room reserved is not equipped as usual with conference tables and chairs but with colorful, round stools, with poser tables and cozy lounge areas, with a coffee bar, and with a green roof terrace. A mix of a colorful learning lab and a stimulating toy store awaits the group. Various creative islands invite to try out and discuss with a variety of material. Two hundred square meters of game, creative, and learning materials are waiting to be discovered. The goal is to initiate within 3 days and further develop the departmental identity as well as the personal professional identity of each individual personnel developer. The creative educational setting is deliberately chosen in order to become clearly aware of the different forms of learning and learning needs. The materials are chosen deliberately and will stimulate the narration of the participants. The participants reconstruct experienced situations and relate their experiences. "Through narratives, new `perspectives' are gained, changed opinions are made possible, and fixed opinions become agile again" (Schierz 1997). Stories start from acquaintances, relate to experiences, and reach beyond the cognitive level. Stories develop tremendous powers that appeal to deep human realms. They affect our minds, enter our hearts, and inspire our fantasy and imagination. Stories appeal to us holistically. Good stories take us from the present to another level of consciousness. They evoke experiences other than those we had and make things real again (Clark and Rossiter 2008). The narrator links his cognitive understanding with his experience, creating new knowledge. Through narration, the experience is lived again, whereby the experience is better understood retroactively and a change can occur (Clark and Rossiter 2008). The work with stories in this methodical-didactical form is used to become self-sufficient, to rework and process experiences, to reflect on own situations from the past, and to stimulate metacognitive processes. Also those processes where you reflect about the thinking are used to revive the past and to repeat it in order to create a deeper understanding and to generate an insight from it.

Before entering the creative circle, there is a short introduction by the seminar supervisor and the boss as a warm-up. With the help of large-scale paper and pens, everyone draws what makes him and his personality. The question "Who am I?" should be discussed here. Michael, the department head, draws his three daughters, his immaculate white shirt as a trademark, and a boat that expresses his passion for sailing. Using three different colored pens, different adjectives are added to the picture in the days to follow. That's how I see myself (self-perception), so the others see me (perception of others), and that's how I want to be in the future. With this exercise, we become aware of who we are, how others perceive us, and how we want to evolve. It is helpful here to recognize that we have changed our roles and identity more than once in life. From student to job starter, to the professional, to the senior professional, maybe even to the leader. Our identity is subject to a permanent process of change and adaptation. On the one hand, we are subject to the influences of our environment; on the other hand, we shape it ourselves. So we can shape our own identity as well as the team or organization, and that's exactly what the group is doing for 3 days.

The agenda of the event is largely open and leaves plenty of room for creativity and leisure. On the basis of picture cards, with pictures of innovative personalities such as Steve Jobs and Hildegard von Bingen, small groups deal intensively at different stations with the respective topic. The small groups work through the different tasks:

Creative Island 1: How are we perceived and seen as personnel developers in the company?

Each participant receives the task of telling stories and describing his impressions. On metaplan cards, the findings are noted and pinned to the wall. The group agrees on a story that best reflects the consensus of the group and uses Playmobil figures for a diagram.

Method:

Discussion about reactions, customer feedback, feedback within the company, the acceptance toward the personnel developer, or the personnel development department is visualized with figures.

Creative Island 2: My personal expectations for a PD. The personnel developer as a customer (change of perspective)

The participants slip into the role of their customers and thereby consciously adopt their customers' expectation of a training program.

Method:

Discussions about personal experiences, about personal expectations of a personnel development department, or a further education institute. The insights are recorded on metaplan cards and pinned on the wall.

Creative Island 3: My company as a fantastic training location

The participants paint or create with clay a heavenly learning place where they would like to work. There are no limits for creativity. The creation of ideas of new education settings and learning atmospheres, also the seemingly impossible, is expressly desired.

Method:

"This is what my dream job looks like" (painted or modeled). Group spinning, painting, dreaming, and designing

Creative Island 4: Benchmark: Innovative education providers. How does the competition work?

The participants view the material collected by the training management about companies and their educational program. Time for internet research is available. Regarding the question: "What are the others doing, and what can we learn from them?" The participants start a conversation, make suggestions, and form ideas. The collected insights are recorded on metaplan cards and clustered in "Dos" and "Dont's."

Method:

Research other educational offerings from other companies and educational institutions. Idea sharing in the small group

It is time to present the results. Some stories are told, all of which imply difficulties, but nevertheless, find solutions in the end. Biographical narratives flow in and, through experience, make the current understanding or current position visible and comprehensible (Watzlawik 2013). Especially the method of "This is what my dream job looks like" gives many possibilities for new and transverse thinking. The originally fictitious ideas, in the aftermath, again and again turn out not to be so absurd and quite feasible.

The next step deals with "Who am I, who do I want to be?" For most of the following time, each participant spends his inner retreat alone, with his own thoughts, his experiences so far, and his wishful thinking from a professional point of view. Visualizing ideas and visions through a collage can be helpful in becoming aware and programming the subconscious mind toward the future in the positive sense of the self-fulfilling prophecy. Inner pictures become, thanks to the imagination, reality (Fig. 2).

The participants are encouraged to mentally slip into new roles and try out new actions in the spirit (probing as an act of Sigmund Freud), because identity development begins in the mind. The imagined scenarios are then put on paper and

Fig. 2 Example of a visualization of personal visions (authors' own figure, 2018)

increasingly detailed. With time the personal story takes over, and a new role and the new identity are defined. Questions like the following can help to take away the fear of the white sheet: Who will I be? How do I want to work? Which tasks do I want to take on? How is the work routine going? How will I master individual tasks? What can I offer? What role do I want to play in the department in the future? How do I want to be thought of by our customers? Which image should the department have in the future? What needs to be done to achieve this image, and what contribution can I make? Maybe writing in the third form can help.

Sarah, for example, a young human resource developer, fresh from university, imagines how she will shape individual educational settings; how she feels, gives, moves, and communicates; how she motivates employees to want to learn; and how she creates new didactic concepts with successful implementation and with stimulating educational settings such as an excavation pit, a forest scene, or a train journey.

After developing their own story, which lies in the future, the next step is the development of the department story. Although identity development means actively changing aspects of one's personality, it can also mean actively transforming the DNA of a department. Through the moderation and the question of the seminar leader, the knowledge about the department is increasingly sharpened. Who would we like to be? What do we want to offer the staff, our customers? What do we value? What do we want to convey? What message do we want to transmit outside the company? How do we want to evolve? What does it take to be what we want it to be? Which story do we want to tell? Based on verbal participation, the seminar leader begins to sketch a first plot of the hero's journey developed by Joseph Campbell and summarized by Frenzel et al. (2013), which is gradually formulated in more detail:

1. Call for Adventure	the personnel development department is called for an adventure. It receives the order from the management level to become more modern and to prepare the workforce for the future requirements and competencies.
2. Departure into the Unknown	The personnel developers set off into the unknown. They do not know yet what to expect and where the journey will go. However, they know that they should start as early as possible, to bring together the clients and the management requirements. They are aware they will have to develop a concept that creates educational experiences and involves new educational settings. They know that they themselves are changing and increasingly should take on the pioneering role of role models.
3. The Way of the Exams	There are going to be some hurdles along the way. There will be employees who don't accept

	the "modern stuff." The development of the new concept will cost time and money that must be demanded from stakeholders, and eventually there will be controversial opinions in the development of the concept within the department.
4. Conquest of the Treasure	The HR developers are working long and hard on their project, but it will be worth in the end. A holistic, future-oriented learning world is conceived which creates a wealth of educational experiences.
5. The Return	The new concept has been developed and implemented in the company. The personnel developers do not want to return, but in the future both directly and promptly will deal with new educational approaches and competence requirements. The department receives a lot of recognition and respect for its services from customers and the managing director. The transformation of the personnel development department as well as each individual personnel developer is visible to the outside world.

At this point, it should be noted that the development of your own identity is never factual; it is influenced by your values. In addition to our own character that each of us obtained through education, our socialization (environment), and tradition such as culture and religion, the corporate culture will also resonate in the processing of the task. Our culture, in which we grew up and live, our environment, and our values, ideas, feelings, fears, but also hopes, they all influence the development of our identity (see also the five pillars of the identity from Petzold).

Identity development is now considered to be a never-ending, automatic process that requires interaction with others (Dorsch Lexikon 2018). The group will be accompanied by the seminar leader afterward. They work on the identity of the workshop and work on the new role model and the attitude toward the outside and the departmental history. Through our thinking and acting, by painting in our imagination with subsequent implementation into reality, we do not only change our behavior but also influence our environment.

After the workshop, the employees of the personnel development department decided to try out new developments and mega trends first in their department, to experiment with them, to internalize them, and then to prepare them in a methodical-didactic way, taking into account stories.

To put it in a nutshell, narration plays an important role in identity construction (Watzlawik 2013; Straub 2000). In stories man always reinvents himself. "He exchanges experiences in conversations, compares himself and his views with those of others, finds compromises, and defends his position. He finds reasons for actions and contradictions" (Watzlawik 2013).

Storytelling helps to rewrite one's own story, that of the team and thus of the company as well. Stories can be used as a tool for a change in coaching but also as an illustration in staff training or as information in a team meeting. Storytelling can also be used by HR developers in their daily work. Because stories increase attention and concentration, show problem-solving approaches, and increase the ability to remember. Above all, stories give us security in a rapidly changing working world. In a "rational world," the longing for emotional elements grows (Fuchs 2013). Stories sweeten the lifelong learning that change brings. In all continuing education areas, they are a small, sustainable, and such a simple treasure that every human resource developer should know. Wherever storytelling in human resources development can be applied, please refer to the final, detailed glossary.

Glossary: Possible uses of storytelling in the 70:20:10 model

Stories in Everyday Working Life (Experience-Based Learning) Constructing stories is not a purely personal process, but it is rather shaped by our cultural values and our history, religions, and traditions, in short, by our social environment. On this basis, we construct stories ourselves but can also decode those of our fellow human beings. Ergo: "Narratives are performances of identity, played out in various ways but always shaped by cultural norms" (Clark and Rossiter 2008). Transferred to the corporate context, stories relating to the working context always refer to the corporate culture. Stories are based on background and experiences. They describe success but more often failures. Experience is a basic learning object in adult learning (Clark and Rossiter 2008).	
Learning by doing	In order to learn from experience or mistakes in the working process, innovative companies rely on the collection of success, failure, experience, and/or role model stories. Employees briefly describe their experience in a narrative, which is collected centrally by companies, but also shared with interested parties in internal and external publications, newsletters, or on the homepage.
Job rotation	For a day, jobs are exchanged with a colleague. What is the colleague doing? What impressions were gained, and what was learned? Job rotation makes it possible to take on new perspectives, get to know other tasks, and understand other interfaces better. A short story is written about the experiences and insights, and it helps to reflect on the day for each individual and to measure the success of job rotation for the personnel development.
Stories in the Professional Environment (Learning from Others) Constructing narratives, reliving experiences and adventures, rewriting history and reflecting on it, as well as taking on new points of view and perspectives allow for ongoing personal development. "The life narrative is repeatedly revised and enlarged throughout one's life to accommodate new insights, events, and perspectives" (Clark and Rossiter 2008). Above all, they offer an exchange with others, a joint development, or further development of stories with new complementary or in-depth thoughts.	
Regular meetings and project work	Stories can be used very well in meetings in order to jointly develop future scenarios, visions, marketing strategies, etc. or to depict complex issues visually and make them more easily comprehensible.

(continued)

Networks and collegial advice	In networks, stories on the one hand provide a social kit that connects and keeps people together. On the other hand, through stories people can learn from each other. “Narration enables people to support and sustain social communities, as well as to differentiate the identity of individuals and collectives” (Scheffel 2005). In addition, “narratives are (...) bridges to the hearts of our fellow human beings” (Kubli 2005). Depending on where and to whom we tell our stories, they can vary in content or be told from different perspectives. Once we can be a hero, sometimes we can be agents or supporters. Narrative can thus be told in many different ways, thus demonstrating the complex identity of the narrator (McAdams 1985; Clark and Rossiter 2008). The narrator shows something about himself, and he makes himself visible, perhaps even vulnerable. Finally stories allow “access to the feelings, thoughts and dreams of others” (Scheffel 2005). They represent the real life of the narrator. Therefore, stories in a professional context should be chosen well-considered and pursue the intention: Why do I choose this story? When networking, it is above all a successful but also an unsuccessful experience, and role model stories that are of use.
Enabling for change, coaching, and mentoring	Change processes in the form of a true narrative, an imitative, or inspirational success story by a leader are more acceptable if they are wrapped up in a story, rather than arguing with data and facts that employees are not interested in and cannot classify. Stories offer opportunities for change. “It is when one can identify with a character who has changed that one can envision and embrace the possibility of change for oneself. Stories of achievement and transformation can function as motivators, pathfinders, and sources of encouragement for struggling adult learners” (Rossiter 2002; Clark 2001). People need to be touched and emotionally reached, so that any change can occur. Or as Erpenbeck and Sauter (2015) put it: “Without feeling, education is nothing.” When coaching, the larger part of talking and finding solutions, however, should lie with the coachee, as he will become aware of things by storytelling. He is the one in with the answer. “Personal stories are not just a way of telling someone (or oneself) about one’s life; they are the means by which identities may be fashioned” (Rosenwald and Ochberg 1992). The writing of experiences and the keeping of learning diaries allow reflection and personal development.
Team development	How storytelling can be used in team development? Prof. Dr. Laila Maija Hofmann from the Technical University of Nuremberg shows with the following examples: “Within the framework of team development processes, storytelling is used in very different forms. For example, the group members are asked through the kick-off workshops to talk about their perceptions of the situation in the organizational unit in the form of a comedy or tragedy, to write a fairy tale or to pour their presentation into a science-fiction version. This can be combined with the request that this description be performed as

(continued)

	a "play" in front of all members or tell the story based on a "painting". It is a regular issue here to "raise for discussion" topics that are usually not put up for discussion in a conventional departmental discussion. The possibility of alienation makes it easier for many to address even unpleasant issues" (Hofmann 2016)
Stories in Classical Education (Formal Learning) This category includes seminars, workshops and trainings in presence, blended learning or e-learning formats and specialist literature, learning apps, etc.	
Seminars	In some larger companies, the teachers or lecturers are not from outside but from within the company. Often personnel developers also take on this role with individual topics. In order to make a lecture or a training session for the learning participants a "narrative experience," according to Scharrelmann, three competencies are needed: linguistic, factual, and social competence (Scharrelmann 1919/1923). Linguistic competence comes into play in the way the story is portrayed. How it is dramaturgically structured? The goals that are pursued, the knowledge that is conveyed, and the facts that are packed into the story represent the factual competencies of the lecturer. Social competencies are almost automatically given when telling stories. How does the narrator respond to his audience? Lecturers do not just tell a story here. Rather, they narrate far beyond the matter and reveal something from themselves and their own personality, attitude, position, etc. Seminar rooms are wonderful places to make stories vivid and relaxing. However, here again, "stories gain weight if they are not used in excess" (Kubli 2005).
E-learning and blended learning	Storytelling is particularly suitable in the field of modern information and communication technology. Digital games, in which the knowledge is packaged into an action and the learner slips into the story (e.g., as an avatar), will be used more frequently and extensively in professional life in the future. The motivation for learning is supported by narrative storylines.
Mobile devices	"Googling" something or translating it: "Look something up online" nowadays is standard German vocabulary. We quickly get information from the Internet and look for something special or less special, or we research one or the other thing more purposefully. We generally learn something new and thereby expand our knowledge. In the changing working world, these forms of rapid information gathering will increase. Mobile devices such as smartphones or tablets, which can be used everywhere by any employee, become standard. Apps, digital libraries, and corporate wiki's that provide us with quick problem-solving approaches are gaining in importance. Personnel development will increasingly be required to create opportunities to keep constantly updated knowledge available. Experience stories showing problem-solving approaches should be considered here.

5 Conclusion

New demands of the working world need new competencies in staff. This changes roles and tasks of the personnel development. It's not about offering seminars only; it's more about finding new ways of bringing knowledge to the people. To provide this, storytelling can help to redefine your own role and identity as a personnel developer and to lay the foundation for new ways of learning for the whole company.

Further Reading

Abels, H. (2010). *Identität*. Wiesbaden: VS.

Hüther, G. (2006). *Die Macht der inneren Bilder. Wie Visionen das Gehirn, den Menschen und die Welt verändern*. Göttingen: Vandenhoeck & Ruprecht.

Keupp, H., & Höfer, R. (1997). *Identitätsarbeit heute. Klassische und aktuelle Perspektiven der Identitätsforschung*. Berlin: Suhrkamp.

References

Clark, M. C. (2001). Off the beaten path: Some creative approaches to adult learning. *New Directions for Adult and Continuing Education*, (89), 83–91.

Clark, M. C., & Rossiter, M. (2008). Narrative learning in adulthood. *New Directions for Adult and Continuing Education, 119*, 61–70.

Daheim, C., & Wintermann, O. (2016). *2050: Die Zukunft der Arbeit. Ergebnisse einer internationalen Delphi-Studie des Millennium Project*. https://www.bertelsmann-stiftung.de/fileadmin/files/BSt/Publikationen/GrauePublikationen/BST_Delphi_Studie_2016.pdf

Dorsch – Lexikon der Psychologie. (2018). *Stichwort: Identitätsentwicklung*. https://m.portal.hogrefe.com/dorsch/identitaetsentwicklung/

Erpenbeck, J., & Sauter, W. (2015). *Wissen, Werte und Kompetenzen in der Mitarbeiterentwicklung*. Gabler, Wiesbaden: Ohne Gefühl geht in der Bildung gar nichts.

Frenzel, K., Müller, M., & Sottong, H. (2013). *Storytelling. Das Praxisbuch*. München: Carl Hanser.

Fuchs, W. T. (2013). *Crashkurs storytelling – Grundlagen und Umsetzung*. Freiburg: Haufe-Lexware.

Hofmann, L. M. (2016). Storytelling als neuer Weg der Mitarbeiterentwicklung. In: K. Schwuchow, & J. Gutmann (Eds.), *Personalentwicklung. Themen, trends, best practices*. Haufe-Lexware, Freiburg Institute for the Future (2018). http://www.iftf.org/uploads/media/SR-1382A_UPRI_future_work_skills_sm.pdf

Koch, A. (2015). Das 70-20-10-Wunschdenken. Zweifel an der Realitätsnähe der "Bildungsformel". Wirtschaft + Weiterbildung. Das Magazin für Führung, Personalentwicklung und E-Learning 05_15, 18–25.

Kubli, F. (2005). *Mit Geschichten und Erzählungen motivieren. Beispiele für den mathematisch-naturwissenschaftlichen Unterricht*. Köln: Aulis Deubner.

McAdams, D. P. (1985). *Power, intimacy, and the life story*. Homewood, IL: Dorsey Press.

Rosenwald, G. C., & Ochberg, R. L. (1992). *Storied lives*. New Haven, CT: Yale University Press. Clearinghouse on Adult Career and Vocational Education Columbus OH.

Rossiter, M. (2002). *Narrative and stories in adult teaching and learning*. Washington, DC: ERIC Digest.

Scharrelmann, H. (1919/1923). *Die Technik des Schilderns und Erzählens*. Braunschweig: Westermann.

Scheffel, M. (2005). *Theorie und Praxis des Erzählens*. Der Deutschunterricht 2/2005.

Schierz, M. (1997). *Narrative Didaktik: Von den großen Entwürfen zu den kleinen Geschichten im Sportunterricht*. Weinheim: Beltz.

Schwuchow, K. (2016). Globales Talentmanagement und weltweite Weiterbildung. Transnationale Führungskräfteentwicklung. In K. Schwuchow & J. Gutmann (Eds.), *Personalentwicklung 2017: Themen, trends, best practices 2017*. Freiburg: Haufe-Lexware.

Sons, G. (2016). Strategisches Personalmanagement in der digitalisierten Wirtschaft. In K. Schwuchow & J. Gutmann (Eds.), *Personalentwicklung 2017: Themen, trends, best practices 2017*. Freiburg: Haufe-Lexware.

Straub, J. (2000). Biographische Sozialisation und narrative Kompetenz. Implikationen und Voraussetzungen lebensgeschichtlichen Denkens in der Sicht einer narrativen Psychologie. In E. Hoernig (Ed.), *Biographische Sozialisation* (pp. 137–163). Stuttgart: Lucius & Lucius.

Watzlawik, M. (2013). Identitätsentwicklung als kreativer Prozess: Wie Ich "Ich" werde und bleibe. In M. Watzlawik (Ed.), *Kreative Entwicklung – Beschreiben, Verstehen, Fördern* (pp. 45–54). Marburg: Tectum.

Wirl, C. (2011). *Personalentwicklung – gestern und heute*. Training no. 7/11, 48–53. https://www.vbc.biz/sites/default/files/presse/personalentwicklung_gestern_und_heute.pdf

Zink, K. J., Schröder, D., & Hellge, V. (2016). Führung und Organisation im digitalen Wandel. In K. Schwuchow & J. Gutmann (Eds.), *Personalentwicklung 2017: Themen, trends, best practices 2017* (pp. 159–170). Freiburg: Haufe-Lexware.

Melanie Gabert, M.A., is an educational scientist with an extension course in e-education/e-learning as well as an external doctoral student at the Martin-Luther-University Halle-Wittenberg, Germany. Her research project deals with forms and functions of narrations in andragogical educational contexts, in short: with storytelling in adult education. She is the director of adult education and study as well as Member of the Executive Board at Kolping Bildungswerk Württemberg e.V. in Stuttgart, Germany, and advises companies and educational institutions in the field of new learning worlds and educational architectures.

Cultural Approaches Toward Time in Global Organizations

Joanna Sell

Abstract

The way we perceive time reveals a lot about our cultural values and differing approaches toward time management. Based on our own historical and societal settings, we have a particular worldview in which a dominant narrative colonizes the time framework and the way we perceive the past, present, and future. Different approaches toward these three "layers of time" lead to differing strategies in organizations and entire communities. They influence decision-making processes, building relationships, and defining sustainability. The aim of this chapter is to review the ways in which time can be perceived in the organizational context in different cultural circles and propose a new approach toward challenges caused by differing time perceptions across cultures. The first section focuses on time orientations in different cultures and the challenge of assigning such orientations to individuals. An examination of time orientations shows that the management of change varies a lot in past-oriented and future-oriented groups and impacts both short-term and long-term planning as well as attitude toward patience and speed in business contacts. When talking about cultural similarities and differences, we need to bear in mind that, in addition to ethnic, national, and regional characteristics, other important layers of cultures must be addressed such as gender, generation (X, Y, Z), social background, level of education, and many more, defined in the cultural mosaic approach presented in this chapter. The interdependence between the cultural layers of belonging to different generations and educational levels unquestionably has an impact on time perception and is addressed in the following section. In times of dramatically changing surroundings it is crucial to challenge not only the black-and-white scenarios that assign static time orientations to entire countries but also "used

J. Sell (✉)
Intercultural Compass, Intercultural Compass Consultancy for Intercultural Competence and Global Team Development, Hannover, Niedersachsen, Germany
e-mail: j.sell@interculturalcompass.com

© Springer Nature Switzerland AG 2019

J. Chlopczyk, C. Erlach (eds.), *Transforming Organizations*,
Management for Professionals, https://doi.org/10.1007/978-3-030-17851-2_18

futures," in which routinized practices are continued despite their "worn off" character. Therefore, the last sections focus on re-narrating time in the organizational context and on the leadership skills necessary to deal with differing time orientations and introduce narrative methods to rewind stories on time.

1 Take a Minute Before Reading on

Have you ever thought about time as a cultural concept? Something that may initially seem obvious in your surroundings becomes much more complex if you take into account an intercultural approach. Is time linear or cyclic? Does the future really lie ahead of us, and if so, do clocks and calendars define it or is it shaped by events? Can time be controlled, and can it be wasted? Can time be interpreted as a resource or as a value, or both?

"Time offers an important basis for helping us to understand our shared and individual experiences in the world" (Briley 2009: 311). According to an Irish proverb, "Time is a great storyteller." It has an impact on our own narratives and is able to change them. Conversely, are we able to change our dominant narratives on time? This text is an attempt at a paradigm shift from the polarized perception of time orientations toward an inclusive approach.

It is important to keep in mind that, in the global business context, those who have power dictate the way time should be interpreted and might tend to use the pressure of time to pursue their goals. Their dominant narratives focus on efficiency, profit, and growth. The set of stories on efficiency in particular impacts time perceptions in the organizational context. As long as the abbreviation HR stands for human resources and not for human relations, employees will be perceived as cogs in the machine, as sources of energy and commitment that can be made use of. However, learning from each other, personal development, and excelling at teamwork are only possible when people know their own and their colleagues' talents and skills and know how to apply them in daily life to reach the common goal. Building strong relationships is an ongoing process that does not happen from one day to the next. As Carlos Valdes-Dapena emphasized, "Strong relationships and trust matter to collaboration, but they are not the starting point. They are outcomes of dedicated people striving together. Connecting collaboration to the motives of success-minded team members is what unlocks productive teamwork" (Valdes-Dapena 2018).

Another myth of efficiency was hijacked this year when the New Zealand-based company Perpetual Guardian announced shortening its working week from 5 days to 4 while keeping salaries unchanged. "Reduced hours for same pay increased successful work-life balance management, cutting stress levels and boosting commitment" (The Guardian, July 19, 2018). The company on the other side of the world hits the nerve of current discussions on the interdependence between time and productivity, particularly in Germany, which is the European leader in working overtime. In 2016 alone, German employees spent 1.7 billion extra hours at work, most of them unpaid (Gurk 2018). And as Ella Saltmarshe pointed out, "We often fail to see the stories that govern our lives. If we want to change specific systems, we first need to make mirrors that enable us to see the narratives we currently live by, and then author new narratives that enable the kind of change we want to see in the world" (Saltmarsche 2018). System changes can involve designing visions of futures in which storytelling, and story sharing can be applied to create different scenarios. Sohail Inayatullah distinguishes among four different perspectives in which futures can be "designed." In the first, the future is predictive; the second emphasizes the interpretive character of the future, where laws are culturally and historically specific; the third is the critical perspective; and the fourth is the action learning approach. As Inayatullah emphasizes, the future forecast is situated in multiple perspectives, nested in multiple worldviews that not only describe but also actively create the world around us. In times of dramatically changing surroundings, it is crucial to challenge "used futures" in which routinized practices are continued, despite their "worn off" character (Inayatullah 2015: 353–355). The 5-day week can serve as a good example of such a worn-off narrative. The same can be said for keeping the black-and-white scenarios in the intercultural context. In the complexity of our times, it is necessary to be aware of culturally based differences toward time and to be able to re-narrate individual time perceptions in order to create a common ground for successful collaboration across cultures. As for a storytelling approach, it is important to remember that "To look to the future we must first look back upon the past. That is where the seeds of the future were planted" (attributed to Albert Einstein).

2 Twentieth Century Time Orientations Across Cultures

Time orientation has been defined as "the relative dominance of past, present or future in a person's thoughts" (Hornik and Zakay 1996: 385). Looking at this definition, we immediately can say that it is originally from the Western and Middle Eastern cultural circle, as it depicts the linear perception of time present in both the Judeo-Christian and the Islamic traditions. Hinduism, Buddhism, and Jainism regard time as cyclical, consisting of repeating events.

The first-time perception is built sequentially, following a timeline from the left (past) through the present to the future (on the right). The instruments to measure linear time are calendars and watches. Any change in the sequence of the activities they measure leads to uncertainty. The second-time perception emphasizes repetitive phenomena such as seasons and rhythms. Apart from the circular character of time in religions, mentioned above, "the Aboriginal concept of time differs from the Judeo-Christian perception of time in that Aboriginal people do not perceive time as an exclusively 'linear' category (i.e. past-present-future) and often place events in a 'circular' pattern of time according to which an individual is in the center of 'time-circles' and events are placed in time according to their relative importance for the individual and his or her respective community (i.e. the more important events are perceived as being 'closer in time')" (Janca and Bullen 2003: 43). Similarly, the concept of time in Hinduism and Buddhism is cyclical, as the process of creation moves in cycles and the end is a threshold to a new beginning.

One of best examples of these two time perceptions is expressed by the procedure of serving meals in different cultures. A clear sequence of serving a starter, the soup, the main course, and the dessert requires keeping a strict schedule, so that the courses are each served at a certain temperature. Such an attitude corresponds with linear time perception. In the cyclic time approach, all the dishes are served at the same time, and it is up to the guests what to taste first.

Similarly, working styles in different cultures mirror differing time approaches.

US anthropologist Edward T. Hall calls the first approach monochronic and the latter one polychronic, putting the emphasis on activities run in parallel (Hall 1959).

The issue of time across cultures has also been addressed in the theoretical frameworks of Kluckhohn, Strodtbeck, Hofstede, Trompenaars, and Hampden-Turner and in the GLOBE Study. All of them agree that cultural groups are influenced by a shared past and shared goals they wish to reach in the present and in the future. In the 1960s, scholars had already pointed out that people from Far Eastern countries such as China, Japan, and Korea tend to have past-time orientations, while Latin Americans are more present-oriented, and Westerners (Americans and Northern Europeans) have more of a future time orientation (Hall 1959; Kluckhohn and Strodtbeck 1961). All these authors treated cultures as static phenomena and limited their research to describing and not explaining cultures. Such approach started to be challenged due to massive changes and transformations at the end of the last century.

3 Twenty-First Century Approaches Toward Time Perceptions

Creating strong polarities in the twenty-first century is artificial, as time perception has changed massively due to globalization and digitalization and to the existence of the cultural identities in flux (cf. Sell 2017: 224). The shift in understanding culture as a phenomenon in process revealed the need to expand understanding through explanation and meaning making. The model of the cultural mosaic captures some aspects of this complexity and offers the basis for a paradigm shift.

3.1 The Cultural Mosaic and the Time Perception

The cultural mosaic approach, emphasizing the process character of cultural identity, can be applied to understand individual time preferences in different contexts without falling into the trap of stereotypes. "Viewing an individual's culture as a cultural mosaic allows for simultaneous observation of global individual culture and localized cultural influences" (Chao and Moon 2005: 1129). It is based on the image of a mosaic, which is composed of distinct colored tiles. Just as every color comprises at its heart the three primary colors, red, blue, and yellow, the individual cultural mosaic comprises three primary categories of culture features: demographic (age, ethnicity, gender, race); geographic (climate, temperature, costal/inland, urban/rural, region/country); and associative (family, religion, employer, profession, politics, avocations). Rather than choosing a particular "tile of the cultural mosaic," such as ethnicity *or* gender (as in twentieth-century research and still practiced by many scholars), individuals draw on combinations of tiles such as ethnicity *and* gender (Chao and Moon 2005: 1130).

Furthermore, cultural values are in constant flux. And so "the biggest paradox of time orientation can be seen in Eastern Asian cultures. They value tradition, family, religion and heritage (short term orientation); yet at the same time, they emphasize thrift, saving, stability, education, secured investment, hard work, stable relationships, and future planning (long term orientation)" (Nguyen-Phuong-Mai 2017: 207). The analysis of individual time perception sheds light on the need to get to know better our own perception of the past, the present, and the future, and this is addressed in the following section.

3.2 Examining the Past, the Present, and the Future

The Stanford Time Perspective Inventory (STPI) developed by Zimbardo and Boyd and tested by D'Alessio et al. (2003) allows individuals to get to know their preferences regarding dealing with time. It measures five dimensions of time: past time, divided into the positive and the negative past; present time, split into hedonist and fatalist perceptions; and future time. Additionally, those researchers defined a sixth category, which they called transcendental future, but this is not part of the inventory. According to Zimbardo and Boyd, the best mixture of time perspectives enabling people to function well in the Western world is as follows:

- *High* **past-positive perspective** (focusing on positive memories and values)
- *Average* **high future perspective** (resisting temptations, following accomplishment of goals)
- *Average* **high present-hedonist perspective** (focused on life for pleasure)
- *Low* **past-negative perspective** (focused on failures and regrets)
- *Low* **present-fatalist perspective** (focused on fate)

"The content of the past is contained in memories, the content of the present is contained in experience, and the content of the future is contained in expectancies. A great deal of the research on time orientation has shown how life experience largely affects one's ability to cognize, derive motivation, or to be emotionally affected by a particular time frame (...). The future is much more likely to be a source of motivation of present-day activities and decisions if there are no serious threats to mere survival in one's past" (Lasane and O'Donnell 2005: 14). That is the reason why sharing stories supports meaning making and building bridges of understanding. Only by sharing stories does it become clear why someone at first sight seems to be demotivated, overwhelmed, and not goal-oriented. Thanks to story sharing, we gain the possibility to better understand different cultural approaches and to offer empowerment to people who have experienced top-down learning and working styles.

It is crucial to remember that the degree to which we focus primarily on the past, present, or future depends on the group culture, individual values, and the context (and not merely, as emphasized in the twentieth-century research, on the influence of national cultures).

For instance, the level of education can play an important role in time orientation. Recent research has revealed "that people with a primary or secondary school degree tend to show a more fatalistic attitude than [college] graduates. These data seem to be of great interest, since they suggest that a low educational standard, known to be associated with a low socioeconomic status, independently from the aptitude for learning, results in a vision of life and time that is independent of the individual's will and ability to make plans for the future which, in turn, produces an attitude of passive submission to events" (D'Alessio et al. 2003: 333). Additionally, belonging to different generations plays an important role in time perception, especially regarding the use of technology. Representatives of Generation Z do not distinguish between being online and offline, and this enhanced connectivity speeds up their sense of time. Expectations of immediate reaction, immediate answer, and immediate solution are just several examples of how time has accelerated for digital natives. A 2012 PEW Research Center survey found that, among millennials, hyper-connectivity can contribute to a need for instant gratification and lack of patience (compare PEW Research Center website). These qualities can therefore make collaboration across different cultures, including generational cultures, challenging.

The newest research provides convincing arguments that, because our time perception, is subjective, we have influence on perceiving time differently in different contexts. The authors of the article "The effect of mindfulness meditation on time perception" (Kramer et al. 2013) emphasize the ability of mindfulness meditation to alter time perception, creating a sense of time slowing down by shifting the brain's attentional resources. In light of brain plasticity and the newest research on neuroscience and mindfulness, is it not high time to re-narrate our black-and-white scenarios regarding time orientations?

3.3 Current Narratives of Time

Currently two powerful narratives mirror differing value systems in the world: "efficiency of time" versus "quality of time." The "time is money" approach, which conquered the Western world and led to capitalism and consumerism, is questioned and confronted with the Eastern worldview, which emphasizes the quality of time spent on different activities. It is worth pointing out that both approaches can currently be found at all longitudes, among people from different cultures. The origins of these two approaches are nevertheless in the western and the eastern hemispheres, respectively.

Time perception centered on the "time is money" approach was recently made excruciatingly clear when Google Chrome launched an app that shows how much working time the purchase of an object over the Internet costs. You enter your hourly wage, and the system calculates the time/money relationship for you. The problem with the "time is money" approach is that we can "buy time," but we cannot purchase "quality time." Buying the time of an unmotivated employee does not add any value. Such a person would remain at work 8 hours a day, but would he or she really be productive when they are convinced that their job is meaningless?

In 1972, when the King of Bhutan realized that the materialization of time is no guarantee of life quality, his advisors introduced as an alternative to the GDP the Gross National Happiness Index. This index includes nine domains: psychological well-being, health, education, time use, cultural diversity and resilience, good governance, community vitality, ecological diversity, and resilience and living standards.

Those authors emphasized that time use should be re-narrated in comparison with the GDP, as focusing on work in order to earn more money leads to distress. Above all, time use in the index should include not only paid but also unpaid (housework, child care) and voluntary work that is normally not included in conventional economic accounts.

At the same time, Western researchers on materialism criticized the "value system that is preoccupied with possessions and the social image they project" (Bauer et al. 2012) and emphasized the danger of the exchange of time against money. Knowing that such time orientation leads to anxiety, depression, and loss of relationships, why do so many individuals persist in this approach?

As Sohail Inayatullah emphasizes, as long as we do not change the metaphor of our surroundings, there is no need to change the litany omnipresent in media, headlines, and, consequently, our thoughts. Moving from the GDP to other measurements such as Gross National Happiness Index can only be possible when the underlying metaphors reflect the value change. (Cf. Inayatullah's keynote speech at the Beyond Storytelling Conference in Hamburg on June 8th, 2018.)

Harry Triandis, a University of Illinois social psychologist considered an expert on the topic of individualism-collectivism, has found that individualistic cultures, unlike collectivist ones, put more emphasis on achievement than on affiliation. The focus on achievement usually leads to a "time is money" mind-set, which in turn results in an urgency to make every moment count. In cultures where social relationships take precedence, however, the attitude toward time is more relaxed (Levine 2006: 18) (compare Table 1).

Due to globalization, we need to rethink this black-and-white scenario. Many countries have multicultural societies, and the number of adult third-culture kids is rising from year to year, due to frequent relocations. Additionally, accelerated digitalization has definitely led to changed time perception. Millennials do not distinguish between virtual and real reality and spend their time in both digital and face-to-face encounters. These are some of the reasons why assumptions about someone's time orientation can be misleading.

As Sohail Inayatullah emphasizes, conventional problem-solving stays at the level of the current litany, and that is why changes in perception do not occur. In order to introduce sustainable change, a new metaphor has to be found that is able to transform a narrative—in our case, the narrative of time perception across cultures. The following section offers my attempt to transform the current narrative with Sohail Inayatullah's CLA.

Table 1 Differences between time perception

	Time as a resource	Time as a value
Time approach	"Time is money"—originally US-American approach	"Do not be afraid of going slowly, but of standing still" Chinese proverb
Approach toward patience	As time is considered a measured resource, there is a strong emphasis on planning and scheduling with little acceptance for interruptions. Patience is not valued	"Losing patience means losing dignity." Indian proverb Interruptions, changes, and ad hoc actions are much more important than plans. Patience is the highest virtue
Approach toward speed	"The faster, the better," is the motto. Speed is considered a highly appreciated value, and the individuals are rewarded for their competitive approach	"If you want to go fast, go alone. If you want to go far, go together." African proverb Investment in collective intelligence is much more important than speed
Decision-making	No decision is considered a lack of progress and therefore a waste of time	Since time is cyclical, the same opportunities occur over and over again. It is wise to make a decision, when there is sufficient knowledge of the context and circumstances. Quick decision-making might be considered as lack of wisdom

Author's own table

4 Storytelling for Dealing with Time in the Twenty-First Century

It is hard to believe that in the twenty-first century, we keep using such strange descriptions as "Western Cultures" and "Eastern Cultures," as the world is round; but people divided the globe into West and East and North and South a long time ago to create and then sustain long-lasting narratives of power. Additionally, "cultures" of both hemispheres (no matter whether polarities are built on the western/eastern axis or the north/south one) are not homogenous due to constant migrations, relocations, and travels as well as the proximity in the virtual world of people from different corners of the blue planet. As shown in the previous chapter, thinking patterns, also those regarding time perception, are above all rooted in the religious heritage. Especially in societies strongly influenced by Christianity, people are used to thinking and communicating in dualistic terms. Something is either good or bad, right or wrong, real or fake, or from heaven or from hell. These black-and-white scenarios do not allow any shades of colors in between. You are either inside or outside. But what about people who were raised in, have been working in, and are exposed to different cultural influences? They think and act at the threshold in many situations and often do not even realize that they are switching their time perception depending on the context. Storytelling works best when we move beyond black-and-white scenarios and talk about nuances of gray.

The best way to understand someone's time perception and time orientations is to listen to the stories this person tells. Their way of dealing with time might change according to the context. These changes are impacted not only by work with people from different countries but also by new contexts.

Coping with perspective change in the intercultural context requires not only knowledge of the local habits, routines, local time management, and communication styles (as shown above, this might be misleading) but above all the capacity to manage the psychological challenges that arise when people try to translate knowledge into action. Story sharing could diminish the uncertainty, which is present in global collaboration. This observation led me to propose a set of skills necessary to deal with different time orientations among global leaders and managers and consequently to some exercises presented in the last section of this chapter and which can be applied to re-narrate time perceptions in intercultural projects (compare Table 2).

Table 2 Time perceptions analyzed with causal layered analysis

The "litany"—official public description of the issue	Time as a resource must not be wasted	Time as a value should be spent in a way that is fulfilling for the person and the people around	Time as a source of life satisfaction und fulfillment at work perceived by one person as a community member. Experience of flow
Systemic causes (social science analysis)	It is important to invest time in individual achievement	It is important to invest time in building relationships and relying on collective intelligence	It is important to find balance between work and leisure time to consciously integrate mindfulness practices in everyday life and encounter the self and other people with emotional intelligence
Worldview (discourse analysis)	Individual success counts mostly and is the basis for climbing the career ladder	Teamwork and collective success counts more than individual achievements	The focus is set on self-reflection on individual and collective talents and continuous dialog with stakeholders
Metaphor/ myth	Successful people are busy and continuously run out of time. They focus on spending time in the most efficient and productive way	Successful people value time spent with people from their surroundings. They value relationships and time invested in building them	Successful people are aware of the importance of the golden cut and the balance in life. They value the "situational" aspect of time and are able to ethically prioritize. They are mindful when they switch between time perceptions

Author's own table

5 Skills Necessary to Deal with Different Time Orientations

5.1 Code Switching Between Cultures

According to Andrew L. Molinsky, "cultural code switching is the ability to modify behavior in specific situations to accommodate varying cultural norms. Code switching requires far more than the right mindset (frequently called global mindset), information, and motivation. It requires a capacity to manage the psychological challenges that arise when someone tries to translate cultural knowledge into action. Executives often feel inauthentic when their behavior conflicts with their ingrained values and beliefs. They may also feel incompetent—anxious and embarrassed about acting in a way so far outside their comfort zone" (Molinsky 2012).

The real challenge is to re-narrate your own stories about time and to act outside your comfort zone. For instance, when you realize that you were taught that being on time is a sign of respect, it is challenging to arrive late. When, however, you kept hearing that interpersonal relations are much more important than punctuality, your values regarding dealing with delay will differ.

5.2 Accepting Disruption

5.2.1 The Impact of Digital Disruption

Global collaboration in the twenty-first century includes dealing with disruption, and virtual meetings are the best example that time perception has changed due to digitalization. Past, present, and future mingle as many actions take place synchronically and asynchronically. Human beings are able to multitask, as our brains are wired that way. Time orientations that used to be rigidly described in cultural contexts (monochronic versus polychronic) do not necessarily correspond with people's nationalities in the virtual setting. More likely they are bound up with whether people are digital natives used to multitasking or those who find virtual communication challenging. If someone persists in acting a certain way, the entire team is challenged to establish its own set of strategies on how to deal with time, for instance, whether to stick to the agenda and treat it sequentially (one step after another) or agree at the beginning of the meeting on what agenda points require more time and energy investment and juggle the agenda points accordingly. The most important aspect of virtual collaboration is the acceptance of disruption and differences in dealing with the time notions of individual team members, as it is not only their cultural roots that play an important role in this regard but also their age, technical affinity, and experience in virtual collaboration and in dealing with interruptions.

5.3 Acknowledging the Dominant Narrative to Create a New, Powerful Story

In order to be able to create a new narrative, it is necessary to listen carefully to the dominant narrative in an unknown culture, especially when the cultural setting is completely new. The following story vividly illustrates these dynamics.

"Unsuccessful efforts to organize a Management of Change seminar with Ethiopian managers led the organizers to listen to the stories, going back to the wealthy era in Ethiopian civilization, as the managers in Ethiopia would not incorporate any developmental principles that were not based in this past. After a discussion with Ethiopian colleagues, we decided to study some Ethiopian history books, looking at them from the perspective of modern management. What had Ethiopia done right in that period to make its cities and trade so flourishing? The company also had a rich history within Ethiopia and these records too were studied. The Dutch manager posed the challenge anew. The future was now seen as a way of recreating some of the greatest glories of the past; suddenly, the Management of Change seminar had captured everyone's enthusiastic support" (Trompenaars and Hampden-Turner 1997: 133).

5.4 Acknowledging the Influence of Experiences Gained in Various Cultures

As highlighted above, in the era of great mobility, there is no other possibility to understand individual time orientations than acknowledging the influence of experiences gained in different cultures. As Robert Levine emphasizes in his *A Geography of Time*, "People are prone to move faster in places with vital economies, a high degree of industrialization, larger populations, cooler climates, and a cultural orientation toward individualism" (Levine 2006: 8–9). Getting to know other team members and listening to their stories with openness and curiosity can deliver many answers when we do not understand their behaviors. Levine proposes ten areas of self-reflection that primarily enable us to understand our own time pace.

6 Storytelling Methods to Re-narrate Time Perceptions

Cultural tools such as Cultural Detective and Diversophy® that are based on sharing stories can bring explanations to many "whys?" regarding time management, decision-making, and working styles. Their authors put emphasis on not only analyzing the given scenarios, scenes, and critical incidents but also sharing one's own stories.

6.1 Time Journey

Time journey is a storytelling intervention in which the story shared with the listeners invites them to initiate change in their perception of stress caused by time frames.

A facilitator reads the following two scenarios and asks the participants to answer the questions related to their thoughts, body sensations, and emotions after having heard each of them.

1

Relax, lie back, and listen to a short account of something that most probably has happened to you many, many times. Imagine that you are late for an important meeting abroad. You are stuck in a traffic jam, your cell phone battery is dead, and you cannot call your business partner to say you will be arriving later. Your charger is out of sight and most probably out of reach.

- Write down three first thoughts that come into your head.
- Now write down what happens with your body, all the physical sensations.
- Write down what emotions you observe while imagining this situation.

2

Now close your eyes and imagine that you have finally arrived. You run to the meeting point, but your business partner is not there. You are trying to catch your breath while searching in your laptop case for your charger. Finally, you find it and start charging your cell phone. Immediately you see a message from your business partner with an excuse: Due to heavy traffic she is going to arrive 40 min later.

- Write down three first thoughts that come into your head.
- Now, write down what sensations you feel in your body.
- Finally, note the emotions you notice while imagining this scenario.

This short scenario intervention allows a perspective change and highlights the importance of mindfulness in dealing with time pressure.

6.2 Rewinding Your Story

The last storytelling method comes from the repertoire of narrative coaching and was designed by David Drake. It can be used to re-narrate situations and choices that challenged clients. The process described below helps them to:

- See and acknowledge the connection between their stories, their behaviors, and their outcomes.
- Accept that they are responsible for all of them.

- Realize that even though some of their behaviors had become automatic and unconscious, people can change the status quo by rewinding their stories.

  Two steps of the process:

1. Reflecting on the story (a conversation or situation you found challenging)
   (a) What did you observe? (Describe the experience as a reporter would)
   (b) What were you telling yourself at the time? (Story)
   (c) What does this say about how you see yourself? (Identity)
   (d) What did you do as a result? (Behavior)
   (e) What happened in the end? (Outcome)
2. Rewinding the story to achieve a different outcome
   (a) What would you like to have had happen in the end? (Outcome)
   (b) What could you have done differently as a result? (Behavior)
   (c) What would need to shift in how you see yourself? (Identity)
   (d) What could you tell yourself next time this happens? (Story)
   (e) What would you observe if "this" were the case? (Experience)

7 Conclusion

It is true that the way we perceive time reveals a lot about our cultural values and differing approaches toward time management. Nevertheless, facing the newest research in neuroscience and brain's plasticity, we know that we can change not only our behaviors but also our mind-sets. In our times when the emphasis is laid on the creation and proactive design of life, it is the highest time to question the world of obviousness and the "worn off futures" rooted in systems that are outdated. The paradigm shift is visible in the growing community of digital nomads and the representatives of the Generation Z whose time perception is massively impacted by living simultaneously in the real and virtual spaces. What we all need is above all the capacity to manage psychological challenges that arise when we need to leave our comfort zone and deal with ambiguity and disruption. Story sharing could diminish the uncertainty, which is present in intercultural collaboration in every single global organization. Only when we are able to gain some distance toward standardized practices regarding coping with time we will manage to re-narrate time perceptions in intercultural collaboration and find balance between the "time is money" and "time is value" approaches. The inspirations delivered by the Gross National Happiness Index can be a first step on this journey. In these turbulent times of rapid development of artificial intelligence, when so many scientists are asking how to make machines acting more like humans, it is our responsibility to ask how to make humans acting less like machines.

References

Bauer, M., Wilkie, J., & Kim, J. (2012). Cuing consumerism. Situational materialism undermines personal and social well-being. *Psychological Science, 23*(5), 517–523. https://doi.org/10.1177/0956797611429579.

Briley, D. A. (2009). Looking forward, looking back: Cultural differences and similarities in time orientation. In R. S. Wyer, C.-y. Chiu, & Y.-y. Hong (Eds.), *Understanding culture: Theory, research, and application* (pp. 311–325). New York: Psychology Press.

Chao, G., & Moon, H. (2005). The cultural mosaic: A metatheory for understanding the complexity of culture. *Journal of Applied Psychology, 90*(6), 1128–1140.

Chlopczyk, J. (2017). *Beyond storytelling*. Heidelberg: Springer.

D'Alessio, M., Guarino, A., De Pascalis, V., & Zimbardo, P. (2003). Testing Zimbardo's Stanford Time Perspective Inventory (STPI) – Short form. An Italian study. *Time & Society, 12*(2/3), 333–347.

Gurk, C. (2018, September 23). Vier Tage arbeiten statt fünf? Eine Idee mit Charme. *Süddeutsche Zeitung*. https://www.sueddeutsche.de/karriere/arbeitszeit-vier-tage-arbeiten-statt-fuenf-eine-idee-mit-charme-1.4139317

Hall, E. T. (1959). *The silent language*. Garden City, NY: Doubleday; reissued 1973, Anchor Books.

Hornik, J., & Zakay, D. (1996). Psychological time. The case of time and consumer behavior. *Time & Society, 5*(3), 385–897.

Inayatullah, S. (2015). Ensuring culture does not eat strategy for breakfast: What works in futures studies. *World Future Review, 7*(4), 351–361.

Janca, A., & Bullen, C. (2003). The Aboriginal concept of time and its mental health implications. *Australasian Psychiatry, 11*(Suppl. 1), S40–S44.

Kluckhohn, F., & Strodtbeck, F. L. (1961). *Variations in value orientations*. Evanston: Row, Peterson.

Kramer, R., Weger, R., & Sharma, D. (2013). The effect of mindfulness meditation on time perception. *Consciousness and Cognition, 22*(3), 846–852.

Lasane, T. P., & O'Donnell, D. A. (2005). Time orientation measurement: A conceptual approach. In A. Strathman & J. Joireman (Eds.), *Understanding behavior in the context of time: Theory, research, and application* (pp. 11–30). Mahwah, NJ: Lawrence Erlbaum Associates.

Levine, R. (2006). *Geography of time*. Oxford: Oneworld Publications.

Molinsky, A. (2012, January–February). Three skills every 21st-century manager needs. *Harvard Business Review*. https://hbr.org/2012/01/three-skills-every-21st-century-manager-needs

Nguyen-Phuong-Mai, M. (2017). *Intercultural communication. An interdisciplinary approach: When neurons, genes and evolution joined the discourse*. Amsterdam: Amsterdam University Press.

PEW Computer Research Center. (2012). Accessed November 11, 2018, from http://www.pewinternet.org/2012/02/29/main-findings-teens-technology-and-human-potential-in-2020/

Saltmarsche, E. (2018). Telling the difference. Using story to change systems. *Gulbenkian*. https://ssir.org/articles/entry/using_story_to_change_systems

Sell, J. (2017). Storytelling for intercultural understanding and intercultural sensitivity development. In J. Chlopczyk (Ed.), *Beyond storytelling* (pp. 221–247). Heidelberg: Springer.

Trompenaars, F., & Hampden-Turner, C. (1997). *Riding the waves of culture: Understanding diversity in global business* (3rd ed.). London: Nicholas Brealey.

[Uncredited 28]. (2018, July 19). Work less, get more: New Zealand firm's four-day week an unmitigated success'. *Guardian International Edition*. https://www.theguardian.com/world/2018/jul/19/work-less-get-more-new-zealand-firms-four-day-week-an-unmitigated-success

Valdes-Dapena, C. (2018, September 11). Stop wasting money on team building. *Harvard Business Review*. https://hbr.org/2018/09/stop-wasting-money-on-team-building

Joanna Sell is an intercultural coach, trainer, and facilitator as well as a fascinated storyteller who believes in power stories. They can bring relief and bring back dignity and can be an eye opener and the reason to laugh together because of culturally based misunderstandings. She is the owner of Intercultural Compass, the company promoting intercultural communication and cooperation in multicultural, virtual teams and coaching for leaders working across cultures. Joanna comes originally from Poland, is currently based in Germany, and brings vast experience in intercultural training and leadership coaching. Her clients are leaders, HR specialists, sales experts, engineers, medical doctors, academic teachers and layers, as well as students from around the world. She offers her programs for global players, middle-sized companies, and universities. She is passionate about applying storytelling in intercultural programs and works a lot with visual storytelling approach. As a book author and author of an intercultural game diversophy Poland, she additionally pursues the goal of working with stories in the intercultural context. For further details, check www.interculturalcompass.com.

MIX
Papier aus verantwortungsvollen Quellen
Paper from responsible sources
FSC® C105338

If you have any concerns about our products,
you can contact us on
ProductSafety@springernature.com

In case Publisher is established outside the EU,
the EU authorized representative is:
Springer Nature Customer Service Center GmbH
Europaplatz 3, 69115 Heidelberg, Germany

Printed by Libri Plureos GmbH
in Hamburg, Germany